From the personal library of
Dave Zatorski

#12

The LIFE and TIMES *of*

RICHARD J. HUGHES

The LIFE and TIMES *of*
RICHARD J. HUGHES
The Politics of Civility

John B. Wefing

RIVERGATE BOOKS

AN IMPRINT OF
RUTGERS UNIVERSITY PRESS
NEW BRUNSWICK, NEW JERSEY, AND LONDON

Frontispiece: Bil Canfield was a longtime cartoonist for both the *Newark Evening News* and the *Star-Ledger*. During his career he regularly portrayed Hughes. He became a great admirer of Hughes and prepared this cartoon especially for this book. It is produced here with his permission.

Library of Congress Cataloging-in-Publication Data

Wefing, John B., 1943–
    The life and times of Richard J. Hughes : the politics of civility / John B. Wefing.
        p.   cm.
    Includes bibliographical references and index.
    ISBN 978–0–8135–4641–4 (hardcover : alk. paper)
    1. Hughes, Richard J. (Richard Joseph), 1909–   2. Governors—New Jersey—
Biography.   3. New Jersey—Politics and government—1951–   4. New Jersey—
Social policy.   5. Liberalism—New Jersey—History—20th century.
6. Judges—New Jersey—Biography.   7. New Jersey. Supreme Court—Biography.
8. Catholics—New Jersey—Biography.   I. Title.
    F140.22.H84W44 2009
    974.9'043092—dc22
                                                                                [B] 2009006170

A British Cataloging-in-Publication record for this book
is available from the British Library.

Visit our Web site: http://rutgerspress.rutgers.edu

Manufactured in the United States of America

Book design and typesetting: Jack Donner, BookType

This book is dedicated to my family—my wife, Dorothea, who, in addition to being my best friend and soul mate, also did a final edit of the book; my son John, a graphic designer; my son Paul, a detective with the Passaic County Prosecutor's Office; and my daughter Dorry, a graduate student and coach. They have enriched my life immeasurably.

It is also dedicated to the memory of my parents, Henry and Freda Wefing.

Contents

Acknowledgments

MANY PEOPLE HELPED in the preparation of this book. Important financial support was given to Rutgers University Press by James C. Kellogg, a long-time friend of Governor Hughes. Financial support for the writing of this book was provided by Seton Hall University School of Law in the form of a one-semester sabbatical and a number of summer research stipends. I thank Deans Patrick J. Hobbs and Kathleen M. Boozang for their support.

I am deeply indebted to many members of the Hughes and Murphy families, including Hughes's sister, Alice, whom I interviewed at the very beginning of my research and has since passed on. She loaned me her extensive scrapbook with innumerable articles and letters concerning her brother. Other members of the family sat for interviews, and a number were regular contributors of information.

George Amick and John Kolesar did a series of interviews with Hughes in the 1980s. The transcripts of those interviews were made available to me by Judge John Hughes and was an invaluable source for the quotes from Governor Hughes himself.

The Lyndon B. Johnson library interviews of Hughes and Betty as well as of Jane Engelhard also provided interesting insights. The Seton Hall Archives provided access to materials relating to Hughes, and I thank the archivist Alan DeLozien.

Seton Hall also provided research assistants. They included Kevin Turbert, Thomas Dyas, Nick Vytell, Peter Jabbour, Michael Laudino, and Vitaliy Galler. All six were very helpful. The staff of the library at Seton Hall School of Law was extraordinarily helpful. Particular thanks goes to Eileen Denner, chief research librarian for the Seton Hall law library, who was an incredible asset in providing terrific research aid.

My brother, Henry O. Wefing Jr., a writer and professor of writing and journalism at Westfield State College, was an invaluable aid in reviewing the manuscript for grammar, style, and content. Cecelia Cancellaro, who was recommended by the editor of Rutgers Press, did a fine job of final editing.

I also wish to thank Marlie Wasserman, director of Rutgers University Press, for her encouragement and advice.

The LIFE and TIMES *of*

RICHARD J. HUGHES

Introduction

RICHARD J. HUGHES, the only person to serve as both governor and chief justice of New Jersey, was also the state's first Catholic governor. He was also the first truly modern governor to lead the state. Known on both the national and international political stage, Hughes won widespread praise for chairing the Credentials Committee at the contentious 1968 Democratic National Convention, and he was one of Hubert Humphrey's finalists as vice-presidential running mate. Hughes was a close and trusted friend to President Lyndon Baines Johnson, leading to his involvement in the historic Glassboro Summit, during which President Johnson and Soviet Premier Aleksei Kosygin engaged in crucial diplomatic talks in the wake of the Six-Day War.

In addition to his governorship, Hughes's multifaceted career included six years as chief justice of the New Jersey Supreme Court, ten years as a superior court judge on both the trial court and the Appellate Division, four years as an Assistant United States Attorney, and many years in private practice. During his eighty-three years, he met hundreds of thousands of people, decided thousands of cases, signed innumerable bills into law, gave thousands of speeches, and appointed hundreds of judges, prosecutors, and other government officials. In addition to Johnson and Humphrey, Hughes forged relationships with many U.S. leaders including John F. and Robert F. Kennedy, and Nelson Rockefeller, and he traveled the world as a U.S. emissary, even monitoring the 1967 South Vietnam elections.

Born to a working-class family with strong commitments to the Democratic Party and the Catholic Church, Hughes did not particularly excel in school; however, he greatly expanded his knowledge as a result of his love of

1

reading. From an early age, he was inspired by his father's deep involvement in Democratic politics, and this homegrown political education impelled the young Hughes to pursue a political path. His admiration for Presidents Woodrow Wilson and Franklin Delano Roosevelt convinced him of the importance of government and its role in helping the less fortunate in society.

Devoted both to his Catholic faith and his Irish heritage, Hughes became an Irish politician of the best kind. A great storyteller, he could win over an audience with wit and humor—much of which was self-deprecating. The father of ten, he was devoted to his family, devastated by the loss of both his wives, and deeply concerned about the futures of his children.

Richard J. Hughes was a man of strong convictions and ideals, but also a man who knew how to compromise. He could argue fiercely with an opponent and immediately afterward enjoy a friendly drink with the same person. There was hardly a person who disliked Hughes, and he was always able to find the good in others. For him, political disagreements were never personal. While he was a strong and dedicated Democrat, he had deep personal friendships with many Republicans.

Early on, Hughes gained the nickname "two buckets." This name reflected his ability to satisfy both sides of a dispute. As one student of his style put it, the name captured his capacity to balance two pails of water on his shoulders without spilling a drop.[1] His son Robert recalled: "He was nicknamed two buckets, given that name by the late New Jersey Congressman Frank Thompson because of Dad's instinctive practice of trying to bring about compromise between warring factions of a political party, or two sides of a litigation. . . . [H]e understood that, in the world of politics, the finding of common ground would enable the party to do the most good for the most people."[2]

People who knew Hughes refer to him as a "great guy," a "considerate person," a "caring individual." They rarely bring up his brilliance or keen intellect. However, one of the lawyers who worked most closely with Hughes throughout his career described him as the smartest person in any room, even though he never projected that image. Hughes was never one to flaunt his intelligence and preferred to be seen as a man of the people. Late in his life, when asked how he wanted to be remembered, Hughes said: "I don't want to be remembered as a great governor. I don't think I was. I'd like people to say, 'He was a good man and he tried his best.' "[3]

Hughes had an extraordinary zest for life. He seemed to enjoy whatever he was doing at the time—whether representing clients in court, speaking on the rubber chicken circuit, campaigning, swimming with his children at the New Jersey shore, having a martini (or more likely several martinis) with friends, or campaigning in Humphrey's losing race for the presidency. This enthusiasm had a downside, however, as Hughes had a tendency to be impulsive, at times having to retract statements and positions and restate them more carefully. Hughes's verve did not allow him to escape life's difficulties and sorrows. He grieved over the relatively early death of his beloved mother, and he was devastated by the very early demise of his first wife, and childhood sweetheart, Miriam. He endured the death of his father on the very eve of his election to the office of governor, the longtime illness of one of his sisters, the early death of his brother, the abuse of alcohol by some family members, the difficult birth of his youngest son, who was legally blind and almost died, the death of his second wife, Betty, and the death of a grandson.

Hughes also suffered when a number of his closest political colleagues abused their positions and ended up pleading guilty to improprieties. Though Hughes himself was never implicated in the improprieties, he often left campaign fundraising in the hands of those trusted advisors, and his trusting nature may have permitted him to ignore the danger signs.

Hughes's devotion to his faith never wavered. He spent a year-and-a-half in a seminary as a young man and remained a devout Catholic until his death. Friends recall having to wait while Hughes stopped to go to confession. His children remember him rousting them out of bed to go to church.

He often turned to Saint Thomas More, the patron saint of lawyers, as his model. He would say that Thomas More's position as Chancellor of England was somewhat akin to the roles he played as both governor and chief justice. A portrait of More hung in his office and he named his youngest son after the saint. Hughes liked the fact that More attempted to compromise with the King of England and persisted until it became absolutely a matter of principle, at which time he knew he would have to die for those principles. Throughout his own political career, Hughes attempted to work out deals through compromise and conciliation, but when all his efforts at persuasion failed, he would rely upon and stand for his principles.

HUGHES'S MEMORABLE YEARS AS GOVERNOR are the focus of this book. His two-term governorship coincided with a time of great change throughout New Jersey and the country. From 1962 through 1970, the United States witnessed the civil rights movement, the beginning of the women's rights movement, the Warren Court, the Vietnam War, and the assassinations of both John F. and Robert F. Kennedy and Reverend Martin Luther King, Jr.

Hughes took office in a wealthy state with few financial resources. Only one of three states in the country that did not have a broad-based tax to support the state government, New Jersey was very much tied to the concept of home rule by local municipalities, utilizing property taxes as the primary mechanism for spending. Upon being elected, Hughes was faced with the serious problem of meeting the increased demand for state services without adequate financial resources.

During his tenure, Hughes increased the role of state government, created a county college system, an office of community affairs, and a public defender's office. He expanded the four-year college system, instituted a sales tax, opened the first public medical school and the first public television station in the state, increased the role of the Port Authority to better serve New Jersey residents, and appointed numerous capable judges and administrators. Many of these initiatives were bold and were greeted enthusiastically; however, the costs associated with these dramatic expansions resulted in both an increase in borrowing and a higher tax burden. Later administrations picked up where Hughes left off and continued to expand these programs, resulting in serious and continual budget crises for the state.

Hughes's years in office also included many destructive civil rights riots throughout the country, and New Jersey was not spared. The Newark riots in 1967, in which 26 individuals were killed, were particularly destructive and had a significant long-term effect upon the viability of the largest city in New Jersey. Many criticized the state for not doing enough to deal with the festering problems in the inner-cities, suggesting that more attention to these issues might have prevented the bloody riots. Hughes had supported measures to improve urban conditions, but his efforts were criticized as being too little, too late.

His work as governor was intense, but it never stopped Hughes from playing an energetic role in supporting Democratic candidates throughout the state and nation. He campaigned for national candidates including John F. Kennedy, Lyndon Baines Johnson, and Hubert Humphrey, and he campaigned for many state candidates as well.

In large measure because of his interest in people, Hughes relished the campaign trail. Reflecting on Hubert Humphrey's decision not to select him as a running mate in 1968, Hughes always said he would have loved the campaign but wasn't so sure he would have liked the position.

In politics, it's important to be in the right place at the right time. While Hughes had great talents and abilities, he also found himself in the right place at the right time on more than one occasion. His selection as governor was serendipitous. He was not expected to win and was chosen because the original favorite had a heart attack. His selection as chief justice was an example of an extraordinary alignment of events. He was appointed by a Republican governor under unusual circumstances.

Hughes excelled in many areas. He was a fine trial attorney, a well-regarded trial and appellate judge, a distinguished chief justice of the New Jersey Supreme Court, and a loving husband and father. Some remember him most for his vigorous campaigning, others for his interest in people. Hughes's life was an extraordinarily rich and active one that blended personal, professional, and public roles in exemplary fashion.

Chapter 1

The Early Days

Richard J. Hughes was born at home in Florence, New Jersey, on August 10, 1909. His parents, Richard Paul Hughes and Veronica Gallagher Hughes, were working people, struggling to make ends meet. His paternal ancestors immigrated from Ireland during the potato famine. Hughes's grandfather, also named Richard, a native of County Clare who arrived in the United States in 1856, served in the Union Army during the Civil War. He married Irish-born New Jersey widow Alice Lynch Duffy, and became a citizen in 1876, signing his citizenship papers with an ✕.[1] The couple's first son, Richard Paul Hughes, was born the same year.

Richard Paul Hughes was not well educated and often told his son that he'd had no schooling past the fifth grade. Despite this lack of formal education, he was intelligent and possessed a great love for reading, with a particular fondness for Charles Dickens. He was also passionate about politics and maintained close personal and professional ties to the Democratic Party throughout his life. He married Veronica Gallagher when she was eighteen, and two years later Richard J. Hughes was born. Richard would become the oldest of four siblings, and the first of two sons. Veronica was a devout Catholic, and a member of Catholic Daughters of America and the Holy Rosary Society.

Richard J. Hughes spent his early years in a white house on Front Street built by his father with the help of friends. While Hughes did not live there long, he "loved Florence"[2] and enjoyed swimming in the Delaware River and hiking in the woods. At the time, that area of New Jersey was quite rural. When he was young, he indulged in a then-popular activity in rural communities—smoking corn silk. He lied about it to his parents, but his conscience bothered him so much that after a few days he confessed. Years later he would use that story to communicate to his own children the value of integrity.[3]

When the future governor was born, his father was a foundry worker. He would soon become a foreman, however, earning a more stable income and acquiring the skills necessary to manage and deal with large groups of people. The foundry employees were a diverse group, and the elder Hughes had a particularly good rapport with the Italian workers, even though, at the time, many Irish were critical of this newer wave of immigrants.

An extremely social man with a distinct political sensibility, Richard Paul Hughes held a variety of jobs throughout his life to earn money, but he always "considered politics his first calling."[4] He was a dapper man who favored tailored suits and a derby, and he seemed to know everyone in town. A member of the Democratic State Committee for thirty-four years, his political career stops included postmaster of Florence, postmaster and mayor of Burlington City, and Democratic chairman of Burlington County. Although the elder Hughes did win a mayoral election, he unsuccessfully ran for state senate and the state assembly, and was unable to secure a nomination to run for Congress. The losses were not surprising considering the overwhelmingly Republican population of Burlington County.

When the younger Hughes was seven, Governor James F. Fielder singled out Richard Paul Hughes for the position of "Keeper of the State Prison." Hughes's father had a personal relationship with Governor Fielder, had entertained him in his home and had served on his campaign committee.[5] This appointment took Hughes away from his work on the Burlington County Board of Taxation and required the entire Hughes family to move to Trenton, where they lived in a house across the street from the Trenton prison. Many years later, Hughes lamented the conditions of the state prison that his father set out to remedy. "[My father] found a large number of psychotic prisoners, who were confined in the dungeons," chained to walls, hosed, and generally mistreated because of their mental state. After he transferred "all of them to the New Jersey Hospital for the Insane . . . [my father was] called a 'bleeding heart.' "[6] He did not, however, hold this job for long. When Governor Walter Edge took office, Hughes was replaced. The younger Hughes's interpretation of the events suggests that the head of the powerful Democratic Party in Hudson County at the time, Jersey City Mayor Frank Hague, who also engineered the election of Edge, was behind his ousting. Hague had been convinced by Harry Heher, the Democratic leader of Mercer County, to give the post to a resident of Mercer County, as opposed to someone from Burlington. When he was not reappointed, hundreds of prisoners signed a petition in protest.[7] It stated that Hughes "has done more toward making the convicts here respect society and become better men than any other warden in the memory of the oldest convicts, some of them more than fifteen years. This warden has been here less than a year and he is respected if not loved by every prisoner in here."[8]

In later years, while the elder Hughes was serving as Democratic leader of Burlington County, he would work with Mayor Hague. His son would later say that his father "was loyal to Hague as every Democrat had to be." His remarks suggest that the father exhibited two characteristics that others would later detect in his son: "the tendency to depersonalize political disputes and the ability to adapt to changed political realities."[9]

After losing the prison position, Hughes and his family returned to Burlington County and lived with Veronica's mother, Katherine Gallagher McCloskey, a Democratic ward leader who also ran a rooming house.[10] In fact, whenever Hughes's father lost a political job, the family would return to McCloskey's house. It was a full and active residence, family and boarders totaling fourteen people. McCloskey was firmly devoted to the Democratic Party, and between her political views and their father's passion for politics, the party loomed large for the Hughes children throughout their early years.

During his young years Hughes was expected to help out with various jobs. His father joked that the future governor was a "migrant worker," since at the age of ten he helped neighboring farmers pick beans.

Hughes did not participate actively in organized sports. In fact, some friends have described him as "non-athletic," even though he took up golf as an adult.[11] The Hughes family lived in a number of different places in Hughes's formative years, so the young boy did not have a large circle of friends. Additionally, his interest in reading probably set him apart.

Hughes started his education at Mount Saint Mary's Academy in Plainfield. He later attended Captain James Lawrence School in Burlington, went on to Wilbur Watts High School, and finally transferred to Cathedral High School in Trenton, where he spent the final two years before graduation. Of that last experience he said: "I loved that school. Came up on the train every morning, there were other commuters, who came up too—who wanted to go to a Catholic High School. That was the nearest; there were none down in Burlington County at that time."[12] He never minded the

train ride, considering it an acceptable price to pay for a Catholic education, and he thought Cathedral was a "very fine school."[13]

In 1922, Governor Edward I. Edwards, with whom the elder Hughes
also had a close personal relationship, appointed him as a Civil Service
commissioner.[14] It was a worthy position; however, it was not nearly as
lucrative as Keeper of the Prison. As commissioner, Hughes virtually sat
as a judge, listening to the complaints of civil servants who believed they
had been improperly treated. This experience played an important part in
his outspoken desire for his son to pursue a career in law. Hughes served
on the Civil Service Commission until 1929, when he was forced out in a
political battle with the Republican Party boss in Camden.

In 1932, Hughes unsuccessfully sought the Democratic nomination for
Congress in the Fourth District. Interestingly, his son would run as the
Democratic candidate for that same seat in 1938 and lose to the same
opponent, D. Lane Powers.

In 1934, Franklin Delano Roosevelt appointed Hughes's father as postmaster of Burlington, reappointing him in 1938, and again in 1942. Finally,
on November 4, 1948, Hughes—at the age of seventy-three—won his only
election, as mayor of Burlington. He was the first Democrat in forty years
to win that position, which he held for one term.

Despite his dedication to the Democratic Party, Hughes told his son,
"Richard, I always want you to remember that in both parties the majority
of the people are fine, decent people and both parties contain a certain
group of no-goodniks. . . . [I]f you ever see somebody on the Republican
ticket, don't hesitate to split your ticket if he's a better person than the one
running on the Democratic ticket."[15] The younger Hughes was known to
use that line in his own campaigns years later, and then conclude: "Now,
would you believe it, I've been voting forty-two years and that problem
has never come up."[16] As a result of his father's constant involvement in
politics, Richard J. Hughes was introduced early to the life of a politician.
As the oldest in the family, he often accompanied his father to rallies
and official political visits. Politics was constantly discussed in his house,
and Hughes spent time as a youngster listening to "governors, mayors and
legislators swapping stories and planning strategies on the back porch of
his home."[17] By the time he was in high school, Richard J. Hughes was a
seasoned Democrat with a true appreciation for public life.

It was at Cathedral High School that Hughes met Miriam McGrory,
who'd been born and raised in Trenton. He was a senior when he first
laid eyes on her. "I followed her all the way out to West State Street until

I found out where she lived, and then I arranged to get introduced to her . . . great humorist, very funny girl, kind of like the sense of humor Betty [his second wife] had."[18] The two became fast friends and were often seen eating together at the Warren Confectionery, a luncheonette just down the street from Cathedral.

Upon graduation Miriam went on to Georgian Court College in Lakewood, New Jersey, where she served as president of her class. Miriam was active in numerous campus activities ranging from religious organizations to the varsity basketball team. The commentary under her yearbook graduation picture described her as "extremely unselfish," interested in making "everyone happy" and a "charming and lovable character."[19]

Despite his attraction to Miriam, Hughes entered the seminary after graduating. "My mother had always encouraged me to go away to be a priest, as most Irish mothers did, and there must have been twelve in our class that went to Saint Charles, a seminary. I was there about a year-and-a-half, but I was always very upset about, you know, doubtful about having a vocation and fortunately I was dismissed."[20]

Hughes describes his expulsion this way: "A very silly thing; some fat kid from Pittsburgh, I forget, he was an Irish kid, and a boy named Mallon from Philadelphia, three of us, decided on, I think Thanksgiving Day, to go off campus which was strictly against the rules. Only because we were starved, we weren't after beer or women or anything of that kind, we were starved for candy."[21] The head of the seminary spotted the truants and they were expelled. Hughes considered it providential. "I might have stayed with it to be a credit to my mother but many kids who didn't have a strong vocation turned out to be bad priests—drinking priests, or hell-raisers, or something. No, I felt a great sense of relief as though a big burden had dropped off my shoulders."[22] But Hughes, who would become the first Catholic governor of New Jersey, never turned his back on his religious heritage. One commentator said: "Hughes's religious training contributed to the political values he articulated as Governor and to the political style he exhibited in office. His theological pursuits taught him to accept imperfections in human nature, work for change within established social structures and institutions, and place the needs of the community ahead of those of the individual."[23]

After his dismissal from the seminary, Hughes attended Saint Joseph's College in Philadelphia to complete the second half of his sophomore year. In those days college students were often immersed in a classical education. Hughes took Latin, Greek, English, history, religion, and chemistry. "Good school," said Hughes of Saint Joe's, "but I just worked enough to pass, and I did pass my sophomore year and then decided to go to law school."[24]

In his own estimation, Hughes was a "mediocre student, bright but lazy."[25] He was, however, always an avid reader. He read the classics, biographies, and history. Like his father, one of his favorite authors was Charles Dickens. Two favorite books which influenced him were *The Last Hurrah*, a book on Boston politics, and *For the Defense, Thomas Erskine: the Most Enlightened Liberal of His Times, 1750–1823* by Lloyd Paul Stryker. Erskine is described in the prologue as "a man who believed in something—believed enough to fight for it. What he believed in was justice and liberty. . . ."[26]

Hughes also loved his Irish heritage, and he often referred to Samuel Lover's *Handy Andy*, a sophisticated novel about life in Ireland. Andy, the title character, is a silly young Irish lad who gets himself into ludicrous situations. But the book is also a vehicle for discussions of the Irish political and legal system. In an introduction to the book, John Sheridan describes it as "a classic in its own right, a book that has vitality, uproarious humour, a zest for life, and no bitterness."[27] The qualities ascribed to the book are qualities Hughes exhibited in his own life. Hughes also enjoyed quoting Irish poems and ballads. His fascination with St. Thomas More spurred his interest in English history.

Hughes entered New Jersey Law School (which would later become part of Rutgers Law School) in 1928, after completing his sophomore year at Saint Joseph's. At the time, an undergraduate degree was not required for law school admission. His decision to go to law school was influenced by his father, who had always been fascinated by the law. His admission, however, was not a foregone conclusion. As Hughes said, "It was a long shot getting into law school."[28] As was often the case in Hughes's life, a friendship helped. Harry Heher, a prominent attorney who would later go on to be a member of the New Jersey Supreme Court and a mentor to Hughes, arranged for Hughes to meet Edward Craig, a friend of the law school dean. Hughes described the outcome of that meeting this way: "Dean Harris reluctantly admitted me with two or three deficient credits. And he said he'd try me for a year. If I made it, fine. And I did make it."[29]

Ironically, the same Harry Heher who helped him get into law school had previously caused Hughes's father to lose his position as Keeper of the Prison. It was telling that a former opponent of his father's would become an ally. Hughes's talent for maintaining friendships with people of opposite views became a hallmark of his career.

Hughes admitted that he was a "mediocre student" in his first year of law school. He attributed his subsequent turnaround to his constitutional law professor, Richard Hartshorn. "This fellow had a knack of teaching the American Constitution kind of in a Boy Scout way, and he just made it come alive."[30] Hughes's love of the Constitution would demonstrate itself often in his later years both as governor and as chief justice. Hartshorn inspired Hughes to become, for the first time in his life, a truly diligent student. "I wound up my final year as I recall with straight As or pretty close to it."[31] Additionally, Hughes was remembered as the "best speaker and most dignified"[32] in the class.

His eventual success in law school was tempered when he failed the bar exam. Although he passed it on his second try, his initial failure made a strong impression on him. "I was very shocked. I was really traumatized by that, scared to death. And in those days there was a four time rule, four failures and you're out."[33] At that time, a lawyer had to pass a separate exam to qualify as a counselor in order to handle more complex cases. Three years after passing the bar exam he successfully passed the counselor's exam on his first try.

Hughes was now poised to begin his active and successful career as both a lawyer and a political leader. As he blended the busy life of a practicing lawyer with dynamic participation in Democratic Party politics, the generosity of spirit and devotion to faith that he learned from his mother, and the understanding of political realities and the need to maintain friendly relationships with all that he learned from his father, would serve as his guide.

Chapter 2

The Young Politician

WHEN HUGHES GRADUATED FROM LAW SCHOOL IN 1932, the country was still in the midst of the Great Depression and employers were not eager to hire a twenty-three-year-old novice lawyer from the non-ivied halls of New Jersey Law School in Newark.[1] Joseph Katz, who served in the Hughes administration, writing about Hughes much later, said, "Given his exquisitely ill-timed entry into the profession, his professional prospects could only improve."[2]

By this time Hughes's father had started a small insurance business. Hughes worked for a while as a single practitioner in an office connected to his father's office in Burlington. Shortly thereafter, he returned to Trenton to work in the law office of Harry Heher, a prominent attorney.[3] It was expected that young lawyers working with senior attorneys would not only help those lawyers with their cases, but would also bring in business. Since the Depression was still affecting the economy, however, it was a struggle for Hughes to attract business. Things became even more difficult when, not long after, Heher became a judge. Hughes was, as he said, "out of luck." According to him, "Had it been say two years later I could have inherited his entire practice and been off to a fast start. But it was just an unfortunate time, and his practice was distributed around to various lawyers, older lawyers of Trenton. Maybe it's just as well, because I had to, you know, work from scratch and make my own way along."[4]

Although Hughes did not take over his practice, Heher was instrumental in helping Hughes get his start in politics. In the early thirties, before the Constitution of 1947, it was still permissible for a New Jersey judge to be involved in politics. In 1932, while simultaneously serving as chairman of the Democratic State Committee and a judge, Heher appointed Hughes chairman of the committee's Speakers' Bureau during Franklin Delano Roosevelt's first presidential campaign. Hughes learned a great deal from Heher about the ins and outs of political life, just as he had from his father. Since his family still lived in Burlington, Hughes called the Trenton Knights of Columbus his home during that time. He was both a member and an officer of this Catholic organization, whose clubhouse had rooms where members could stay.

The romance Hughes began with Miriam McGrory back at Cathedral High School continued during his law school days and beyond. The couple married in 1934, not long after Hughes passed the bar. They lived with Miriam's parents in Trenton until they were financially secure enough to find their own place. Miriam, who was described as refined and retiring by Hughes's sister, Alice Hulse, gave birth to two sons, Richard and Robert, during the early years of their marriage. Two other children, John and Mary, would be born several years later. The young Hughes family became accustomed to difficult financial situations. It was challenging for a young lawyer to provide for a growing family in the Depression era. Years later, Hughes's sister remarked, "They never had any money."[5]

Claire McQuade, who would later become Hughes's sister-in-law when he married her sister Betty after the death of his first wife, recalled that Hughes and Miriam were a striking couple. When they came into Blessed Sacrament Church with their children all heads would turn to see the charming young lawyer and his handsome family.[6] Miriam had grown up in the Blessed Sacrament parish, and it was an important part of their family life. Her sons were altar boys at the church and Hughes regularly attended mass there. Miriam played an active role in her community and particularly her parish, serving as president of the Blessed Sacrament School's Parent Teacher Association.

While Miriam was not particularly interested in political life (her son Robert described his mother as "detesting politics"[7]) she was devoted to her husband and she supported his efforts. When Alice Hulse was asked about Miriam's attitude toward Hughes's political activity, she said, "He [Hughes] could engage in politics because that was what he wanted—they were very happily married."[8]

At the time, Hughes was active in the Young Democrats, an organization that remained central to his life until he became an Assistant United States Attorney in 1939. Reminiscing about those years, Hughes said, "So then those years went by '34, '35, '36. I was a hot young Democrat."[9] Following in his father's footsteps he got to know all the important people in the Democratic Party, and in 1937 he became president of the local Young Democrats organization. He then ran, successfully, for a position on the Democratic State Committee. This was an especially daring move because he did it without the approval of party leaders. Hughes ran against Judge Irwin E. Marshall, who was the Mercer County prosecutor and a former judge.[10] But as Hughes said, Marshall was "an inactive politician; and I beat him about 12,000 to 7,000 or 5,000."[11]

Congressional Candidate

In 1938, only six years after his father had unsuccessfully sought the nomination to run for Congress from the Fourth Congressional District but was passed over for a Democrat from Mercer County rather than Burlington County, the party asked Hughes to seek the same seat against the incumbent Republican, D. Lane Powers. Hughes described himself during this experience as a "sacrificial lamb." Not only was the district heavily Republican, but President Franklin Roosevelt, a Democrat, was unpopular, having just ended a controversial effort to enlarge the Supreme Court to make it more supportive of his Great Depression agenda. The existing court had declared some of the legislation supporting Roosevelt's agenda unconstitutional, and in an attempt to obtain a more agreeable court, the president suggested increasing the membership, and allowing him to appoint more supportive justices. This "court packing" proposal was very unpopular.

Nonetheless, during his congressional campaign, Hughes trumpeted his support for Roosevelt, adopting the campaign slogan, "Hughes, a Roosevelt Democrat." His campaign speeches demonstrated his liberal views, and he criticized his opponent for being a reactionary who would take the country back to the days of monopolies. Hughes told voters that, "Today liberal thought pervades the thinking of the people of this country and of the Fourth Congressional District particularly."[12] Apparently, voters in the Fourth Congressional District did not agree. Powers easily won reelection. Ironically, Hughes had previously attributed the loss by the former Democratic candidate for that seat to his failure to hitch his wagon to the right star—Roosevelt.[13] It seems clear that Hughes lost, at least in part, because he did hitch his wagon to Roosevelt.

Hughes knew he was likely to lose, but he knew that the campaign would increase his visibility and demonstrate loyalty to the party. The process also allowed him to discover just how much he enjoyed the political game, including going door-to-door to garner votes. Years later, he would say that the congressional campaign provided great training for his run for governor.

Hughes also learned the importance of taking care of constituents during that campaign. Much later, when talking about the race, he remembered that while he disagreed with Lane Powers on policy matters, he respected his attention to the problems of constituents. He recalled that Powers had hired a newsman to see to it that every letter he received was answered over the Congressman's personal signature within 48 hours. While Powers was not on the same page as many of his constituents politically, they still voted for him because of his concern for their needs.[14]

Even though Hughes ran as a Roosevelt Democrat, he very much opposed the court-packing plan. He later stated: "[A] vastly popular American President [Roosevelt] elected in 1936 by the electoral votes of 46 of 48 states, attempted in 1937 to 'pack' the United States Supreme Court which had been less than friendly to his New Deal legislation (the latter itself was supported by a clear majority of the people). Yet in 1938 this same electorate administered a severe rebuke to this challenge to judicial independence, refusing to displace many Congressional members of the President's own party, who had opposed his plan, and against whose election he had mounted a vigorous campaign. His own reelection had he been a candidate that year, would obviously have been at risk."[15] Hughes had great respect for Roosevelt, but he believed that the independence of the judiciary was crucial. He would argue for judicial independence throughout his career.

Hughes worked full-time on his campaign for Congress, to the great detriment of his personal finances. This was not easy on his family, but for Hughes, politics was an essential element of his being. He stopped working on July 4 and campaigned virtually full-time until the November election. He owed nothing at the start of the campaign but by the end he was $10,000 in debt, which was a fortune at the time. Luckily Hughes had friends who could help him out. One of them was Mary Roebling, one of the first women to preside over a major bank, the Trenton Trust Company. Hughes constantly rolled over loans from the bank, later acknowledging, "It was an uncomfortable thing to be that much in hock."[16] Ironically, the Roeblings, who were quite helpful to Hughes, were wealthy Republicans.

When asked how he spent the $10,000, Hughes said: "Oh, it slips away, you know, you stop in Bordentown at the local tavern and you'll spend $12, buying beer for people and so forth and so on, you don't want to look cheesy. We had a candidate for Congress one time who was a Princeton professor, and he didn't understand spending; he was in the same bar one time, and I was campaigning with him and he opened his little wallet to pay for his own beer, lost a lot of votes, I think."[17]

Hughes wrote a letter many years later to a "Sis Bernhardt" reminding her of a "generous beer-bust" she had given for him when he was running for Congress in 1938. "As Miriam and I left, I heard later that you said to your friends—'See that little Irish Mick over there—he's going to be Governor of New Jersey someday!' This was possible because of my windbag performance at your party, but it *was* somewhat prophetic."[18]

Assistant U.S. Attorney

Hughes's political involvement and legal ability led to his appointment, in 1939, to the position of Assistant United States Attorney. The job was part-time, so he was able to practice private law simultaneously. Hughes believed that Thorn Lord, whom he met when they were both active in the Young Democrats and was then serving as an Assistant United States Attorney, had recommended him. The routine F.B.I. investigation of Hughes at the time he was appointed shows that, in fact, Lord had supported his application.[19] However, a number of other prominent members of the bar and judiciary had also spoken on his behalf.

Hughes handled many different types of cases as an Assistant United States Attorney. After the attack on Pearl Harbor, on December 7, 1941, the office became extremely busy. Many cases dealing with war fraud came to Hughes, and he tried the first war fraud case in the country.[20] It involved a defendant named Herman, who was accused of bribing a sergeant to sneak 6,000 pairs of pants out of Fort Dix. Hughes handled the prosecution, and Herman was convicted.

Hughes also tried the case of *United States v. German-American Vocational League*.[21] The league was accused of masquerading as a social and fraternal organization while really acting as a propaganda agency of the German Reich. In 1938, Congress passed, and the president signed, the McCormack Act, a national security measure requiring anyone performing public relations of any nature on behalf of a foreign government to register. The German-American Vocational League failed to register and was charged with conspiracy to violate the act. Hughes handled the case through trial and appeal, winning at both levels. Rather than exploiting the evident patriotic angle, he focused on the legal issues. At the conclusion of the trial, District Court Judge Thomas F. Meany described Hughes as "a most effective trial lawyer . . . he gives tremendous attention to detail."[22] Hughes loved trial work of all sorts.[23]

During his time as an Assistant United States Attorney Hughes worked with Judy Sarosky, the only secretary in the office who could keep up with the fast-talking attorney as he dictated his briefs, letters, and memoranda. Sarosky would remain his secretary, through all his careers, until the time he died. Hughes always said that he was lucky about the women in his life, including his mother, his mothers-in-law, and his wives. He and his family would come to recognize his secretary's place in this group of women. Judy was an immense help to Hughes in his private practice, and in his work as a judge, governor, and chief justice. A friend, who was unaware that Sarosky was married, once asked Hughes, after observing the close working relationship he had with his secretary, why he had not married her. Hughes responded that the presence of Bill, Judy's husband, was a major obstacle, and besides, why would he want to take a perfectly fine secretary and make her his wife?

During his years at the United States Attorney's office, Hughes forged a close personal and political relationship with Thorn Lord, the man who had recommended him for the job. They were an unlikely pair but the two were constant companions who consistently supported each other's political careers. While Hughes was gregarious and outgoing, Lord was withdrawn and taciturn, even described as "eccentric, moody and saturnine."[24] He was "aloof, diffident, cavalier about money, he dressed oddly, and gave the appearance of a typical, absent-minded professor."[25] Despite all of that, Lord had many friends in Washington who had been part of the New Deal, including Justice Abe Fortas, Thomas Corcoran, and Walter Lockheim.[26]

Alvin Felzenberg, the author of a study of three New Jersey governors, including Hughes, said: "Together Hughes and Lord forged one of the most successful political alliances in the history of their state. . . ."[27] They worked together to invigorate the Democratic Party in Mercer County. Ronald Grele, who wrote about the development of liberal Democratic ideology in Mercer County at the time, wrote: "Thorn Lord, who succeeded [Crawford] Jamieson as the dominant influence in party politics after 1944, was a brilliant tactician of politics. His registration drives, his clever manipulation of ethnic politics, and his awareness of the liberal imagination allowed him to forge the Democratic constituency of industrial, working-class Trenton into a solid political base."[28] Richard Leone, a major figure in New Jersey political life and currently the head of the Century Foundation, said of

Hughes and Lord, "Together they transformed the solidly Republican County [Mercer] into a solidly Democratic one. . . ."[29]

While serving as Assistant United States Attorney, Hughes was elected Mercer County Democratic leader. In an editorial, the *Trenton Evening Times* criticized Hughes for continuing to work at the United States Attorney's office after the election,[30] stating that it was a violation of the Hatch Act, which prohibits federal employees from engaging in political activities. Hughes did not actually assume the position, however, until after his resignation as an Assistant United States Attorney. In the interim period, Frank Katzenbach held the position as acting county leader. Apparently Hughes believed that the interim appointment of Katzenbach eliminated any violation. However, the editorial writers for the *Trenton Evening Times* thought differently, and accused Hughes of serving in both capacities simultaneously, and of "fence-straddling" and "double-talk" by having Katzenbach fill-in.[31] The editorial writers concluded by saying that it was unlikely that the United States Attorney's office would prosecute one of their "own."[32] There was never any formal complaint made against Hughes for this activity.

During World War II, while Hughes was still serving as Assistant United States Attorney, he attempted to gain a commission in the Navy. He was turned down because of his bad eyesight. He was eager to serve, so he asked what he could do to remedy the situation. He was told to drink a lot of orange juice and eat a lot of carrots and try not to use his glasses. Hughes would later recollect, "We had dinner that night. I drank about a quart of orange juice and at breakfast another quart, a lot of damned carrots, all that crazy stuff. I'd go out in the street without my glasses on and pretty nearly got killed by a cab."[33] When he went back for the next test, not only were his eyes still bad, but he also tested positive for diabetes from all the sugar he'd consumed from drinking so much orange juice. He was turned down again.

Later, when the need for soldiers intensified, he was drafted. "I had to go to Camden to take a draft examination. And it was the funniest thing, talk about psychology . . . when I was Assistant U.S. Attorney, you know, these United States marshals are holding your coat, 'Can I get you a glass of water on the table? And 'Can I carry your bag out to the car?' and so forth and so on, very obsequious. Now, on examination day, down at Camden Armory, the same assistant marshals are there, to supervise the examination, you know, watch the people so no one gets away. And they're altogether different. Now you're a civilian again. It was a good lesson for me."[34] He was also amused by the draft examination itself: "Everybody's naked in a row with their wallet, and the guy with a lot of hair on his chest, the sergeant says, 'You so and so, I told you to leave the sweater in the locker.' But, it was an experience, I enjoyed it very much."[35] After the physical he was called in to meet with the draft officers. "There was an Army captain and a Navy lieutenant commander. The Army guy looked through the whole sheet, and he said, like this, nodded his head, 'No Way,' in disgust, turned me over to the Navy guy. And I had about half vision in this eye (left), which had been detected when I tried to get a Navy commission two years before this incident, and it was good enough now so they accepted me for limited service."[36] Hughes never served, however, because just before he was to be inducted, President Roosevelt declared that no pre-Pearl Harbor fathers over twenty-six, categories Hughes fell into, were to be sent to war. Additionally, he'd been worried about the induction because of the physical fitness demands (he was told he would have to do fifty push-ups, and even with practice, he could never get past eighteen).

County Democratic Leader

In 1945, Hughes had returned to private practice and joined Thorn Lord, who had also left the United States Attorney's office. For the next three years, Hughes threw himself into the practice of law and into politics. Hughes said of this time, "I had a general practice and was doing rather well."[37] He was also involved in charitable as well as political activities. Sometimes those activities combined, as when he joined with the Republican leader of Mercer County to raise money for cancer prevention research.

Politics certainly played a major role in the lives of Hughes and Lord at the time, as they worked to expand the liberal voter base in Mercer County so Democrats could take control and increase their influence statewide. This effort, undertaken by these two men, seemed unlikely to some. Grele wrote, "Richard Hughes and Thorn Lord could not, on the surface, have seemed less qualified to express this new liberalism and to reorganize the local and state parties. Hughes has been described by most who knew him as a 'glad hand,' a man who consistently compromised and thus earned the sobriquet of 'two buckets.'[38] Hughes was always ready to say yes to whoever asked for something. His wife quipped that the only time he said 'no' was when he misunderstood the question."[39] Lord was an even more unusual choice to become a political leader in New Jersey. He was a newcomer, having been raised in the South. Quiet and shy, he feared "crowds so much that he hid from them during his unsuccessful senatorial campaign of 1960."[40] He hated to make decisions and often just let things happen. Unlike Hughes he never said yes, but he never said no, either. In spite of these perceived shortcomings, however, Grele explains the many reasons that the two men were actually perfect to develop the liberal agenda. Hughes had his father's liberal philosophy and his memories of the anti-Catholicism of the Al Smith campaign of 1928[41] to guide him as he "remained committed to equal rights throughout his career."[42] Lord, too, came from a family devoted to liberalism and was an early supporter of the New Deal. The two would work assiduously to bring liberal Democratic ideals to the forefront in Mercer County.

When asked to explain their success in this endeavor, Hughes replied, "[the Republicans] didn't work as hard as we did. I had a corps of Young Democrats, maybe 300 members, we would go out and we would canvass door to door, in a hot July, August, summer. We'd have what they called mobile registration, say at a certain public school. We would canvass the neighborhood, anyone who looked like a Democrat or an independent, take them to the place and get them registered. Make a note, take them to vote on election day. And we registered thousands of people. Thorn Lord and I, and Thompy [Congressman Frank Thompson] was so enthused about that technique that [Thompson] ran the nationwide registration campaign for President Kennedy in 1960, which was very successful. But the seed was planted right here. And that made it; the Republicans never even thought of such a thing."[43]

Thompson was a close associate of Hughes and Lord. He was elected to the House of Representatives in 1954 and reelected twelve times. "A leader of Democratic liberals in the House, he oversaw passage of major education and labor bills in Congress and the Civil Rights Act of 1964."[44] Hughes would later, as governor, work closely with Congressman Thompson to obtain support for New Jersey from the federal government.

Hughes was very proud of his work in organizing the Democrats. Although some of the older members of the party were not happy with his new procedures, he was able to convince party leaders to let him run the show. One of Hughes's techniques was the use of "street money." "We used to have a great committeewoman named Sarah Harkins down on Centre Street, good territory for Democrats, and I'd call her up, I'd say, 'Hey, Sarah, I want to come down and see you. I'll be there 5:15. I'll have a bottle of booze. I want you to get your committeemen, your two election officers, and your two best workers in. I want to talk to you and them.' So I'd go down and we'd go over the cost, one guy could work a half a day so he got $7.50, say Joe Doakes. Another guy could work a whole day and use his car, he got, in those days, $25. The committeewoman got $50. I slipped her an extra ten; I said, 'Don't let the committeeman know this.' You had to do all that stuff. But the district was tightly organized; nobody had ever done this before. So that on Election Day, when I'd drive down the street and look across, everybody would be huffing and puffing and working, bringing people in. And that did it."[45]

Hughes saw his street-level involvement as a way to meet the committeemen and -women directly. "I must have talked to thousands of people. And it showed for years. It established a kind of pattern of personal attention by the guy in charge, to the little guys as well as the big shots."[46] Hughes's attention to the "little guys" would continue throughout his career. He was just as happy talking with a secretary, janitor, or workman, as he was talking to Presidents Kennedy or Johnson or the Duke and Duchess of Windsor. And Hughes remembered the names of those "little guys." Many marveled at his ability to remember names, an important talent for a politician. When Hughes's son Michael Murphy was asked about this he said, "Dad had some tricks that helped him, but basically it was a gift."[47] One of those tricks was a Rolodex loaded with names and information about the people he met.

While working to invigorate the Democratic Party in Mercer County, Hughes knew he had to work with Democrats of all stripes, particularly the other county leaders, if he hoped to reach his ultimate objectives. During 1945, Hughes worked with Jersey City Mayor Frank Hague on a number of political matters, despite Hague's earlier harsh treatment of his father. Hughes never really liked Hague himself, but he recognized that Hague had been a dominant political force in the state for many years, able to turn out huge numbers of voters in his Democratic stronghold in Hudson County.[48]

One example of Hague's political prowess was his successful courting of Franklin Roosevelt. In the Democratic primary in 1932, Hague had supported Al Smith, the former governor of New York and 1928 candidate for the presidency. When Roosevelt beat Smith, Hague quickly displayed his loyalty to the chosen Democratic candidate.[49] "If FDR opened the presidential campaign in New Jersey, Hague promised to stage the biggest political rally in the nation's history."[50] And he lived up to his promise. With amazing efficiency, the Hague organization shipped more than 150,000 Democrats from Hudson County "to Sea Girt, site of the summer residence of New

Jersey's Democratic governor, A. Harry Moore."[51] Hughes, who was at the event, recalled that Roosevelt "was very impressed . . . became a Hague man right away."[52] Hague subsequently became the party's spokesman in New Jersey and controlled the patronage from the federal government. John Cunningham's book on New Jersey refers to "'Rice Pudding Day,' the annual day for 'contributions' to the Democratic machine" when each government employee in Hudson County was expected to pay for the privilege of working for the government. Cunningham takes note of "the mayor's [Hague's] immaculate attire and the uncanny budgeting ability of a man who never officially made more than $8000 a year, yet paid $7000 annual rent for his apartment in Jersey City, had a $125,000 summer home in Deal, and owned a handsome villa in Miami Beach. He lived like a millionaire on a Jersey City's mayor's salary: he traveled only first class, spent big, and dazzled his followers with personal splendor."[53]

By 1945, when Hague and Hughes were working together, however, Hague was beginning to lose his control over the Democratic Party. He had both local and national problems. According to Hughes, toward the end of his presidential career, Roosevelt was beginning to lose respect for Hague and "Truman never had any time for Hague, at all. Always hated him."[54] When Truman became president after Roosevelt's death, Hague lost most of his control over federal patronage, and he faced opposition within his own party. In 1947, Hague resigned the mayoralty of Jersey City—a position he'd held for thirty years—and installed his nephew as mayor. Others in the party, incensed, began to plot Hague's downfall. Hague felt he could regain some of his stature by getting a Democrat elected to the Fourth Congressional District, and was desperate for a Democrat to win that congressional seat. But despite the efforts Hughes and Lord had made to turn Mercer County into a Democratic bastion, they were unable to deliver the vote in that particular case. While he did not like Hague, Hughes's pragmatism made him willing to work with Hague because it was their mutual objective to win the congressional seat. However it was this willingness to work with the bosses, and clearly Hague had been the most powerful in the state, which would lead to criticism particularly in his first run for governor. Hughes, in part, blamed himself for the loss. As Mercer County party leader, Hughes chose Frank Katzenbach, a former judge and well-regarded person, to run for the position. "I was the county leader then, harmony leader, both sides were playing friends with me, and we blew it because I had thrown the C.I.O. [Congress of Industrial Organizations] out of my office; they wanted to nominate the congressional candidate.

So they persuaded George Pelletierri, a city district court judge, to resign from the bench and run, and he got all C.I.O. labor votes, he was a big man with labor, and we were beaten by 7,500 and George Pelletierri got 10,000 Democratic votes in between us. So we blew that election, and Hague kept on going downhill."[55] The C.I.O. was a federation of unions that organized workers and it was a very powerful force in elections. The Republican candidate, Frank A. Mathews, won the seat.

Hughes described Hague's political strategy: "[H]e had a magnetic personality. He showed me a picture in his office one time; 'Now,' he said, 'Hughes or Hughesie,' whatever he used to call me, he said, 'I want to tell you something. You see this picture?' Picture of an infant child, with footprints, like fingerprints, in the corner. And a little dedication to the kid's mother, Italian name, signed by Mayor Frank Hague. He said, 'I gave a duplicate of that picture to that family. She delivered that baby at Margaret Hague Hospital; no cost.' He said, 'Do you think they're ever going to take that family away from me?' See, that was his technique. As it was the technique of all the Irish politicians at the turn of the century, during depressions. Somebody would move into a district and the Democratic committeeman would be around the next day offering to help in getting hold of Public Service to turn on their power, and telling them which day the garbage was collected, did they need anything for Thanksgiving, did they need a job, like that. It was personal attention to these people, which, you know, made lifetime friends. The political club would dig up some money and send out 2,500 frozen turkeys in the area. Of course, people now, with welfare and changing times, don't need this but they needed it very much back in the 1920s, 1910s. That's when the big machines in New York and Boston and Jersey City were built. I don't excuse . . . what would now be called corruption, then it was regarded as everybody did it, the Republicans the Democrats, but, you don't excuse that but you accept it as a fact of life."[56] Hughes's acceptance of those political facts of life led to some criticism in later years that he was too close to people like Hague.[57] During 1945, Hague urged Hughes to run for state senate, but Hughes decided against it. Perhaps his decision was based on the debt he had built up when he ran for Congress. He often described his mistake in funding his own campaign, and years later when his son Brian ran for the same congressional seat he urged him not to spend his own money on the race.

In 1948, Hughes served as an alternate delegate from New Jersey to the Democratic National Convention. He and his father, who was still serving as Burlington County Democratic leader, both attended. Hughes continued to serve as Democratic leader of Mercer County until he was appointed to the Court of Common Pleas in 1948.

While politics were important during those years, Hughes was also successfully practicing law. One of the prestigious positions to which lawyers in New Jersey aspire is membership on the editorial board of the *New Jersey Law Journal*. Hughes was chosen to serve on that eleven-member board. Many of those eleven would go on to be prominent jurists and leaders of the bar, including the future Justice of the United States Supreme Court, William Brennan. One of the editorials that Hughes wrote as a member of the board during that time praised the creation of the new state constitution but worried about continuing problems related to the juvenile justice system.[58] When Hughes joined the bench he continued to have concerns about juvenile justice and served on a number of committees examining that system. His combined successes as an Assistant United States Attorney, practicing lawyer, member of the editorial board of the *New Jersey Law Journal*, as well as his involvement in politics, were all factors that led to his next career as judge.

Chapter 3

The Bench

I N 1948, GOVERNOR ALFRED E. DRISCOLL, a Republican, appointed
Hughes, a Democrat, to a judgeship. This was in keeping with the New
Jersey tradition of balancing Democratic and Republican membership
on the courts. Some felt that it was not only Hughes's proven legal abilities that led to his appointment. They speculated that Driscoll wanted to
remove this effective organizer from the political scene.[1]

The year 1947 had been a turning point in the history of New Jersey. A
constitutional convention dramatically changed the structure of the state's
government. The first New Jersey Constitution was hastily drafted during
the Revolutionary War in 1776. Prior colonial governments were controlled
by royal governors appointed by the Crown. The former colonies created
new governments that gave very little power to governors and placed most
of the power in the hands of legislatures. The second Constitution of New
Jersey was adopted in 1844. That constitution continued what is known
as a weak governor format. It had a judicial article that provided for a
convoluted and difficult court system. The 1947 constitution radically
changed the distribution of power that had been established in 1844, and
gave governors major new powers. Previously, governors had three-year
terms and could not succeed themselves. Under the new constitution,
governors had four-year terms and could succeed themselves for one additional four-year term. Governors were also given dramatic appointment
powers—empowered to appoint all judges, prosecutors, and cabinet officials—although the Senate was given the role of advising and consenting.
Due to the Constitution of 1947, New Jersey's governorship was considered
to be one of the most powerful in the country.[2] The conservative columnist

George Will, commenting on the extraordinary powers of the New Jersey governor, compared the position to "an American Caesar."[3]

The judicial system was also dramatically revised. Prior to the new constitution, the *Journal of the American Judicature Society* called New Jersey's judicial structure the worst in the country. After the new constitution was adopted, that same journal considered it the best in the country.[4] Under the earlier constitution, there were many levels of courts, each with its own procedures and requirements.[5] There was a strict division between law and equity, which led to endless delays as lawyers took their cases through a labyrinth of procedural minutiae. The highest court of the state was the Court of Errors and Appeals. It was an unwieldy and ineffective court consisting of sixteen appointed judges, some of whom had little knowledge of the law and were appointed based not on merit but on politics.[6] The most notorious example was the appointment by Governor A. Harry Moore, who had owed his election to Hague, of Hague's son, Frank Hague Jr., an inexperienced and ineffective lawyer. The governor openly admitted that he had appointed the younger Hague to "please his daddy."[7]

The 1947 Constitution and the appointment of Arthur T. Vanderbilt as New Jersey's first chief justice under the new constitution ended the political abuses. Vanderbilt was an extraordinary force in legal and political circles both in New Jersey and across the country. He was a prominent trial attorney, dean of the New York University Law School, Essex County Republican leader, and president of the American Bar Association. As president of the Bar Association, he crusaded for the improvement of judicial systems across the country. He was a dynamic, behind-the-scenes force in moving the New Jersey Constitutional Convention to adopt a streamlined judicial article. While chief justice of the New Jersey Supreme Court, he was seriously considered by President Eisenhower for chief justice of the United States Supreme Court—a position that would eventually go to Earl Warren.[8]

The New Jersey judicial system devised at the Constitutional Convention of 1947 had a strong, seven-person Supreme Court at its apex. The Superior Court was divided into a number of divisions, including an Appellate Division. While the new system continued to have a Chancery Division to deal with equity matters, it was now included within the Superior Court. This inclusion eliminated delays by permitting a simple system of transferring cases from the Division of Law to the Chancery Division.

Under the new constitution, the chief justice was the administrative head of all the courts in the state. As head, the chief justice could assign Superior

Court judges to the various divisions, including the Appellate Division. This gave the chief justice great power over the entire court system.

Hughes's appointment in September 1948 occurred just as the system was changing from the old to the new. He was the last judge appointed to the Court of Common Pleas, a position that was to be eliminated under the new constitution. Hughes described the situation this way: "And when I was sworn in which was [on] September 13, I became the last common pleas judge under the old court system, under the 1844 constitution. Because the 1947 Constitution created a new court system but said it would be implemented on September 15, 1948, to allow them time to set up, I was a common pleas judge for two days, and then all the common pleas judges in the state were sworn in at one time as county court judges in Trenton . . ."9

One of the desires of the framers of the constitution was to divorce judges from political involvement. Once Hughes was appointed, therefore, he could no longer participate in any political activity. Hughes makes reference to the fact that he might have violated the ban when he gave his parting words of advice to Thorn Lord, who took over as leader of the Democratic Party in Mercer County. Hughes said: "And I had a talk with Thorn after I was appointed a judge, I shouldn't have done it I guess, but we sat in the car and I said, 'Listen Thorn, don't forget this. You terrorize these freeholders, now you've got control. First thing you know somebody's going to be taking a case of booze at Christmas or taking something else.' I said, 'You tell them that you're eccentric and the first thing you hear anything about that [impropriety] you're going to call for the attorney general.' And I said, 'Scare the hell out of them.' And he apparently did because there wasn't a hint of anything. He apparently scared them straight."10

Hughes was an outstanding judge. Chief Justice Vanderbilt, a tough taskmaster, assigned him many difficult cases. Hughes said Vanderbilt used him as a "troubleshooter." It was ironic that Vanderbilt, a former Republican County leader, placed his trust in a former Democratic County leader. During his time on the bench, Hughes sat in eleven of the twenty-one counties in the state. He sat in Cape May County in the southeast corner of the state as well as Sussex County in the northwest corner. Handling cases in so many different locales was very unusual. This familiarity with the people was no doubt helpful in his later campaigns.

As a judge in Mercer County, where he sat for a good part of his early years, he handled numerous petitions from the Trenton State Prison. These were petitions from prisoners who believed they had been unconstitutionally convicted. Judge Catherine Hayden, a recipient of the Richard J. Hughes Award at Seton Hall Law School, commented on Hughes's handling of those petitions: "He had to sit down and write opinions time and again. . . . When an explosion of prisoner habeas applications broke over the state courts in 1950, it was Richard J. Hughes sitting in Mercer County, home to Trenton State Prison, who presided."[11] Judge Hayden then noted that Hughes had an incredible ability to review a large number of these cases and give each of them a careful and thoughtful assessment.[12]

Despite his busy schedule as a judge, Hughes had more time to spend with his family because he was precluded from attending political events. His son, Robert, recounts that for the first time his father was available to participate in family activities, even helping him with his homework and spending summer weekends at the Jersey shore with the family.[13]

The Death of Miriam

In 1951, during his third year on the bench, Hughes experienced one of the great tragedies in his life. His wife Miriam died unexpectedly at the age of thirty-eight. Hughes was devastated. His sister, Alice Hulse, said, "The shock broke his heart."[14] Years later when talking about her death, Hughes still expressed dismay that he had not been with her when she died. He was serving on a committee examining the juvenile court system and had been scheduled to go to Detroit to meet with people from the Detroit system. Miriam had not been feeling well, and they had gone to the doctor. Various tests were done and nothing was detected. Her doctor assured Hughes that it was safe for him to travel. When Miriam took a turn for the worse, members of the family had trouble reaching him. When he finally got the word, he flew home immediately, but he arrived ten minutes after she died.[15] Hughes and Miriam had dated since their high school days and he was deeply devoted to her. At the time of Miriam's death, sons Richard and Robert were teenagers, John was four, and Mary was only one. The McGrorys (Miriam's parents) subsequently moved in with Hughes to help with the children. Jim McLaughlin, a coworker, said that Hughes coped with the death of Miriam by throwing himself into his work. Hughes later said, "I was very down in the dumps of course, and I didn't have any social life, go out at all, until I suddenly started going out to play golf with some friends of mine, who came around, wanted to be helpful. So we went out stag and played golf at Shawnee and other places."[16]

Hughes's trauma over the death of Miriam stayed with him even after he had happily remarried. When Senator (later Vice President) Joseph Biden was first elected to the Senate in 1972, just before taking office, his wife and daughter were killed and his two sons were severely injured in a car crash. Biden was devastated and seriously considered not taking his seat. Hughes, remembering the trauma of Miriam's death, quickly reached out to Biden and told him about his own trauma and how he dealt with it. He recommended that Biden get a notebook and judge each day on a scale of zero to ten. He told him that in the beginning he would have many zeros but as time went by he would begin to have better days. The Hughes family had never heard the story until many years later, when Biden met Hughes's son Brian at a political event and communicated the story. Biden, it turns out, had followed the simple strategy suggested by Hughes and said that it probably saved his political career.[17]

Miriam had never enjoyed political life. According to one family story, she even tried to discourage Mercer County political leaders from gathering for coffee in the morning at the Hughes household by keeping a fresh pot for the family, and a stale, unappetizing pot for the politicians. Perhaps the politicians got the message, because eventually the morning ritual ended. Robert Hughes views the end of those morning gatherings as fortunate for his father's career on the bench. While Hughes continued to play some minor political role, it was less obvious than the morning ritual. "Being the resourceful person that he was, Dad got around Judge Vanderbilt's political prohibition by encouraging the other members of the secret seven [a group of political friends] to drop by our home in the morning for coffee." When those meetings ended, with some help from Miriam's two-pot system, Robert Hughes said, "Dad was forced to make other arrangements for obtaining his political information and for transmitting, unofficially of course, his suggestions to the party leadership. His was probably the first and last occupation of the office of county chairman in absentia. But it all came down to this: he lived his life as he thought his God would have him live it. He did what he thought was the right thing to do, even if it meant bending the rules in the process."[18]

In 1952, when Judge William J. Brennan, who later served for thirty-eight years on the United States Supreme Court, was appointed to the New Jersey Supreme Court, a Superior Court position became available and Governor Driscoll decided to appoint Hughes to Brennan's old seat. Driscoll called Hughes and asked him to come see him. Hughes described the meeting:

So I went up to see him that afternoon, and he said, "Now, I haven't made up my mind fully about this, and I may not appoint you to the Superior Court but I am thinking about it, giving it serious consideration.[19] And in case I do, after I make up my mind, I want you to promise me three things." This was kind of funny talk to me. He said, "Now I want you to promise me that you'll always be fifty-fifty. Absolutely fair in the middle. According to the best of your ability. Don't give a minute's thought to what would please Governor Driscoll or what would please Arthur Vanderbilt, right down the middle." And he said "Number two, I want you to promise me that even though you'll have what's equivalent to life tenure, that you'll keep on being a student, reading the law reviews, enriching yourself professionally, intellectually in the law." "I'll promise that." All right, now I wondered what the third thing was. Now, he says, "Also, I have information that you still see the boys occasionally." That would be like Thorn Lord and the politicians, you know, that I'd have lunch with or have a sandwich with them or something, and he said "I'd like you to arrange to have a good successor recommended." And I promised him all those things. And I often, except for the recommendation for a successor, I often repeated that same stuff to people that I appointed. I must have appointed 100 judges, I suppose, when I was governor, and I would give them that same statement of my hopes for them. So then he did appoint me, and I was approved by the Senate.[20]

Four high-level judicial appointments were made at the time Hughes was appointed to the Superior Court: Brennan to the New Jersey Supreme Court; Hughes to the Superior Court to replace him; Nathan Jacobs to the New Jersey Supreme Court; and Sidney Goldman to the Superior Court to replace Jacobs. Hughes said: "Two great appointments, Bill Brennan and Nat Jacobs. But Jacobs and Goldman were Jews, and Brennan and I were Irish Catholics. And I don't know if it's true, but the fiction was that some group of WASPs [white Anglo-Saxon Protestants] came down to Driscoll, who was himself a WASP, and criticized him for being partial to Jews and Catholics on these appointments."[21]

Hughes's penchant for "seeing the boys," as Governor Driscoll put it, almost got him into hot water with the court. In 1952, Chief Justice Vanderbilt saw a newspaper story and picture about a dinner at which a number of politicians had honored Hughes. Vanderbilt demanded an explanation. Hughes responded in detail:

On my appointment to the bench in 1948, I left public life at the height of my activity. Since then I have been besieged by proposals from all sorts of civic and other public groups, including persons of both political faiths, to permit a testimonial dinner of imposing proportions and I have refused same for obvious reasons. A few weeks ago, I agreed to attend a small private dinner in my honor, the invitation list to be confined to the survivors of the original nucleus of the Young Democrats of 1933 vintage. I laid down as conditions that the attendance would be so limited and that no persons, regardless of their importance, politically or otherwise, would be invited outside of that group. These terms were followed and a rather innocuous pleasant occasion resulted with a few humorous and nostalgic speeches and I do not recall that politics was even mentioned, and if so, was in a jocular vein.[22]

Hughes went on to further explain the circumstances and to apologize for any embarrassment to the judiciary caused by the event. Two days later the chief responded, indicating that the court was satisfied with his response.

One of the most interesting cases that Hughes handled as a trial court judge was the case of Walter G. Winne. Winne had an impressive resume. He had held numerous prestigious positions, including United States Attorney for the State of New Jersey, Republican leader of Bergen County, president of the Bergen County Bar Association, and prosecutor of Bergen County from 1944 to 1950. He was indicted in 1951 for criminal nonfeasance for failing to investigate and prosecute known gambling activities as the Bergen County prosecutor.

Chief Justice Vanderbilt directed Hughes to handle this politically charged case from Bergen County, even though Hughes was not sitting in Bergen.[23] This selection demonstrates the confidence that Vanderbilt had in Hughes's ability to be fair and just despite the important and political individuals involved in the case. The case also demonstrates Hughes's careful and analytical style in dealing with a complex issue.

Generally, prosecutors have a great deal of discretion in determining what cases to prosecute. In New Jersey, prosecutors are appointed by the governor, as is the attorney general of the state, who has significant powers over the local prosecutors. In this case, the Bergen County Board of Freeholders passed a resolution requesting that the attorney general supersede Winne as prosecutor.[24] Nelson F. Stamler, an assistant attorney general, was assigned to take charge in the Bergen County Prosecutor's Office. Governor

Driscoll indicated that he had no authority to remove the prosecutor, who as a constitutional officer could only be removed by impeachment.[25] Subsequently, Stamler was asked to focus his attention on the gambling investigation. Many of the detectives in the Prosecutor's Office resigned.[26] A special grand jury was set up to investigate, and Winne was indicted. There were nineteen counts alleging misconduct in office—all basically involving failure to prosecute various types of gambling operations. Other members of his staff were also indicted.

Hughes ruled that the indictment of Winne should be dismissed. In the opening paragraphs of his opinion, Hughes acknowledged that the failure to enforce the gambling laws had grown out of the Prohibition era, when it became commonplace for people to violate the law.[27] He also acknowledged the involvement of organized crime in these activities and recognized that gambling profits helped to support organized crime, and the failure to enforce led to a general breakdown in law enforcement.[28] He then turned to the particular terms of the indictment. He found that a number of the counts could not stand because they merely alleged that Winne was "a corrupt public official" but did not recite what Winne was alleged to have done or not done that made him "a corrupt public official." This, Hughes concluded, was improper.[29] Hughes determined that those counts could not be upheld because the mere act of being "a corrupt public official" was not sufficient without a recitation of "things done or omitted by such officer bringing about such a status."[30]

Hughes went on to indicate that the other allegations revolved around the role of the prosecutor. Hughes wrote a lengthy review of the role and authority of the prosecutor, concluding that prosecutors are "ministers of justice" and "in the very nature of things the dispensation of justice by such minister must be a quasi-judicial function and call for the exercise of discretion. . . ."[31] Hughes then turned to the doctrine of immunity, which protects judges and prosecutors, holding that such doctrine is indispensable to the administration of justice. Hughes felt that the prosecutor had to possess immunity in order to carry out the responsibilities of his office.[32] He then concluded that in order to allow prosecutors to make decisions without fear of constantly having to defend themselves from lawsuits, the doctrine of malfeasance "must be based upon some corrupt or evil motive."[33] Finally, Hughes held that the wording of the indictment did not "meet the constitutional requirement of informing defendant of the 'nature and cause of the accusation' and that it does not charge the offense with the certainty required of indictments."[34]

The government decided to appeal the case. The decision by Hughes was reversed by the New Jersey Supreme Court in a five–two decision. Chief Justice Vanderbilt, writing for the majority, reviewed the history of the role of the prosecutor and came to a conclusion different from Hughes's. He said: "The statutes reflect . . . a fixed legislative policy to cast on the county prosecutor responsibility for the detection, apprehension, arrest and convictions of criminals in his county."[35] Justice Vanderbilt continued: "The indictment clearly sets forth breaches of official duty by the defendant in his failure to act with respect to matters concerning which he is expressly charged to do so by statute."[36] Vanderbilt also rejected the argument that because of immunity, the prosecutor could not be charged unless there was a showing of corruption on his part.[37] Vanderbilt recognized that the prosecutor has to have some level of discretion but that it is not absolute. Vanderbilt also stated that the indictment was not invalid for failing to allege corruption. He concluded: "The power to quash an indictment rests in the sound discretion of the trial judge, but this discretion should not be exercised 'except on the plainest ground . . . or on 'the clearest and plainest ground' . . . or unless the indictment is 'palpably defective.' "[38] Justices William A. Wachenfeld and A. Dayton Oliphant dissented, and would have affirmed the decision by Hughes. Some years later, the United States Supreme Court came to the same conclusion as had Hughes, that one could not be convicted simply for one's status as opposed to one's conduct.[39]

The case subsequently went to trial. Judge John J. Francis, who would later serve as a justice of the New Jersey Supreme Court, handled the case, which lasted fifty-three days with close to 150 witnesses. At the time it was the longest case in New Jersey history involving just one defendant.[40] One of the character witnesses called on behalf of Winne was the former governor, Walter Edge, who had also served as ambassador to France. During the course of the trial, Judge Francis dismissed all of the counts except for two. The jury deliberated for five hours and thirty minutes and acquitted.[41]

Hughes was very proud of his opinion. When his son, W. Michael Murphy, was sworn in as prosecutor of Morris County many years later, Hughes told him to read his opinion in that case to understand the role of a prosecutor. Murphy did read the opinion and quoted from it in his speech after being sworn in. The overturning of Hughes's decision in the *Winne* case did not injure Hughes's judicial reputation. Many lawyers in the state felt that Hughes's decision was correct. Furthermore Chief Justice Vanderbilt later appointed Hughes as chairman of the Supreme Court

Committee on Juvenile and Domestic Relations Court, and assigned him as assignment judge of Union County, an important position within the judiciary. A few years later a new chief justice, Joseph Weintraub, a brilliant lawyer who would lead the court for the next sixteen years, assigned Hughes to the Appellate Division, the court that handles the vast bulk of the appeals that occur in New Jersey. It is considered a very demanding court, requiring great legal, analytical, and writing skills of its judges. All of these positions recognize Hughes's various talents as a judge.

The New Jersey judiciary is divided for administrative purposes into geographical districts called vicinages. Each of the larger counties is its own vicinage; smaller counties are joined together to make up vicinages. Each vicinage has an assignment judge selected by the chief justice to be the chief administrator for that vicinage. The chief justice chooses assignment judges very carefully. Chief Justice Vanderbilt's selection of Hughes as assignment judge of Union County occurred after Hughes had been on the bench for a relatively short time. Hughes often said how much he enjoyed that position. As assignment judge, there was more reason for him to attend Bar Association events and to interact with county leaders to make the courts work efficiently. The position requires more administrative talents than most judicial positions and the constant interaction with others suited Hughes's gregarious personality. Hughes said, "I had been Assignment Judge in Union County and I just loved it. Good county, 600,000 people, 21 municipalities, a lot of action, good Bar, fine group of lawyers, good judges, colleagues. I liked that assignment. That's the best of my assignments on the bench, except for being Chief Justice."[42]

Edward Beglin, who served as assignment judge in Union County from 1983 to 2004, recalled that when he was still a law student and clerking in a law firm in Union County, he would watch Hughes handling motions on Fridays. He said the room was hot and it was noisy from the railroad trains going by. Beglin remembered that Hughes would pace around the bench while listening to the lawyers. He also recalled that Hughes was very popular with the attorneys despite the fact that he increased the length of the court day.[43] Previously, the trials would begin at 10:00 A.M. After Hughes arrived the trials started at 9:30.

Brendan Byrne, who served as governor from 1974 to 1982, recalled his days as a young trial attorney appearing before Judge Hughes. He described how Hughes would regularly call the attorneys into chambers after the case was over and discuss their performance. He would discuss their strengths and weaknesses, but always in a kind manner.[44]

Betty Hughes

Two years after the death of Miriam, Hughes met Elizabeth (Betty) Murphy, whom he eventually married. Betty was a widow with three children, Michael, Patrick, and Timothy. Her husband, William, a captain in the Air Force, had been killed in a plane crash off the coast of the Azores. His remains were never recovered. At the time of her husband's death, Betty's children were very young. She was shaken by her loss and had endured a number of lonely years.

Hughes and Betty met by chance. While Betty Sullivan Murphy had grown up in Blessed Sacrament parish, she was about ten years Hughes's junior. Their paths had never crossed. On Halloween 1953, after taking the children trick-or-treating, Hughes dropped in to visit friends, the Moonans. The Ridolfis, other friends of Hughes, also stopped by. Betty was with them. Hughes described the meeting this way:

> We had a couple of drinks and I was very much impressed with her, naturally. It was a great evening. I was impressed with the fact that Betty had gone two years to Chestnut Hill [a Catholic women's college in Pennsylvania] and then had gone to Douglass [the women's college of Rutgers University], and was a journalism major and had this fine educa-tion, and had worked for Opinion Research and had a pretty responsible job, and would go all over the country, Albuquerque and all over, put ads in the paper to hire interviewers and work on product investigations and so forth. . . . Anyhow, I said I was impressed with this college career and business career and she was an Air Force wife before her husband was killed. I said, "Mrs. Murphy, you're articulate, you're well-educated, you look great, you should go into politics, you should run for the Assembly. I'll come down and talk to you about it some time." She says, "Do that." And she always joked that we got married, and then I put her at the washing machine and taking care of the kids and so forth, and she never got a chance to run for anything.[45]

In spite of the fact that she never ran for political office, Betty did eventu-ally enjoy a fulfilling and rewarding career of her own. During Hughes's years as governor, Betty had her own television show as well as a regular weekly column that appeared in a number of newspapers. There was family precedent for her independence. Her mother, Helen Sullivan, had been widowed at an early age, and worked a full-time job while providing for her five children.

Miriam and Betty were similar in many ways. Both were intelligent, thoughtful, and humorous. Betty, however, was far more attuned to political life than Miriam had been. Betty, while sometimes complaining about the political life, reveled in it. In later years, Hughes would say "When we were governor," including Betty in the plural pronoun. Associates remember Betty as having been involved in many different issues.[46]

Hughes would say later that he and Betty "just clicked." They were married on May 7, 1954, in a quiet ceremony presided over by Hughes's brother, Father Joseph Hughes. While Hughes had been warned that the kids from the two families would never get along, he said of his family life: "They got along so beautifully that one of the kids, Pat (one of the Murphys), who was being spanked for some misdeed started to cry and said 'I wish I had my first mother back.' He believed that he was a Hughes, you see. And so the kids meshed perfectly. In all those years there was never a bit of disharmony."[47] But this last comment undoubtedly involves some touch of Hughes's penchant for exaggeration. A favorite family story recounted that Hughes would sometimes get pulled out of a meeting for a call from Betty, telling him that his kids and her kids were beating up their kids (Brian, Helen [Honey], and Thomas, the three children Betty and Richard subsequently had together).

While the family was generally harmonious, its size put greater strains on Hughes's finances. In some jurisdictions, judges can make additional money by teaching, writing, or lecturing, but in New Jersey there are strict rules against judges earning any outside income. And, of course, judges may not practice law. Confronted with his growing family obligations—by that time, the first of their children, Brian, was born—Hughes began to consider the necessity of leaving the bench to earn more money. At the same time, there was a movement building to have Hughes selected for the next vacancy on the New Jersey Supreme Court. Hughes described the situation: "Thorn Lord and several of my friends were thumping the drums and talking to the papers and all about the possibility that I would be appointed. Then Governor Meyner called me one night . . . and he said, 'Hey, Dick, I want you to know that you're not on my promotion list tomorrow, this time, but I want you to know that I will give you every consideration when the next vacancy comes along.' The next vacancy would be Justice Heher [Hughes's early mentor], who would be bound to retire in three years or so. I said, 'Well, that's all right, governor, I've about made up my mind I've got to get out of here anyhow, for financial, personal reasons.' And, well, he said, 'I'm sorry, but don't forget what I said, if you're ever interested I'll certainly consider you for the position.' "[48]

Shortly after learning he would not be appointed to the Supreme Court, Hughes resigned from the judiciary to open his own practice. Some newspapers suggested that he resigned because he had not gotten the Supreme Court appointment. Hughes said that his resignation was for financial reasons. By this time, the family had added a ninth child, Helen. A letter written by Hughes's father at the time, however, suggests that Hughes may have been very much interested in the Supreme Court position. In it Richard Paul Hughes writes, "I received your letter today and have already read the entire contents over twice. To me it was very interesting and I continue to wonder why in the hell they don't recognize your talent as compared with some I personally know and put you on the high court—however I suppose we will have to be patient."[49] Two years later Governor Meyner called Hughes and offered him the appointment.[50] By then Hughes was busy making money in private practice. He declined the offer. It would be many years later, only after Hughes had been governor for two terms, that his father's wishes would be fulfilled and Hughes would become a member of the New Jersey Supreme Court.

Chapter 4

Private Practitioner

AFTER RESIGNING FROM THE BENCH IN 1957, Hughes opened a private practice in Trenton. He divided his time between Trenton and Newark, where he had a working relationship with the law firm Bilder and Bilder. As his Trenton practice grew, Hughes asked a young attorney, James McLaughlin, to join him. Later, he added Mary Jo Dixon as an associate. McLaughlin said that the former judge and future governor always handled his own cases, even researching and writing briefs. Hughes said the hiring of McLaughlin was one of the best things he ever did. For McLaughlin the experience was equally satisfying. He viewed Hughes as a father figure and he described the four years he spent working with him as the best four years of his life.[1] He said that he never met anyone who did not like Hughes. McLaughlin came from the same Irish Catholic area of Trenton where Hughes and his family lived. He had even attended Blessed Sacrament School with Betty Hughes's brother.[2]

Hughes's large circle of friends—professional, political, and personal—played a significant part in his thriving practice. Joseph Katz, who would later work in public relations for Governor Hughes, said, "Clients streamed in; he was soon earning multiples of a judge's salary."[3] Perhaps the firm's most important client came as a result of Hughes's relationship with another professional, John Pindar. Pindar was a well-known trial attorney from Newark. While a partner at Shaw, Pindar, Connell, Foley & Geiser he tried a number of cases before Judge Hughes. At the conclusion of one of the cases, Hughes complimented Pindar on the excellence of his presentation. Pindar was impressed by the quality of judicial craftsmanship exhibited by Judge Hughes. The two men became friends. Pindar, who handled all the defense work for New Jersey Manufacturers Insurance Company in the northern part of the state, arranged for Hughes's new practice to get the NJM work in Mercer County. This client became an important one for the practice, although there were many other sources of work as well.

Grover Richman, Governor Robert Meyner's attorney general, appointed Hughes as a rate counsel before the Public Utility Commission. The rate counsel position, which paid very well, was seen as a political plum.[4] Thorn Lord, Hughes's close friend and former partner, had, as Democratic leader of Mercer County, strongly supported Meyner's quest for the governorship. Hughes's many political friendships were also responsible for his service as legislative counsel to the railroad industry. Edward O'Mara, a senator from Hudson County who headed a prominent law firm in Jersey City, arranged for Hughes to represent the railroads. Hughes said, "I was recommended by Senator Edward O'Mara. They had a representative, a Republican named Harry Towe used to be a congressman from Bergen County [served as Representative for the Ninth District from 1943–1951], a lovely man, very fine man, we were good friends. His job was to handle the Republican members of the legislature and I was supposed to know something about the Democrats. And the job, the Brotherhood of Railroad Workers had always special legislation that would hurt the railroads financially, we were supposed to fight that. So it was quite a job, had a lot of fun."[5] In this position Hughes willingly opposed unions, in spite of his strong Democratic values. At the time, he was trying to build his practice and was happy to have the work. His lobbying efforts on behalf of the railroads brought in $15,000 a year.

Hughes also handled an important case involving the Seabrooks—a wealthy family who owned Seabrook Farms, a large frozen food company. A major family feud had erupted when the patriarch of the family, C. F. Seabrook, tried to cut his sons out of the business. The sons hired Hughes to represent them, and he worked to call into question the competency of the patriarch. However, just before the case was to be heard, the patriarch sold the company, making the matter moot.[6]

Nevertheless, Hughes won some of the early skirmishes in the case by bringing in an expert in the area, Alfred Clapp. While on the Appellate Division, Hughes sat with Clapp, one of the giants of the legal profession in New Jersey. Prior to becoming a judge, Clapp had been a state senator, a professor, dean of Rutgers Law School, and chairman of the editorial board of the *New Jersey Law Journal.* At the time of the Seabrook case, he had left the bench and was in private practice. One of the issues in the Seabrook case revolved around the interpretation of a state statute which had been drafted while Clapp was chairman of the Advisory Committee on Review of Statutes. Hughes brought in Clapp to argue this particular issue and won. As described by James McLaughlin, Judge Clapp told the court that he had drafted the statute and could interpret its meaning.[7] Years later, Clapp, a Republican, would play a much less helpful role in the life of Hughes, serving as chair of James Mitchell's gubernatorial campaign against Hughes.

Another prominent attorney Hughes became friendly with during his years of private practice was Alan Lowenstein, founder of Lowenstein Sandler and a major figure in the New Jersey Bar. He, too, would play a role in the 1961 gubernatorial campaign, but in his case, a supportive one, serving as chairman of Essex County Citizens for Hughes. In recollecting their friendship, Lowenstein recalled, "In 1960, I served as counsel for an applicant for a bank charter in Hillside, and found myself opposed by several eminent attorneys representing opponents of the charter application, including Richard J. Hughes [serving as counsel to Union County Trust Company]. . . . This litigation experience with Dick Hughes was the beginning of my friendship with him that lasted until his death."[8]

The most interesting case Hughes was involved in during this time was noteworthy because the lead counsel was Thomas E. Dewey, the former two-term governor of New York. Dewey had achieved a reputation for racket-busting as a prosecutor. He ran for president in 1944 and lost to Roosevelt. He ran again in 1948 and lost to Truman in an upset. Hughes worked with Dewey as local counsel in a case representing Eli Lilly, a pharmaceutical company, in a matter involving the Salk vaccine. Under New Jersey court rules, as an out-of-state attorney, Dewey was required to have a New Jersey lawyer as local counsel. In a most serendipitous manner, Dewey's firm, Dewey Ballantine, chose Hughes. William Reiss, a well-regarded labor law attorney at the firm of Pitney Hardin and Ward in Newark was instrumental in this selection. He was also a close friend of John Pindar. Reiss was apparently well-regarded by the people at Dewey Ballantine. When he was asked for a recommendation for an attorney in Trenton, he said, "Well you couldn't get any better than Dick Hughes."[9] When Hughes was being considered for the New Jersey Supreme Court, however, Hughes had heard through the grapevine that Reiss had made some derogatory comments about him. Apparently, this must have been misinformation in light of Reiss's later recommendation to Dewey Ballantine. Although Hughes had said that he had left the bench for financial reasons, he still must have been disappointed about not receiving the position on the Supreme Court because he later said, "When I heard this reputed remark I was mad, and it's easy to reach out for a fellow and call somebody up and give them hell but I forbore and didn't do it. Two years later he put me in probably as big a case as I ever had."[10] Some years later Reiss would work with Hughes on his campaign for governor.[11]

Hughes spent quite a bit of time on the Lilly case, although Dewey actually tried it. Hughes was particularly delighted to be involved because Dewey was used to the higher fees New York lawyers usually received. He told Hughes, "Just send your bills to me . . . don't stint yourself, just send fair bills and I'll see they're paid."[12] Hughes was a conservative biller. When he considered charging $7,500 in his last bill, Betty convinced him to change it to $15,000. When his check arrived, a note was included from the president of Eli Lilly thanking him for his "extremely moderate bill and statement for your services, well earned."[13] Hughes quoted Betty as having said, "You see? Give me my half."[14]

Hughes considered Dewey a great lawyer. Dewey "worked like a dog on that case; a great lawyer. Seven day a week lawyer."[15] Hughes observed, however, that Dewey was not exactly a man of the people. Hughes liked to tell an illustrative story: There is a well-known restaurant in Trenton, Lorenzo's, which was frequented by politicians. While not fancy, Lorenzo's had very good food and was located near the courthouse. Hughes and Dewey ate there the first day of the trial. Dewey was content with the surroundings until he had to use the men's room, which did not have doors on its stalls. As Hughes told it, "Then he went to the bathroom and sat down, and some very rough looking guy came in to use the urinal, said 'Hiya, bud' he says 'Hi.' But then he says to the rest of us. 'This is too informal for me.' So he made us go up after that to the Stacy Trent."[16] This was a fancier restaurant, but it was fifteen minutes farther away, and so they had to rush through their meals. But Hughes understood. "It was embarrassing, because there are pretty tight quarters there [in Lorenzo's]. He was seated in the stall, and the guy was using the urinal, but there's no door, and he said 'Hi bud.' "[17]

Hughes's relationship with Dewey was yet another example of his ability to work and get along with people with whom he disagreed. "I never liked him politically, but I got along beautifully with him. There's a picture around someplace of Dewey and myself shaking hands the first day of the trial. And I was smoking a pipe, I think, or he was smoking a pipe. A very friendly, natural picture. Yeah, I thought very highly of him. He was the best trial lawyer I ever heard in my life."[18]

Hughes was also serving in an "of counsel" position with the law firm of Bilder and Bilder. Larry Bilder, who later served in Hughes's administration and then as a judge, recalled Hughes's excellence as an attorney. His skill in taking depositions revolved around his simple direct style and his excellent memory. He would begin questioning and then veer off the subject and then later return to the earlier subject, remembering exactly what the deponent had previously said, and often being able to find inconsistencies in the answers. Bilder remembered that Hughes wanted everything short and to the point.

Stanley Van Ness, who also served as counsel to the governor and went on to be public advocate for the state, also recalled Hughes's remarkable talent to focus and remember. He talked about a memo he had prepared for Hughes on a difficult topic. After Hughes read the memo, the issue was put on the back burner for some weeks. In a surprise move, a reporter raised the issue at a press conference. Van Ness was amazed that Hughes had total recall of all the important facts and issues contained in a memo he had read weeks earlier.

During these years, while he was running his own law firm in Trenton and serving as "of counsel" at Bilder and Bilder, Hughes was making significant money for the first time in his career. The large Hughes family was able to move into a thirteen-room house in the Blessed Sacrament parish. So Hughes was understandably hesitant when politicians first approached him with the possibility of running for governor. Thinking about a governor's salary, which was about one-third of his private practice income, he said, "a big family kind of soaks up money like a sponge."[19]

Even during his private practice years, Hughes was always involved in politics. He worked hard for John F. Kennedy during the 1960 campaign and helped his old friend Thorn Lord, who was running for Senate that same year.

Joel Sterns, who worked on Lord's campaign, recalls that Hughes was often with Lord on the campaign trail. He also said that the first time he met Hughes was at a large political dinner in Washington. Hughes and Betty were hosting a large reception for the New Jersey delegation attending the dinner. Hughes was ostensibly hosting it in his capacity as a lobbyist for the railroads, but Sterns sensed that he had other ambitions.[20]

Senator Richard Coffee, who was active in Mercer County politics in the years when Hughes was serving as a judge, remarked that he had always heard about the legendary leader of Mercer County, Richard Hughes, but had not known him personally until Hughes began practicing law. During that time, Hughes became county chairman of the United Fund drive. Coffee, who served under Hughes in that drive, said that Hughes expended a great deal of energy in this effort and significantly increased its success.[21] This was an example of Hughes's ability to boost his own name recognition and reputation, while simultaneously supporting a worthy cause. He knew that kind of public activity would help his law practice and that it would prove beneficial if he decided to run for political office in the future.

Lord was still serving as Mercer County Democratic leader at that time, a position he loved. He regularly lunched at Lorenzo's surrounded by other active Mercer County Democratic politicians. These lunches were nicknamed the Zoo.[22] As Democratic leader, Lord was involved in the selection of judges and he consistently turned to his friend Hughes for advice on those appointments. One of his appointees, Judge J. Wilson Noden, who would go on to serve for many years in various judicial positions, recalled that after he was appointed to the bench he was shocked by the cost of the robes. In New Jersey, judges are expected to supply their own. Noden mentioned this to a group of friends, including Hughes. Hughes immediately offered Noden his own robe. Noden accepted the offer and wore Governor Hughes's robe for some time. He considered Hughes to be an excellent judge, saying there was "no one smarter."[23]

While Hughes was keeping his hand in politics he was primarily engaged in the practice of law. Hughes was so adept at handling many different things at once that his partner, James McLaughlin, who worked very closely with him on his day-to-day legal work, felt that he was not involved in politics much at all, whereas those in the political world recognized his level of involvement. At this point he had nine children and his wife was busy taking care of them. She would not start her career as a television personality and columnist for some years to come; therefore, the family was dependent upon his salary. He likely thought of himself as a hard-working lawyer with an avocation for politics, who was supporting and raising a large family. At that moment, there was no indication that he would soon shift gears and run for the governorship.

Chapter 5

Governor Hughes

The First Campaign

ALFRED DRISCOLL AND ROBERT MEYNER were the first two governors to serve under the New Jersey Constitution of 1947. Driscoll, a Republican, served under the old constitution from 1947 to 1950 and under the new from 1950 to 1954. Meyner, a Democrat, served from 1954 to 1962. The new constitution gave the governor far greater powers than the earlier constitution had. The authors of the new constitution believed that the times required a powerful executive to deal with the growing problems of decaying cities and the large-scale exodus to the suburbs, the latter a nationwide movement,[1] particularly pronounced in New Jersey. Even though the state's population had grown by almost 2 million between 1940 and 1960, a 50 percent increase, virtually all the major cities had lost residents.[2] The increasing suburbanization reinforced the historic emphasis on home rule. With home rule, each of the 567 units of New Jersey local government controlled its own destiny. Schools were controlled and financed by the local governments rather than by the state, and local governments also controlled planning and zoning within their cities or towns. While New Jersey was not alone in taking this approach,[3] it certainly was in the forefront of its development. As the author Lizabeth Cohen said, "Citizens who prized the independence of their local governments not surprisingly had little interest in sharing power with more distant levels of political authority, be it county, region or state."[4]

There was very little state control over these municipalities. Because New Jersey had no broad-based tax at the time (being one of only three states that had neither a sales tax nor an income tax),[5] it had limited financial resources. Property taxes paid to local municipalities provided for most governmental services. Funding for the comparatively small state government was achieved through excise taxes on various items, including tobacco and gasoline, a corporate tax, and a small inheritance tax. There was then—and there had been historically—great antipathy toward a broad-based tax, but there was an attempt to create one in 1935, when New Jersey adopted a sales tax for a brief period as a result of a bipartisan coalition led by Republican Governor Harold Hoffman and the Democratic boss of Hudson County, Frank Hague. A quick and angry reaction followed. Described as Hague's "raid on the public treasury," according to Richard Leone, the tax was revoked within weeks of its enactment.[6]

Governor Meyner developed a number of major new initiatives including "legalization of bingo and raffles, substantial increases in state aid to education and the restructuring of Rutgers University, as well as increases in teachers' salaries and aid to mentally ill and handicapped children."[7] However, he never pushed for a broad-based tax.

Meyner was selected as a compromise gubernatorial candidate by a group of Democratic Party leaders during a meeting at Thorn Lord's house in Princeton. Despite that, Meyner soon gained a reputation for distancing himself from party leadership. His relationship with party leaders, particularly with John V. Kenny of Hudson County, began to deteriorate shortly after his election and declined steadily during his two terms of office.[8] The Democratic leadership was determined not to let Meyner play any role in the selection of his successor. Meyner's credibility was further weakened by his failure to support John F. Kennedy for the presidency. Due to his own desire to run for president, he participated in a favorite son campaign for that position. Meyner's presidential ambition was not entirely quixotic. He had received a good deal of positive national press during his governorship. He was also featured prominently in a *Time* magazine cover story on November 24, 1958, which pictured six potential Democratic candidates for president: Meyner, Senator John F. Kennedy, Senator Lyndon B. Johnson, Senator Hubert H. Humphrey, Senator Stuart Symington, and California Governor–elect Edmund G. Brown. Adlai Stevenson was pictured in the background.

At the Democratic National Convention of 1960, Meyner did not release his delegates to Kennedy despite strong pressure from the Kennedy camp. Theodore White, a well-known chronicler of presidential politics, reported that New Jersey was bitterly split. While pledged to its own governor, the New Jersey delegation was generally in favor of Kennedy. Joseph P. Kennedy had won the loyalties and votes of the Northern New Jersey political leaders for his son. But the elder Kennedy's lobbying had embittered Meyner.[9] A commentator summed up the situation: "Governor Robert B. Meyner of New Jersey was a big loser in terms of national prestige. He not only persisted in his own Presidential candidacy long after it was apparent he had stirred no interest beyond New Jersey, but he also tried desperately to slow down the Kennedy drive."[10] Meyner, realizing that he had no shot at the presidency, was still hoping for a chance at the vice presidency. Some years later, Meyner said that he had strong indications that he would have been seriously considered for the vice presidency if Lyndon Johnson received the presidential nomination. "Yes, it is true that I was suggested as Senator Johnson's running mate in 1960. A few months before the convention, I was in Texas visiting Johnson supporters in Dallas and Fort Worth. They did suggest me for the vice presidency on the Johnson ticket and, when reporters confronted Johnson with this information, he nodded his approval."[11] Meyner then explained that he had agreed to hold the delegates as a favorite son on behalf of Johnson even though "70 of the 84 persons in the New Jersey delegation were for Kennedy. I gave my word to the Texas delegation and kept it."[12] Kennedy, however, was furious, and it became known that no major patronage would go to New Jersey while Meyner was still in control of the party.[13]

In the same election in which President Kennedy eked out a victory in New Jersey, Lord ran for the United States Senate against incumbent Clifford Case. Case was a formidable candidate, a moderate Republican who appealed to both Democrats and Republicans. *Time* magazine described Lord as, "Democratic Kingmaker Thorn Lord (full name: Balfour Bowen Thorn Lord). A big-time lawyer, Lord works in Trenton, lords it over a claque of intellectuals at home in Princeton."[14] *Time* also noted that he was a shrewd politician. "He was one of the earliest advocates of all-out registration drives . . . and masterminded Bob Meyner's rise to the governor's mansion."[15] Despite Lord's political abilities, Senator Case soundly defeated him, partly because Lord's personality made him an incompetent campaigner. Joel Sterns, who was working on the campaign with Lord and would later serve as counsel to Hughes, said that Lord was irascible, that he did not trust anyone, and that the bigger the crowd, the more nervous he would become.[16] Lord's shyness was underscored during a Kennedy campaign stop in Paramus in September. A large crowd had come to hear the young senator, but Lord, according to observers, hovered in the background. In fact, he had to be coached to stand up when Kennedy introduced him. He said, "The next U.S. Senator, Thorn Lord . . . why don't you stand up, Thorn."[17] Even an accomplished campaigner would have been hard put to unseat Case, the popular incumbent, and Lord did not come close. Robert Hughes recalled that his father had been "deeply involved in Mr. Lord's campaign and was deeply troubled when he lost the race by more than 300,000 votes."[18]

Joel Sterns believes Lord sacrificed himself for the good of Kennedy's candidacy. A key issue facing Kennedy was his Catholicism. Lord thought that if the Democrats ran any of the leading Senate possibilities, all of whom were Catholic, Kennedy's chances would suffer. So Lord arranged for himself, a Protestant, to run, even though he knew he had no chance.[19] However, it was also generally accepted that anyone running against Case would have had an extraordinarily difficult time.

The split between party leaders and Governor Meyner that intensified during the Kennedy campaign helped Richard J. Hughes become the surprise candidate for the governorship in the next election, in 1961. The party's leaders were determined to block anyone supported by Meyner. While Meyner had thought enough of Hughes to consider making him a justice of the New Jersey Supreme Court, he did not originally back him for governor, thus giving Hughes a lift.

Meyner supported several candidates for the governorship—perhaps the kiss of death for them.[20] The president of the Department of Public Utilities, William Hyland, who had previously served as speaker of the Assembly and would later serve as attorney general of the state, was one. The wealthy industrialist Charles Engelhard, who was a major contributor to the Democratic Party, but who had never held elected office, was another. Engelhard had previously run for State Senate in Somerset County against Malcolm Forbes, the flamboyant publisher of *Forbes Magazine* and another multimillionaire. Engelhard lost in a very close race. In 1957, Forbes was the Republican challenger against the incumbent Governor Meyner, who was running for his second term. Forbes lost. Meyner also considered United States Senator Harrison Williams as a potential candidate. Williams had recently defeated Congressman Robert Kean, the father of future Governor Thomas Kean, to become the United States senator from New Jersey.

Hyland, one of Meyner's favorites, would have had a very good chance if Meyner had not supported him. Instead, the party leaders settled on Grover Richman, who had served as attorney general in the first Meyner administration and also served as United States Attorney. Richman had strong support in South Jersey. He had been considered as a candidate for governor when Meyner was selected. However, when Richman suffered a heart attack, the party leaders selected Hughes. Several factors came into play. Thorn Lord's support was one. There was also little time to select a candidate. Additionally, the general belief was that it was time for a Republican to take over and that it was unlikely that any Democrat could win. The leaders, aware of this, decided to go with the well-liked but little known former judge, who had a reputation "as a party regular."[21] The expected Republican candidate, James Mitchell, labor secretary under President Eisenhower, was bound to be favored because of his name recognition. Hughes said that he never expected to get the nomination. "They had maybe sixteen or eighteen names, that you would read about, hear about, and I was not on that list at all."[22] Hughes speculated that each of the leaders would have his own candidate, "Denny Carey would want Mayor Leo Carlin or half a dozen other possibilities, [State] Senator Don Fox, Mayor Kenny would want John Grogan [mayor of Jersey City], Governor Meyner would want Ray Male, Senator John Waddington, he had quite a list."[23] The fact that Hughes was not perceived as the first choice of any of the major leaders was probably a significant factor in making him the perfect compromise candidate.

Throughout the ensuing campaign, the issue of bossism would be a prominent theme. The Republicans accused Hughes of being the candidate of the bosses. Hughes's description of his own selection supports that argument. "There was a conference at the Newarker restaurant[24] attended by Thorn Lord, leader of Mercer County, David Wilentz, former Attorney General and Democratic leader of Middlesex County, John Kenny, Mayor of Jersey City and Democratic leader of Hudson County, Senator Anthony Grossi, Democratic leader of Passaic County and State Senator, Jim Kenneally, Democratic leader of Union County and Dennis Carey, Democratic leader of Essex County, who participated by telephone."[25] At that meeting the leaders coalesced around Hughes. "I was having dinner with my family and I get a call from Wilentz. He said, 'Hey, would you consider running for governor?' I said, 'Certainly not, Dave, for heaven's sake. I'm just getting started in the law business. I'm doing well. I'm making money, I can't afford to spend $75,000, $100,000 on a long shot campaign.' 'Well,' he said 'you wouldn't have to spend that,' he said, 'just don't say no.' I said, 'All right, I won't say no.' He says, 'I'm going to call you back next week.'"[26] While Wilentz made the call to Hughes, Lord, Hughes's long-time friend and former partner, undoubtedly led the charge. *Time* magazine reported, "The awed northern Jersey bosses acknowledged his [Lord's] political genius" and his support for Hughes was extremely important."[27]

Sterns says that Lord initially suggested the name of Congressman

Frank Thompson.[28] Thompson was a friend of Hughes but also an important supporter of President Kennedy in Congress. Kennedy convinced Thompson not to run.[29] With Thompson out of the running, Lord then raised the name of Hughes. This floating of Thompson's name may have been a strategic move on the part of Lord to eliminate the idea that Hughes was Lord's hand-picked candidate.

Betty Hughes, who generally handled the family finances, was not happy with the idea of her husband running. They had just started to earn enough money to support their large family. Adrian Foley, a close friend of both Hughes and Betty, recalled that Hughes called upon him to help convince Betty to support the candidacy.[30]

At the outset, Hughes himself was not in favor of running. In a letter to his father he said he would not take the chance. However, when Wilentz called again and urged him to accept the position, Hughes's love of politics prevailed. He agreed.

In later years Hughes admitted his embarrassment at having promised two different potential gubernatorial candidates that he would talk to Lord on their behalf. One of them, Senator Donald C. Fox of Essex County, was particularly upset. Hughes showed Fox the letter he had written to his father in order to prove that his decision to accept the candidacy was a last-minute one and that he had not deliberately misled him. Later, Fox supported Hughes's run for governor.[31] But Fox was not the only possible candidate from Essex County who was upset. Leo P. Carlin, the mayor of Newark, Conservation Commissioner Salvatore Bontempo, and Congressman Peter Rodino all believed that they would have had a shot at the nomination if Carey pushed for an Essex person.[32] However, when it became clear that Hughes was the consensus choice, they all supported him. Bontempo even became his campaign manager. The Newark Evening News reported: "Bontempo was one of the party's most eager aspirants for the nomination himself, but quickly became one of Hughes' top boosters after the party's leaders picked the former Superior Court Judge as the candidate to succeed Governor Meyner."[33] Later, Bontempo stepped down as campaign chairman to accept a high position in the United States State Department.[34]

Before an official announcement was made about his candidacy, Hughes met with John M. Bailey, the head of the national Democratic Party, whom Hughes described as a "good friend," and with Mayor Grogan of Jersey City, who had been seeking the nomination. Grogan agreed to step aside in favor of Hughes.

Subsequent to the meeting with Grogan, a formal meeting of the Democratic leaders took place at Morven (the governor's home in Princeton) with Governor Meyner. Twenty of the twenty-one county leaders were present. They unanimously chose Hughes as their candidate. Meyner, who had not originally supported Hughes, enthusiastically announced the selection, saying, "Richard Hughes has all the qualifications necessary to be a successful candidate and a fine governor. He is articulate, intelligent, well informed, a lifelong Democrat and from a family of Democrats. I am pleased we have chosen him."[35]

Congressman Peter Rodino, who would later serve as the distinguished chairman of the House Judiciary Committee during the impeachment hearings on President Richard Nixon, recalled that Hughes asked him to serve as chairman of his campaign after Bontempo left. Mayor Carlin of Newark, however, was adamantly opposed to Rodino as chairman. Rodino was rooming with Congressman Hugh Addonizio in Washington at the time, and Carlin perceived him as a supporter of Addonizio, who was contemplating a run for mayor of Newark against Carlin. He believed that being chairman of Hughes's campaign would give Rodino stature that he would eventually use to support Addonizio. Carlin refused to support Hughes's candidacy if Rodino were to be his chairman. Rodino withdrew, not wanting to hurt Hughes's chances for the governorship.[36] Some time later Hughes did give Rodino a position in the campaign—"personal campaign assistant."[37] In place of Rodino, Hughes chose John C. Giordano, a former Monmouth County judge, as chairman of his campaign. While Giordano was the chairman, the two people actually in charge of the day-to-day running of the campaign were Robert Burkhardt and John Kervick. Burkhardt had worked on Meyner's campaigns, as well as in his administration, and Kervick was the state treasurer in the Meyner administration and the chief fundraiser in Hughes's campaign.

There were three candidates in the Republican primary—Walter Jones, James Mitchell, and Wayne Dumont. While some considered Mitchell the favorite, others thought Jones was the favorite because of his closer ties to New Jersey. However, the *Newark Evening News* and the *New York Herald Tribune* supported Mitchell. He was viewed as a "Rockefeller Republican," meaning a moderate Republican. The newspapers' support and his identification with the moderate wing of the Republican Party led him to victory in the primary.[38] In the Democratic primary, Hughes had only nominal opposition. Three people, Essex County Supervisor Weldon R. Sheets, Hackensack Councilman Eugene E. DeMarest, and

Fort Lee attorney Michael Kearney, were on the ballot, but none had any organizational support.

Once Hughes gained the nomination, he announced his intention to recommend Thorn Lord for the Democratic Party state chairmanship. Governor Meyner was also seeking this key position, which basically controlled federal patronage in the state. The Democratic leaders of Hudson and Essex Counties supported Lord, and President Kennedy and others in his administration remembered Meyner's role at the 1960 convention and refused to back him. With Hughes's continued support of Lord, Meyner withdrew. On April 26, 1961, Lord became State Democratic Chairman.[39]

The Campaign

Hughes's campaign was a rigorous one. He estimated that he shook more than 300,000 hands during the months between his selection and the vote. James McLaughlin, who was then Hughes's law partner, said that Hughes had tremendous energy.[40] One of his great abilities was to sleep at a moment's notice. When he was campaigning, he would nap between stops at the many rallies, dinners, and meetings he would visit each night and awaken refreshed. Senator Raymond Bateman, who would later run for governor himself on the Republican ticket, said that Hughes went everywhere. Bateman recalled that Hughes used to talk about being the only candidate to go to Shellpile, a tiny town in Salem County literally built on shells.[41]

Although Hughes had been promised financial support from the party, he played a significant role in fundraising. Joseph Katz, who worked actively in the campaign, recalled that Hughes had to raise much of his own finances.[42] At one point, the Hughes team sent out an appeal to every lawyer in New Jersey. When asked why they were sending out requests that would reach Republicans and nonpolitical types, Lord replied, "They're lawyers and they know and love Dick Hughes."[43] The campaign did, in fact, receive contributions from unlikely sources, including Republicans. One Republican contributor was Robert W. Johnson, board chairman of Johnson & Johnson and a leading spokesman for the conservative wing of the Republican Party. When Johnson was asked why he contributed to the campaign, he said, "I try to help anyone I think is deserving."[44] *Time* magazine reported a month before the election that the Hughes campaign had over one million dollars and intended to spend it, as compared with Mitchell's $500,000.[45]

On July 8, the *Newark Evening News* commented on the ability of Hughes to bring people together. "Win or lose in November, Richard J. Hughes, the Democratic gubernatorial candidate this week reserved for himself a niche in recent Essex County political history."[46] The article was referring to the fact that Hughes had been able to get the feuding members of the Essex County Democratic Party to come together. Those now united included Essex Chairman Dennis Carey, Senator Donald C. Fox, and Congressman Peter Rodino. "It was difficult to remember that as recently as April, Fox and Rodino were fighting to depose Carey as chairman."[47] The *Newark News* went on: "If his feat needed any icing, Hughes also brought together the two men who are expected to battle it out next May in Newark's mayoralty election—Mayor Leo P. Carlin and Rep. Hugh J. Addonizio."[48]

The influence of Democratic bosses was perhaps the biggest issue in the campaign and it was raised continually, especially by the Republican candidate, James Mitchell. Hughes stoutly defended his independence, repeating again and again that he did not owe allegiance to anyone. The campaign sought various resources to combat the charge of bossism. An organization called Mercer County Lawyers for Hughes sent out a letter strongly challenging the allegation of bossism and stressing the failure of Mitchell to debate the issue. The letter also stressed the integrity Hughes had demonstrated while a state court judge.[49]

Some newspapers, however, decided to endorse Mitchell based on the bossism charge. For example, the *Asbury Park Press*, after conceding that both candidates were men of "competence, integrity and personableness," endorsed Mitchell, saying the discredited system of bossism was employed in the selection of Hughes, thus denying the Democratic voters the chance to pick their candidate.[50] Other papers editorialized in favor of Hughes. The *Trenton Evening Times* said: "It is our conviction, based upon a thoughtful study of campaign developments as they have unfolded up to the present time that the cause of progressive and effective government in New Jersey would be served best by the election of former Judge Richard J. Hughes, the Democratic candidate for Governor."[51]

Joe Katz, Hughes's campaign coordinator, remembered how difficult it was to get publicity, even though the campaign worked hard to get stories in the papers. He specifically noted that the *Newark Evening News*, which was supporting Mitchell, never gave much coverage to Hughes. Katz recalled the campaign's staging of a big birthday party for Hughes. They had Hughes's father attend and said they were taking the party to Hughes because he was too busy campaigning to stop for a party. Katz said, "Even the *Newark News* had to run a picture of that party."[52]

The *Bergen Record*, however, gave Hughes extensive coverage. Hughes recalled that Mitchell had gotten into a conflict with Donald Borg, one of the publishers of the *Bergen Record,* at the Correspondents' Dinner. The dinner is held each year in New Jersey with all the major political figures, and all the members of the press who cover the political scene, in attendance. "They almost had a fistfight at the correspondents' dinner one night. Mitchell was in the sauce a little, they say (in the campaign year) when he beat Walter Jones, and then shortly after the primary came the correspondents' dinner, and I guess both of them had a little, as everybody does there, but Mitchell, big guy, was poking Don Borg in the chest and said, 'You shouldn't be for Jones [Walter Jones, another candidate in the primary] and those things you said about me weren't true' and Don Borg kept poking him back and he gave him hell, and it showed. He says, 'I've got a right to say what I want. And I'm going to keep on doing it.' "[53]

Hughes usually had good relations with the reporters. This was true even when the publishers were in favor of the other candidate. For example, Angelo Baglivo, who was a reporter for the *Newark Evening News*, personally preferred Hughes, even though his paper favored Mitchell.[54]

Joe Katz, who had worked as a newspaper reporter and was in charge of writing press releases and speeches for the Hughes campaign, dictated that Hughes's first name for the campaign would be "Judge." Every piece of literature and every reference to Hughes referred to him as Judge. The reasoning was that since Hughes often came across as a genial backslapper, it was important to invest him with gravitas.

The initial polls indicated a sizable lead for Mitchell. Some polls had Mitchell leading right to the end of the campaign. There was never a real turning point where Hughes surged ahead. Instead, a series of small successes by Hughes and mistakes by, and problems for, Mitchell, turned an expected rout by Mitchell into a narrow victory for Hughes. For one thing, Mitchell, who was never an aggressive campaigner, was forced to limit his campaigning even further when he fell and broke his leg in the final weeks of the campaign.

Early in the race, Hughes challenged Mitchell to debate. Mitchell refused, and Hughes harped on the issue throughout the campaign. Katz has said that Hughes was lucky that Mitchell turned down the invitation, not only because Hughes wasn't a good debater, but because Mitchell's refusal gave Hughes a viable criticism that served him throughout the campaign. Katz thought

Mitchell basically sat on his hands and relied upon his lead. "He counted on the *Newark News*, and the *Herald Tribune* to carry him through."[55]

A review of the campaign records illustrates that Hughes covered dozens of different issues. His campaign turned out press releases on everything from how the state pension funds should be handled, to access to the beaches, to education, to civil rights. Hughes clearly was on the more liberal side of many of them. For example, on education the campaign literature said: "Our higher education system is not keeping up with demand. Our college age population is growing by leaps and bounds. If you want your children to be able to find space in a New Jersey college, then we must expand Rutgers University and also the system of two year technical institutes and junior colleges."[56] At one point during the campaign, Mitchell apparently said that too many people were going to college and that admission standards should be raised. Hughes immediately jumped on that statement, emphasizing his support for increasing opportunities for students to receive higher education.

Instituting a broad-based tax was an important issue during the campaign, and one that Hughes played very close to the vest. Across the country states were becoming increasingly financially involved in the problems of their communities, and there certainly was some feeling that New Jersey needed to do more for its citizens. Hughes took the first tentative step toward increasing taxes by announcing that he would ask his party to drop the no-new-tax plank of the 1957 and 1959 state platforms.[57] But while recognizing the need for the state to do more, particularly in the area of education, Hughes was still not prepared to say whether a sales or income tax was needed. Instead he said that he would do everything that he could to avoid imposing such taxes. He was testing the waters, and it would not be until his second term that he would make an all-out push for new taxes.

Campaign Problems for Hughes

First, Hughes feared that the Mitchell campaign might bring up $80,000 in fees Hughes earned for representing the state in a major rate case before the Public Utilities Commission. He took the initiative and raised the topic himself, stating that he had saved the state $26 million annually in gas and electric charges. He also said that it was his toughest case ever, with 106 hearing days before the Public Utilities Commission. When Mitchell did, in fact, address the issue, Meyner came to Hughes's defense, stating that he had named Hughes as a rate counsel and that his fee was fixed by law. Mitchell also emphasized the fact that Hughes had worked as a lobbyist for the railroads. In response, Hughes offered to open his personal financial records to public review.

Another such issue that arose during the campaign was the charge that Hughes had offered a federal judgeship to Congressman William Cahill in order to get him to stop campaigning actively for Mitchell.[58] The charges came from various newspaper reporters citing unnamed sources. At that time Cahill was serving as head of the Mitchell campaign in Cahill's congressional district.[59] Cahill, a Republican, had argued cases before Judge Hughes and the two had become acquainted. They were friendly and had similar Irish-Catholic backgrounds and political styles. There were three judicial vacancies at the time, but Hughes would not have been in a position to fill these openings, since federal judgeships are in the domain of the President of the United States. Of course, Hughes did have a relationship with President Kennedy, and it is not out of the question that he could have provided a recommendation and influenced the choice. When asked about the claim, both Cahill and Hughes refused to comment. The *Newark Evening News* reported, "Questions put by the *Newark News* to both Hughes and Cahill brought neither denial nor confirmation. Both men declined to comment."[60] Subsequently, Hughes released a statement: "I have read an account in a newspaper that is apparently dedicated to the candidacy of Mr. Mitchell to the effect that I had visited the office of Congressman Cahill to offer him a federal court judgeship in exchange for his abandonment of support of Mr. Mitchell. This statement is unqualifiedly false and I categorically deny it."[61] The *Newark Evening News* subsequently reported: "James P. Mitchell said today that he has 'no information' on the truth of the reports that Republican Rep. William T. Cahill, 1st. Dist. was offered a federal judgeship by Richard J. Hughes, the Democratic nominee for governor."[62] However, when the press persisted and asked whether the issue had been discussed, Hughes refused to answer.[63] A commentator stated: "Cahill's refusal to comment on the issue and the awkwardness with which Hughes tried to explain it away kept the story alive for weeks."[64]

Cahill continued to campaign for Mitchell and after a while, no further mention of the incident appeared. Cahill never became a federal judge. In fact, while he was congressman he was also practicing law, and with his reputation as a fine trial attorney,[65] he was making a substantial amount of money. He had a large family, and earning money might have been more important than a federal judgeship. Later, Cahill would succeed Hughes as governor of New Jersey and would appoint Hughes as chief justice of the New Jersey Supreme Court.

Another, potentially more embarrassing attack occurred when Mitchell alleged that the Democrats raised $80,000 at a dinner with 160 people who did business with the state. Hughes dismissed these charges as "fringe trash of the Republican campaign."[66] Meyner defended the Democrats, saying that asking for contributions was common practice among both parties. He also denied ever pressuring contractors or employees for money.[67] Alfred Clapp, Mitchell's campaign manager, demanded that the Democrats disclose the list of all contributors who paid $500 to attend the dinner and also did business with the state. John Kervick, executive director of the Democratic State Committee, agreed to disclose the list if the Republicans would disclose their list of contributors. The Republicans insisted on a distinction, arguing that they wanted the specific list of those who attended that dinner and also did business with the state.[68] Governor Meyner strongly supported Hughes, stating that he saw nothing wrong with accepting contributions from those doing business with the state.[69] That practice, often referred to in later years as "pay to play," continued in New Jersey and many other states for years after the Hughes campaign.

Shortly after that flap, yet another controversy arose. The Mitchell campaign alleged that Theodore Botter, then First Assistant Attorney General who would later become a well-respected state court judge, told the lawyers on the staff of the attorney general's office that under the Democratic administration of Governor Meyner, their salaries had been raised and they might suffer financial reverses if the Republicans took over. Therefore, they should financially support Hughes.[70] Attorney General David Furman, who also would go on to a distinguished career as a judge, responded "it is common practice of both parties to ask all persons holding government appointments at federal, state, county and local levels to contribute."[71] However, he added that no pressure had been brought to bear on members of the staff. At that time the Supreme Court had issued an order barring court employees from participating in any way in political campaigns. That was consistent with the desire of the court, after the adoption of the new constitution in 1947, to keep the court system completely free from politics. Mitchell argued that the same type of prohibition should be applied to the attorney general's office.

Despite the necessity to defend against those allegations, Hughes took the offensive on a number of issues. He attacked Mitchell for not being a liberal. At that time in the history of this country, and in New Jersey in particular, liberal philosophy was on the rise. President Kennedy, who campaigned on liberal principles, was very popular. The Republican senator, Clifford Case, was a liberal Republican and was campaigning for Mitchell. The Republicans were trying to position Mitchell in the same light. Hughes, in remarks to the Retail Clerk's Union after attacking Mitchell for not supporting an increase in the minimum wage, said, "He's no liberal no matter what they try to tell you."[72]

Hughes showed his own liberal sentiments by speaking out strongly in favor of civil rights. "We have been educated by the great series of United States Supreme Court decisions. We have been bitterly educated by Little Rock and by New Orleans, Montgomery and Jackson, Mississippi. What we need is constant action to abolish second-class citizenship in New Jersey and in the nation."[73] He announced that if he was elected he would transfer the State Division on Civil Rights from the Department of Education to the Department of Law and Public Safety. He believed that this would bring about greater enforcement of the civil rights laws.

The fact that Hughes was Catholic and would become the first Catholic governor in New Jersey was not an issue in the campaign, even though just one year earlier, John F. Kennedy's Catholicism had been a major concern. Kennedy had to convince skeptics that he would not be a tool of the pope.[74] He won the election despite continuing anti-Catholic sentiment, particularly in the South. But New Jersey had a large Catholic population and relatively little anti-Catholic sentiment. Perhaps, most important, Mitchell was also a Catholic. Thus, no matter which side won, there would be a Catholic governor.

Hughes profited from Mitchell's failure to unite the Republican Party. Walter Jones, who was defeated by Mitchell in the primary, did not actively support him.[75] Some Republicans saw Mitchell as an outsider and were not personally invested in his campaign.[76] Additionally, many conservative Republicans considered Mitchell the hand-picked candidate of the liberal Republican Senator, Clifford Case, and simply decided not to vote.[77]

Both candidates sought support from national figures. Hughes received endorsements from Adlai Stevenson, Secretary of Labor Arthur J. Goldberg, President Harry S Truman, and ultimately President John F. Kennedy. Mitchell had the active support of President Dwight D. Eisenhower, in whose cabinet he had served throughout most of Eisenhower's presidency. At a campaign appearance in Newark, Eisenhower said, "I do not know a finer man."[78] Mitchell also received support from other Republican heavyweights including New York Governor Nelson Rockefeller and New York Senator Jacob Javits.

Hughes took advantage of the popularity of President Kennedy by meeting with him in Washington to update him on the progress of the campaign. This provided him with needed publicity, and support for the idea that he would have access to federal funds and a sympathetic ear if he were elected. During the campaign, Secretary of the Interior Stewart L. Udall came to New Jersey to announce that the Defense Department would turn over 460 acres of the Sandy Hook Peninsula to be used as a state park. On the same day, Udall gave a campaign speech on behalf of Hughes.[79]

Another Hughes campaign strategy was the "Hughes Girls." Jacqueline Beusse, who had served in the Kennedy campaign as a "Kennedy girl" the previous year, had organized a large contingent of 210 young women—ten in each county—to support Hughes's campaign. These women in matching outfits designed by Beusse in the state colors would appear at every type of campaign event including breakfasts, dinners, whistle-stop tours, etc. Beusse said: "I thought of it as a publicity campaign to build awareness for his name in the newspapers and among the potential voters as he traveled the state." Beusse described the role of the young women: "They were briefed on the issues. They distributed his campaign literature. They sang his campaign songs and were able to speak intelligently on the goals he hoped to attain as the next governor." They generated significant public attention, which aided in the attempts to gain publicity for Hughes.[80]

Looking back in 1969, Edward Mullin of the *Herald News* in Passaic County described Hughes as a candidate who made campaigning "a lot of fun." Mullin referred to him as "a master politician, and as the greatest New Jersey campaigner of his day."[81] After the election, *Time* said, "Hughes earned his own win. Working 20 hours a day, he logged a remarkable 60,000 miles in crisscrossing New Jersey. He visited each of the state's 21 counties at least twice, concentrating on Republican strongholds. By his own estimate he shook some 300,000 hands; he turned up at so many political and civic luncheons and dinners that he gained ten pounds."[82] His son Robert said that Hughes would get back from a night of campaigning with his hands bleeding.[83]

Not all reviews of the campaign were favorable. Alan L. Otten, writing for the *Wall Street Journal*, was not impressed by either candidate. "For all their differences, there are strong similarities between the candidates. Both are big, heavy men, tireless chain-smokers. . . . Mr. Mitchell talks slowly and softly, Mr. Hughes rather shrilly and quickly; neither is a moving speaker. Both tend to rely on cliches and make speeches in answer to questions. Neither seems to enjoy the contest much: it is a humorless campaign."[84] Alvin Felzenberg described the campaign as lackluster because the candidates basically took similar positions on most of the major issues and relied on the support of national figures.[85]

John Miller, who was running for the assembly at the same time, often campaigned with Hughes. He said there were times when just the two of them would show up for meetings in citizens' homes. He particularly recalled one night when they went alone to a home in a poor section of Newark. They sat in the kitchen, talking and answering questions for about half an hour. When they started to get up to leave for another event, they found that they were stuck to their chairs. The host, in an attempt to make his home more presentable for the candidates, had painted the chairs before the meeting and they still hadn't completely dried. Hughes, undaunted by the experience, simply laughed. They went on to the next meeting with paint stripes across the backs of their clothes.[86]

Hughes, a strong proponent of the labor movement, received the endorsement of the New Jersey Congress of Industrial Organizations (C.I.O.). Hughes's securing of the endorsement was an impressive demonstration of his powers of persuasion. The C.I.O. executive board had recommended that the organization remain neutral. After 650 delegates listened to the two candidates speak at a meeting of the organization, they rejected the recommendation of the executive board and overwhelmingly endorsed Hughes.[87] That the C.I.O. supported Hughes was particularly impressive in light of his earlier dispute with it when he was Mercer County Democratic leader.

Hughes had other campaign advantages, including nine children and an outgoing wife. There were numerous stories during the campaign about "Hughes the family man." His wife and children were prominently depicted in campaign literature and in stories about Hughes. The papers loved the family pictures. Early on in the campaign Betty Hughes was depicted worrying whether or not the large family could all fit into Morven, the governor's mansion. In the *Newark Sunday News* magazine section on the Sunday before the election, a big spread pictured both candidates and their families. The pictures of the Mitchell family were much more staid than those of the large Hughes clan. Mitchell appeared in one picture with his wife in a rather formal pose, and in another less formal picture with his wife, daughter and granddaughter. Hughes was portrayed in a demonstrably loving picture with two of his young children and in another with his wife and eight of his children.

Betty Hughes enjoyed campaigning and she was never hesitant to speak her mind. One commentator tells the story of her rejoinder to a reporter for *The Star-Ledger*, who often said Hughes was too old. "After reading a number of articles to that effect, Betty Hughes called the writer responsible to tell him he hadn't made much effort to uncover the truth. 'Why didn't you check with me first?' she asked. I'm his wife. I should know. I sleep with him.' And bang went the telephone receiver."[88]

Betty's comments vividly described what life was like with Hughes. One of her often repeated remarks was, "If three men are installing a manhole cover in Teaneck, Dick Hughes will be there to make a speech." She also complained that Hughes would never take her out for a quiet dinner because her husband believed that a dinner without a microphone and a dais was not worth going to.[89]

President Kennedy's Visit

President Kennedy's visit to New Jersey to campaign for Hughes was another opportunity for the Hughes family to receive prominent press coverage. The *Trenton Times* carried a banner headline about Kennedy as well as a photograph and story about the Hughes children meeting the president. The caption read "Children's hour at Kennedy reception."[90] According to a favorite family story, Hughes's ten-year-old stepson Pat Murphy ended up arm-wrestling with the president while he waited to go on stage for his speech. Hughes wrote about the incident some time later. "He [Kennedy] was warm and kind in a private greeting to my wife and family, including most of my children. Waiting to go on stage, JFK challenged my stepson Pat Murphy, then 10 years old, to a contest of 'hand wrestling,' which the President won handily."[91]

There had been a question as to whether Kennedy would participate in the campaign. New Jersey is one of only two states that have a gubernatorial election the year after the presidential election. Thus, there is a great deal of media attention to these races, the results of which can be seen as a reaction to the policies of the president. Because the race was close and most polls were still saying that Mitchell would win, President Kennedy was hesitant to put his prestige on the line.

On October 24, a number of Democratic leaders from New Jersey went to Washington in the hope of getting the president to campaign for Hughes. The group included Thorn Lord, David Wilentz, and Robert Burkhardt. They met with John Bailey, the national Democratic chairman, and Kenneth O'Donnell, a political aide to Kennedy.[92] As of October 25, there was still no indication that the president would appear in New Jersey on behalf of Hughes, even though he had expressed support for him. A press release stated: "The White House said today that President Kennedy believed Richard J. Hughes would make 'an excellent Governor' of New Jersey."[93] It was a late poll by John Bucci, indicating that Hughes had pulled into the lead, that helped persuade Kennedy. On October 27, the White House announced that Kennedy would campaign for Hughes.

Kennedy visited New Jersey just four days before the election. It is unclear how much his visit helped, but it certainly received a great amount of media attention. The newspapers were filled with banner headlines about the arrival of Kennedy. He gave a short (12-minute) but rousing speech on behalf of Hughes, again pointing out the failure of Mitchell to debate. Kennedy said, "I am all for debates, because I believe—and I am going to debate when I am a candidate, if I am again—because I believe that this is the way the people of this State or other States of this country can make a judgment as to the competence and knowledge of those who present themselves for office."[94] Kennedy went on to emphasize what he and Hughes wanted to do for the country and New Jersey.

> If we can keep this country moving ahead and keep the people working, give to them and to the world an example of a free society moving ahead, then we meet our responsibilities to freedom. And I believe that that is what we are trying to do in the nation's capital. That is what your governor has tried to do in this state. That is what Judge Hughes will try to do when he is elected governor of New Jersey on next Tuesday. He has had a long and uphill campaign. He has been written off on more front pages of more papers supporting other candidates than any candidate I know, with the possible exception of myself about 18 months ago. And I believe that day by day, because of his knowledge of the problems of this state, because he runs on a record which he is proud to stand on of a previous Democratic administration, because he recognized that New Jersey and the country must move ahead, I believe on next Tuesday if you move and do your job from now until then, this state will be in the Democratic column again, and Judge Hughes will succeed Governor Meyner and Governor Wilson and the other distinguished governors of this state who have meant so much to New Jersey.[95]

Just days before the election, a poll by the *Newark Star-Ledger* predicted that Mitchell would win by 100,000 votes. Brendan Byrne, who would serve as governor from 1974 to 1982 and was very close to Governor Meyner, recalled that prior to the election he was so sure that Hughes would lose that he thought it was almost cruel when, before the election, Mrs. Helen Meyner took Mrs. Hughes for a tour of Morven. Michael Murphy recalls going to see Morven with his mother. A number of the children went and swam in the pool while they were there. Betty was convinced that her husband was going to lose and constantly told the children not to get their hopes up. Michael Murphy recalled that the family considered it a nice outing but did not expect to be moving into Morven any time soon. In fact, Betty, while the campaign was going on, bought a new house in Trenton. Betty had always admired a particular house on their street, owned by a Dr. Walters. When he told Betty that he was planning to sell the house, she immediately offered to buy it. And they shook on it. When Hughes got home from a long day of campaigning, Betty greeted him with the news that she had just bought Dr. Walter's house. Hughes pointed out that he believed they would soon be moving to Morven. He then asked whether she had signed a contract. She said no. He then asked if she had shaken on it. She said yes. To Hughes a handshake was as good as a contract. They agreed to buy the house.[96]

During the waning days of the campaign, Hughes's father was quite ill. He, too, was convinced that his son would not win. He died just two days before the election on November 5, at the age of eighty-three. Hughes suspended his campaign to participate in the wake and services for his father. Out of deference, Mitchell also stopped campaigning.

In the end, Hughes won by about 34,920 votes (1,084,194 to 1,049,274). He won in eleven counties and lost in ten.[97] Hughes reported a presidential phone call: "When my victory count was almost complete, about midnight, I received a phone call from JFK who was hearing the returns in the White House, his congratulation led to a close relationship with him during my first administration, until his tragic assassination."[98] This come-from-behind victory gave Hughes a great deal of national publicity. Kennedy was able to take partial credit for it, and he used it to suggest support for his own programs and policies. The exciting election, combined with the president's support and the buzz around New Jersey, were responsible for Hughes's immediate prominence, presaging a governor who would play a role on the national stage.

In an editorial published on November 8, 1961, the day after the election, the *Trenton Times* said: "The election of Mr. Hughes was largely a personal triumph. In comparison with his Republican opponent, former

Labor Secretary James P. Mitchell, who had served long in the national administration, he was virtually unknown. He overcame this disadvantage through an aggressive, hard-hitting campaign, gaining strength gradually as he went along. But even up to the last moment he was conceded only a fighting chance. His surprising victory may be attributed primarily to his forceful campaign, also to the effectiveness of the Democratic organization in the state, to the inspirational effects of President Kennedy's visit to Trenton and to an adverse reaction which Mr. Mitchell suffered by reason of his refusal to debate the issues with his opponent."[99]

The funeral for Hughes's father occurred very shortly after the victory. More than 500 people, including many of the political leaders of New Jersey, attended. After the rigors of the campaign and the trauma of the death of his father, Hughes took a short vacation before he began the transition. Betty accompanied him on a Caribbean cruise with a number of other couples. No doubt planning for the new administration took place on the ship, because one of the people who joined the cruise, Arthur Sills, would subsequently become attorney general.

Hughes was sworn in on January 16, 1962. Inauguration Day was sunny and mild with a slight nip in the air. The day's activities demonstrated his deep devotion to religious faith and practice. He received Holy Communion at the 7 A.M. Mass at Blessed Sacrament, his parish church, which was his daily custom. He then assisted at a Votive Mass in honor of the Holy Spirit at Saint Mary's Cathedral, attended by more than 1,000 people.

Approximately 5,000 people gathered to watch the ceremonies. There were major state dignitaries in attendance, including two former governors, Robert Meyner and Alfred Driscoll. Chief Justice Joseph Weintraub of the New Jersey Supreme Court swore in Hughes. Even so, one reporter described the atmosphere on the platform as more like "a family picnic"[100] than a formal inauguration, as the governor and his first lady were busy keeping the large Hughes family organized.

In his inaugural address, he said: "Having taken an oath before Almighty God, I stand here in full awareness of my particular and heavy responsibility as Chief Executive of the State of New Jersey. I respect but do not shrink from the magnitude of the task before me. For as I stand before you today I sense as I did during the campaign, a new spirit, a new pride of the people. It is this pride, tempered by the humility of an abiding trust in the Almighty, which convinces me of our ability as a people, together, to look with hope upon the sobering face of the modern world."[101]

The address also outlined Hughes's compassionate liberal activist view.

"Good government is government with a sense of social justice, acting not as a patronizing busybody, but as a friend of the migrant laborer in his underprivileged status, the worker replaced by automation, the poultry farmer with his problem of overproduction, the Negro in search of a decent home to mention but a few of the many—the all—for whom government really exists."[102] Reflecting the growing national concerns about economic and educational issues, Hughes focused on the need for economic progress and the need for the state to shoulder more of the burden of aid to education at all levels. He also announced his intention to create a new Department of Urban and Suburban Affairs to deal with the decay in the cities and the rapid, haphazard growth in the suburbs.

One of the attendees more than likely was sixteen-year-old Ridgewood High School student Kathleen Hughes, who was no relation to the new governor. She'd written to Hughes saying that she was the only Democrat in her class and had proudly stood up for her position. Her staunchly Republican teacher would ask her regularly when she would be getting her ticket to the inaugural. When Hughes received her request, he replied by sending a ticket for Kathleen, her parents, and the Republican teacher.[103]

On the same day that Hughes was sworn in, the Senate confirmed the appointment of two of Hughes's most important cabinet officials. Arthur Sills was confirmed as attorney general and Robert Burkhardt was confirmed as secretary of state. Hughes had come to know Sills when they both served as rate counsel for the Public Utilities Commission. He was a partner of the Democratic leader of Middlesex County, David Wilentz, and considered to be an excellent attorney. Burkhardt had been the central political operative in Hughes's campaign and served in Governor Meyner's administration. As the transition swung into full force, Hughes indicated that he would keep on many of the cabinet officials who served under his predecessor.

Hughes was ready and eager to take on the role of governor even though he faced many daunting tasks. The legislature was split, with one house controlled by the Democrats and one house controlled by the Republicans. There was little state money to deal with the mounting problems of transportation, education, civil rights, urban deterioration, major demographic changes, and crime and public safety. Before long, Hughes would confront these and other issues as well.

Chapter 6

The Early Days as Governor

G OVERNOR HUGHES TOOK OFFICE in 1962 while John F. Kennedy was president. Kennedy's Inaugural Address, which included the famous line, "Ask not what your country can do for you—ask what you can do for your country,"[1] had stirred the country. It seemed a time of great potential. On the horizon, however, were signs of the issues that would make the sixties a decade of tumult: civil rights, women's rights, the sexual revolution. The Vietnam War would tear at the very fabric of the country. The assassinations of President Kennedy, Martin Luther King, Jr., and Senator Robert Kennedy would devastate the morale of the nation.

During the 1960s, the United States Supreme Court under the leadership of Chief Justice Earl Warren was actively expanding constitutional rights. The court had begun applying many of the provisions of the Bill of Rights, originally intended to be only applicable to the federal government, to state governments as well. As a result of these decisions, states would have to deal with issues of reapportionment, the rights of criminal defendants, and issues of religious freedom. While some of these issues were already being considered by state courts under provisions of their own constitutions, states would now be bound to follow United States Supreme Court precedent. Hughes would deal with all of these issues during his tenure as governor, and he would also face a host of other concerns that were more local in nature.

When Hughes assumed office, he realized that there were many pressing issues facing New Jersey. He also realized that because of his slim margin of victory in the election, he did not have an overwhelming mandate.

Furthermore, his party did not control the Senate, so Republican cooperation was essential in order for him to succeed. Finally, many of the legislators from his own party were more beholden to county leaders than to the governor. The New Jersey Senate was composed of twenty-one senators, one from each county. The county leaders generally determined who would get the Senate seats, giving them a great deal of control and power. In order to achieve any important legislative breakthroughs, Hughes would have to work with both the Republicans legislators and with both parties' leaders. His great ability to do this was to be a key to his success. However, some did not view his relationships with county leaders favorably, because he occasionally had to trade patronage for their support, at times even taking their recommendations on gubernatorial appointments. Richard Connors, in his book on Hague, relates that Hughes appointed James A. Tumulty, Jr. as prosecutor of Hudson County. It was quite clear that Tumulty was the choice of John V. Kenny, the Democratic leader of Hudson County. Connors writes, "When being sworn as prosecutor in February, 1963, James A. Tumulty, Jr. made his position quite clear: 'I'm Kenny . . . Lest there be any misunderstanding, for the record make that John V. Kenny.'"[2] Connors goes on to say, however, that during the Hughes administration, Kenny's power was limited.[3]

During the entire eight years that Hughes was governor, the state chairman of the Republican Party was Webster Todd. (His daughter, Christine Todd Whitman, would serve as governor of the state between 1994 and 2001.) Hughes developed a good working relationship with Todd. A letter that Hughes wrote to Todd, after a report stated that the governor had made critical remarks about the Republican state chairman, illustrates Hughes's constant effort to stay on the best of terms with everyone. The letter read, "Under extreme fire in Bergen County on a very hectic afternoon when I was confronted with a very tough statement about the bond issue made by the Republican State Committee, I referred to the decrepit Republican Party. This turned out in the press to be a personal reference by me to you as a 'decrepit leader.' I never intended, and am quite sure I did not say such a thing, and for that reason, I take the opportunity to state that I never considered you to be decrepit but, unfortunately, to have too much youthful enthusiasm in your work."[4] And in another letter from Hughes to Todd, Hughes said, "As you know, I have deeply appreciated your personal friendship and that of Eleanor [Todd's wife] over these years and am looking forward to working with you for the common good of New Jersey during the years ahead."[5] However, Hughes was not always this conciliatory. Responding to a letter in which he felt Todd had impugned his integrity, Hughes attacked Todd's position vigorously.

Raymond Bateman, a leading Republican figure throughout Hughes's governorship, wrote about the relationship between Hughes and Republicans. "During his four years with Republican legislatures Hughes became a celebrated compromiser."[6] According to Bateman, he and Hughes became close friends when they both ended up being treated at the same hospital. When Hughes learned that Bateman was also a patient, he immediately invited him to his room to share some "marvelous martinis." These meetings continued for the five days they were hospitalized. Bateman said they "became forever friends. His friendship has been a marvelous tonic for me."[7] He also mentioned that Hughes "didn't have a nasty bone in his body" and that he "was my kind of man, my kind of politician—my ultimate hero in politics."[8]

It was fortunate for Hughes that he learned early on to work productively with Republicans. When Hughes took office in 1962, the Republicans had a slight majority in the Senate (11 to 10) and the Democrats controlled the Assembly (38 to 22). In the midterm elections during Hughes's first term, this changed dramatically. The Republicans gained control of both houses by substantial margins. But when Hughes ran again two years later, he helped effect a decisive Democratic takeover, carrying majorities in both houses. Two years later in the midterm elections, however, the Republicans regained control of both houses with overwhelming majorities. As a result of the United States Supreme Court's reapportionment decisions,[9] the number of senators in the Senate changed twice and the number of assemblymen in the Assembly changed once.[10]

When Hughes was elected, he took over one of the most powerful governorships in the country. As the only elected statewide official, he had the power to appoint virtually all important public officials in the state, including the attorney general. He also had the power to appoint the prosecutors in all twenty-one counties, and all state judges, including the members of the Supreme Court, in addition to having line-item veto power and extensive control in the issuing of executive orders.

Despite those sweeping powers, Hughes was still limited by the absence of a broad-based tax. Money for significant initiatives was unavailable. The sources of income for the government were limited to various excise taxes on railroads, utilities, cigarettes, gasoline, and alcoholic beverages, a corporate business tax, and a transfer inheritance tax.[11] The budget was minute and insufficient to provide for programs Hughes believed necessary to improve the state. During the campaign, Hughes had insisted on removing from the Democratic platform the previous pledge not to raise taxes. The option to institute a broad-based tax, however, could not be easily exercised in a state that had so strongly opposed such an initiative. Hughes faced a dilemma. How could the government help the people of the state in the absence of any significant source of revenue? In the early days of his administration, he indicated that while a tax would not be necessary in the first year, he would urge the creation of a broad-based tax in his second year. In fact, he did not get a broad-based tax instituted until his second term in office.

Hughes undertook enormous responsibility in a difficult financial situation, but he did so with the same energy and commitment that he had given to his campaign. He seemed to be everywhere. He gave numerous speeches and was constantly on the road. Almost every night, after a full day in his office, he attended some sort of gathering. A reporter was given regular access to the governor in order to make note of his activities. After one day keeping up with Hughes, he reported that he was exhausted. The reporter detailed myriad activities in which the governor had been engaged: meeting with staff, taking telephone calls, signing correspondence, reading briefing pages, and then attending a number of events.[12]

One of the lessons Hughes learned early in his career was the necessity of being accessible to his constituents. Early on, he instructed his staff that any letter that came to the governor's office should be answered and answered promptly. If the issue concerned an agency within the executive branch, the staff sent the letter to the agency requesting a proposed response. The governor's staff kept track of the issue and followed up if the agency did not respond. The staff, and often the governor himself, then reviewed the response. If it seemed appropriate, the response was sent out, and if not, the matter was sent back to the agency for further work.[13] While many of the response letters were routine, a good many bore personal touches from Hughes. He signed the vast majority of the letters himself.[14] He often used his travel time to read and sign his correspondence. Governor Byrne recalled that one of the secretaries in his office, who had also been a secretary when Hughes was governor, would sometimes complain that Byrne was not enough like Hughes. According to Byrne, Hughes would come in on Monday mornings and dictate letters to all the different people he had met with over the weekend, thanking them for their help or simply keeping in touch with them.[15]

He was also extremely accessible in person. One reporter quipped that Hughes "admits his daily routine is still not exactly orderly. One reason is that the governor is only a little more difficult to get to see than the lady who runs the information desk at the State House entrance. It seems almost anyone, from party faithful to old school chum or visiting foreign student can get in to talk to the governor."[16] In describing the governor's day, the reporter talked about Hughes getting up early and calling all the children on the intercom system at Morven to get them going and then spending a few minutes with them during breakfast while reading the paper and listening to Betty discuss the plans for the day. He would then leave for work with a handful of papers that he would peruse on the way. Once at the office, he would begin a hectic series of meetings. He often had a lunch appointment and a number of events in the evening. Another article pointed out that Hughes averaged 183 conferences per day, counting only the important ones.[17] Hughes also had a telephone and a steno-recorder in his car so he could work while traveling from appointment to appointment.

Unlike most states, New Jersey did not have a lieutenant governor during Hughes's tenure. When asked whether the state should adopt a lieutenant governor, Hughes said that although he didn't oppose the concept, he just did not think it was right for him as governor. He said, "Theoretically, the lieutenant governor is in place so he can go around the state dedicating high schools, snipping ribbons and performing other ceremonial functions that would otherwise require the presence of the governor. Then the real governor can stay back in his office and work. But I had a real liking for getting around to meet the people; I liked to do that outside work myself. So I was both the governor and lieutenant governor in a sense."[18]

Senator Stephen Wiley, who served as counsel to Governor Meyner and would later be partners with Meyner in a law firm, stayed on with the Hughes administration for a short period to help with the transition. He noted that although he had the greatest respect for Meyner, Hughes had a different, more outgoing personality and that the atmosphere in the Governor's Office under Hughes was much more open and relaxed.[19]

Early on in his administration, the governor met with the members of the New Jersey congressional delegation and developed a good working relationship. Whenever the delegation was seeking support from the federal government for any New Jersey projects, Hughes would work closely with them. He would then defer in the public announcement, allowing the congressman from the district, whether Democrat or Republican, to state where the money would be used. This allowed the congressman to announce the grant and get credit for it. With this united front, the state was able to obtain a good deal of federal money for important projects.

Larry Bilder, who served as assistant secretary and later counsel to the governor, would often travel to Washington on behalf of Hughes and work with the congressional delegation on these matters. Bilder was very close to the governor, and when he spoke, it was known that Hughes was speaking.[20] Hughes's close relationship with President Kennedy and the members of his administration was also helpful.

Many politicians consider the press an obstacle. Hughes considered the press a potential ally. He enjoyed them and enjoyed many good friendships within the press corps. He was described as having a "buddy-buddy relationship" with a wide variety of media representatives.[21] James McLaughlin, who served for a brief period as secretary to the governor, described an example of how Hughes dealt with a new reporter. When Peter Carter was assigned to the state house press corps, Hughes immediately asked him out to dinner at Lorenzo's in Trenton. The reporter was so pleased by the personal attention that he became a friend for life.[22]

Hughes had two regularly scheduled meetings with the press each week, one on Tuesday afternoons designed to benefit the morning papers, and one on Thursday mornings designed to benefit the afternoon papers. Reporter George Amick described the press conferences this way: "It's the governor's show. He fields the questions without visible signs of distress. He sits back in his chair, smokes cigarettes and sometimes fingers his necktie thoughtfully as he answers. He draws on his background as a lawyer and a judge for Latin phrases—amicus curiae, sui generis, ex parte—that sometimes stop the reporters short in their notebooks. . . . Sometimes Hughes turns a question aside with a quip—he has a quick wit and a keen sense of humor. . . ."[23]

Even before his inauguration, Hughes had begun to prepare for his time in office. One developing issue involved the creation of the World Trade Center in New York City. For some time New Jersey and New York had participated jointly in the Port Authority, a bistate agency created to deal with issues concerning transportation and other matters between the two states. New Jersey was very concerned about its railroad system and, particularly, the bankrupt Hudson and Manhattan Railroad Company, which carried passengers under the Hudson River between New Jersey and New York. At the same time, plans had been made for the Port Authority to erect a large office building on the East River in New York. Governor Nelson Rockefeller was supporting that plan and was willing to support a Port Authority takeover of the Hudson and Manhattan Railroad Company as well.

Governor Meyner viewed the takeover of the Hudson and Manhattan Railroad Company (the tubes) favorably, but felt that New York was getting the better bargain in the construction of the office building, which was to be built and owned by the Port Authority. There had been no agreement between the two parties when Hughes was elected, and "Hughes initiated a series of meetings with Rockefeller at his midtown office to discuss commuter taxes and transportation issues."[24] It is hard to imagine two more different men. One was a multimillionaire Protestant Republican; the other was a down-to-earth Irish-Catholic Democrat. They were seeking a compromise permitting both projects to go forward.

At about the same time, planners at the Port Authority, who were studying the takeover of the tubes, realized that the old terminals were in such decrepit condition that it made little sense to try and rehabilitate them. They began to consider merging the two projects—moving the proposed new office complex from the east side to the west side of Manhattan, and having the tube station as part of the new World Trade Center. Austin Tobin, the executive director of the Port Authority, was beginning to accept this new possibility when governor-elect Hughes stopped by his office for an informal visit. With Hughes was Thorn Lord, a former Port Authority commissioner.[25] During the discussions, Hughes revealed his sense of frustration and disappointment over the continuing inability to break the existing deadlock on the Hudson and Manhattan/World Trade Center issue. Hughes indicated his desire to make the deal more palatable to New Jersey. Tobin then mentioned the fact that his staff had been giving very preliminary study to the possibility of merging the two topics.[26]

Hughes was intrigued by the idea and felt that it might be acceptable to the New Jersey legislature. After broaching the idea with legislators, he reported back to Tobin that there was an enthusiastic reaction. Tobin then met with Rockefeller, who was also enthusiastic about the merger of the projects. Subsequently, Rockefeller and Hughes met and agreed to have their staffs begin drafting the necessary legislation. In addition to the takeover of the Hudson and Manhattan tubes, the new plans also included other programs of benefit to New Jersey.

On February 13, 1962, less than a month after Hughes took the oath as governor, both houses of the New Jersey Legislature unanimously passed the Hudson Tubes–World Trade Center Bill, and the governor signed it the same day. A parallel bill passed the New York Senate and Assembly,[27] signed by Governor Rockefeller. There would be subsequent complications, however. Business owners who had property in lower Manhattan where the new World Trade Center was to be built, brought suit, arguing that there was no justifiable public purpose for condemning the property. The Appellate Division in New York declared the statutes unconstitutional.[28] Subsequently, New Jersey, New York, and the Port Authority appealed those decisions. Theodore Botter, then serving as First Assistant Attorney General of New Jersey,[29] argued in his brief that, with the vast movement toward the suburbs in the early sixties, there was concern that the cities would deteriorate. Botter argued that development of world trade was essential to the future strength of the cities. This and other arguments convinced the New York Court of Appeals that condemnation was appropriate and it reversed the decision of the appellate court.[30] The process that led to the building of the World Trade Center and the creation of a new terminal for the Hudson and Manhattan Railroad involved Hughes and Rockefeller working together for the benefit of both states.

Another issue involving New York and Governor Rockefeller centered on Hughes's effort to find new sources of revenue. Hughes had to balance the budget for the first term. He had a small surplus from the former administration but he had scant financial resources for the initiatives he hoped to undertake. He first tried to get the money from a tax that New Jersey had recently placed on commuters who worked in New York. New York had an income tax, and since 1919, commuters from other states working in New York had to pay that tax. At the same time, because New Jersey had no income tax, New Yorkers commuting to New Jersey were not required to pay tax to New Jersey. New York's income tax law provided for reciprocity—if commuters to New York paid income tax to the state from which they commuted, that tax would be a credit against the tax they would have to pay in New York. Instituting a New Jersey commuter tax was seen as a great solution, because this money was already being paid by commuters, and the tax would not increase their payments, but simply reduce the taxes that New York would receive.

The new commuter tax was proposed in 1960 by then-Governor Meyner and passed into law in 1961. However, New York was still collecting the full New York income taxes from the commuters. Even before Hughes was inaugurated he had announced that he would take legal action to obtain the tax money that New York had received from New Jersey commuters. New York argued that the tax was unconstitutional in that it only applied to New Jersey residents who worked in New York. It did not apply to anyone else who worked in New Jersey or anyone who commuted to Pennsylvania or Delaware.

Rather than battling the various legal issues, Hughes and Rockefeller worked out a deal. The agreement called for each state to receive the funds that commuters to each state would be charged. New Jersey would get taxes from the approximately 70,000 New Yorkers who worked in New Jersey, and those workers would be able to deduct that money from what they would otherwise have to pay New York. At the same time New York would be able to continue to receive the income taxes from those who commuted into New York. While New York would still receive a larger percentage because more commuters went into New York from New Jersey than went into New Jersey from New York, it still provided New Jersey an anticipated $8 to $11 million in revenue, which enabled Hughes to expand the budget. The argument over the constitutionality of the tax was a close one and Hughes chose to accept the arrangement rather than continue to contest the issue, which the state might have lost. Hughes stressed that the agreement had been reached in the interest of promoting "interstate cooperation."[31]

Responding to Crises

Before Hughes could devote his attention to the new initiatives on which he had campaigned, he had to deal with a blow from nature. Shortly after his inauguration, a massive storm struck the shore area of New Jersey. From March 6 to March 8, 1962, the coastline was battered with high winds and torrential rain. Many areas were flooded, hundreds of homes were literally washed away, and a number of deaths occurred. Long Beach Island, a long, narrow stretch of land along the coast that is connected to the mainland by only one bridge, was completely closed off. Hughes immediately telegraphed President Kennedy requesting emergency aid. Kennedy approved the request, granting funds from the Federal Disaster Relief Agency. Hughes called upon the National Guard and the New Jersey State Police to deal with the problems.[32] On March 14, Hughes, together with federal, state, and local officials, made an aerial inspection of the ravaged area. He then met with 500 officials from seashore communities at the Claridge Hotel in Atlantic City to explain the plans for federal and state aid. He emphasized that the state had requested $30.5 million in federal assistance and that the state was prepared to provide $2.5 million. At first, Kennedy requested $30 million for all the states affected by the storm. Hughes urged him to increase that amount. Eventually Hughes was able to increase the state commitment to $12 million.[33] Some of the Republican state senators from the shore area would later complain that not enough had been done by the federal government. Hughes responded by saying, "I don't recall any instance where a disaster state was aided more quickly than New Jersey was."[34] He also said that the shore area was recovering well, and that the recovery was demonstrated by a very successful Easter weekend for the shore's establishments.[35] Hughes's quick response increased his support throughout New Jersey. Richard Leone, in a doctoral dissertation, said the hurricane actually gave Hughes an opportunity to win public acclaim by proposing timely schemes for disaster relief.[36]

In addition to dealing with a natural disaster, Hughes had to grapple with the effects of a controversial court decision. In 1962, Hughes's first year in office, the United States Supreme Court decided *Engel v. Vitale*,[37] one of the most controversial cases in the history of the court. It involved the meaning of the provision of the First Amendment of the United States Constitution prohibiting the establishment of religion. The original purpose of the Establishment Clause was to prohibit the federal government from establishing religion. In later years, the court held that the clause also prohibited the states from establishing religion. The issue in the *Engel* case was whether the saying of a prayer at the beginning of the public school day constituted the establishment of religion. The prayer in that case was: "Almighty God, we acknowledge our dependence upon Thee and we beg Thy blessing upon us, our parents, our teachers and our Country."[38] The New York Court of Appeals held that, as long as no student was required to say the prayer, the practice was constitutional. The United States Supreme Court disagreed, holding that saying the prayer in the public schools was a violation of the Establishment Clause.

Many people in New Jersey and the many other states that permitted school prayers were enraged by the court's decision. New Jersey had provided for the reading of several verses of the Bible or the reading of the Lord's Prayer, provided there was no commentary on the part of teachers. Hughes received a great deal of correspondence about this case, with opponents outnumbering proponents by 20 to 1.[39] Perhaps living up to his moniker of "two buckets," Hughes responded in two ways. First, he affirmed the role of the United States Supreme Court in interpreting the United States Constitution and the need of the people to respect those decisions. Second, he argued that because the system in New Jersey was different from the system in New York, the New Jersey system was still constitutional. Hughes also pointed out that the New Jersey Supreme Court had upheld New Jersey's practice, of readings from the Bible or reading of the Lord's Prayer without comment.

Hughes's own views and experiences may have contributed to his ambivalence. While Hughes attended public schools during his early childhood, he savored his time at Catholic schools, and many of his children received a Catholic education. The Catholic schools were developed in the United States, in large measure, out of the belief that the public schools were, in fact, Protestant schools teaching Protestant doctrine.[40] As a result of the strong anti-Catholic bias displayed during the presidential campaign of Alfred Smith, and in a lesser degree during Kennedy's campaign, Hughes knew that Catholics still faced remnants of discrimination. His strong religious views may not have been offended by the elimination of prayer in the schools because he believed that those who wanted religious education for their children could obtain it by creating their own religious schools. His public position, however, was in favor of continuing prayers in the schools.

One year after the *Engel* decision, the United States Supreme Court decided that the reading of biblical passages did not pass constitutional muster.[41] That case was focused on other states, but their practices were basically the same as New Jersey's. Immediately after the decision was issued, Hughes and other state officials refused comment. The New Jersey Council of Churches condemned the decision, while some other religious groups supported it.[42] On June 18, 1963, Hughes made a statement in which he again straddled the issue. He said he disagreed philosophically with the decision and that he would not like to see all mention of the Deity disappear from the schools. But he reiterated his support for the Supreme Court as the ultimate interpreter of the Constitution, adding that he would not support any attempt to amend the Constitution to make school prayers legal.[43] The governor also recognized that the opinion, while dealing with the laws of other states, did have the effect of making the laws in New Jersey unconstitutional. Subsequently, the attorney general of New Jersey, Arthur Sills, issued an opinion that the New Jersey system fit within the decision of the United States Supreme Court and, therefore, the system in New Jersey was unconstitutional.[44] Despite that, some school districts tried to continue the practice of Bible reading in the public schools. The Hawthorne Board of Education passed a resolution to the effect that Bible reading was not to be halted.[45] The attorney general challenged that conduct, and Judge (later Justice) Morris Pashman wrote an opinion ordering the school district to comply with the attorney general's opinion. Judge Pashman's opinion recognized that the decisions from the Supreme Court in this sensitive area were not popular. It concluded, however, that once the United States Supreme Court has spoken, citizens must abide by its decisions. Otherwise, it said, there would be anarchy.[46]

The Hatch Act (which bars federal and state employees who are engaged in activities financed with federal funds from political activities) became an issue in the early part of Hughes's governorship when a member of his cabinet was accused of violating it. The charge was that Raymond F. Male, the state commissioner of Labor and Industry, who had held that position during the end of the Meyner administration and had been retained by Hughes, had violated the act when he gave speeches supporting Hughes during the gubernatorial campaign. The attorney general, Arthur Sills, took the position that the Hatch Act did not apply to Male because, while some activities in the Department of Labor and Industry were supported by federal funds, most were underwritten by the state and Male's salary was not paid from federal funds. The State of New Jersey instituted suit in Federal District Court to declare that the Commissioner of Labor and Industry was not covered by the Hatch Act.[47]

Hughes was apparently convinced that the charge was bogus, because he attempted to use his political clout to make it disappear. He argued that Male had made public statements only after Mitchell, Hughes's Republican opponent, claimed that the state lost jobs during the Meyner administration. Male, as commissioner of Labor and Industry, cited statistics to rebut those charges. Because on the surface those statements supported the Democrats in office as well as Hughes, a complaint was filed with the Civil Service Commission accusing Male of violating the Hatch Act. Years later in discussing the case Hughes said, "Now I went to Kennedy about that because it was a disgusting case, a very grievous overreaching kind of case. . . . I went to J.F.K. figuring he might call Bobby [Robert Kennedy was then the Attorney General of the United States] and he just looked up to the ceiling, whistled, he'd look into it. But I could see there was nothing there."[48] He then approached Vice President Lyndon Johnson and again presented his argument that Male was a victim and that something should be done. According to Hughes, Johnson responded a few days later with a call saying that Hughes would be hearing from the chairman of the Civil Service Commission. Hughes said the chairman did, in fact, call him and indicated that the problem with Male would be resolved.[49] Eventually there was a resolution of the case but it was not until Male testified for a full day before the United States Civil Service Commission. His argument was that he had been told that he was not covered by the Hatch Act and that it was absurd to think that a member of the governor's cabinet could not engage in political activity.[50]

Ultimately, the United States Civil Service Commission determined that Male was not guilty of a Hatch Act violation because of a statutory exemption. At the time of his support for Hughes during the campaign, Male was serving as mayor of Princeton, and the Hatch Act specifically exempted mayors from its requirements.[51] Hughes expressed his pleasure with the result and indicated that he considered Male one of the best commissioners of Labor in the country.[52] Male continued to serve until well into Hughes's second term. Whether the case was won on the merits or because of the intervention by Johnson is unclear, but Hughes defended his actions, saying, "It wasn't fixing a case or anything like that. But it would have dragged on for years and be propagandized by the opposition all that time, and it was a nothing thing."[53]

Hughes, like other governors, attended many of the meetings of the National Governors' Conference as well as the Democratic Governors' Conference. He held various positions within those organizations during his two terms. Shortly after he was elected, he was selected to serve on the 1963–1964 executive committee for the National Governors' Conference and continued in that position in 1964–1965. Hughes, in trying to persuade her to go along with his gubernatorial ambitions, told his wife Betty about the interesting places the governors held their meetings. She was disappointed when the first meeting they attended was held in the neighboring state of Pennsylvania at Hershey Park. Many of the later meetings were held in more distant places. Bolton Schwartz, a reporter who covered the governors' meetings that Hughes attended, said, "I got to follow Hughes through a portion of the United States and found that he was as popular with the other governors as he was in New Jersey."[54]

Another gathering in which Hughes participated enthusiastically was the annual Correspondents' Dinner. The dinner, hosted by political reporters, draws a crowd of political movers and shakers. The correspondents put on skits and tell stories roasting the politicians they cover. Hughes participated in those dinners during and after his terms as governor. He was the featured speaker assigned to respond to the reporters' slings and arrows. Schwartz, who regularly helped organize the dinners, said, "The only problem we had with him was that he was funnier than the show."[55]

William Hyland, one of the potential candidates for governor when Hughes was selected, recalled that no one wanted to speak after Hughes because the crowd often made an exodus after he finished. Hyland, who held many political positions during the Hughes years, recalled how effectively Hughes used stories. Whenever he introduced Hyland at political events, Hughes would tell the story about the decision to select him over Hyland. He would talk about Hyland's competence and his great potential. He would then say, "It was destiny, which had given Bill Hyland an angelic, youthful face with golden blond curly hair, which cheated him of the nomination. His appearance on TV evoked images of choir singers and altar boys, and the Democrats preferred a more ugly and mature appearing, even haggard looking, candidate. Thus I was chosen and elected Governor."[56]

Toward the end of his first year in office, Hughes was back on the campaign trail on behalf of the congressional candidates in New Jersey. President Kennedy returned to New Jersey on Columbus Day, October 12, to support the reelection of two Democratic candidates, Cornelius Gallagher and Peter Rodino. As he traveled with Hughes and other leading Democrats from New York to New Jersey, many thousands of spectators cheered as his motorcade passed through Newark.[57] He spoke before 9,000 people in front of Newark's City Hall, stressing the contributions of Italian Americans as well as the importance of a Democratic Congress. Of the fifteen House seats in New Jersey, Democrats held only six. They gained one additional seat in the election. Both Gallagher and Rodino, supported by Kennedy at that stop in Newark, were reelected.

Just a few days later the world was threatened by nuclear war. The Soviet Union's placing of nuclear weapons in Cuba, just ninety miles from the United States, precipitated what came to be called the Cuban Missile Crisis. Hughes was quick to offer moral support to President Kennedy during this time. In a telegram to the president, Hughes said, "Drawing strength from your determined leadership, the people of New Jersey stand firmly with you at this crossroads in our Nation's destiny. With you, we are ready to reaffirm that the historic meaning of America is freedom. And with you, we pray that we can yet achieve both peace and freedom in the hemisphere and around the world."[58] Two days later Kennedy responded, "I wish to express to you and to the people of New Jersey my gratitude for your message of support and confidence in the current international crisis. It is most heartening to have this expression of national unity and this evidence of our common purpose during these critical days."[59] Fortunately, the threat was eventually avoided. The correspondence showed that Hughes believed in constant communication, not only with his constituents, but also with the president and other leaders across the country.

Prior to Hughes becoming governor, Thorn Lord, Hughes's former law partner and Democratic kingpin, had created an informal think tank composed largely of Princeton faculty members with whom he had forged relationships during the 1950s. After some hesitation, Hughes began attending those gatherings,[60] and after his inauguration, the think tank became a functioning committee of policy advisors within the Democratic Party.[61] Larry Bilder, special assistant to the governor, who met regularly with the committee, said there was an agreement that he would take all the committee recommendations to the governor for a fair hearing. In exchange, the committee members agreed that their deliberations would be confidential and that no members would publicize any disagreement with policies ultimately adopted by the governor.[62] Many prominent academicians and lawyers attended these meetings, and experts were brought in from various disciplines when matters arose that required specific expertise. Committee members included professors from the Eagleton Institute at Rutgers and the Woodrow Wilson School at Princeton. One of the individuals who was often invited to those meetings, who provided a different perspective, was Raymond Brown Jr., the leading African American lawyer in New Jersey. Brown was involved in many of the most prominent criminal cases in the state, and also represented the Black Panthers and other activist groups. Additionally, he was the head of the National Association for the Advancement of Colored People (NAACP) in Jersey City. It was Brown who brought many civil rights issues to the table. Bilder recalled the important dimension that Brown brought to the work of the committee. When they were discussing some of the problems facing the African American community, Brown told them of a town where the streets of white residents were paved, while the African American sections were not. Bilder was incredulous until Brown brought him to the town in question so he could see it for himself. Bilder, Brown, and Hughes became close and Hughes would often turn to Brown for advice on civil rights issues. This relationship proved very valuable during the civil disturbances in Newark some years later.

During the Hughes administration, many of the proposals ultimately enacted originated with the think tank/committee formed by Lord. However, most of the committee's progressive suggestions, including a broad-based tax, the creation of the Department of Community Affairs and the Board of Higher Education, and the restructured Department of Transportation, had to wait for implementation until Hughes's second term. In 1964, in the middle of Hughes's first term, the Republicans had taken control of the legislature. Although Hughes worked well with Republicans, he and his administration recognized that they had to wait until Democrats regained control of the legislature to pass some of the more progressive legislation they were proposing.[63]

Family Life at Morven

Shortly after the Hughes family arrived at Morven, Betty gave birth to their tenth and last child. The family named him Thomas More Hughes because of Hughes's abiding interest in St. Thomas More, the patron saint of lawyers. The child was born with a heart condition that required him to stay in an oxygen tent for two weeks. That condition eventually disappeared, but Thomas was also born with congenital cataracts in both eyes that required surgery and that left him with some sight, but legally blind.

Morven, a historic landmark, had been remodeled to accommodate the large Hughes family. According to Bolton Schwartz, Betty had been concerned that there was no fire escape. "A spokesman for the overseeing commission said such an addition [the fire escape] would ruin the colonial appearance of the house." The earliest section of the house was built in 1701 by Richard Stockton on a tract purchased from William Penn. It would later be expanded, but at the time the Hughes family came to live there it was basically as it was at the time of the Revolutionary War, and thus no fire escapes. "When she persisted, she was told that her 'excess children' could be housed in what used to be the slave quarters. . . ." Betty's cold response was "I have no excess children!" In the end a fire escape was installed, hidden in the rear of the building so as not to offend the history buffs. Several years later Mrs. Hughes had cause to wonder about her "victory," "when the fire escape became a means of surreptitious exit and entrance for the older children."[64]

Morven is in the wealthy town of Princeton, the home of Princeton University. Some local residents were less than delighted when the large Irish Hughes family moved into the neighborhood, even if it was the governor's family. A favorite family story revolves around a porcelain pig that stood in the living room of this stately home. Betty bought it after overhearing a conversation between two women in one of the stores in Princeton. The women had no idea that the governor's wife was in the store. Their talk focused on the large boisterous family moving into historic Morven. One of the women said, "They will probably have a pig in the parlor."[65] It was just like Betty to respond with humor to this kind of snobbery. Her mother, Helen Sullivan, would often hide the pig in the closet. Jacqueline Beusse, a family friend, recalled the pig as being made of Belleek china and rather attractive.[66]

Betty was fortunate that her mother was available to help with the family. The first lady of the state had many obligations and it was often Helen

Sullivan who held down the family fort. Hughes would often talk about his three mothers-in-law. "There was a time in my life when I had three mothers-in-law at one time; that would be Miriam's mother, she was a mother-in-law, Betty's mother, Helen Sullivan, she was a mother-in-law, and then I had the mother of Betty's first husband, Bill Murphy, whose name was Martha Murphy, she was a school teacher, retired. So these mothers-in-law; and they said I was entitled to a lot of credit—getting along with these mothers-in-law."[67] He was also fond of an old gag—Behind every successful man stands a surprised mother-in-law.

Betty, who had participated actively in the campaign, was becoming a celebrity in her own right. Newspapers loved to feature the large family in their pages. The "his, hers, and ours" story made great journalistic fodder and helped endear the governor to the people of New Jersey. A sampling of headlines from Hughes's first year in office included, "Governor Hughes Rushes Ill Baby to Children's Hospital," "Honey Helps Her Mother Meet the Press," "State's First Lady Gay at Press Parley," "Hughes Baby to Be Operated On," "N.J.'s First Lady Needs 30-Hour Day," "Baby Sounds the Alarm to Start Mrs. Hughes's Day," "A Governor's Wife Is Busy, Even Without an Election," "Only a First Lady Could Take This Moving Madness." These and dozens of other stories brought the humanity of the state's first family to the fore, and allowed the public to get to know them. The private Hughes came into focus as a man who forever seemed to be roughhousing with one of his ten children, or worrying through an eye operation for his youngest.[68]

Chapter 7

Dallas, 1963—Atlantic City, 1964

THE ASSASSINATION OF PRESIDENT KENNEDY on November 22, 1963, was a traumatic event for the United States and the world. Initially, many people could not believe the news. Hughes, who had come to know the president well, and who believed that Kennedy's support during his campaign had made a difference in his election, was truly shaken by the event.[1]

Immediately after the devastating news broke, Hughes issued a statement extolling the virtues of the president. He said later: "I wrote that myself. I felt very bad because he did many things for us."[2] Hughes's son John said, "I remember going home to the Governor's Residence in Princeton the night President Kennedy was assassinated, with the house surrounded by State Police, (many feared that the assassination was part of some organized attack) and my father reassuring us all by saying, 'Don't worry, kids. America's institutions and its people are strong.'"[3]

Hughes and Betty attended Kennedy's funeral in Washington. They were invited to a special viewing with other governors and dignitaries. Years later Hughes would say, "I remember being in line with [Congressman] Frank Thompson and Frank Thompson was in tears too. He had always been very close to Kennedy."[4] Hughes described the church service as a "very impressive ceremony, very sad one."[5] The governor and his wife then went to the burial at Arlington National Cemetery. Hughes remarked, "The crowds, it was remarkable, the quietness of the crowds. There were a lot of tears. Black and white, young and old, and it was a very impressive thing. It must have been a million people along the streets and there was hardly a word, no noise, nobody shouting. Very impressive."[6]

After the assassination, Hughes and other public officials had to pay more attention to security. Hughes said, "Bobby Kennedy was Attorney General, and he ordered every governor in the country to have twenty-four hour state police coverage. So after that a state policeman slept at Morven every night."[7] An F.B.I. report on Hughes records a number of threats against him while he was governor. Most of the threats were considered to be the work of cranks, but Hughes recalled that one of the threats was taken very seriously. "There was one very heavy thing that even had the F.B.I. scared. Betty and I had our kids down in Jamaica. . . . We rented Grace Palmer's villa one time for a week. Billy Hyland and some other friends were down with us at the time. Anyhow, we were in this other villa and I had three or four kids with me and a death threat came in to the F.B.I., somebody was going to kill Governor Hughes. They knew where I was, they knew what plane I went down on, they knew how many kids were with me."[8]

Everyone got very upset. The head of security for the resort contacted the high police commissioner in Kingston who then furnished guards. Hughes was concerned and "wouldn't let them have guns so they had machetes."[9] He was concerned that they might end up accidentally shooting his children. He also noted the authorities were so concerned "they dismantled the whole Pan Am plane that I had come down on or that we were going back on before we got on."[10] The threat turned out to be nothing. Hughes also mentioned another person who regularly sent him threatening letters, but when he was checked out it was determined that he was simply, in Hughes's words, a "blabbermouth." Still, after Kennedy's assassination, Betty was very pleased that Attorney General Kennedy had ordered extra security. The assassination of Kennedy would have lasting influence. Although there had been earlier assassinations, there had been a widespread belief in the country that such an event could not happen in modern America. For many, the trauma of this event was further exacerbated by the subsequent assassinations of Senator Robert Kennedy and the Reverend Martin Luther King, Jr.

President Lyndon B. Johnson, who took office immediately after the assassination, became very friendly with Hughes and often attended events in New Jersey, including those surrounding the 1964 Democratic National Convention. For example, in June of 1964, Johnson transferred 271 acres of land belonging to the Army, to the State of New Jersey in order to expand Sandy Hook State Park. The park had become so popular that it was often overcrowded. The New Jersey leadership worked together to convince the federal government that the park needed expansion. When he came to New Jersey to officially transfer the land, Johnson congratulated Hughes and the members of the congressional delegations of both political parties for working together to help the state.[11]

Urban riots were common throughout the United States during the 1960s. In 1964 a number of them occurred in New Jersey. Focusing on civil rights issues, the riots often started as peaceful requests for equality but turned into violent disturbances. The most violent riots occurred in 1967 during Hughes's second term.

The 1964 Democratic National Convention in Atlantic City was thought to be a logical target for demonstrations. Hughes urged all the civil rights organizations to refrain from demonstrating at the convention. While Hughes was a supporter of equal rights, he was also strong on law and order, and he was willing to use force to contain violence. He had heard that two groups, the Congress of Racial Equality and the Student Nonviolent Coordinating Committee, were planning demonstrations in favor of a strong civil rights plank in the platform of the convention. Those groups also planned to protest against the seating of the all-white delegations from Mississippi and Alabama. Just before the convention, Hughes urged those groups to refrain. He argued that Johnson had been the strongest proponent of civil rights the White House had seen so far, and that demonstrations would be an affront to him. He also feared that any demonstration could easily get out of hand.[12] Fortunately, no demonstrations interfered with the convention.

President Kennedy had selected Atlantic City as the convention site before he was assassinated. He did it by a process of elimination. At first, there were six cities besides Atlantic City in the running—Baltimore, Chicago, Detroit, Miami Beach, Philadelphia, and San Francisco. Originally, Kennedy hoped to combine the convention and a vacation with his children on the Pacific Coast, so he pushed for San Francisco. But the Republicans were already scheduled to have their convention there and it was considered too difficult to schedule two conventions in one city in the same year. Kennedy then considered Chicago. But Chicago leaders were unwilling to make the necessary financial contribution. Miami and Atlantic City ended up as the two finalists, but since Miami included many Cuban refugees, it was feared that demonstrations against Castro might erupt and embarrass the president. Atlantic City was ultimately selected as the convention site, helped by the fact that New Jersey Democrats promised to raise $625,000 for the event. The money came from a number of different sources, including the Democratic State Committee, the New Jersey Legislature, Atlantic City businessmen, and the city of Atlantic City.[13]

Hughes, and others, hoped that the convention would showcase Atlantic City. Hughes said, "It was a great thing for us in New Jersey. We had never had a national convention of any kind here, and we were quite excited about it."[14] He was not alone in believing that it would be great for the state. According to a story in the *New York Times*, "Public officials and business and industry executives agreed the convention would do much to stimulate the state's economy and enhance its prestige."[15] Unfortunately, Atlantic City, while still an important resort community and a major convention setting, had become seedy, and was not ready to host a large national event. State Senator Frank S. (Hap) Farley, Republican leader of Atlantic County and a major force in state politics, was eager to see the convention take place in his city. Hughes had a good relationship with Farley, another Irish politician. Nelson Johnson described Farley as "possibly the most powerful legislator in the history of New Jersey."[16] He added, "Farley had an excellent relationship with Hughes and every governor he worked with."[17]

Among the many events leading up to the convention was a dinner and party hosted at the convention center by Charles and Jane Engelhard at which President Johnson was the guest of honor. Charles Engelhard, who had been a possible candidate for the governorship when Hughes was selected, was a multimillionaire and a devoted Democrat. He and his wife were jet-setters with homes in many different countries. He was the inspiration for the character "Goldfinger" in the James Bond novel and movie. Jane Engelhard had been part of the small committee helping Mrs. Kennedy redecorate the White House and the Engelhards had contributed a great deal of the furnishings that made that redecoration so successful.

Charles had been a classmate of President Kennedy and had wonderful access to the president prior to his assassination. Jane Engelhard described the relationship. "He had known him very well in prep school. He had gone to many dances with him, and there was a friendship between the two men."[18] Engelhard had been a delegate from New Jersey at the Democratic National Convention in Los Angeles where President Kennedy had been nominated. The Engelhards were also very friendly with Johnson, and after Kennedy was chosen to be the presidential nominee, Charles Engelhard worked behind the scenes to help get Johnson on the ticket.

The dinner and party at which Johnson was the guest of honor and major speaker was scheduled for the month of May preceding the 1964 summer convention. The Engelhards invited friends, including the Duke and Duchess of Windsor, to stay with them at Cragwood, their estate in Somerset County prior to the dinner. The Duke of Windsor was eager to attend an American political event.[19] Hughes described the event: "We had him [President Johnson] up here in 1964, for a big fundraiser at the Atlantic City Convention Hall, which was attended by all our brass and the party. Charlie Engelhard was there, Jane Engelhard and they had as their guests the Duke of Windsor and his wife the Duchess and this was a big deal. And I had set up through a nationalities division you know, all the different ethnic groups in this room and that room, and labor would be here and you had to separate different factions of labor, so we had about twelve little cocktail receptions, all of which I had promised the President would visit, before the big dinner. About 3,035 at the dinner, it was a success."[20] Hughes's plan to show off Johnson at a dozen different receptions had to be changed when the president told the governor that he was tired. Hughes said the only time Johnson ever leaned on him was that night when he said he needed a rest. Hughes reported telling the president, "You go on up and have a rest and we'll consolidate all these groups and they'll come together and they'll be just delighted to see you."[21] In his speech, Johnson encouraged the attendees to work for the election of more Democrats to join those who were already part of the delegation. He also spoke of the many successes under the Democratic administration.[22] The president must, indeed, have been tired because Jane Engelhard said that when she greeted Lady Bird Johnson at the reception, Lady Bird asked her not to invite her husband to the party after the dinner because she felt he should rest. The president, however, said: "I can't wait to come to your party."[23]

Jane did not know whether she should abide by the wishes of the president or his wife, but her decision was made for her. "Right in the middle of dinner and right in the middle of the President's speech," she said, "a Secret Service comes and tugs on the bottom of my skirt. He was crawling on the floor and he said, 'Get going.' I said, 'How can I get going when the President is speaking and the Duke of Windsor is still eating his steak?' He said, 'Never mind. Get going. The President will be at your apartment in two minutes.' I sent word over to my husband and said, 'We have to get going.' It was very embarrassing. He was the host. We were in the front row at the main table. But we did get going. There were Secret Service men waiting for us outside. They drove us to the hotel a few minutes from there. The elevator hadn't gone up to our apartment and I hadn't had time to fix my hair and put some powder on my nose when the President was there, big as life, and Mrs. Johnson. Mrs. Johnson was not too happy."[24] But, the president who started off the evening too tired to attend a group of political cocktail parties had a good time and stayed until late in the evening. Perhaps the presence of an interesting group of people intrigued him. The success of the evening cemented the relationship between the Engelhards and the Johnsons. Hughes's thoughtful managing of the evening so that Johnson could rest and enjoy the later party furthered his standing with the president. Later that same year, the Engelhards hosted Lynda Bird Johnson at a campaign event for her father at their estate, Cragwood. Thousands of people attended and Sammy Davis Jr. entertained. It was a great success for the campaign.[25]

Holding the convention in Atlantic City did not succeed in showcasing and revitalizing the city as Hughes and the other leaders of New Jersey had hoped. In fact, it showed Atlantic City at its worst. While future years would see some revitalization of Atlantic City from gambling casinos, which were approved in 1976 and brought in many tourists and provided thousands of jobs, the 1964 Convention was a disaster for the city. The convention drew 5,260 delegates and more than 5,500 newspeople and media technicians. The newspeople and technicians, who had just come from the "sparkle and elegance of San Francisco suffered from what could be called 'culture' shock—which they immediately transmitted to the nation."[26] Hawkers sold busts of John F. Kennedy and Lyndon Johnson. The hotels were overcrowded, provided poor service, and charged exorbitant prices. The restaurants were equally overcrowded and the food was often bad. The appearance was one of tawdriness.[27] Hughes, himself, came down with a case of food poisoning during the convention.

In discussing the convention some years later in an interview with her husband, Betty Hughes said, "Dick, in retrospect, thinking about that convention, you know we had gotten very bad press. There are simply not the facilities, unfortunately, in Atlantic City that would be in either Chicago or Miami."[28] She also discussed her nervousness at the thought of being hostess for such a huge event. Betty expected that since Atlantic City was a resort, many delegates would bring their families, thus further swelling the crowd. That expectation turned out to be true, and resulted in overcrowding, overbooking, and jacked-up prices. But Betty and Richard tried to make the best of the situation. In the words of Hughes, "Betty got the idea of having a buffet party every night beginning at midnight, on a big terrace outside of our hotel suite. . . . We had the big people in the Democratic Party at these parties in our suite; had several bars, and it was well done from the logistics standpoint. But it was remarkable to me to see a man like our friend Governor John Connally and his wife Nellie Connally, or Adlai Stevenson or some other great figure in history standing and talking seriously to a little committeewoman from the third ward in Hoboken or Paterson, New Jersey, about the future of the Democratic Party. We had a great mix of humble people, the grassroots of the party, and the big people."[29]

Betty worried over what kind of food to serve at the parties. She assumed that most delegates attended cocktail parties in the late afternoon and then went to the convention. Accordingly, she felt they needed a substantial meal at the end of the evening. The menu was heavy on food and light on alcohol. Betty said, "Let's have great, big serious roasts of beef and hot rolls and Lobster Newburg, and real, true food, and big urns of coffee."[30]

Betty was clearly delighted to find a special guest on her hotel terrace one evening. "Surprise visitor of the week: Coming in from one of the first of Perle Mesta's parties and finding Carol Channing on our terrace with her husband her friend Mrs. Carpenter [press secretary to Mrs. Johnson] and three or four others. She's the greatest! She walked across the street to the Colony to help us greet the New Jersey delegation and they loved her. Next day, she brought the house down with her version of 'Hello, Lyndon.' "[31]

The Hughes's children and other family members were very much present. Betty describes the rather chaotic scene. "Our children were everywhere. We'd invited each down for one day and evening in pairs. Ran into a snag because two kept arriving each day, catching convention fever, and declining to go home. On the last day they were sleeping all over town. One was at the Colony with Janice and Phil Levin, who had an extra bed in the room with their 15-year-old son, Adam. Still another stayed overnight on the Paul and Olga Roebling boat, based at the Atlantic City Marina. One bunked in with Father Joe Hughes, my husband's brother, one was with Nana Sullivan, my own mother, another with Senator and Mrs. Si Ridolfi of Mercer; and one ended up with one of the state troopers."[32] They may have been particularly pressed for space for the family because they also made one of their rooms available to Governor and Mrs. Frank Morrison of Nebraska, who arrived with reservations but found there was no room at the motel where they planned to stay. Governor and Mrs. Hughes put them in a room adjoining their suite at the Claridge Hotel.[33]

While the convention was a disaster for Atlantic City, it was a triumph for Johnson, who was chosen as the nominee for the presidency. The day he was nominated was also his birthday, and the celebrations were extravagant. There were fireworks, a parade of 200 boats just outside the breakers of the Atlantic Ocean, thousands of marchers along the Boardwalk in ethnic costumes, and thirty-one drum and bugle marching bands.[34]

Hughes, always a strong supporter of Johnson, had committed his delegation to Johnson early on. He said, "We never had any doubt about President Johnson. It was a unanimous delegation, very high on him."[35] The Republican National Convention in San Francisco had already chosen Barry Goldwater and William Miller as its presidential and vice presidential candidates, respectively. Ultimately, Johnson would defeat Goldwater decisively, but at the outset of the campaign, Hughes was concerned about Johnson's prospects. "I was worried very much about Senator Goldwater's strength. I thought I felt a backlash coming in this country. I remember being down to the White House with Mrs. Hughes on August 22; the Convention began on August 24, and the Democratic governors and their wives were invited to a luncheon at the White House on the Saturday before the convention opened. The president had a little receiving line, only on the way out. I had previously expressed my worries about Goldwater to him, and I remember him saying, 'Are you still afraid of that man Goldwater?' I said, 'I sure am, Mr. President, and I hope you will campaign very hard.' He said, 'I shall, and I think we will beat him.' So he was confident, supremely confident."[36] In his memoirs Johnson said that even at the time of the convention, he was still thinking that he might decide not to run. He even wrote a statement announcing his decision not to run, just in case it came down to that decision.[37]

Once Johnson put aside any doubt about running, the next big decision was his choice for vice president, because President Johnson had been serving without a vice president since his ascension to the presidency after Kennedy's assassination. Today, if the vice president becomes president for any reason there is a process to select a new vice president. That did not exist in 1964.

Many were hoping that the nominee would be Attorney General Robert Kennedy, but Kennedy had been ruled out even before the convention. Robert Kennedy and Johnson never had a cordial relationship. Johnson had opposed John Kennedy in 1959 when Robert had been his brother's campaign manager. When Kennedy was nominated and then selected Johnson as his running mate, Robert opposed the choice. President Kennedy had come to like and appreciate Johnson. A biographer of Robert Kennedy wrote, "Despite the gulf separating Jack's East Coast sophistication from Lyndon Johnson's Texas earthiness, JFK had liked his vice president. LBJ's drawl, his outlandish stories, his barnyard vocabulary, had amused the urbane president."[38] Robert, on the other hand, had never liked Johnson and his view did not change after Johnson became president. In fact, his dislike of Johnson may have increased.

Hughes believed that Johnson had always been extremely respectful of President Kennedy. He said, "I have never seen in public life the deference and courtesy [shown by Johnson to Kennedy]. For instance I would ask Vice President Johnson if he would come to New Jersey for a speech, and he would say he would like to, but of course this depended on whether President Kennedy wished him to do it at a particular time and so forth. So he was just, I think, the perfect vice president, carrying his share of great responsibility and yet leaving the limelight to the President and not trying to encroach on it. . . . I think he did it as he did most of the other things that he did and didn't do, because he loved this country.[39] Johnson himself saw his self-effacing work as vice president as reason for Robert Kennedy to wait his turn. Johnson said, "Every day, as soon as I opened the papers or turned on the television, there was something about Bobby Kennedy; there was some person or group talking about what a great Vice President he'd make. Somehow it just didn't seem fair. I'd given three years of loyal service to Jack Kennedy. During all that time I'd willingly stayed in the background; I knew that it was his Presidency, not mine. If I disagreed with him I did it in private, not in public. And then Kennedy was killed and I became the custodian of his will. I became the President. But none of this seemed to register with Bobby Kennedy, who acted like he was the custodian of the Kennedy dream, some kind of rightful heir to the throne. It just didn't seem fair. I'd waited for my turn. Bobby should've waited for his."[40]

Johnson made some efforts at reconciliation, but those efforts foundered, apparently over Johnson's belief that Kennedy had no respect for him.[41] C. David Heyman, a biographer of Robert F. Kennedy, wrote: "Johnson knew that he was the butt of ridicule among what he called the 'Bobby crowd,' who referred to the vice president and his wife, in a phrase coined by Jackie, as 'Colonel Cornpone and his Little Porkchop.' "[42] In Johnson's own memoirs, he said that the major reason for not selecting Kennedy as his running mate was geographic. He felt it was important that the ticket gain support in the Middle West and the Border States and stir as little adverse reaction as possible in the South. Johnson believed this was necessary because he thought Goldwater would have strong support in the South, the Southwest, the Border States, and possibly the Middle West.[43]

In September 1964, Kennedy resigned as attorney general to run for the United States Senate in New York. Johnson campaigned for him in that election but they would never become friends. Lester Shapiro, a former newspaperman who worked for Charles Engelhard as a political advisor, and who was working with Robert Burkhardt at the convention, recalled that the Johnson people were worried about the possibility of a draft-Bobby movement. He recalled that the Republican leader of Atlantic County, Hap Farley, wanted to display a bust of President John F. Kennedy at the convention. Johnson operatives led by Marvin Watson tried unsuccessfully to stymie the idea. The bust was set up in front of the convention center. A flame similar to the light that burns at the president's grave in Arlington National Cemetery was lit by Hughes. The recent assassination of the president was still on the minds and in the hearts of many of the delegates as they arrived in Atlantic City and saw that flame. The Johnson people sought to mute the press coverage of the installation of the bust.[44]

After Kennedy was eliminated as a potential vice president, much of the attention turned to Hubert Humphrey. Humphrey had long been the subject of vice presidential speculation. After Kennedy's death, Humphrey's friends began urging him to seek the vice presidency. Humphrey's response had been, "Whatever Lyndon Johnson wanted Lyndon Johnson would get."[45] Other names were being considered as well and there was even some suggestion that Hughes was among them. In 1968, there would be considerable support for Hughes as a vice presidential candidate; in 1964 he was just one of the many potential candidates mentioned but not seriously considered. Johnson did not make his decision until the convention was in progress. Because his own renomination was basically assured, Johnson hoped to maintain some suspense by delaying his selection of the vice president until the last moment. This was difficult for Humphrey. Even though most expected Humphrey to be selected, Humphrey himself was never sure until the very end.[46] In describing the support that was gathering for Humphrey, Theodore White said, "Governor Hughes of New Jersey had already reported to Johnson his strongest support of Humphrey's candidacy."[47] Hughes confirmed that. "I had actually, I think, been the first Democratic governor to ask for the nomination of Humphrey as vice president."[48] But Johnson was always ambivalent. He set Humphrey one last task prior to selecting him. He asked him to help work out a compromise on the seating of the Mississippi and Alabama delegations.[49]

The seating of the Mississippi and Alabama delegations was a major issue. The regular delegation from Mississippi was all-white. It was being challenged by an African American Freedom Party delegation, which claimed that African Americans had been systematically excluded.[50] Additionally, both the Mississippi delegation and the Alabama delegation were refusing to sign a pledge that they would support the nominees of the convention. Before the convention, Johnson was worried about the divisiveness of the disputes. Texas Governor John Connally reported that the president had been so distressed by the challenge that he could barely sleep for fear that it would cause a serious fight on the convention floor, disrupt the convention, divide the party and damage his election chances.[51] In tapes of phone conversations later released to the public, Johnson said it was a difficult problem to solve because of the failure of the regular members of the Mississippi and Alabama delegations to sign the pledge. Johnson said, "I don't see how a fellow like Dick Hughes and Governor Lawrence and Dick Daley . . . can possibly go back to their states and say that they were for seating the Alabama group and the Mississippi group when they won't say they'll support their nominees."[52]

After a great deal of discussion, Hubert Humphrey and other Democratic leaders worked out a compromise permitting the seating of two members of the Mississippi Freedom Democratic Party as at-large delegates.[53] Johnson was aware of the compromise being worked out but told Humphrey to keep his name out of it.[54] While the compromise was being negotiated, the leaders of the party selected a number of young Democratic workers who were not from Mississippi to sit in the seats of the delegates until the compromise was reached. James Florio, who would go on to be governor of New Jersey, was a young aspiring Democrat at the time, and spent the early part of the convention sitting in one of those seats.[55]

The credentials committee required that the members of the Alabama and Mississippi delegations sign a pledge that they would support the nominees of the party. The compromise did not please everyone and most of the delegates from both Mississippi and Alabama continued to refuse to sign the pledge and did not participate in the actual voting.

After the compromise was accomplished and the convention was already in progress, Johnson called Humphrey and asked him to come to Washington. But even then Humphrey was nervous because he learned that Senator Thomas Dodd from Connecticut would also be on the plane. Although he was assured Dodd's presence was window-dressing so the press would not know that Humphrey was the choice, Humphrey was still unnerved.[56] At their meeting in Washington, Johnson asked Humphrey to be the vice presidential candidate.

The convention then unanimously selected Johnson and Humphrey as their candidates. Later, Johnson would say, "Atlantic City in August was a place of happy, surging crowds and thundering cheers. To a man as troubled as I was by party and national divisions, this display of unity was welcome indeed. But ovations, however deafening, can be short-lived. As I stood there warmed by the waves of applause that rolled in on us, touched to the heart by the display of affection, I could only hope that this harmonious spirit would endure times of trouble and discouragement as well."[57]

After the convention's ratification of Johnson's choice, Humphrey and his wife participated in a last-minute press conference in the Hughes suite. After the press conference, the Humphreys had a short wait before leaving for other places. Betty Hughes said, "After the reporters, photographers and TV folks left, the Humphreys had 20 minutes before time to leave for their plane. Muriel admitted they hadn't had time together in three days, so our family volunteered to vacate the living room of the suite and give them time to be alone together while we waited in the bedrooms. Sen. and Mrs. Humphrey were en route to the LBJ Ranch and the young people [family of the Humphreys] were leaving for Washington and Minneapolis, so it was their last chance for some quiet family talk."[58]

For Hughes, as host of the convention, there was much to be done and priorities to balance. One time he found himself caught between taking a call from the president and greeting Lady Bird and her daughters as they arrived in Atlantic City. He opted to greet the women and gathered a crowd of more than 3,000 to accompany him. When it started to rain, some in the crowd left, but there was still a fair contingent braving the showers to greet Mrs. Johnson. Hughes said, "I began to leave the hotel room to go out front to greet Mrs. Johnson and her daughters. As I did, I was halfway out along the grounds, an aide said, 'The President wants you on the phone right away and it's important.' So now I had to choose between receiving Mrs. Johnson and answering the President's call. I decided in her favor. I said, 'I will have to call the President back,' and then I went out. Just at that moment her helicopter set down, can you believe it or not, the sun came out. It stopped raining and I made a little speech introducing her. I said, 'The sun shines on Lady Bird Johnson. This is a good luck symbol.' Then we introduced the girls and so forth."[59] When he finally got back to the president, he discovered Johnson had been watching the arrival of Mrs. Johnson and the greeting by Hughes on television. The president had called to praise Hughes for his kindness to his wife.

As the host of the event, Hughes also had to give a welcoming speech. The *Newark Star-Ledger* described the speech. "Gov. Richard J. Hughes, in the most momentous speech of his political career, rallied the Democratic Party to a fever pitch of enthusiasm last night in welcoming its 1964 National Convention to New Jersey."[60] Hughes set a tone for the convention with praise for the Democrats and withering derision of the Republicans without ever referring to Goldwater by name. He brought rounds of applause from the 18,500 delegates and spectators. The speech in many ways was vintage Hughes. It included proud references to the history of New Jersey, citing its role in the Revolutionary War, the importance of New Jersey's former governor, President Woodrow Wilson, as well as the industrial might of New Jersey and its progress in the area of civil rights.

The Engelhards had invited the Duke and Duchess of Windsor to attend the convention itself, in addition to the dinner that preceded it. In the excitement of Johnson's arrival at Convention Hall, the Windsors were almost forgotten. Adrian "Bud" Foley and his wife Mary were also at the convention. They were close personal friends of the Hughes family and Mary was helping with the hosting obligations. Foley recalled that when President Johnson was making his triumphant entrance into the Convention Hall just before his nomination, his wife Mary observed an elegantly dressed couple entering the convention center through another entrance. The couple seemed lost. She suddenly realized it was the Duke and Duchess of Windsor. She greeted them and sought to make them feel at home.[61]

Perhaps the most important decision of the convention was one that applied to future Democratic conventions. It was decided that in 1968, all delegations would be required to insure all voters had an opportunity to participate in party affairs and vote in presidential elections "regardless of race, color, creed or national origin."[62] This was a dramatic decision requiring fundamental changes. The new requirement led to significant controversy. Hughes would be involved in that controversy when he subsequently served as chairman of the Credentials Committee at the 1968 Democratic National Convention.

One of the most memorable moments at the 1964 convention was a tribute given by Attorney General Robert Kennedy to his brother, the late president. Many who saw that tribute will never forget it. The nominations had been completed, and a memorial film dedicated to John F. Kennedy had been scheduled. Robert Kennedy went to the enormous convention hall to introduce the film. He dressed in a black suit and black tie as he had dressed on public occasions since his brother's assassination. A *New York Times* account of the speech described it this way: "A surge of applause rose from the standing delegates and spectators, but there was no shouting, no music, no parading and only modest waving of state placards. Kennedy stood impassively before the massive arena for sixteen minutes of thunderous tribute, only a suggestion of a smile on his face, before he began to speak in a small, boyish voice, thanking the delegates for all they had done for his brother."[63] He then urged the delegates to support the nominees as they had supported his brother. He quoted Shakespeare's words: "When he shall die, take him and cut him out in little stars, and he will make the face of heaven so fine that all the world will be in love with night, and pay no worship to the garish sun."[64] Betty Hughes described her own emotion at that moment. She said it was a "thrill to stand directly behind Mrs. Robert Kennedy and watch her grow taller during the thundering ovation for her husband. I moved a little to see her face. There were a few tears glistening but her chin stayed high."[65]

The last day of the convention was a bad one for Hughes. He had contracted salmonella poisoning and could not attend the final receptions even at the president's urging. He ended up in the hospital for ten days. After his recovery, he took to the campaign trail for Johnson and Humphrey.

Hughes enjoyed telling the story of what happened one day when he and his good friend, William Hyland, were campaigning with Johnson in Bergen County. Hyland was then serving as chairman of the Department of Public Utilities for the state. Someone in the crowd threw a rotten egg at the president but missed him and struck Hyland. Apparently, the president was not even aware of the incident until Hughes told him about it. The president laughed. Hughes said, "We had to take Billy to a gas station and wash his hair on the way home."[66] For years afterwards, Hughes would tease Hyland about taking an egg for the president.[67] Hughes also talked about Johnson's willingness to step out of his car when he was surrounded by a crowd despite the possible danger.

Hughes worked hard for Johnson, who won New Jersey by more than 900,000 votes. Hughes's view of Johnson's opponent, Barry Goldwater, reflected the concerns that many had expressed about him: that he was appealing to racism and would dramatically increase international tensions. Hughes offered this interpretation: "Goldwater obviously was appealing to prejudice against the minorities. Maybe he didn't mean to do it, I don't know. But certainly there was a great target, I think, against President Johnson on the ground of his forthright, honest dedication to things like the war against poverty and civil rights law and so forth. I was afraid he was going to suffer from it. Now as it turned out, however, there was a great flocking-in to his support of Republicans and independents alike. In New Jersey I, myself, addressed many Republican meetings in the most conservative type towns which went for President Johnson. They were definitely afraid of Goldwater and his potential escalation of the war and so forth."[68]

When Johnson came through victorious, the governor and Betty attended the Inaugural. Hughes described the day's events: "Then we went to the parade, and the inauguration day was great. I remember the President and Vice President Humphrey standing in the stands and giving me a big hand as the New Jersey car went by, and Betty and I waved. Then at a reception in some big place, I guess in the Wardman Park or the Sheraton Park Hotel, we have a picture that we cherish. The President was going around to visit all the state delegations, including Republican as well as Democratic governors, and he came to my box and he grabbed my wife and gave her a very resounding kiss. It was a very nice reunion."[69]

Chapter 8
Civil Rights

HUGHES SPOKE OUT IN FAVOR OF CIVIL RIGHTS during his first campaign, and this issue bedeviled society throughout the entire period of Hughes's governorship. Martin Luther King, Jr.'s famous "I Have a Dream" speech at the March on Washington, organized by many African American leaders, gave a great boost to the civil rights movement and spawned similar actions all over the country.[1] On October 26, 1963, a large group of African Americans and their supporters marched to the State House in Trenton and presented demands to Hughes. The marchers were led by Bayard Rustin, a major civil rights leader. The demands focused especially on discrimination in housing and employment. Hughes had already agreed to meet with civil rights leaders, and, in fact, a number of members of the coalition supporting the march were actually in the governor's office when the group arrived. Priscilla Reed Chenoweth, a member of the coalition, recalled that "beautiful Indian summer day" in Trenton. She was a member of the committee that met with Hughes, but she viewed the meeting as a formality because "he supported our legislative goals." Chenoweth believed that the march and other similar actions were partly responsible for the breakthrough legislation passed the next year, the Civil Rights Act of 1964.[2] Even with the passage of the Civil Rights Act, racial discrimination and civil rights were issues that Hughes, and the rest of the country, would deal with for many years to come.

Hughes worked cooperatively with New York's Governor Rockefeller on many issues. Hughes said, "We were always very friendly and cooperative to the extent that we, when one was going to release some kind of news bombshell, critical of the other, we'd forewarn him the day before so that he could have an answer ready."[3] But Hughes and Rockefeller tangled over civil rights at a governors' meeting in Miami in 1963. At that time the majority of governors were Democratic, and the Democrats could generally control the Governors' Conference. Many of the Democrats, however, were from southern states and were less supportive of civil rights. Hughes believed that Rockefeller would intentionally introduce a proposal to split the Democrats. According to Hughes, "He put on his usual civil rights speech, wanted the governors' conference to adopt a strong civil rights plank and immediately a debate broke out between the northerners and the southerners, Democrats. So, I got in, got the floor, went to the podium, I said, the Governor of New York constantly puts in these resolutions with the obvious intent of dividing and splitting the Democratic governors. . . ."[4] He went on to point out that Rockefeller could do more good by getting the legislators in his own state to be more supportive of civil rights. After extended debate, Rockefeller withdrew his proposal. The *New York Times* reported that Hughes had invoked "his best sarcasm" in response to Rockefeller having said that the GOP had become the party of civil rights. Hughes described the Republicans' conversion as a "24 hour miracle."[5] On the way out of the meeting, Rockefeller said to Hughes, "All right, Hughes, I won't forget that."[6] Nevertheless, Hughes and Rockefeller continued with their usual healthy personal relationship despite their policy disagreements.

One example of Hughes's efforts to end racial discrimination involved housing. In 1963 Hughes planned a conference on housing bias. He met with leaders of the African American community, including the president of the state conference of the National Association for the Advancement of Colored People, and announced that he would promulgate a state policy to end racial discrimination in public housing.

As Hughes attempted to get the fair housing bill passed, he lobbied many different groups. In a speech to the National Council of Catholic Men, Hughes said that supporting the cause of racial justice was a moral imperative. He found that duty enunciated in Pope John XXIII's recently issued encyclical, "Pacem in Terris."[7] During much of Hughes's first term Republicans controlled the legislature and regularly blocked the governor's efforts on behalf of a fair housing measure.[8] But when the legislature became overwhelmingly Democratic in 1966, Hughes's persistent efforts paid off. Early in 1966, at the urging of Hughes and as one of the first acts of its session, the New Jersey State Legislature passed an amendment to the Law against Discrimination[9] that strengthened and expanded its scope. The amendment created both a Commission on Civil Rights and a Division on Civil Rights within the attorney general's office. It broadly expanded the definition of a "place of public accommodation" in order to ban discrimination in public places. The new law also eliminated loopholes in antidiscrimination laws affecting public accommodations, employment, and travel, and specifically targeted swimming clubs and resort establishments along the shore.[10] The Division of Civil Rights was empowered to "investigate and act upon complaints alleging discrimination against persons because of race, creed, color, national origin, ancestry or age. . . ."[11] The controversial fair housing measure assured the right of an African American or anyone else to purchase any home anywhere in New Jersey.[12] The legislation also banned discrimination in employment. At the signing, Hughes said, "We are witnessing a momentous event in the history of our state. . . . We have removed one more impediment. We have only reaffirmed a right which every American accepts as fundamental."[13] These legislative breakthroughs came about after Hughes was reelected and after he had emphasized civil rights in his Inaugural Address, saying: "To those citizens too long denied an open door into New Jersey life—into its communities, its schools, its jobs and opportunities—I mean to keep my solemn promise that this will be a human and civil rights administration. Because we care, because we include every man in our society, together we can form the living tissue of a democracy whose work is never done—as progress is never done, and equality is never done—as justice, the sure foundation of every government is never done. We can no longer tolerate half-freedoms and half-citizens. We can no longer suffer the social and moral stigma with which discrimination marks all of us—majority and minority alike. The barriers must come down. And I call every citizen of New Jersey to the good fight in the only war Americans seek, the war against bigotry, poverty, hate, ignorance and injustice."[14]

Hughes also fought to desegregate New Jersey's schools. At one point he urged the school systems to work out flexible pupil placement policies to remove racial barriers in education. The neighborhood system of student assignment often resulted in segregation because most African Americans lived in one part of town, while nonminority members of the community lived in others. Hughes said, "Where it [the neighborhood school policy] collides with the concept of equality in educational opportunity, its adaption to circumstances to prevent de facto segregation is not only necessary but normally feasible."[15]

The Bergen County community of Englewood was a litmus test for school desegregation in New Jersey. Englewood had a large wealthy population and a substantial number of poorer minority citizens. The wealthy, who tended to be white, congregated in certain sections of town, and the less economically advantaged residents, who were mainly African American, lived in others. There were five elementary schools in Englewood, and the wealthy, white children were concentrated in the same schools since students were assigned by neighborhood. Likewise, the schools in predominantly African American neighborhoods were attended mainly by African American students.

During Hughes's first year as governor, integrationists in Englewood asked him to intervene. At the time, Hughes said that he was unable to get involved in the matter.[16] The turmoil continued, and numerous hearings and various legal actions followed. At one point, a number of parents were charged as disorderly persons for refusing to send their children to a segregated school.[17] There were sit-ins, boycotts of white-owned stores, and a federal suit was filed to prohibit the neighborhood school system. Commissioner of Education Frederick M. Raubinger ordered the Englewood school system to reduce the concentration of African Americans in the Lincoln School, whose student body was 98 percent African American. He later issued a directive to all school officials to modify the neighborhood assignment system to avoid racial segregation. Those measures and others offered temporary solutions, but these matters would not be fully resolved until long after Hughes completed his governorship.

As governor, Hughes sought to diversify appointments. When the New Jersey Youth Division was created, he appointed William S. Hart, an African American, to be its leader. Hart was the first African American in the history of New Jersey to hold such a high post in the governor's office. In 1964, Hughes appointed the first African American woman to the Board of Governors of Rutgers University, Bessie Nelms Hill. Ms. Hill was a civil rights activist who had been a teacher and guidance counselor in Trenton for more than forty years. Hughes worked to improve conditions for African Americans throughout his years in office. The Columbia University oral historian Ronald J. Grele noted that "Hughes appointed blacks to public office in large numbers."[18] He also pointed out that "black counselors like Stanley Van Ness had a sympathetic ear, and within the party (Democratic Party) Hughes established a Minorities Division under C.B. Cargyle, expressly to deal with black and Puerto Rican political participation."[19] Raymond Brown, the African American lawyer and leader of the NAACP in Jersey City who worked on many civil rights issues with Hughes, found the governor to be sympathetic to the concerns of African Americans. Brown delighted in telling a story that demonstrated Hughes's sympathy. When Brown told Hughes of some of the indignities he had faced as a black man, Hughes responded with stories about the indignities the Irish had to suffer in the early days of their immigration to this country and the posted signs saying "No Irish need apply."[20]

Hughes also worked to protect the civil rights of other groups. When the legislature voted for a statute that would have made it compulsory for all school students to salute the American flag despite objections by certain religious groups, Hughes vetoed the bill, saying, "It ill becomes a state legislature to turn its back on the Constitution by seeking to curtail anew the religious and civil liberties of those whose individual beliefs, however unorthodox, are protected from invasion by the First and Fourteenth Amendments."[21]

Hughes used the governor's power to issue executive orders to push for equal rights. In 1965, he issued an executive order creating a Governor's Code of Fair Practices. This code was intended to assure that the executive branch of government accorded equal protection to all its citizens. In the preface to that order, Hughes said, "In accordance with the principles of fair practices, we must strive to recognize the abilities and talents of every individual, while denying to no person his rightful opportunity because of race, creed, color, religion, national origin, ancestry, age, sex or liability for service in the Armed Forces of the United States."[22] The code itself then set forth standards to assure that there was no discrimination in the workforce of the executive branch. It urged the Civil Service, for example, "to take appropriate steps to insure that all examinations oral and written and appointments from certified lists shall be carried out on a non-discriminatory basis."[23] It required that contractors doing business with the state act in a nondiscriminatory manner. Furthermore, the executive order supported the decisions of the commissioner of education to insure that de facto segregation in the schools be eliminated. It also mandated that private schools that received support from state programs adopt a policy against discrimination.

In 1965, Hughes spoke approvingly of the steps his administration was taking to combat discrimination and poverty. "The poor in New Jersey concern us very much, especially that 35 per cent of all non-white families who earn less than $3,000 a year. This is why I established, just a few months ago, a special New Jersey Office of Economic Opportunity to place New Jersey in the first ranks of the Federal economic opportunity or anti-poverty program. There are probably more anti-poverty programs underway now in New Jersey than in any other State."[24] The same year, the governor spoke at the statewide conference for all municipal Civil Rights Commissions in New Jersey. He said that it was the obligation of the members of those commissions to educate the public about the problems of discrimination. "And education doesn't just mean holding brotherhood programs or awarding plaques," Hughes said. "It means getting into the modern civil rights era by actively working at the grass roots for better understanding and observance of the State Law against Discrimination. It means making better known the voluminous information on the positive contributions of minority groups to American history. It means local discussions within the Commission of real or alleged civil rights grievances, recognizing that some of those grievances may be based on past events rather than present facts. But you must work to dispel the myths held both by the majority community as well as the minority community."[25]

In a letter in 1967, Hughes outlined much of his position on equal rights. He was responding to a letter from David Frost, chairman of New Jersey Political Alliance for Peace and Human Rights, who had complained about the failure of the Democratic Party to field more African American candidates. Hughes said, "In seeking candidates for public office, the Democratic Party should, at all times, make every effort to find the men who are best qualified to hold public office. The question of color should not enter the picture whatsoever. However, I do want to make clear that we have always made it our policy to do everything in our power to assure Negro involvement in the affairs of this state and community by encouraging him to register and vote, by inviting his participation in the Democratic Party and opening our doors to him, as to all other citizens, in party organizations at every level."[26] Hughes stopped short of backing affirmative action. In 1967, it was a step forward just to believe in equality.

The issue of segregated schools arose again in 1967 when the new commissioner of education, Carl Marburger, caused a great stir by suggesting the merger of urban and suburban schools to achieve racial integration. Marburger, considered an education innovator, had previously served as an assistant commissioner in the Federal Bureau of Indian Affairs. There was significant controversy over his appointment to replace the former commissioner, Frederick Raubinger. The established education community in New Jersey supported an inside candidate and worked to block Marburger's appointment. But Hughes, who considered Marburger to be one of the leading educators in dealing with the urban poor, used all his weapons to fight for Marburger's approval, including announcing that all patronage appointments would be held up until Marburger was confirmed.[27] Eventually, the Senate confirmed him. Marburger soon began proposing innovations, including the contentious merger suggestion, which seemed to suggest busing as a solution.

In *Brown v. the Board of Education*,[28] the United States Supreme Court in 1954 struck down segregation and prohibited its use in the public schools. Great consternation greeted that decision and years of controversy ensued. New Jersey prohibited segregation in the schools by virtue of language in the 1947 Constitution, prior to the decision in *Brown*, but because of the neighborhood school system, de facto if not official segregation continued. While, in later years, the United States Supreme Court would permit the Federal District Courts to mandate the use of busing to achieve racial integration within the same educational district,[29] it never required the use of busing to integrate across school district lines.[30] Marburger's suggestion would undoubtedly have resulted in busing across district lines to achieve integration. Marburger was attacked widely and Hughes defended him, while simultaneously defending the system of neighborhood schools. Hughes pointed out that Marburger never used the term "busing" in his proposal. Hughes accused Republicans of injecting racial issues into the 1967 legislative campaign.[31] The issue would ultimately be one of the factors which led to the Republicans gaining control of both the Assembly and the Senate in 1968, thus requiring Hughes to deal with an overwhelmingly Republican Legislature during his last two years in office.

In 1967, Hughes appointed Stanley Van Ness, an African American who had been a member of his staff for a number of years, to be his chief counsel. Van Ness was the first African American chief counsel in the history of New Jersey. In 1969, Hughes named Horace Bryant to be the commissioner of Banking and Insurance, making him the first African American cabinet member in the history of New Jersey. Bryant, a noted civil rights leader and a two-term commissioner of Atlantic City, was the founder of the first African American financial institution in Atlantic City.

The movement for women's rights was only beginning during the administration of Hughes. His cabinet and administration were predominantly filled with males. However, he was certainly not opposed to the appointment of women. In 1963, he appointed Millicent Fenwick, a Republican, to his Committee on Equal Employment Opportunity. In a letter written years later, Hughes described Congresswoman Fenwick, who would later be immortalized in the *Doonesbury* comic strip as Congresswoman Lacey Davenport, by saying: "I doubt, in the history of New Jersey any

Republican [and Democrat] . . . were closer in philosophy and affection than Millicent and yours truly. And that without any worldly romantic tie—just love for the people—all of them. Millicent often risked a punch in the jaw, at least when she invaded union meetings in Newark and insisted on the recruitment of black apprentice members—a great lady, one devoted to the world and the hungry. . . ."[32] Fenwick was not the only Republican on that committee. Its members included Bernard Shanley, who had been in President Eisenhower's administration, and Webster Todd, the chair of the New Jersey Republican Party.

In 1964 Hughes nominated—and eventually the Senate confirmed—June Strelecki as the first woman director of the Department of Motor Vehicles. Strelecki would later become a judge of the Superior Court. Judge Strelecki believed that when she was appointed, Hughes was actively seeking to appoint women. She thought this was partly the result of his close relationship with his wife Betty and the high regard he had for his wife's intellect. She added that the fact that she was Polish (at that time there was no Polish person in the higher levels of the Hughes administration) was also a help.[33]

Later that year, Hughes appointed a commission to study women's issues and how to get them more involved in the political process. The executive director of that commission was Beatrice Tylutki, a young deputy attorney general.

When Hughes became governor, there was only one woman sitting in all of the state courts. Aldona E. Appleton was a judge in Juvenile and Domestic Relations Court in Middlesex County. By the end of Hughes's tenure, Judge Appleton was joined by Judge Inez M. Stanziale, whom Hughes appointed as a judge of the State Division of Tax Appeals. New Jersey was not unlike other states at the time, in having a small number of female attorneys and very few female judges.

Hughes appointed a number of women to state education boards. His appointments included Katharine Auchincloss and Marion Epstein to the State Board of Education and Ruth Ford and Deborah Wolfe to the State Board of Higher Education. He also appointed women to the Public Health Council and the State Board of Control of Institutions and Agencies.

Under New Jersey law, when the governor is out of the state, the president of the Senate serves as acting governor, and when both are out of the state, the speaker of the Assembly serves. In 1965, the speaker of the Assembly was Marion West Higgins, the first woman to hold that position. When Hughes was attending the inauguration of President Johnson,

Senator Charles W. Sandman, the president of the Senate, was serving as acting governor. Sandman decided to travel outside the state in order to permit Speaker Higgins to become the first woman acting governor. Much later, Christine Todd Whitman would serve as the first full-fledged woman governor of New Jersey.

Years later, in 1985, Hughes fought for the reappointment of Judge Florence Peskoe. Judge Peskoe worked with Hughes as clerk of the court when he was chief justice, and he had always been very impressed by her. When the time came for her reappointment there were some criticisms of her as a judge, and there was an effort to block her reappointment. Hughes jumped to her defense. In a letter written to the Chairman of the State Bar Committee on Judicial Appointments, he combined his ever-vigilant emphasis on judicial independence with his personal support for Judge Peskoe. The letter stressed in glowing terms the work she had performed for the Supreme Court while he was chief justice but also emphasized his concern that judges who hear matrimonial matters are frequently targeted for criticism by people who lose in the courts, and that "it is only for the gravest reasons, that an honorable career on the bench should be terminated by failure of reappointment."[34] A compromise was worked out. Normally, in New Jersey if a judge is reappointed after initial appointment, that judge is granted tenure and can serve until the mandatory retirement age of seventy. However, that only applies if the reappointment occurs within the period of the first term. In Judge Peskoe's case her reappointment was delayed and thus she did not receive tenure. Later on Judge Peskoe was again reappointed and granted tenure.

These issues and appointments show Hughes's deep commitment to equal rights for everyone regardless of race or gender. Hughes's own remembrances of discrimination against the Irish, reinforced by his deep commitment to the liberal agenda first demonstrated by his devotion to Woodrow Wilson and his confidence in the agendas of Franklin Roosevelt, John Kennedy, and Lyndon Johnson, would be demonstrated throughout his years as governor, chief justice, and beyond.

Chapter 9

Making a Difference

Hughes Confronts New Jersey's Challenges

IN ADDITION TO THE VOLATILE ISSUE OF CIVIL RIGHTS, Hughes had to face many other challenges throughout his years as governor, including the death penalty, the minimum drinking age, education, transportation, and many others. These challenges continued throughout his two terms in office.

The Death Penalty

In the early years of Hughes's governorship, the death penalty was still in effect in New Jersey, as it was in most states. In 1972 the United States Supreme Court would strike down the death penalty,[1] and then issue a subsequent decision to reinstate it under certain carefully circumscribed conditions.[2] Hughes had an early introduction to the death penalty when his father was warden of the state prison. The elder Hughes opposed the death penalty, but Hughes himself had a strong law and order streak, formed during his years as an Assistant United States Attorney and on the bench. Although he had some qualms, he was willing to support it.

As governor, Hughes held the ultimate decision in death penalty cases through the power of executive clemency.[3] If he thought it appropriate, he could commute a death sentence to life imprisonment. In the first case that came before Hughes during his first year in office, he turned down the appeal for clemency in a death penalty case. After a hearing in the presence of the condemned man's family and the lawyers on both sides of the case, Hughes permitted the execution of a man who had killed his four-and-a-half-year-old stepdaughter during a sex offense.[4] The New Jersey Supreme

Court had affirmed the conviction 6–1.[5] The dissenting justice sought to reverse the sentence based on a technical issue which did not raise doubts about the defendant's guilt.[6] At that time it would have been difficult for even a governor as committed to civil rights and protection of defendants' rights as Hughes was, to have rejected the jury's death penalty decision in such a heinous case.

The last New Jersey case leading to an execution involved Ralph Hudson, who was convicted of murdering his wife in 1959 and executed in 1963.[7] In the presence of a number of witnesses, Hudson announced that he was going to kill her. There seemed to be no substantial doubt as to his guilt. Hudson had previously been convicted for assaulting his wife. A number of arguments were raised during the case's appeal, but the New Jersey Supreme Court rejected those arguments. At the time, there was still a great deal of support for the death penalty. It would have been unlikely that Hughes would find any justification for clemency, particularly since Hudson indicated that he wanted to be executed, and he was executed. Nonetheless, the qualms about the death penalty that Hughes had learned from his father made it difficult for him to permit the executions. W. Michael Murphy, Hughes's stepson, said in testimony to the New Jersey Department of Corrections on the death penalty, "The last execution in New Jersey, of Ralph Hudson in 1963 for the murder of his wife Myrtle, was carried out during my father's administration. The painful decision to allow Hudson's execution to go forward profoundly impacted him."[8] That concern, however, was not enough to lead Hughes to push for the abolition of the death penalty. The climate was still one of support for the death penalty and Hughes had seen firsthand the consequences of crime from his time on the bench.

When Hughes created a state commission to study the death penalty in 1964, the commission's recommendations included retaining the death penalty but instituting reforms in the trial process. In 1967, the New Jersey Supreme Court nullified two death penalties because of mistaken instructions given by the trial judge concerning the possibility of parole. Again there were calls for the abolition of the death penalty, but Hughes responded that he still approved of the death penalty and would veto any legislation that would abolish it.[9] Subsequently, the New Jersey death penalty as it was being applied in New Jersey, was declared unconstitutional as a result of a decision of the United States Supreme Court.[10]

During Hughes's six years (1973–1979) as chief justice of the New Jersey Supreme Court he did not hear any death penalty cases because at the time there was no death penalty statute in New Jersey. In the late

1970s, after the United States Supreme Court decided that the death penalty was constitutional under certain carefully defined circumstances,[11] there were a number of attempts by the New Jersey Legislature to reinstate it. Governor Byrne, a strong opponent, continually vetoed such legislation and the legislature was unable to garner sufficient votes to override his veto. When Thomas Kean became governor in 1982 he signed a death penalty statute. While a number of individuals were convicted and sentenced to death during the following years, no one was ever executed, and in 2007 under another Democratic administration the death penalty in New Jersey was abolished.

The power of executive clemency extends to matters beyond the death penalty. The governor can, for example, commute a sentence. In one case, Hughes considered the request of an escapee who had been convicted of a number of car thefts. He had served five years of a seven-to-ten year term when he escaped. He then lived under an assumed identity in a community as a good and decent citizen for thirteen years. He had married, fathered six children and worked at a trade. Hughes commuted his sentence to time served, saying, "The past 13 years of his life has reflected demonstrable rehabilitation and a complete adjustment to the community."[12]

Hughes also showed sympathy in a case dealing with extradition. Extradition is the process whereby state A requests that state B return a person accused of a crime in state A back to state A for trial. In this particular case, Alabama requested that an individual living in New Jersey who had escaped from a prison camp in Alabama twenty-five years earlier be returned to Alabama. Hughes refused, saying that his investigation revealed that the individual had become a "model citizen" during his twenty-five years of freedom in New Jersey and that there was no reason to extradite him.[13]

The Drinking Age and Safety Concerns

The drinking age in New Jersey was twenty-one when Hughes became governor. The drinking age in New York was eighteen. This discrepancy prompted persons from New Jersey between the ages of eighteen and twenty-one to go to New York to drink. After drinking, many of them drove home to New Jersey. That practice resulted in a substantial number of deaths and injuries caused by drunken drivers. Greatly distressed by this, Hughes lobbied Governor Rockefeller and the New York Legislature throughout his two terms to change the drinking age in New York. Hughes never succeeded. At one point, in 1966, a New York state senator suggested a compromise: the states of New York, Connecticut, and New Jersey would all agree to set the drinking age at nineteen and one-half. New Jersey and Connecticut strongly rejected that idea.[14]

A change did occur in the voting age during Hughes's governorship, however. In 1967, the Democratic State Convention recommended changing the national voting age from twenty-one to eighteen. Hughes originally opposed the change. Ultimately faced with the argument that if young people were old enough to fight (the conscription age was eighteen) they were old enough to vote, he reversed his position and supported the reduction. He said, "I'm not ashamed to change my mind."[15] He then supported an amendment to the United States Constitution that would change the voting age to eighteen. On July 1, 1971, the United States Constitution was amended to provide that anyone eighteen or older could not be denied the right to vote because of his or her age.[16]

With the drinking age disparity remaining, Hughes worked with the legislature in New Jersey to tighten the laws on youthful drunk driving. In 1965, New Jersey passed legislation that provided for mandatory suspension of driving privileges for at least two years, or until the offender reaches the age of twenty-one, whichever is greater, for a first offense of driving while intoxicated[17] or under the influence of narcotics or habit-forming drugs.[18] The *New York Times* reported: "Gov. Richard J. Hughes signed a bipartisan measure that, in his words, 'gets off the road' any teen-ager convicted of drunken driving at least until he is 21 years of age."[19]

Additionally, in 1966, Hughes pushed through a bill to make the drunk-driving laws more stringent. The legislation provided that anyone operating a motor vehicle on the public roads of New Jersey and suspected of being intoxicated would be deemed to have consented to taking a breath test for the purpose of determining his or her blood alcohol level. Any person who refused to take the test would lose his or her license.[20] The legislation also added penalties for driving while impaired. By 1966, Democrats were in control of the legislature, but even with the Democratic majority, Hughes had to push hard for passage. When the legislature first failed to put the issue to a vote, Hughes was quoted as saying, "I think they should take it up even if they don't have the votes . . . if they do not want to save 400 lives or so annually, let them put it on the record."[21]

Another safety concern Hughes addressed while governor had to do with motorcycle safety. His position on this issue suggests that he occasionally listened to his family in judging legislation. Legislation had been proposed to mandate the use of helmets by motorcycle riders. The bill also required motorcycles to have an iron bar protruding from both wheels. Proponents said the bar would help protect the rider in a crash. Hughes's son Pat, a motorcycle enthusiast, was opposed to both measures. He and a group of other enthusiasts were able to prove to Hughes that the iron bar requirement would make riding more, rather than less, dangerous. Pat was unable, however, to convince his father to reject the helmet proposal. In 1967, Hughes signed a law requiring motorcyclists to wear a helmet. That law remains in effect today.[22] Additionally, in June 1965, the legislature approved a bill requiring all passenger cars manufactured after July 1, 1966, and sold in New Jersey to have front-seat safety belts.[23]

Hughes, who had been very involved in juvenile crime issues while a judge, also signed a law that strengthened measures against the use of drugs. There had been an increase in youth, particularly in urban areas, using drugs, particularly barbiturates or tranquilizers referred to as "goof-balls." The new law made it a crime to purchase or possess barbiturates, tranquilizers, amphetamines, and other specified drugs without a doctor's prescription. The punishment was a $1,000 fine, a year in jail, or both.[24]

Birth Control

Hughes's easy and relaxed relationship with the press, as well as his tendency to exaggerate, occasionally got him into hot water. He was asked at a news conference whether the state welfare agencies should supply birth control to welfare recipients as a method of reducing the number of illegitimate children. Hughes replied: "One solution would be to execute her (the unwed mother). Another solution would be to sterilize her. Another would be to teach her birth control. I put all three in the same category as far as the morality is concerned."[25] Hughes's opposition to birth control probably reflected his own moral position and the views of the Catholic Church. When his hyperbole was reported, however, there was widespread criticism. Hughes later modified his position and said that his "extemporaneous comments . . . produced interpretations which I did not intend and which do not reflect my views . . . as governor, on birth control."[26] Here the wording was much more careful, indicating that his personal moral stance was not his official position as governor. He rejected the use of contraception or sterilization as the appropriate public policy for the state. He acknowledged that many people in the state did not view contraception as immoral and that its use was certainly permissible under state law. Summing up Hughes's position, a newspaper article said the governor viewed birth control as "a matter of individual conscience and religious freedom and it is not the function of the state to interfere in this area of private life."[27]

The Bond Debacle

A bond proposal was the primary reason Hughes lost the Democratic majority in the legislature after the elections of 1963. Hughes was struggling with a paucity of money. Knowing he would be unable to institute a broad-based tax, he recommended the passage of two big bond issues. The issues passed the legislature, but under the requirements of the State Constitution these bonds had to be placed before the voters. [28]

The two bond issues were presented to the people in the November 1963 election. The first called for $275 million in bonds for construction of public institutions and colleges; the second, $475 million in bonds for public roads and highways.[29] Both were bigger than any previous bond issue in the history of New Jersey. The largest before then had been $83 million. In an astute move, Republicans insisted that the full cost of repaying the bonds be included on the ballot. This made the amount appear even larger.

Hughes staked his reputation on passage of the bond issues. He campaigned intensely, making numerous appearances every day.[30] He threatened that if the bond issues did not pass, he would have to seek a broad-based tax—either a sales tax or an income tax. But numerous groups opposed the bond issues. Some were opposed because they favored a broad-based tax and felt that the bonds would delay implementation of such a tax. Others believed that the bond issues were unnecessary and that expenditures should be cut. Even the League of Women Voters favored an income tax and opposed the bond plan. On Election Day, the voters decisively defeated both bond issues.[31] They also voted against many Democratic candidates who were on the ballot. Edward Hulse, the husband of Hughes's sister, Alice, was running for the state senate from Burlington County that year. He was one of those who were defeated. Alice blamed the loss on the bond issue and she was not alone.[32] Many local Democratic officials blamed the legislative and local losses on Hughes's emphasis on the bonds.[33]

After the defeat, the *Newark Evening News* called for Hughes to resign. The newspaper never supported Hughes and had editorialized strongly against the bond issue. While Hughes had said he would seek a broad-based tax if the bond issue failed, the losses suffered by the Democrats in that election made it impossible for him to garner sufficient support. After the Republicans gained control of the legislature in 1964, they clearly stated that they would not support a broad-based tax.[34] In the following year, the Republicans sponsored a bond issue of $90.1 million for college and institutional building. A college bond issue of $40.1 million would provide housing for more than 10,000 additional students, and an institutions bond issue of $50 million would include money for a second hospital for the mentally retarded, a medium security prison, community health centers, and other capital projects. Hughes said that he would campaign for the bond issues despite believing that they were too little too late.[35]

Despite the defeat of the bond issues and the Democrats' loss of control in the legislature in 1963, there was general optimism in the state. The economy was healthy and business leaders were hopeful. The population continued to increase and personal income was expected to rise to $20 billion. That sense of optimism would help Hughes overcome the problems caused by the defeat of the bond issues.

The Transportation Challenge

Transportation issues loomed large during Hughes's governorship. The development of roads and mass transit had not kept pace with the state's rapid suburbanization. As early as his first annual report to the legislature, Hughes championed improvements to both highway and mass transit systems. Hughes had achieved some success in the area of mass transit by reaching an agreement with the Port Authority to take over the old Hudson and Manhattan Railroad. In 1962, Hughes approved a $115 million state highway construction program and, at the same time, signed an agreement with the Federal Bureau of Roads to receive federal grants much more quickly. The federal government would end up paying for about $78 million of the $115 million project.

As the automobile became increasingly popular and more resources were being devoted to it, many railroads began facing significant financial difficulties. In 1962, New Jersey began providing state subsidies to a number of railroads (Pennsylvania, Erie-Lackawanna, Pennsylvania-Reading Seashore Lines, and the Reading) to assure continued commuter services.[36] While the railroads needed help, the toll roads in New Jersey—the New Jersey Turnpike, which had opened in 1951, and the Garden State Parkway, which had opened in 1955—were financially successful. More and more people used these roads, eventually leading to serious congestion that required additional lanes and other improvements.[37]

In 1963, the Jersey Central Railroad threatened to cut or eliminate its commuter services if it did not receive increased public subsidies.[38] In 1964, the railroads asked for tax relief and government aid totaling $405 million over 10 years.[39] The state responded with a subsidy of approximately $7 million for that year, with the largest portion going to the Central Railroad.[40] Meanwhile the Central Railroad was still finding it necessary to lay off workers as a cost-cutting procedure.[41] There was a growing recognition of the need for regional planning in this vital area.

In March 1965, Hughes and New York Governor Rockefeller agreed on the creation of a tristate transportation agency. The states of Connecticut and New York had already agreed on such an agency, and during a meeting at Morven, Rockefeller and Hughes agreed that New Jersey would join this planning operation.[42] Shortly thereafter, Hughes proposed a plan for continuing and improving commuter services. The plan had been developed in conjunction with the state highway commissioner, whose department had a Division of Railroad Transportation. The plan included various proposals to help the railroads, including money for capital improvements supported by both the state and federal government, as well as new scheduling and service changes to increase ridership.[43] Eventually, the state received federal funds, as well as funds from the Port Authority, to implement some of these plans.[44] There was also talk of various railroad merger plans at the time, which Hughes had to monitor in order to protect the interest of New Jersey riders. He met with the leaders of a number of the railroads to try to insure continuing service. By December 1965, the executive director of the Port Authority, Austin Tobin, was urging New Jersey to create an independent state agency to deal with the commuting crises affecting 77,000 railroad passengers. Tobin speculated that $130 million was needed for improvements on the Erie-Lackawanna and Jersey Central Railroads.[45]

At the same time, efforts existed to get another bond issue passed. Even though Hughes's earlier transportation bond proposals were defeated, the new calls for a significant bond issue were strong. The New Jersey committee of a regional planning agency suggested the need for $300 million over the next ten years for modernization of the railroad lines. It said half of that could come from the federal government and the remaining portion from the state. In 1966, there was significant movement involving these issues. It was estimated that there were 189,000 commuters going into New York City on a daily basis—the majority by rail and bus and the rest by auto.[46] The governor presented a special message to the legislature in May of that year, in which he proposed the creation of a Commuter Operating Agency that would be a part of a new State Department of Transportation. He also asked the legislature to approve a $375 million, ten-year commuter rail program,[47] anticipating that much of those funds would come from the federal government. In October 1966, Hughes announced a $176 million highway program focused primarily on improving safety on existing roads.[48] At virtually the same time, he announced a $30 million overhaul of railroad commuter service.[49]

Highway construction was also going forward. In 1965, another major road construction program for $152 million was approved. More than $96 million was scheduled to come from the federal government. These funds would mainly cover major east-west roads, including Route 280, Route 78, Route 3, and Route 46.

Hughes had been pushing for several years for a restructuring of the system for controlling transportation. It was late in 1966 when the governor finally achieved his goal and a new Department of Transportation was created.[50] The new department brought all divisions of transportation together under state authority, including the State Highway Department, the Division of Railroad Transportation, and the aviation responsibilities of the Department of Conservation and Economic Development. The New Jersey Turnpike Authority and the New Jersey Expressway Authority, "although retaining their 'politic and corporate' autonomy," were also transferred to the new department.[51] The department would have two divisions—one for public rail and bus transportation and one for highways. Hughes appointed his counsel and close confidant, David Goldberg, to be commissioner of the new department.[52] Goldberg was referred to as the "unofficial lieutenant governor" because of his important role in planning and developing the governor's policies.[53] His selection indicated the importance that Hughes gave to the new Department of Transportation. Soon after the appointment, Hughes and Goldberg were embroiled in the problems resulting from the Jersey Central Railroad's bankruptcy. They indicated that they would do everything possible to maintain the operation of the railroad.[54]

At approximately the same time, the New Jersey Turnpike Authority began expanding the number of lanes on that important north-south toll road through New Jersey.[55] A major new bridge across the Delaware River, built as a twin to the Delaware Memorial Bridge, was designed to ease the congestion on the existing bridge, which only had two lanes in each direction. When the Delaware Memorial Bridge opened in 1951, it was estimated that it would carry 3.6 million vehicles a year. By the time the new bridge opened, the original bridge was carrying 15 million vehicles annually.[56]

In 1968, the voters, who refused to support a bond issue for transportation in 1963, would approve a large bond issue to support transportation improvements. The $660 million bond issue earmarked $440 million for highways and $200 million for mass transportation. In spite of the passage of the bonds, and the complete overhaul of the transportation department, transportation issues would continue to arise for Hughes and New Jersey, the most densely populated state in the country.

Saying Goodbye to a Friend

On June 15, 1965, Thorn Lord, Hughes's close friend and political confidant, committed suicide at the age of fifty-eight. Lord, whom Hughes had chosen as the state Democratic leader in 1961, committed suicide in the home of Judge Clifton C. Bennett, where he had been staying for a few days. In a letter, addressed to Bennett, Lord indicated that he was "despondent over the estrangement from his second wife."[57] Lord's death was a traumatic event for Governor Hughes. The two men had been close friends for years, and Hughes knew that without Lord, he probably would never have become governor. In spite of their closeness, the governor had often commented on the fact that Lord steadfastly refused to discuss his personal affairs and problems. In a public statement, Hughes said, "New Jersey has lost one of its finest citizens, and I have been deprived of a dear personal friend. His sole concern as a conscientious civic leader was good government and the well-being of the people of this state. Our loss is indeed a great one."[58] Hughes recalled years later that he had no inkling that Lord was so depressed. "I saw him the week before [he committed suicide] when he was elected, reelected as chairman of the Democratic State Committee, I saw him in my office in Trenton, no he was an inside man, he kept all his troubles to himself."[59]

Since Lord had just been elected to lead the state Democratic Party for another four-year term, his sudden death was both a personal and political blow to Hughes, who was about to start campaigning for a second term and would undoubtedly have looked to his old friend for support and advice. Congressman Frank Thompson replaced Lord as Democratic state leader for a short time, until Robert Burkhardt was appointed to fill the position.

Medical Education

When Hughes took office, there was only one medical school in the state, run by Seton Hall University, a Catholic university of the Archdiocese of Newark. That school, located in Jersey City, had been chartered in 1954 as a result of efforts by the Jersey City Medical Center, Seton Hall, and the archdiocese. It began accepting students in 1956.[60] After a hopeful start, the school ran into serious difficulties. It was facing a multimillion dollar debt when both the president of the university and the first dean of the medical school died. Conflicts with municipal authorities in Jersey City had also been disruptive. In the mid-1960s, Seton Hall was looking to divest itself of the medical school.

New Jersey had sought unsuccessfully in the late 1940s to develop a state medical school.[61] Voters turned down a proposed $25 million bond issue to finance a state medical college at Rutgers University. Some observers blamed Catholics for voting against that bond issue, believing that many Catholics, while supporting their own schools, were not interested in paying additional taxes to support other universities and schools. Rutgers consequently was not supportive when Seton Hall looked to the state to take over its medical school.[62]

In April 1964, Hughes appointed a committee chaired by George F. Smith, the president of Johnson & Johnson, a pharmaceutical company, to study the possibility of state acquisition of the Seton Hall Medical School. Sensitive to possible criticism because he was a Catholic, Hughes said, "We have no idea of helping Seton Hall . . . we are interested only in preserving New Jersey's only medical school."[63] Senator Raymond Bateman, later a Republican candidate for governor, indicated that the Church expected Hughes, as the first Catholic governor of the state, to help Seton Hall out of its difficulty.[64] After careful investigation, the committee eventually recommended that the state take over the school. On May 3, 1965, the state paid Seton Hall $4 million and Hughes signed into law an act creating the New Jersey College of Medicine and Dentistry.[65] Some months later the medical school ceased operating out of the Jersey City Medical Center and relocated its clinical facilities to the 640-bed Newark City Hospital and the 950-bed East Orange Veterans Administration Hospital. President Johnson "personally directed that the East Orange Veteran's Administration Medical Center be at the complete disposal of the medical school."[66]

A debate then ensued as to whether the school should take up new quarters on a suburban tract of 138 acres in Madison, or on a 185-acre campus in Newark. The faculty of the medical school as well as others supported the suburban location. Mayor Hugh Addonizio of Newark and Governor Hughes pressed for consideration of Newark. In the end, Newark was selected as the location, but the number of acres was significantly reduced. The political lobbying to have the school in Newark had good intentions. It was thought that the school would be an economic stimulus for the community and improve medical care for Newark residents. The proposed taking of properties in the Central Ward of Newark, however, provoked community antagonisms that would play a part in fueling the destructive Newark riots some months later. Those riots, which will be discussed at length later, caused immense and long-term harm, both in loss of life and destruction of large sections of Newark, but did lead to increased recognition of the problems in the inner-cities.

Shortly after those riots, in an effort to make more housing available in Newark, the medical school agreed to further scale back the amount of land it needed. Additionally, state officials met with Newark community leaders. Together they formulated what one commentator called, "a remarkable social contract with Newark and its citizens, the Newark Agreements of 1968."[67] This effort was designed to bring community leaders into the work of the medical school and to demonstrate the importance of that institution to Newark.

It would be many years before the completion of the new medical school. Today, it is part of a major medical school system in New Jersey that includes numerous schools and programs, operating under the umbrella of what is called the University of Medicine and Dentistry of New Jersey.

Working with the Kennedy and Johnson Administrations

The Hughes administration worked hard to participate in the many new programs created under the Kennedy and Johnson administrations. Larry Bilder, who worked in Hughes's administration, would regularly go to Washington and meet with administration officials, particularly Kenneth O'Donnell, who served as a special assistant to both Kennedy and Johnson.[68] Hughes always wanted to be involved in new proposals coming from the White House, and especially wanted to be sure that New Jersey would be ready to participate, and get its fair share of the funding provided for those programs.

One of the new federal initiatives was Head Start, instituted in 1965 and designed to help poor preschool-age children get a jump on their education. New Jersey was the first state in the country to participate in the program. Lady Bird Johnson traveled to New Jersey in 1965 with Sargent Shriver, who was heading up the administration's antipoverty initiatives, to highlight the success and great potential of Head Start. In her memoirs, Lady Bird said, "Soon we were in Newark, with Mayor Addonizio and Governor and Mrs. Hughes at the foot of the ramp. Mrs. Hughes proved a most outstanding person in that crowded day, combining good common sense, infectious humor, and industry."[69] Dr. Charles Kelley, the coordinator of Head Start in New Jersey, took Mrs. Johnson to see the program in action at Cleveland Elementary School in Englewood. In addition to education, Head Start provided balanced meals, and medical and dental care, including inoculations and hearing and speech tests. Mrs. Johnson was impressed by what she saw. She felt that the students were learning to pay attention, to get along with others, to increase their vocabularies, and to see things they had never seen before.[70] Mrs. Johnson hoped that the program would make a difference in the lives of the students who participated.

The group then visited another Head Start program in Lambertville, a much more rural town, but one with its share of poverty. The program was full of children whose parents worked on the truck farms and lived in shanties along the Delaware River. Mrs. Johnson described the scene: "The little church was as bleak and poverty-stricken as any I have ever seen in the backwoods of East Texas or Alabama, but it opened its arms to people in need."[71] Despite the dreariness of the setting, Mrs. Johnson was impressed by the teacher in charge of the Lambertville project, describing him as "earnest, devoted, full of life, [and] excited by the improvement in the children in the course of eight weeks."[72] After meeting with the students and their parents Lady Bird expressed her hopes for the program. "I do not want to turn America over to another generation as listless and dull as many of these parents looked. I yearn for better from their children."[73]

At the end of the tour, the party returned to Morven, where a group of educators were taking part in a seminar on the Head Start Program. There, Mrs. Johnson had an opportunity to relax with the Hughes family. "One of the happiest moments of the day had been my arrival at Morven. At least eight of the ten Hughes children were waiting for me—some his, some hers, some theirs! They are a remarkable family and my admiration for Mrs. Hughes grew minute by minute."[74]

Appointments

Hughes made hundreds of appointments during his time as governor. Surprisingly, however, he never got the opportunity to appoint a member of the New Jersey Supreme Court. Throughout his eight years in office, the same seven justices sat together. He did, though, reappoint five members of the highest state court. He reappointed Chief Justice Weintraub, who had essentially been his superior when he himself served in the judiciary. He also reappointed Justice John Francis, who had gotten the appointment to the Supreme Court when Hughes was also being considered by Governor Meyner. The other reappointments to the Supreme Court were Justices Haydn Proctor, Frederick Hall, and Vincent Haneman. One of his Superior Court appointees, Alan Handler, was later appointed to the Supreme Court by a subsequent governor.

In 1967, Hughes entered into a compact with the New Jersey State Bar Association to allow that organization to vet all candidates for judicial appointment. The association would review the credentials of all potential state judges and make recommendations pro or con.

Hughes, the consummate politician, took into consideration the wishes of the various party leaders when he made appointments. But because of his tremendous knowledge of the state from his experience as a lawyer, judge, and political leader, he often knew personally the individuals who were being appointed. In fact, Larry Bilder, his counsel, recalled that when Hughes was making judicial appointments, he often went through the Lawyer's Diary looking for the lawyers who had impressed him.

Governor Brendan Byrne remembered the dispute over his own reappointment as prosecutor by Hughes. Byrne, who had been secretary to Governor Meyner, was appointed by Meyner as Prosecutor of Essex County over the objections of Dennis Carey, the Democratic leader of Essex, who had another candidate in mind. Ultimately Meyner prevailed and Byrne became prosecutor.[75] When he came up for reappointment, however, the then-mayor of Newark, Hugh Addonizio, urged Hughes not to reappoint Byrne. In an effort to appease both parties, Hughes offered Byrne the statewide position to head the Alcoholic Beverage Commission. Byrne demurred, indicating he wanted to stay on as prosecutor.[76] Hughes ultimately reappointed Byrne, who later became a successor to Hughes as governor.

John Gibbons, who served as president of the New Jersey Bar Association and later chief judge of the United States Court of Appeals for the Third Circuit, described Hughes's appointments as generally good. He said appointees from the opposing party were "superb" and from his own party were "at least very good."[77]

One appointment that went sour was that of Judge Ralph DeVita. In the early 1960s, DeVita was the First Assistant Prosecutor in the Union County prosecutor's office. He was seriously considered for prosecutor when that position opened up in 1964. After Attorney General Arthur Sills indicated that DeVita might have a possible mob affiliation, Hughes rejected DeVita and appointed Leo Kaplowitz. Two years later, however, Hughes appointed DeVita as a county court judge. DeVita had the backing of the Union County Bar Association and the Union County Democratic Party. When questioned about the appointment, Hughes was reported to have said that the allegation of DeVita's possible mob affiliation was "hearsay "and "unsubstantiated" and that "he could not reject a nominee of the Democratic party in Union County unless the law enforcement authorities had more concrete evidence against him."[78] This decision may have reflected loyalty to both his party and people whom he knew. Because Hughes served as assignment judge in Union County during the time DeVita was First Assistant Prosecutor, they must have known each other, and Hughes would have had the opportunity to observe DeVita. Additionally, as a Democratic loyalist, he would have been impressed by the wishes of the Democratic Party. This may have been particularly true because the Democratic leader of Union County was still James J. Kenneally, who was present at the meeting at which Hughes was selected as the Democratic candidate for governor

Some years later, the warnings about Judge DeVita appeared to have substance. He was indicted for attempting to bribe the Somerset County prosecutor, Michael Imbriani, to drop charges against two men in the county who were charged with bookmaking. Donald Horowitz, who had returned to private practice after serving as First Assistant United States Attorney for the District of New Jersey, was recruited to handle this sensitive case. DeVita took the stand in his own defense and denied the allegations. Instigated by Imbriani, the state police had taped conversations between DeVita and Imbriani, but the discussions on the tapes were general and vague. The main evidence was the testimony of Imbriani. The *New York Times* reported that many prominent lawyers and businessmen appeared as character witnesses for DeVita. After twenty-seven hours of deliberation, the jury found DeVita guilty of obstructing justice but not guilty of bribery. He was sentenced to one to two years in jail.[79]

Imbriani continued as Somerset prosecutor until 1971, when he was appointed to the bench. In an ironic twist, Judge Imbriani was himself later charged with embezzlement, pled guilty, and was subsequently disbarred.[80]

Chapter 10

The Second Campaign

Hughes was selected to run again in 1965 without any significant opposition within the Democratic Party. There was, however, some opposition within his family. Betty was not in favor of a second term. Hughes said, "It never occurred to me not to run for a second term. I liked the job, I had a lot to do. I hadn't accomplished what I had hoped to accomplish because I was opposed by mostly Republican legislatures. Betty Hughes and a close friend of ours, Paul Troast, the man who ran against Meyner in 1953, became very close to us and I remember him and Betty sitting together in Morven trying to argue me out of running again. He pointed out that I could be four years ahead on returning to a pretty good law practice and make some money and that I had been governor and he said they were kidding about the obituary, that it would not recite that he served two terms, but they'll just say he was a former governor, and I would get rid of the aggravation, etc. etc. But I thought about my programs that I wanted and I thought about the hundreds of people in state government and county government who depended on me."[1] Hughes went on to say that ultimately Betty did not object too strenuously. He quoted her as saying, "Where you go I go Amigo."[2]

Hughes had only token opposition in the primary. His opponent in the general election, Wayne Dumont, a state senator from Warren County, who had been selected by the Republican screening committee as its candidate, had to survive a hard-fought primary campaign against a conservative Republican, Charles Sandman, state senator from Cape May County. In the primary contest against Sandman, Dumont, recognizing the need for greater state revenues, supported a sales tax. Sandman ran on an antitax position.

On the pressing issue of whether or not to have a broad-based tax, Hughes and Dumont held the same view. They differed on the kind of tax, however. Hughes felt an income tax would be fairest to the average person. He knew he needed additional funds to support his ambitious programs for the state, but he campaigned heavily against a sales tax, arguing that it was regressive and unfair. He constantly harped on the unfairness of a sales tax and only in asides did he indicate that he was in favor of an income tax. In a notably careful statement during one of the gubernatorial debates, Hughes, when accused by Dumont of waffling on the tax issue, was reported in the *New York Times* as saying, "that he would not press with 'dogmatic insistence' for a sales tax, nor for what he said was his own preference, an income tax, but would rather 'fight to make the Legislature respond to the 20th century needs of New Jersey with any responsible fiscal measure.'"[3]

Dumont was an excellent public servant, but he was not widely known. In later years, Hughes would write that he knew Dumont would have been a fine governor. For obvious reasons, Hughes had far greater name recognition, and he was generally well-liked. Additionally, the economy remained healthy during Hughes's governorship. In the last year of his first term, personal income rose by 8 percent, retail sales rose 6 percent, and unemployment was down from previous years.[4]

Despite Hughes's efforts to expand the opportunities for New Jersey residents to attend in-state colleges, there was still a major exodus of students from New Jersey, for which he was criticized by Dumont. Ironically, publicity that resulted from Dumont's criticism may have strengthened Hughes's hand in his subsequent efforts to obtain more funding for higher education.

Dumont recognized that his chances of winning against Hughes without some cutting issue were negligible. He had depleted his finances during the primary fight, and thus, he could not rely on extensive advertising. He was looking for an issue that might electrify his campaign.[5] He found that issue in the Genovese case.

The Genovese controversy began in a rather innocuous manner, with a letter from a constituent to Hughes. The writer complained about a Professor Eugene Genovese, of Rutgers University, who was criticizing the war in Vietnam. The writer wanted the governor to fire Genovese. Opposition to the war was not a new phenomenon, but Genovese was using graphic language and calling for a victory by the Vietcong, all while teaching at a public university. A young, new assistant in the governor's office, Richard Leone from the Woodrow Wilson School at Princeton, was given the task of responding to the letter. He wrote a reply strongly supporting the right to freedom of speech. He showed it to Hughes, and after some changes, Hughes approved it. When the issue was publicized, Dumont seized it in an attempt to invigorate his campaign. The press also jumped on the issue, and it became a major factor in the race. There was still a great deal of support for the war in Vietnam. Hughes, while a very loyal and ardent supporter of President Johnson and his position on the war in Vietnam, was also a strong advocate of free speech.

Hughes made his position very clear. He disagreed vehemently with the statements made by Genovese, but defended Genovese's constitutional right to express them. His position delighted some New Jersey voters, but alienated others. It was particularly well-regarded in academic circles,[6] and he received many messages of support. Critics, however, were vociferous, and Hughes received a great deal of mail deploring his position. Some say that even Betty was not happy with her husband's position on this issue. A few years later, when Hughes was pushing for a sales tax, Betty wrote a column criticizing some aspects of the proposal. Hughes was upset. When he brought it up, Betty said that if he could run around the state supporting the free speech rights of some Commie, he could support her free speech rights, too.[7] The Genovese issue may have been the primary reason that Senator Robert Kennedy, riding a crest of pro-Kennedy sentiment, agreed to campaign for Hughes. On October 14, 1965, Kennedy gave a rousing series of speeches supporting Hughes. Kennedy and Hughes campaigned together in Elizabeth, East Orange, Paterson, and Newark.[8] The senator emphasized his support for Hughes and his support for Hughes's position on Genovese.

Hughes later described the day he spent campaigning with Kennedy. "Bobby Kennedy came to campaign for me in '65 and we had a pretty good go-around and we went past some big Catholic girls school up in Essex County, I think. We stopped to make a speech and there were several hundred people around including the kids, some nuns. Bobby Kennedy clambered up on top of the limousine and made a speech and I started to climb up too, thinking I was young as he and as athletic and I had to get a couple of boosts from the state policeman to get up there. So we stood on top of the limousine, he was great fun and signed some autographs. A very magnetic personality. He spoke and said he wouldn't be here if it weren't for the stand Governor Hughes took on the Genovese case, and 'I believe in free speech too and I believe in the Constitution, and if he had done other than he did I wouldn't come and speak for him.' So he made a pretty good point."[9]

During his second campaign, Hughes had the support of many of the leading newspapers, including the *New York Times*, the *Newark Star-Ledger,* and the *Record* of Bergen County. In an editorial endorsing Hughes, the *New York Times* criticized Dumont for his position on the Genovese issue. It characterized Hughes as a good chief executive for the state who recognized the need for "modernization."[10]

Many Republican leaders supported Dumont during the campaign, including President Eisenhower and Richard M. Nixon, the former vice president who would eventually become president. Some of the leading Republican officials in New Jersey, however, disagreed with Dumont on the Genovese issue, including Walter Jones, head of the Republican Party in Bergen County.[11]

Years later, in a letter to Senator Bill Bradley,[12] who was considering his vote on an amendment to the Constitution concerning flag burning, Hughes recalled the Genovese affair. "As you may know, Bill, I am a simplistic man and reached a simplistic conclusion. I always loved the Constitution, and it was plainly the constitutional right of Genovese to speak, however offensively. So I upheld that Constitution, taking a chance that would have doomed me in the McCarthy Era, when he had convinced Americans, that there was a Communist 'under every bed.' But, as you know the people of New Jersey responded affirmatively to my defense of the Constitution."[13]

Once elected, and throughout his second term, Hughes waged a high-profile defense of the right to free speech. When Governor George Wallace, who was campaigning for the presidency in 1967, campaigned in New Jersey, his racist views had already drawn protests, some of them violent, in other states. When Wallace came to New Jersey, state police were assigned to protect him. Catherine Graham, president of the Trenton branch of the NAACP, objected, calling the police protection "red carpet" treatment. In a letter responding to her criticism Hughes labeled as dangerous her position suggesting that "If Mr. Wallace chooses to travel from area to area on a political campaign preaching hate and racism, he should take the consequences."[14] Hughes said "Quite frankly, I think there is danger in this position. As you very well know, there have been unfortunate incidents in our country in recent years in which distinguished civil rights leaders have been the victims of violence because of the failure of local and state governments to assure these citizens of their right to free speech without fear of bodily harm. Indeed, these shameful incidents have happened because of the attitude that these people should suffer the consequences if they choose to travel throughout the country preaching equal rights and racial justice."[15] He also said that the alleged "red carpet" treatment was done to assure Wallace "his right to express his [views] at a peaceful assembly."[16] But he also indicated his own disagreement with the views of Wallace stating, "Let me make it perfectly clear that I, too, strongly disagree with most of the views held by Governor Wallace on any number of issues."[17]

Free speech would again become an issue during the second term when the legislature enacted anti-obscenity legislation. Hughes vetoed that legislation, saying that the statute "presented a very clear challenge to the constitutional protections of speech and press set forth in both our state and Federal Constitutions."[18] In spite of his own beliefs, values, and views, when free speech was threatened, Hughes always came out squarely in favor of it. As a strong Catholic, Hughes opposed obscenity. He backed the war in Vietnam. Flag burning outraged his patriotic sensibilities. The views of George Wallace were antithetical to his own. Yet on all these issues he came down in favor of free speech rights. On the matter of obscenity, once again demonstrating a capacity to see two sides, he noted that New Jersey already had a law banning the distribution of obscene material to juveniles under the age of eighteen.[19]

Another important issue during the campaign was gun control. Hughes was in favor of gun control and Dumont was against it. Eventually, Hughes would get a bill passed creating stringent gun control legislation despite strong opposition from the National Rifle Association.

Hughes campaigned with the same fervor that he had in the past, attending event after event. Bob Burkhardt, chair of the state Democratic Party, and John Kervick, state treasurer, continued to be the main operatives directing the overall campaign and fundraising. Congressman Peter Rodino, passed over for the chairmanship of the first campaign, became the campaign chairman.

While a great deal of controversy surrounded Mitchell's refusal to debate Hughes during the first campaign, the second campaign included a series of debates in which the candidates discussed many issues including taxes, funding for school busing, penalties for narcotics law violators, and many others.

President Johnson, hospitalized for gall bladder surgery, did not participate actively in the campaign. During that time, he temporarily ceded his presidential powers to Vice President Hubert Humphrey. Humphrey did campaign on behalf of Hughes.

Hughes traveled all over the state during the campaign, often relying upon a helicopter provided by the State Democratic Committee. On one of these trips, the excitement was far greater than he would have liked. While traveling with his nineteen-year-old son, John, to a campaign event, the engine suddenly lost power. The pilot had to make an emergency landing on Route 532. No one was hurt, but that was not the end of the day's mishaps. Hughes then broke his finger when his car door accidentally closed on it. The finger injury was probably more traumatic for Hughes than the engine malfunction, because as a result, the glad-handing campaigner was unable to shake hands for some time. Hughes decided that helicopters were no more dangerous than car doors and was off on another helicopter trip the next day.[20]

Betty Hughes had originally announced that she would not participate actively in the campaign. On June 20, 1965, the *Sunday Times Advertiser* reported, "When Elizabeth Sullivan Murphy Hughes, wife of Governor Richard J. Hughes who hopes to be reelected in November, was asked what she would do to help her husband with his electioneering, she answered, 'Nothing! I don't speak from overconfidence because my husband doesn't need me, but because my children need me more.' "[21] However, three months later, the *Asbury Park Press* reported, "Mrs. Richard J. Hughes is campaigning heavily to retain her title as New Jersey's first lady for the next four years—against her better judgment."[22] Although she had counseled Hughes not to run again, she pitched in with gusto at the tail end of the campaign, averaging ten to fifteen speeches a week.

Working closely with Hughes during the second campaign was a young African American, Stanley Van Ness. Van Ness was an attorney in the Governor's Counsel's office. He would later become the public defender for the state, and then later, the public advocate. Van Ness was a great help to Hughes in dealing with African American voters. Van Ness described what it was like to campaign in African American churches with Hughes. "At the first church we went to, he introduced me as a member of his staff, and said that he looked for very good things from me. At the second church we went into, I was one of his most trusted confidants. At the third church, I was the most brilliant lawyer he'd ever met."[23] Van Ness would often add "One more church and I would have been Attorney General." The newspaper article that reported Van Ness's story recalled it as just one example of the "consummate political man, who was known for his soaring hyperbolic oratory."[24]

Hughes won the second election by an overwhelming majority— 1,278,568 to 915,996—and swept in large majorities in both the

Senate (19–10) and the Assembly (41–19). Exhausted after his energetic campaign, Hughes took a twenty-two-day Caribbean cruise, fulfilling a promise he made to his wife many years earlier.[25] After his impressive victory, some newspaper reports suggested that Hughes had become a major political figure in the nation who might have political ambitions beyond the governorship. Responding to those reports, Hughes said that he was not a wealthy man and that he had promised his wife that he would return to the practice of law to make some money at the end of his governorship.[26]

Chapter 11

The Second Term

THE MORNING OF HUGHES'S SECOND INAUGURATION was very similar to the morning of his first. After a Mass at Saint Mary's Roman Catholic Church, he led a procession of major state dignitaries to the State House. His brother, Father Joseph Hughes, gave the invocation, and Robert Burkhardt, the secretary of state, presented the certificate of election. In an exaggerated manner, Burkhardt carefully and slowly stated the word "seal" in reaction to his predecessor's presentation four years earlier, in which he presented Hughes with the "great steal" rather than "great seal" of New Jersey.[1] Given the closeness of the first race, the error of the former secretary of state might have been interpreted as a Freudian slip. Chief Justice Weintraub, for whom Hughes had worked when he was a judge and whom Hughes had reappointed as chief justice, swore the governor into office.

Hughes's Inaugural Address was full of hope and promise. He began by thanking the people of the state of New Jersey for the faith they had exhibited by reelecting him, and "for the challenge and opportunity of completing a task only partially finished."[2] He promised a "government unafraid to act in the people's service."[3] He called for cooperation between the Democratic and Republican Parties to do what was best for the state. He said, "After every American election, no matter how bitterly fought, old enmities are forgotten, political strife is muted, and people come together to face their common problems."[4]

"As I look out upon the face of New Jersey I see a people and a State destined to be great from the moment of its birth as a colony more than three hundred years ago. But we have too long been hidden in the shadows of great cities to the east and west, too long a mere corridor without our own identity, too long rich in private wealth but poor in public services, too long afraid to come to grips with our own destiny. And I tell you today that we must release the full energy and resources of this State and seek from New Jersey's own abundance fuel for the engines of our social and economic growth.[5]

In light of his overwhelming victory and the fact that he had ushered in Democratic majorities in both the Senate and the Assembly, Hughes felt that he now had the mandate to carry out many of the ambitious plans his administration had been working on. This was the moment for the various programs prepared by the Lord Committee (the committee originally created by Thorn Lord to provide private advice to Hughes) to go forward. Shortly after his victory, the *New York Times* reported that Hughes "promises one of the most hectic six months in New Jersey's history."[6] His agenda included a minimum wage law, a fair housing law, strict laws against drunk driving, a tight gun control law, air and water pollution control programs, a new department of community affairs, massive expansion of college facilities, more mental health facilities, better highways, and judicial reorganization.

Mrs. Kennedy

Just as Hughes was beginning to effectuate his second term agenda, he was momentarily sidetracked when an unexpected issue arose. Jacqueline Kennedy, the widow of President Kennedy, purchased a home in Bedminster Township in rural Somerset County, New Jersey. Her primary residence was in New York City, but being an avid horsewoman, Mrs. Kennedy wanted a country home where she and her children could indulge their passion for riding. Somerset County had a large number of estates that fit that description. Despite Mrs. Kennedy's avowed intent to devote her time to her children, a rumor spread in New Jersey Democratic circles that Mrs. Kennedy might be considering a run for the Senate seat then held by long-time incumbent Clifford Case. The thought of Mrs. Kennedy running delighted New Jersey Democrats, because Case, a Republican, was extremely popular and had a virtual lock on the seat. Without informing Mrs. Kennedy or Hughes, the Ocean County Democratic Party endorsed Mrs. Kennedy. When the endorsement became public, other Democratic leaders also expressed support for the idea. Senator Robert Kennedy criticized the actions of the Ocean County Democratic leaders as a "discourteous bandying of the name of this wonderful and distinguished lady," and Hughes immediately called Senator Kennedy to apologize for the actions of the Ocean County Democratic Party.[7] He said that he had heard rumors about supporting Mrs. Kennedy on the cocktail party circuit, but had not believed that anyone would take them seriously.

At the time, Mrs. Kennedy and her children were skiing in Switzerland. When the press approached her about the idea of running she responded with her normal no comment. Hughes also indicated that he would send a letter of apology to Mrs. Kennedy when she returned from vacation.

Income Tax versus Sales Tax

Of the substantive issues on his agenda, Hughes considered increasing state revenues his first and most important goal. His first proposed budget of the second term was in excess of $900 million. To spend that much money, the state would have to institute an income tax. To win legislative passage of the income tax, Hughes sought first to reform the legislative procedures. Specifically, he sought to eliminate the caucus system used in the Senate, which he had fought against, unsuccessfully, throughout his first term. The caucus system permitted a political party to meet privately, vote, and then present the vote as the majority will of that caucus without each member having to take responsibility for his or her vote. The Republican senators were able to meet in a closed caucus, vote on bills and appointments, and afterwards, simply state the overall results of the vote. No one would know how any one particular senator had voted on an issue,[8] and senators could claim they supported a proposal, even if they hadn't voted that way, and vice versa. During his campaign Hughes had vigorously condemned "the secret Republican caucus."

Hughes argued that the legislative committee system should be reinstated and the caucus abandoned. Hughes's position seemed to resonate with the public during the campaign, and he felt that victory on this issue would be helpful in his fight for the income tax.[9] One commentator said, "All realized that public and editorial sentiment was strongly behind the Governor."[10] The governor won. He obtained commitments to change the Senate rules and to revitalize the legislative committee system.[11] Despite having an agreement, Hughes wanted to make sure it was executed. In order to pressure the Senate to change its rules, he included a reference to the fact that the Senate had changed its rules in the prepared text of his not-yet-delivered annual message to a joint session of the legislature. Before giving the speech, he inquired whether the Senate had in fact changed the rules. When he learned that they had not yet done so, he–with a certain dramatic flair—delayed his speech to give the Senate time to make the changes. The Senate acquiesced and voted to abandon the caucus system.[12]

With the legislative reform accomplished, the next order of business was winning approval of the income tax. Because of the strong antitax sentiment in the state, this would be a significant battle, even though no one would deny that the state needed a new source of revenue if it was to provide its citizens with the services they needed. When Hughes started campaigning for an income tax, the state was sending more than half of its prospective college students out of state for their education. The educational systems in poor communities were failing. The transportation system was woefully inadequate. Services provided for the poor were insufficient. And the mental health system was in disarray. The dramatic move of thousands of city dwellers to the suburbs had significantly decreased the urban tax base. The cities housed most of the poorer members of New Jersey society, but the vast majority of voters now lived in the suburbs. Legislators representing the suburbs had little incentive to provide for the needs of the urban poor. The income tax was seen by many as a way to redistribute wealth from the wealthier suburbanites to the poorer city dwellers.

Although New Jersey was one of the wealthiest states in the nation, it lagged behind many other states in providing services. One advantage Hughes had in the battle for a new source of revenue was the economic growth in New Jersey. The private sector had been booming for the previous five years. The *New York Times* reported, "Just about every economic indicator showed dramatic gains."[13] Arguably, there were resources that could be tapped to gain additional financial support for state government. There were two questions: whether any broad-based tax was necessary, and what form it should take. During the 1965 campaign both candidates agreed that a broad-based tax was necessary, Hughes favoring the income tax and Dumont favoring the sales tax. Hughes spent more time talking about the problems presented by a sales tax than he spent arguing for the income tax. But once reelected, he began a concerted effort to gain support for the income tax. He firmly believed that a progressive income tax was fairer than a sales tax. His plan to support an income tax was included in his Inaugural Address, and in his annual budget message, he predicated his budget projections on the existence of such a tax. Specifically, he proposed a 1 to 5 percent graduated personal income tax that would produce about $180 million in revenue a year.[14] He also set forth the intended uses for that money. Much would go to education, state aid to local school districts, and construction funds for higher education. As he often did, Hughes relied in part upon work done by members of the academic community. He received a report from Lester Chandler of Princeton University, who had a significant reputation in the field of economics, endorsing the use of an income tax as opposed to a sales tax, and Hughes publicized those views widely.[15]

The *New York Times* and other newspapers supported the governor, but legislators were still wary. Hughes was disappointed that he did not get stronger support from such groups as the League of Women Voters. "Even the President of the League of Women Voters, with a long history of support for the income tax, noted that while the League supported such a tax, 'We don't endorse all the particulars of the Hughes plan.'"[16] But Hughes pressed on, buoyed, in part, by his overwhelming election victory. He now determined to use his powers of patronage as a tool to push the Democratic legislature to support his plan. He announced that all appointments would be delayed until after the tax issue was resolved.[17] He also delayed action on reapportionment, an issue of great importance to the legislators. The decision to delay most legislative action until the tax issue was resolved was a dangerous tactic. If he had lost on the tax issue, the rest of his legislative agenda might have suffered, and many legislators used their potential support for the tax as leverage to try and get promises and concessions on other issues from the governor.

At the beginning of the fight, the only county leader supporting the plan was David Wilentz, the former attorney general who was Democratic leader of Middlesex County.[18] Hughes was surprised that the elected officials of the major cities that would benefit from the increased state aid did not endorse the plan. Only Mayor Art Holland, of Trenton, Hughes's home-town, was in favor of the plan at the outset. The *Newark Evening News*, always an opponent of Hughes, strongly opposed the plan. The opposition of the Newark newspaper, located in Essex, the state's largest county, was especially influential because Dennis Carey, the leader of the Essex County Democratic party, controlled the largest legislative delegation and bucking the newspaper could have risked his clout in Essex County. Therefore Carey was wary of the income tax from the beginning.

There seemed to be relatively little support for Hughes's proposal. Even the mail the governor was receiving ran strongly against an income tax. Yet Hughes was optimistic. After reviewing the support for and opposition to the income tax in late November, Hughes announced that he thought success was probable.[19] This confidence was derived from the large Democratic majorities in both houses, and the fact that he was prepared to use all his powers to convince the legislators, and the leaders who controlled them, to support the tax. As one commentator put it, "Hughes, in a sense, was asking for the leaders' support in return for being one of their own, for being their kind of Governor, for being like them a party regular. . . . The Governor was more than an old colleague of the state's other leading Democrats. He was, and some of them admitted it, among the best of them: better education, more honest, more issue-oriented, more intelligent, more articulate, and even (since every major leader save one shared Hughes' Catholicism) more religious."[20]

Senator Anthony J. Grossi, leader of the Democratic Party in Passaic, who had been at the meeting during which Hughes was selected to run for the governorship back in 1961, was one of the first, aside from Wilentz, to show signs of support. Hughes's hopes were bolstered. Grossi controlled the entire Passaic delegation.

Although members of his staff urged Hughes to use more direct appeals to the electorate, the governor stuck, primarily, with his own strategy of appealing to the party leaders and the members of the legislature. Originally, the governor had wanted the tax to be retroactive for six months, but he agreed before the measure came to a vote to eliminate the retroactivity proposal. This permitted some of the legislators to claim that they had succeeded in limiting the scope of the income tax.

The large Hudson delegation was almost as important as the Essex delegation. The leader of Hudson County, Mayor John V. Kenny, like his Essex County counterpart Dennis Carey, was a longtime Hughes supporter. In early 1966, the governor, John Kervick, and Robert Burkhardt visited Kenny at his winter residence in Florida to seek his support. Hughes knew that Kenny wanted backing for a state lottery and night harness racing in exchange for his support of the tax. Hughes was willing to consider those requests. (In fact, a referendum to legalize night-time racing and betting was approved in the general election in 1966.) After their discussion, Kenny agreed to support the tax, and most members of the Hudson County delegation lined up behind him.[21] One member refused to support the tax proposal, but Hughes believed he would not need that one vote.

Carey, the Essex County leader, proved to be the most difficult to convince. He had previously indicated his opposition to the income tax. As time went on, however, Carey seemed to be more amenable to the governor's persuasion. He had sided with the governor on the Senate rules debate and was accepting of the more merit-based appointments the governor was making. As the tax proposal was nearing a vote, Carey "assured the Governor privately . . . that Essex would support the tax."[22] The *Newark Evening News* continued to editorialize against the tax and criticized the "bosses" for supporting it. One editorial even threatened the legislators with voter retaliation. The victory, nonetheless, seemed sure. The schedule called for the Assembly to receive the bills on Monday and vote by Wednesday, and then the Senate would receive the bills on Wednesday and vote by Friday.

At a breakfast meeting with the Essex legislators the day before the scheduled vote, the governor heard from those present that "a recent pledge of support from the Essex leader was firm."[23] However, the next day, March 16, the day of the anticipated vote, a reporter told the governor's staff that the leader of the Essex delegation had told him "there would be no Essex votes for an income tax."[24] Hughes brought the Essex delegation into a conference, in which the members informed him they would not support the tax. Apparently, at the last minute, a number of labor leaders from the union of operating engineers convinced Carey not to support the income tax proposal.[25] Years later, Hughes would talk about this as the "double-cross," but Carey had been in a difficult position. Prior to his arrival on the scene, Essex County had been a predominantly Republican county. Carey worked hard to bring it into the Democratic column, and he was wary of doing something that would imperil the Democratic control of the county. After Hughes learned that Carey would not support the proposal, he went into high gear. He first worked on the members of the Assembly. That very day he called the thirty-one Democratic legislators into meetings that lasted all day. He used his persuasive powers, as well as all the political power at his disposal. It was an emotional time. Richard Leone wrote: "Reward and punishment were explicitly discussed with Assembly members as never before."[26] "He soothed fears and calmed nerves. He appealed to loyalties and to conscience. He threatened stark political retribution, often accompanied by references to the righteousness of his case."[27] Some of the legislators, particularly those from Union County, began demanding specific promises of political favors, but Hughes was unwilling to go that far. "He not only refused to discuss Union County's 'demands' but also backed the Assemblymen out of his office with a series of admonitions."[28]

Hughes's efforts worked and the bill was passed by the Assembly. He now had to turn his attention to the Senate. At one point, the governor and the Senate agreed to a delay so that Senator Grossi from Passaic County could recover from an operation and be able to vote, but in fact he was never available to vote because the recuperation took longer than expected.[29] Every vote was essential. Support from Essex was crucial, but Carey was hiding. The governor could not reach him. For part of this time Carey was apparently at a New York Knicks basketball game.[30] Efforts were made to try and swing some other votes, but those efforts failed. Tom Giblin, who would later be Democratic leader of New Jersey, recalled how his father, John Giblin, one of the senators from Essex, went into hiding so he would not have to face the governor.[31] Ultimately, Hughes recognized that he could not obtain the fifteen votes he needed. (At that time there were twenty-nine senators.) Hughes then released the Senators from the commitments they had made to him to vote for the income tax so that those who wanted could make public their decision not to support the income tax before the governor announced he was giving up the fight. On March 23, 1966, Hughes announced to the public that he did not have enough support for the income tax and that, while pessimistic, he hoped he would find support for a sales tax. Political leaders from both parties considered this one of the greatest defeats for Hughes. They compared it to the loss of the bond issue in 1963.[32]

Hughes and his closest associates were drained by the defeat. In later years, he would still recall the disappointment and anguish he felt. But, as usual, Hughes was the "first to recover."[33] Larry Bilder, who was on the governor's staff at the time, recalled that while Hughes thought that Carey had double-crossed him, he recognized that Carey had supported him on all the other important initiatives he put forth. Some reports at the time indicated that there would be retribution. The New York Times even quoted an unnamed administration official as saying, "Carey is through."[34] But Hughes did not retaliate, recognizing Carey's prior support, and knowing that he might still need him in the future for other programs.

The next step for Hughes was to turn to the Republicans, who were already in favor of a sales tax. He met with Senator Raymond Bateman and others who supported the tax. Bateman recalled that Hughes was great at interacting with everyone, including the Republicans.[35] The Republican candidate in the previous campaign, Wayne Dumont, had spoken out strongly about the need for a sales tax. Although Hughes still believed that an income tax was fairer, he recognized how urgently the state needed a broad-based tax, and was willing to back a sales tax out of necessity. The Republicans were willing to support a sales tax, but in return, they wanted input into how the increased revenue would be spent, which Hughes acceded to in order to achieve the goal of gaining a broad-based tax. They were eager to spend more on county roads and less on college construction, for example. Slowly, Republicans began to line up behind the sales tax, but some GOP legislators, including Senators Charles W. Sandman Jr. from Cape May County and Frank S. Farley of Atlantic County, remained opposed to any broad-based tax.

Hughes knew that some Democrats were hesitant about immediately jumping on board in favor of another tax plan, so he quietly began approaching groups that had previously supported some form of broad-based tax. The newspapers, including the *Newark Evening News*, which recognized the need for some increase in state funds, began to editorialize in favor of the sales tax. Groups such as the New Jersey Education Association got on board.[36] On March 28, Hughes announced publicly that he would work for the enactment of a sales tax. He worked behind the scenes with legislators and campaigned around the state. He utilized his press conferences and as much television and radio as possible to push the tax. "In general, he used his unparalleled access to the public to promote his program," one student of the campaign noted.[37]

Labor was still a major opponent,[38] but it appeared that there was little commitment to the position. Observers believed that several legislators were swayed by the unions' antitax stance. "Overall, however, these negative effects were more than compensated for by the widespread pressures in the press and among other interest groups for passage."[39] Two leading Republicans, Raymond Bateman and William E. Ozzard of Somerset County, worked hard to help Hughes garner sufficient support within the Republican Party.

Bateman worked with the state treasurer, John Kervick, and the counsel to the governor, David Goldberg, to develop the state sales tax proposal. They wanted the tax to be as fair as possible to the less wealthy members of society. Bateman recalled that the three of them met in Princeton for two days reviewing sales taxes from states across the country.[40] The bill they ultimately devised was not as regressive as many others because it exempted from the proposed 3 percent sales tax basic staples such as food, medicines, gas and electric services, and some clothing.[41] Bateman, noting that the governor was never really a "detail man" said Hughes was satisfied when the three of them told him that it was a good bill and the least regressive sales tax in the country.

The legislature was ready to vote on April 26, 1966, but the Assembly refused to take the lead for fear of voting for it and having it defeated in the

Senate. The Senate, then, first approved the budget, which was calculated on the assumption that there would be a sales tax. This made the Assembly more comfortable, and they voted to approve the tax. The Senate followed suit. Even the *Newark Evening News* gave credit to Hughes for his fight for the broad-based tax. The measure was approved on the one-hundredth day of Hughes's second term.

There were many reasons why the sales tax proposal won acceptance and the income tax proposal did not. Despite the fact that the majority of citizens in New Jersey would have paid less tax under the income tax plan than under the sales tax, they were more supportive of a sales tax than an income tax. This could have partly been the result of a feeling that if they opened the door to the proposed small state income tax, it would soon begin to increase. Their only familiarity with income taxes came from federal income taxes, which were much more substantial. Many of the unions opposed any broad-based tax but were less vehement in their opposition to the sales tax. Finally the Republicans, many of whom had good personal relationships with Hughes, tended to represent the wealthier members of society and were willing to go along with a sales tax, which would not impact their constituency as much as an income tax.

In a doctoral dissertation, Jennifer Plotkin praised the leadership Hughes exhibited in attempting to attain an income tax and assessed his subsequent success in attaining a sales tax as daring and innovative. "He altered the fiscal structure of the state,"[42] she wrote, and was able to do so with "one of the least regressive taxes of its kind."[43]

Chapter 12

A Flood of Legislation

WITH THE LARGE DEMOCRATIC MAJORITIES in the Senate and Assembly, Hughes spearheaded an ambitious legislative program in his second term. More than 300 bills were passed in 1966. A minimum wage bill was just one of the proposals he put forth. There was no state minimum wage law and Hughes proposed a phased-in increase with an hourly minimum wage of $1.25 in 1966, rising to $1.50 by 1969. The federal hourly minimum wage was $1.25, but many New Jersey workers were not covered by the federal law. At the time, $1.25 per hour was sufficient to lift a family of three with a single, full-time, year-round worker out of poverty.

Living up to his reputation for keeping everyone happy, Hughes was able to keep business and labor content by backing bills that benefited each of them. As the *New York Times* reported, "Richard J. Hughes showed today that a Governor can be all things to all men. He did that when big business and organized labor walked out of his office here singing his praises."[1]

Hughes signed a bill described as a "sweeping reform of the state's chaotic local business taxes on personal property."[2] Businesses had sought the reform. At the same time another bill dealing with the Workmen's Compensation Act was also signed, and labor was pleased by the measure, which substantially increased the maximum weekly payments for death or temporary or total permanent disability.[3] The governor had separate bill signings with each group. He told the labor leaders, "He who forgets the workingman forgets the substance of democracy." To the business leaders he said, "He who forgets the businessman forgets the substance of democracy."[4]

Gun Control

Hughes, who had supported gun control legislation during his second gubernatorial campaign, acted upon his promise during his second term. In a letter Hughes wrote years later to Congressman Peter Rodino, who was fighting for federal gun control legislation, he said, "I had to fight hard to win this law [the gun control legislation] (by *one vote*) because of the opposition of the NRA [National Rifle Association]. Decent Legislators, who had campaigned with me for gun control, later came to me, trembling because they had received thousands of letters from constituent 'sportsmen,' boiler-plated and dictated by NRA."[5] In that same letter, Hughes used some of the harshest words he ever used to describe the NRA, referring to it as an "evil lobby devoted to the principle of murder for profit."[6] The gun control legislation passed in 1966 required "all prospective gun buyers to go to their local police stations for identification cards and to be fingerprinted. Anyone ever convicted of a felony or known narcotics addicts, alcoholics, former mental patients, subversives, or persons with physical handicaps which would interfere with the proper handling of weapons would be denied a permit."[7] The bill also imposed additional penalties for persons who commit other crimes while possessing a dangerous weapon. Hughes wanted an even stronger bill that would have required the registration of every gun sold, but he compromised to gain passage. On May 31, 1966, the Senate passed the gun control bill on a 16–12 vote after much debate and verbal fireworks.[8] The passage of the legislation was seen as a victory for Hughes because of his vocal support of it during the campaign and his hard lobbying. Two days after the vote Hughes signed the bill, ending what was described as one of the "bitterest legislative struggles in years."[9]

Subsequently, the legislation was challenged in court, with the plaintiffs alleging that it was unconstitutional. One major argument was that it violated the Second Amendment of the United States Constitution. The New Jersey Supreme Court rejected that argument, following the general precedent that the Second Amendment was not applicable to the states and thus states are permitted to regulate the use of firearms. In dealing with other arguments presented by the plaintiffs, the court held that the gun control law was designed to prevent criminals and other unfit elements of society from obtaining guns, with minimal burdens on those who should have the right of possession. The court recognized that such legislation was clearly within the police power of the state and that the interests of the state in protecting society were paramount.[10]

Some years later Hughes strongly criticized Congress for not enacting strict gun control laws. Hughes charged that New Jersey's weapons control statutes were being "subverted" by the absence of supportive federal gun control legislation. He said, "I believe that the people of this country now know the truth, and that is that the Congress of the United States is encouraging lunatics, addicts and criminals to use the mails to get guns."[11]

Teacher Benefits

Hughes had pledged during his various campaigns to improve benefits for teachers. Since 1955, the pensions of public school teachers in New Jersey had been tied to their Social Security benefits, providing for one combined pension benefit.[12] For years, teachers had been demanding to get out from under this provision, which significantly reduced their pensions. The teachers' union in New Jersey has always had significant political muscle, especially within the Democratic Party. Hughes, a strong supporter of the unions, supported the abolition of the 1955 pension law. With his backing and a Democratic majority, the legislature passed a bill that permitted teachers to retire and collect both a full state pension and full Social Security benefits.

Governor Meyner, an extremely frugal governor, had repeatedly rebuffed efforts to change the 1955 law.[13] Hughes, on the other hand, recognizing the importance of teachers, felt they should not be required to give up the additional Social Security payment simply because they were also receiving state pensions.[14] The change in this law may have had a beneficial effect upon morale of the teachers and it may have been instrumental in attracting teachers to New Jersey. It would also, however, substantially increase pension costs for the state. In later years, the overall pension costs in New Jersey would become a significant financial drain.

The Elections of 1966

The national elections of 1966 were difficult for the Democrats. While the governor and the legislature were not up for election that year, there were important races in the United States Senate and the House of Representatives. Clifford Case, the popular, moderate incumbent Republican Senator, was up for reelection. The Democratic candidate was Warren Wilentz, the son of David Wilentz, the person who originally called Hughes to suggest that he run for governor. Hughes campaigned hard for

Wilentz, and he convinced President Johnson to campaign in New Jersey. The speech Johnson gave was described as "a bare-knuckle, hard hitting speech." Obviously relishing his return to the political wars after his medical convalescence, Johnson alternately attacked the Republicans and boasted of the accomplishments of his and President Kennedy's administrations.[15] He also praised Warren Wilentz, calling him a "great friend," a "war hero," and a "public servant."[16] Despite the support of Hughes and Johnson, however, Wilentz lost.

It was generally not a good year to be a Democrat running for office. The war in Vietnam was beginning to undermine the strong support that had swept Johnson to election in 1964. Antiwar groups were marching in the streets. The early successes in civil rights achieved by President Johnson seemed forgotten, and Democrats suffered significant losses in the midterm elections. In one of her columns Betty Hughes reflected on the loss, "We realized early on election evening that it wasn't very chic to be a Democrat this season."[17] She sympathized with her friend, Lady Bird Johnson, because although her husband had not been on the ballot, the losses reflected negatively upon him. Betty said, "It must have been hard for her. After that wearing Asian trip, she had to face her husband's surgery, and still try to buck him up after a series of political losses."[18]

Betty also noted that the governors' conferences would be somewhat different because for the first time since she had been attending, there would be a woman governor: Lurleen Wallace had been elected governor of Alabama. Her election, however, could not be seen as a victory for women's rights, because Lurleen was not going to govern herself but merely be the voice of her husband. Lurleen Wallace replaced her husband, George Wallace, who had been governor for three years but could not be elected to a consecutive term. He arranged for his wife to be elected and "the couple admitted frankly that if Lurleen was elected, George would continue to make the administrative policies and decisions."[19] Betty also noted the loss of governor and Mrs. Pat Brown of California but was looking forward to meeting the Reagans. Ronald Reagan, who would eventually serve as president, had just been elected governor of California.

Corporate Law

Hughes's ability to use outside advisors and commissions to improve the legal system in New Jersey was demonstrated in the creation of a new corporation law, which by the late 1950s was in need of revision. In the latter part of the nineteenth century, New Jersey had developed a modern corporation law that drew many of the largest corporations in the country to incorporate in the state. According to one study, "By 1904, the seven largest business corporations in the United States, with an aggregate capitalization of over two and one-half billion dollars, all were incorporated under New Jersey law."[20] New Jersey received significant financial benefit from the fees these corporations paid. The New Jersey law made it financially beneficial for the corporations to incorporate in New Jersey by making it easy for the corporations to cooperate by combination and thus get around some of the antitrust laws. A historian noted, "At the end of that century, [the nineteenth century] the empire of corporate law was New Jersey. Known by muckrakers as 'the traitor state,' 'the mother of trust' and a variety of other less printable epithets . . ."[21]

While Woodrow Wilson, Hughes's favorite president, was governor, he convinced the legislature to toughen the antitrust laws. "During his lame-duck days, he [Wilson] induced the legislature to adopt the so-called Seven Sisters Acts of 1913, seven laws that severely limited the privileges of corporations in New Jersey."[22] This led to an exodus of companies from New Jersey to Delaware. Later, New Jersey again changed its law to be more welcoming to companies, but the exodus of corporations had already occurred and New Jersey never regained its prominence in the area of corporate law.[23] As time went on, Delaware continually modernized and improved its corporation statutes while New Jersey fell behind.[24]

Plans began in the 1950s to rewrite the corporation law in New Jersey. In 1958, the legislature created a Corporation Law Revision Commission. The bill creating the commission was drafted by Alan Lowenstein, a distinguished corporate lawyer. The commission consisted of some of the best legal minds in the state.[25] For ten years, it studied various state statutes and models. It also drew upon the expertise of others in the field of corporate law, and held hearings on the proposed legislation.[26] Subsequently, a bill was introduced in the legislature to update the corporate law. Hughes had asked Senator Frank McDermott, the Republican majority leader, to sponsor the legislation. McDermott, a labor lawyer, looked at the detailed, lengthy bill and asked the governor if he had to read it. Hughes assured him it was not necessary. They then added other prominent legislative sponsors including another Republican, Raymond H. Bateman and two Democrats, J. Edward Crabiel and Norman Tanzman. The Joint Committee of the Senate and the Assembly on Revision and Amendment of Laws then held hearings of the bill and the legislation passed. McDermott believed that the legislators had not actually read the bill, but relied upon the representation of the members of the commission.[27] While this may not be the best method of enacting legislation and it would be preferable if all legislators carefully reviewed all legislation, the sheer bulk of new laws probably precludes that possibility.

The enactment of the new corporation law demonstrates the benefit of creating legislation by relying on the expertise of a highly regarded commission. At the time of the legislation's approval, Hughes said, "The Commission produced an entirely new law providing for New Jersey the best in modern American Corporation statutes. . . . Already widespread interest in our new law is evident. . . . I urge those who would seek an exemplar in the best of modern draftsmanship to consult the Report and compare it with existing law here in New Jersey and with the law of several other states. . . ."[28] Most scholarly commentary at the time seemed to agree that the new corporation law was a decided improvement over the previous law.[29]

School Busing

On May 26, 1967, Hughes signed a bill to extend bus service to almost all private and parochial school pupils at public expense. State payment of student busing had been an issue in New Jersey for many years. Originally, the legislature had provided that if school districts financed transportation expenses for public school children, they were also obligated to pay for busing expenses for students attending nonpublic schools if they used the same bus routes as the public schools. The legislation was attacked as a violation of the Establishment Clause of the Constitution. The United States Supreme Court, in an opinion written by Justice Hugo Black, determined that the legislation was not unconstitutional.[30] Subsequently, after *Everson* the New Jersey Constitution of 1947 made it clear that such aid to private and religiously affiliated schools was also not unconstitutional under the New Jersey Constitution.[31] In 1968, the limitation that the nonpublic schools had to be on the same bus routes was eliminated. Hughes, who had pushed for the legislation, based his support of the change on safety considerations. "It is my firm belief that one of our major considerations in improving educational opportunity in New Jersey must be the safety and well-being of all school children, and the availability of a safe, dependable means of transport is crucial to such safety and well-being."[32]

Meadowlands Development

One of the most significant areas in New Jersey is the Hackensack Meadowlands just across the Hudson River from New York City. This large expanse of land (approximately 20,000 acres) is washed by tidal waters. Its location made it ideal for development, but the wetlands nature of the property made development difficult and expensive. The Meadowlands were situated in fourteen different towns and in two different counties, Bergen and Hudson. Each town and county had its own rules and regulations for development. Additionally, there was a significant question concerning the ownership of the property. Because it was considered tidal land, the state of New Jersey claimed ownership of much of it. This made private individuals and companies claiming ownership of the property hesitant to use the land for high-level development. Much of the Meadowlands was being used for warehouses and garbage dumps.[33] The garbage industry was making substantial profit using the property this way and was opposed to other kinds of development.[34]

For years, the state and the various municipalities had tried to grapple with the problems attendant on development of the Meadowlands, but no comprehensive plan had ever been drafted.[35] Differences among the municipalities over the right approach made cooperation difficult.[36] Numerous commissions studied the issues, but none was able to come to a successful resolution of the many conflicting concerns. It was widely recognized that because of its closeness to New York City, this area could become important and vibrant, but the problems seemed insurmountable

During his years as lawyer and judge, Hughes, whose home was in Trenton, had not paid much attention to the Meadowlands, which are in northern New Jersey. But during his gubernatorial campaign he became aware of its potential. "While I was campaigning in Bergen County in 1961, driving through and around this huge, undeveloped area right in the center of the most highly developed, most densely populated section of New Jersey,"[37] Hughes said he began to envision a bright future for the area. In 1963, the legislature created the New Jersey Commission to Study Meadowlands Development and Hughes appointed former governor Meyner as chairman. This commission was to devise a plan to both resolve the title problems and develop the area.[38] The commission issued its final report in June 1965. The report, which called for the creation of a state Meadowlands authority,[39] was greeted with strong opposition, and never turned into legislation. Seeking a compromise solution, the legislature reestablished the commission in 1966. A report issued by the reestablished commission also called for the creation of a state authority, but one that lacked the broad powers necessary to end the wrangling over development. This report attempted to mollify the opponents of the proposal which gave the state strong powers over the Meadowlands but was inconsistent with the desires of Hughes and his administrations to have a commission that was controlled by the state rather than by the local interests.

At this point the Lord Committee got involved (despite Lord's death, the committee continued). It agreed with the Meyner Commission that action was urgently needed, but it feared that the creation of a strong state agency was not politically feasible. The political worries were based on the committee members' belief that the legislature would not support any legislation opposed by the local communities on home rule grounds.[40]

But the governor and his aides decided it was time to test the assumption that the legislature would not support a strong state authority in the Meadowlands. They quickly drafted a bill that was proposed by Senator Alfred Kiefer of Bergen County. It proposed "to establish a new political subdivision of the state government to take control of the Meadowlands development."[41] That new subdivision or agency would have an eleven-member board: four state cabinet officers; three members appointed by the governor from the state at large, without the advice and consent of the Senate (nonlocal members); and four local members appointed by the municipalities and county freeholders. The bill gave the agency major control over zoning and building controls. It also had extensive development and financing authority of its own, and perhaps most important, the legislation established a method for settling the title disputes.

Many people thought this legislation was doomed. However, a relatively new face in state government, Paul Ylvisaker, led the fight for the new authority. At the beginning of his second term, Hughes increasingly called upon members of the Lord Committee and other sophisticated national figures to help him staff the various state departments. In 1967, with the help of Joel Sterns and other members of his staff, Hughes convinced Ylvisaker to leave the Ford Foundation, where he had served as director of public affairs for more than ten years, to head up the newly created Department of Community Affairs. Ylvisaker accepted the position and subsequently strongly supported a legislative campaign to create a Meadowlands Commission.[42]

The bill proposed by Senator Kiefer was drafted in such a way as to allow room for compromise. One commentator noted, "The legislation was termed a 'discussion piece' or 'starting point' to which changes were expected and welcomed."[43] But there was no denying its bias toward state control. Generally, the mayors and local officials adamantly opposed the plan.

Politics, of course, affected the inevitable bargaining. The bartering between the Democrats and Republicans worked in this manner: The Republicans from South Jersey wanted the dispute regarding riparian title (who had the ownership of property on the banks of waterways) resolved in favor of private rather than state ownership. Under the Democratic legislature of 1966 they could not get the constitutional amendment they wanted supporting the private rights of the landowners to the properties in the Meadowlands over the state's riparian rights. The opposition of Governor Hughes would stymie that effort.[44] Hughes would not agree to trade his support for the constitutional amendment for their passage of the Meadowlands bill. But as this issue was developing, the legislative elections of 1967 occurred, which the Republicans won overwhelmingly. When the Republicans took over the legislature in 1968 they had the 3/5 plurality necessary to get on the ballot the amendment resolving the land dispute in favor of private ownership, and eventually they would use that plurality to get the issue passed.[45]

Meanwhile Hughes and Ylvisaker continued to push for the Meadowlands Commission. Ylvisaker held numerous meetings to demonstrate that local people had been included in the discussions. The strategy was not to convince the mayors and officials in the area of the Meadowlands to support the legislation—that was deemed impossible—but rather to present to the entire state the argument that a hypothetical reasonable person uninfluenced by local interests would support a Meadowlands Commission with broad powers. Clifford Goldman, who wrote a dissertation on this subject, said, "Hughes was at the height of his popularity as he approached the end of his second term."[46] He also noted that Hughes had the ability to command the attention of the media and speak for a statewide constituency in contrast to the special and local interests represented by the members of the legislature. "With a statesman's image and highly developed political skills," Goldman said, "Governor Hughes was able to enhance the natural advantages of his office in contests with the legislature. Repeatedly, he offset the large majority against him. He seemed to thrive on the partisan battles with the disorganized Republican opposition."[47] Alan Marcus, an active Republican from Bergen County, recalled Hughes's meetings with Republicans in which the governor used his "Irish political touch in conjunction with his strong command of good government" to cajole the Republicans into supporting his positions.[48] Marcus viewed Hughes as a "spectacular politician and policy maker."[49]

In the early days of the debate, Ylvisaker gained support from much of the media and worked with the Army Corps of Engineers to plan for utilizing the Meadowlands in a major flood control system. This added to the regional importance of the plan, and a consensus was building in favor of creating a strong Meadowlands Commission. But within the legislature there was still no agreement. On April 29, the senators traded votes and both the new Hackensack Meadowlands Commission bill favored by Hughes, and the resolution to put the constitutional amendment on the ballot, which was opposed by Hughes, passed the Senate.[50]

But there was still opposition in the Assembly to the Meadowlands Commission bill. At that point, Hughes pushed to release the Meadow-lands Commission legislation before the summer recess, and at the same time decried the resolution placing the constitutional amendment on the ballot.[51] There were many attempts to amend the Meadowlands Commis-sion act, but Hughes became more and more involved, calling meetings in his office and urging support for the bill as originally drafted. Despite Hughes's efforts, at that point he failed and the amended bill passed. Hughes debated whether to take half a loaf or veto and fight for the whole loaf. He vetoed the bill. In his message Hughes ripped into the legislature for accepting a poor bill and giving in to local and special interests. Some of the Republican leadership recognized that the amended bill was not a good one and the Republicans found themselves in an untenable position. They could not continue to support the amended version of the bill. The Senate Republicans then voted to pass the original bill Hughes wanted, but the Assembly was still balking. "Hughes called in the Hudson County delegation, and began ripping up papers denoting judicial appointments."[52] Ultimately, they agreed to vote for the emergency authorization (permitting the matter to be voted on despite the normal time requirements). Hughes used his power of appointment to win concessions on his legislative agenda. Because this vote permitting the legislation to be voted on was being done as an emergency authorization it needed sixty votes, whereas normally a majority of forty-one is sufficient. In the Assembly chambers there was an electronic tabulator recording the vote. It stood at fifty-eight, then fifty-nine, then back to fifty-eight, and then to fifty-nine. When it finally hit sixty the vote was immediately closed. Ultimately, the legislation itself, which required only a majority vote of forty-one, passed fifty-four to ten. At the same time, the resolution approving the constitutional amendment passed. Hughes responded by complimenting the legislature on passing the Hackensack Meadowlands Commission but attacking it for approving the constitutional amendment. He called the proposed amendment "New Jersey's Teapot Dome, the billion dollar giveaway," referring to a famous scandal during the administration of President Harding.

Clifford Goldman attributes the passage of the Hackensack Meadowlands legislation to a number of factors: raising the issue from one of local concern to one of general concern; effective champions, Paul Ylvisaker for the administration and Fairleigh Dickinson in the legislature; effective bartering of votes; and the ability of the governor to take advantage of the legislature's disarray.

After the Meadowlands bill passed and the commissioners were appointed, Hughes attacked the constitutional amendment in earnest. He appointed William Brennan III (son of Justice Brennan of the United States Supreme Court) as a special counsel to bring a suit challenging what he argued was the confusing wording of the ballot question. The selection of Brennan was a blow to the Republicans because he had earlier, as a deputy attorney general, argued that some members of the legislature were too involved with members of organized crime. His selection in this case seemed to suggest that Republicans might have ulterior motives for their support of the amendment, perhaps implying that the constitutional amendment also was inappropriate.

On February 13, 1969, Hughes sent a special memorandum to the legislature. He described the proposal as "a constitutional amendment which, if approved, would strip the People of New Jersey of their entire interest in some 150,000 acres of riparian, or tidal lands. These lands constitute a potential asset of at least $1 billion for the State School Fund—an asset that could be wiped out by your action."[53] He went on to suggest that he would exercise his veto power and he intended to fight the constitutional amendment with all his power. He concluded the memorandum by saying, "I believe you should rescind S.C.R. 41 [the resolution amending the constitution]. As I have indicated, I am exploring every possible remedy including legal action, to see to it that this gigantic giveaway is not perpetrated on the people of New Jersey. But the most certain means of protecting our schools against a potential one billion dollar loss, and of safeguarding our people against a handover of invaluable natural lands–in short, the best way to correct your most unfortunate action of last year—is to immediately rescind S.C.R. 41."[54]

Faced with the relentless attack upon their position led by the governor, the Republicans ultimately withdrew the resolution. Many years later in talking about this fight Hughes said, "The money realized from the sale or quitclaim of tideland areas, such as along a lake or a river, as well as the sea, was dedicated—the only dedicated fund in our constitution—to the school fund. I could get nowhere with the sponsors of this resolution, which was actually passed, I think by the assembly [and the senate]. So I called on the media and I pointed out that the resolution threatened the school fund. I talked about all these little kids without their jelly sandwiches and milk and so forth. I admit I overdrew the issue a bit, but I felt justified because things about titles and lawyers do not interest the public the way little kids do. And the press got onto it. The *New York Times* took the lead. There was so much noise about it that the legislature finally withdrew the resolution."[55]

In 1969, toward the end of his term, Hughes said, "The historic Hackensack Meadowlands Reclamation and Development Act is a piece of legislation I consider one of the proudest achievements of my administration. What an extraordinary and exciting opportunity for responsible growth and progress this Meadowlands reclamation offers to the People of New Jersey."[56]

The state has clearly benefited from the establishment of the Meadowlands Commission and the eventual creation of the New Jersey Sports and Exposition Authority. In later years, numerous professional teams would make their homes in the Meadowlands including the Giants football team, the Jets football team, the New Jersey Nets basketball team, and the New Jersey Devils ice hockey team. It also became a popular venue for concerts and other events. New Jersey superstar Bruce Springsteen performed regularly in both Giants Stadium and the Byrne Arena, subsequently renamed the Continental Airlines Arena and then the Izod Arena. He sold out forty-four concerts at the arena and fifteen at the stadium.

The Constitutional Convention and Other Legislation

For many years, the United States Supreme Court refused to consider reapportionment issues, viewing them as "political questions." In 1962, the Supreme Court held in *Baker v. Carr*[57] that reapportionment was not a "political question" and could be considered by the courts. In New

Jersey, the Assembly was apportioned by population, and the Senate was composed of one senator from each of the twenty-one counties.[58] Since the populations in the various counties varied dramatically, this gave the counties with smaller populations disproportionate representation in the Senate. It would be just a matter of time before that system would come under challenge.

Immediately after the United States Supreme Court decision, a New Jersey suit, *Jackman v. Bodine*, challenged New Jersey's system. The New Jersey attorney general's office defended the case. Judge Morris Pashman agreed that the case could be considered in light of the decision in *Baker v. Carr*, but upheld the New Jersey system. He read the Supreme Court case as only declaring systems that were invidious or irrational to be unconstitutional.[59] Finding the system to be neither irrational nor invidious, he upheld its constitutionality. While the *Bodine* case was pending in the New Jersey Supreme Court, the United States Supreme Court decided *Reynolds v. Sims*.[60] Chief Justice Earl Warren wrote that any state system had to be based on one-man one-vote. This effectively rendered the system in New Jersey unconstitutional. The New Jersey Supreme Court then ordered re-argument of the New Jersey case and in a unanimous decision declared the New Jersey system to be unconstitutional.[61]

After the decision in *Reynolds* and before the decision in *Jackman v. Bodine*, the Republican members of the Senate voted to provide for weighted voting. This meant that the senators from the smaller counties would have fewer votes than the senators from the larger counties. The senator from the smallest county, Cape May, for example, would have one vote, while the senator from Essex would have nineteen votes.[62] That system met with general derision, even though it could be argued that it was actually consistent with the decision of the United States Supreme Court, which held that each voter should have equal representation in each state senate.[63] Hughes, who favored having more senators rather than some senators having more votes, ordered the attorney general to file suit to block the weighted voting plan.[64]

The New Jersey Supreme Court then decided *Jackman v. Bodine*, and set forth certain requirements. Among those requirements was that the next legislative elections in November 1965 be consistent with the Equal Protection Clause. The court was willing to permit the legislature to set up the system for that particular election and it endorsed the use of a Constitutional Convention to determine the ultimate system. Shortly after the opinion was handed down, Hughes delivered a special message to the legislature calling upon the Senate to rescind its decision on weighted voting, and urging the creation of a special commission to recommend a plan for the interim legislature. The commission he proposed would have given him the power to appoint eight of the sixteen members. The legislature, which was controlled by Republicans, rejected Hughes's proposal. It adopted a different proposal by concurrent resolution, which does not require the governor's approval. The commission created by the Republicans was a bipartisan commission of twelve members appointed by the legislature.[65] The Republicans voted for the plan as a unified bloc. All the Democrats voted against it.[66]

The case dealing with weighted voting was argued before the New Jersey Supreme Court on December 14. The next day the court ruled against the State Senate, primarily on procedural grounds.[67] The court noted, "Some members of the Court wish to state now that both constitutions [federal and New Jersey] bar weighted voting."[68] On December 17, the Senate unanimously rescinded the weighted voting rule.[69]

Eventually, the New Jersey legislature voted to have a Senate with twenty-nine members elected from 14 Senate districts.[70] This would be an interim plan awaiting the Constitutional Convention, which would make the final decision. A study commission was created to plan for the Constitutional Convention.

Originally, the commission was asked to deal with both the issue of representation in the state legislature and congressional representation. Former Governor Meyner was appointed to head the commission, whose early work was dogged by partisan politics largely due to the controversy over congressional redistricting. The Democrats had done extremely well in 1964, winning eleven of fifteen congressional districts on the coattails of President Johnson's large margin of victory. In the New Jersey election a year earlier, the Republicans had gained control of both houses of the legislature. The Democrats had little interest in tampering with congressional redistricting when they had a majority of congressional seats for the first time since 1912.[71] In addition, Democrats feared dissent within their own party because any change in congressional districting would force the two most powerful political machines, the Democratic organizations in Hudson and Essex Counties, to compete for representation. Hughes, acting preemptively to avoid potential partisan in-fighting, made it clear that he would veto any bill that included a revision of congressional districts.[72] This was an effort to preserve Democratic Party strength, particularly in Hudson and Essex counties.[73] Ultimately, the two issues were treated separately.

On May 10, 1965, the legislature passed a statute creating a Constitutional Convention limited to the state reapportionment issue. In order to ensure the bipartisan nature of the convention, there was to be an equal number of delegates from each party. The statute said, "The constitutional convention shall revise and amend the provisions of the present Constitution relating to the representation of the people in a Legislature, to comply with the requirements of the United States Constitution."[74]

On March 1, 1966, the convention delegates, sixty-three from each party, were elected. The voter turnout for the election was the lowest ever in a statewide election, with only 3 percent of eligible voters casting ballots.[75] Hughes's role was specific and limited. He was to "open the convention and to preside until permanent officers had been chosen. He also was given the power, while presiding, to break ties in voting."[76] Republicans and Democrats struggled for control of the convention before it had even gotten under way. Adrian (Bud) Foley, a close friend of Hughes, was selected as chairman of the convention.

The convention began in late March at the Rutgers University gymnasium in New Brunswick and lasted until June 14. The convention rejected a proposal to create a unicameral legislature in place of the existing bicameral legislature. The excess power that the smaller counties enjoyed was stripped from them as the one person–one vote requirement mandated by the United States Supreme Court governed any change to be made. The size of the legislature was increased minimally (80 members in the Assembly and 40 members in the Senate). The system decided upon in March 1966 is still the system in New Jersey. Hughes did not attend the convention except for brief opening remarks, but he communicated his positions through Robert Burkhardt, the secretary of state and Democratic state chairman, and David Goldberg, his counsel.[77]

The convention also devised the system that would be used for carrying out the redistricting process. The system chosen was a commission with five Democrats and five Republicans. If that commission could not reach consensus then the chief justice of the New Jersey Supreme Court would appoint a tie-breaker.

Hughes had been able to avoid combining the congressional and legislative redistricting issues, but it remained imperative to deal with the congressional districts. As a result of United States Supreme Court decisions, the states were required to ensure that each of its congressional districts was equal in population. New Jersey congressional districting (there were fifteen seats) had become imbalanced as a result of a population shift to the southern part of the state. When negotiations broke down on how the congressional districts would be revised, there was talk of the state's having all the congressional candidates run as at-large candidates. Many Republicans favored that at-large solution because the head of the Republican ticket in the election would be the popular Republican Senator, Clifford Case. It was thought that he would have extensive coattails to bring in other Republicans.[78]

The Democrats opposed an at-large election system and Hughes led their campaign. At the time, five congressmen represented Hudson and Essex. Hughes pushed a plan to eliminate the district of Paul Krebs, who had been in office for only a year and was seen as a likely loser in the next election. Reluctantly, the Democrats fell in line and voted to eliminate that seat and give another district to South Jersey. Dennis Carey, the leader of Essex County, was concerned about losing a congressman from his own county, but he was even more concerned with the potential ramifications from the labor unions if he was seen as sacrificing Krebs, a strong union supporter. Congressman Frank Thompson, a major force in Congress as chairman of the House Labor Subcommittee and a close associate of Hughes, was instrumental in getting the influential national labor leaders, George Meany and Walter Reuther, to convince the local labor leaders to recognize the necessity of giving up Krebs.[79]

The Republicans challenged the new district lines on the grounds of gerrymandering and the fact that the district lines did not meet the requirements of the United States Supreme Court, which mandated that district lines be drawn in such a way as to result in almost exact population equality in each district. The New Jersey Supreme Court, in effectuating the United States Supreme Court's ruling, held that the plan adopted by the Democrats did not meet the court's requirements of population equality, but they rejected the arguments based on gerrymandering. However, because of the shortness of time from the court's decision to the next election, the court permitted the plan to be used for that election.[80] Subsequently, a new plan was devised, and the court eventually accepted that new plan as constitutional.[81]

Public Defender's Office

Another major decision of the United States Supreme Court affecting every state in the country was *Gideon v. Wainwright*.[82] That case required that in all serious criminal cases the government had to provide counsel to indigent defendants. While many states, including New Jersey, had previously developed some form of appointment of counsel for indigents, the *Gideon* case required expansion of those efforts.[83]

In 1966, Hughes and the legislature created a Commission on the Defense of Indigent Persons Accused of Crime. In March 1966, the New Jersey Supreme Court ordered that beginning January 1, 1967, lawyers had to be paid for defending indigents.[84] The court further ordered that the counties pay the lawyers, basing its position on the fact that the counties were responsible for prosecuting criminal cases and that this should include the cost of the defense of indigents.[85] This led to great pressure on the state to create a Public Defender's Office to take the burden off the counties. In November 1966, the commission created by the legislature indicated that it would recommend the creation of a public defender system.

In the process of creating the legislation there was some dispute about the method to be used in appointing the public defender. The president of the New Jersey Bar Association, John Gibbons, argued for appointment by the chief justice of the New Jersey Supreme Court. Others argued for appointment by the governor. The latter suggestion was adopted. On December 29, 1966, the Commission formally recommended the creation of a Public Defender's Office as part of the executive branch of government. The office would not be under the jurisdiction of the Attorney General's Office because of the attorney general's responsibilities with respect to the prosecution of crimes. Placing the Public Defender's Office within the Department of Institutions and Agencies avoided both the appearance and potential for a conflict of interest. On April 10, 1966, New Jersey became the first state in the nation to adopt a statewide Public Defender's Office when the legislature voted overwhelmingly in its favor.

At that time, representation was only provided for offenses which carried a penalty of more than one year. Shortly, after the creation of the Public Defender's Office, a legislative commission suggested that any indigent facing a possible jail sentence of any length should have free representation. Eventually, the New Jersey Supreme Court extended the requirement of free counsel to "whenever the particular nature of the charge is such that imprisonment in fact or other consequence of magnitude is actually threatened or is a likelihood on conviction."[86]

Family Time

In 1966, Hughes combined business with family life by taking most of the family to Los Angeles, where the country's governors were holding one of their conferences. The family traveled in two station wagons. Two sons, Michael Murphy and John Hughes, drove one, and Betty and Hughes drove the other. Betty's version of the trip has the three younger children riding with her and her husband. Michael Murphy has a different version. He recalled that each day would start with the young children in the car with Hughes and Betty and the older children with Michael and John. Halfway through the day, the young ones would be assigned to the car with Michael and John and the older ones would join their parents. Betty described the trip in one of her memos from Morven. "It's hard to believe we're finally here. We've put 5,500 miles on each of our two station wagons. We've spent two and a half weeks 'Seeing America First' and we know why it is called America the Beautiful."[87] Betty wrote a lengthy article for *McCall's* magazine describing the trip. She recalled that she thought after the two station wagons were packed that they had forgotten something. Only at the end of the first day did she realize that her own two suitcases had been left behind.

In a letter written many years later, Hughes reflected on the importance of spending some time with the children. He had been talking to W. Cary Edwards, then attorney general in the Kean administration. He learned that Edwards was being pressured by his wife, Lynn, to go on a cross-country trip with their children. Hughes immediately wrote to Lynn enclosing a copy of the *McCall's* article, saying, "As she mentions in the article, her first hurdle was to convince me (I was then Governor) to try to overcome my bizarre notion that New Jersey would sink into the ocean if I were to take a month off."[88] He went on to say that since the Edwards children were then eight and fifteen, it was one of their last chances. "Once kids are 17 or 18, they have their own fish to fry, dates, friends, etc., and are not too interested in a trip with parents."[89]

In a column in August 1966, Betty described some of the social events that took place regularly at Morven. "We began our weekend early with our annual press and staff party here at Morven on Thursday evening. Friday night was the 50th birthday of my brother-in-law, Father Joseph Hughes, and that called for a family party. Saturday evening we attended the Turf Charity Ball at the Monmouth Park Race Track. It all added up to a busy, but enjoyable weekend."[90]

Many parties were held at Morven. In a letter written to Charles and Marion Sandman many years after his governorship, Hughes reflected on one of those parties. Sandman was one of the most conservative of the Republican politicians in the state.[91] Hughes wrote: "I wish Betty had written a column about her luau at Morven, when Charlie offered his sculpted head on a silver platter, in lieu of a boar's head which we could not locate: or about our hilarious trip to N.Y. in 1965 to greet Pope Paul VI; or about the time you folks and Hap and Honey Farley stayed over at Morven in 1962 after the Senate party. I mentioned the N.Y. incident in an interview in the New Jersey Reporter, April issue. I also made some irreverent remarks about Charlie, not nearly as bad as the libelous statements he always made about me. But these are fun memories—thank God for them."[92]

Pollution

In his fifth annual address to the legislature, Hughes began to focus heavily on the problem of pollution. He recognized that for too long the state had been using its natural resources without sufficient concern for protecting them. He noted that in the previous year, the state had made a start with full funding of the State Public Sanitary Sewerage Facilities Act of 1965. He argued for further developments in that area, but he also began emphasizing the problem of air pollution. He urged an increase in fines for those who violated existing air pollution rules, as well as the creation of new laws to protect air quality. He also emphasized the need to work with the surrounding states on environmental issues.

An Air Pollution Control Commission had been created in 1954. There was concern that the commission was dominated by industry officials and was not sufficiently vigilant. Hughes at first suggested that he was going to shake up the membership of the commission.[93] That suggestion provoked a strong reaction from its chairman. Hughes, in turn, said he was thinking of abolishing the commission in favor of a new agency in the Department of Health. That new agency was established by legislation passed later that year. The legislation provided: "The Air Pollution Control Commission is hereby abolished. All of the functions, powers and duties of the Air Pollution Control Commission in the Department of Health are hereby transferred to the Department of Health."[94] The new agency had the power to "receive or initiate complaints of air pollution, hold hearings in connection with air pollution and institute legal proceedings for the prevention of air pollution and for the recovery of penalties."[95] The legislation increased the possible fines from $500 to a maximum of $2,500 a day for each violation.[96] The statute also permitted local municipalities, counties, and boards of health to impose more stringent standards,[97] and provided for a clean air scholarship intern program to train individuals to work with the department of health in monitoring compliance with the requirements of the act. The recipients of the scholarship had to agree to work for at least three years for the department.[98]

On the very same day that it created the new agency, the legislature passed an act creating a regional agency to deal with the problems of air pollution. The states of New Jersey and New York initially agreed with the federal government to form a Mid-Atlantic States Air Pollution Control Commission. Other states, including Delaware, Connecticut, and Pennsylvania, would have the opportunity to join as well.[99] The major role of the commission was "to abate existing air pollution and to prevent and control future air pollution in the region."[100]

Water pollution was also a significant problem. On the same day that the other legislative actions were taken with regard to air pollution, the legislature also created a Clean Water Council. The council was part of the Department of Health. It created a scholarship program to train individuals to work as monitors of the Clean Water Act.[101] Larry Bilder, who worked with Hughes in developing these laws, considered them among Hughes's great accomplishments.

Community Affairs

For some time, Hughes had been pushing for the creation of a Department of Community Affairs. He first suggested such a department at the beginning of his first term, but when opposition to it developed, he put off the idea until he was reelected. This department was to include the existing divisions of housing, redevelopment and taxation, aging and youth and a new office of community services. Some concern was voiced that the department might interfere with home rule, but Hughes countered that objection by saying it was to be a service organization that would help communities.[102] In 1967, he achieved this goal. The first head of the new department was a nationally known figure in urban concerns, Paul Ylvisaker, the leader in the Hackensack Meadowlands Development plan. When he was director of public affairs for the Ford Foundation, Ylvisaker directed the distribution of more than $200 million in grants to city and state governments. He believed the current crises in the cities were of extreme importance. It would not be long before he would face that crisis directly in the form of urban riots that sprang up the same year he was appointed.

Hughes's plan to name Ylvisaker to head the Department of Community Affairs drew opposition. Some Republicans feared that Ylvisaker would "steer funds to community activists."[103] Hughes followed through on the appointment, nonetheless, and Ylvisaker was soon experimenting with various ideas. He created a housing finance agency with the goal of providing monetary incentives for developers to build and rehabilitate middle-income housing. He also set up state programs that piggybacked on new federal programs to create model-cities grants to aid urban areas. Additionally, he expanded state regulations over multifamily dwellings.[104]

Hughes pushed for increased funding for the housing agency to create more low- and-moderate income housing and to rehabilitate blighted neighborhoods. Many of these programs were aimed primarily at the urban centers. Consequently, they had only tepid support from rural and suburban legislators. However, many other states began looking at the work that New Jersey was doing through its Department of Community Affairs and were considering emulating it.[105] Massachusetts Governor John Volpe indicated, for example, that he was considering creating a similar agency in his state.[106]

Ylvisaker was not universally admired. His proposal to put the finances of Newark under the control of the state, for example, was criticized by proponents of home rule. Republicans in the legislature, at one point, tried to get rid of Ylvisaker by proposing a bill to abolish the department. That move was quickly squelched. Hughes continued to support Ylivsaker, who continued to propose new programs and ideas. Hughes's successor, Governor William T. Cahill, did replace Ylvisaker, even though there was a good deal of editorial support in the newspapers for keeping him on.[107]

Abortion

In March 1967, the abortion debate began heating up in New Jersey. New Jersey, like most states, had a statute outlawing abortion, which had been in effect for 118 years. It was still some years before the famous decision of the United States Supreme Court, *Roe v. Wade*,[108] which held that the statutes in the states which prohibited abortion were unconstitutional. The abortion issue had come to the fore as a result of a decision by the New Jersey Supreme Court dealing with a malpractice case brought against physicians who had not recommended an abortion for a woman who had contracted German measles during her pregnancy and had subsequently given birth to a child with serious disabilities.[109] The trial court had dismissed the malpractice case, and the New Jersey Supreme Court affirmed that decision, stating that no damages could be paid because the New Jersey statute provided criminal sanctions for abortions performed without lawful justification, and "the only justification so far held lawful by our courts is preservation of the mother's life."[110] The majority went on to say that a claim for [damages] would be precluded by the countervailing public policy supporting the preciousness of human life."[111] There were three dissenters in that case: Chief Justice Weintraub and Justices Nathan L. Jacobs and C. Thomas Schettino. Justice Jacobs, in his dissenting opinion, argued that the phrase "without lawful justification" could be read more broadly to permit abortions in situations like the instant one.[112]

Discussions were taking place all across the country concerning abortion at that time, and in many states there were movements to liberalize the laws. At one point, Hughes refused to comment on the issue.[113] It was a difficult issue for the devoutly Catholic governor with ten children. But eventually it became clear that Hughes was opposed to liberalization of the law.[114]

After the court's decision in *Gleitman*, Arthur Sills, the attorney general, announced that he had ordered a review of the administration and enforcement of the law.[115] Subsequently, the legislature decided not to take up the issue. Newspaper reports at the time gave the reasons for this decision: New York, which was also studying the issue, had rejected a liberalization of the New York law; the legislature would be up for election in a heavily Catholic state; and the Catholic Church was adamantly opposed to any change in the abortion law and it was perceived that Hughes was opposed to any changes in the law as well.[116] The *New York Times* reported, "The Democratic majorities in the Legislature supported by Gov. Richard J. Hughes, killed a bill . . . that would have created a commission to study the 118 year old abortion law."[117] But a year later, the legislature did approve a study commission.[118]

Some years later the United States Supreme Court stepped into the abortion debate and decided, in *Roe v. Wade,* that all the abortion statutes in the United States were unconstitutional in violation of the right of privacy found in the Fourteenth Amendment's concept of personal liberty. The issue has never been totally resolved and debate continues as to the scope of the right accorded by the United States Supreme Court.

Chapter 13

Working for Peace

At Home and Abroad

I N JUNE 1967, Hughes was involved in an important international diplomatic event, the Glassboro Summit, held at Holly Bush, the home of the president of New Jersey's Glassboro State College (later renamed Rowan University).[1] A major summit meeting between Soviet Premier Alexei Kosygin and President Lyndon Baines Johnson on the Middle East took place there.

In 1967, the conflict between Israel and its Arab neighbors escalated, culminating in the Six-Day War.[2] The Israeli forces quickly destroyed much of the Arab Air Force and marched into Arab territories. The United Nations was attempting to create a ceasefire resolution.

The Soviet Union supported the Arabs; the United States supported Israel. The Soviet Union objected to a proposed ceasefire, but eventually the Russians, recognizing that delay was costing their Arab friends ground and prestige, gave way and supported it. The Security Council then focused on the warring parties, issuing a simple ceasefire proposal that Israel quickly accepted, contingent on agreement by its enemies.[3] The United Nations's call for a ceasefire was met with initial rejection by the Arab countries. However, they soon agreed. The agreement was, at least in part, the result of vigorous pressure from the Soviet Union. Eventually, Premier Kosygin went to the United Nations. On the morning of Kosygin's speech, President Johnson, though not at the U.N., delivered a speech to the nation outlining his proposals for settlement of the crisis. Later in the day, Kosygin spoke, condemning the actions of Israel. There was a belief that both Johnson and Kosygin wanted to defuse the situation; however, neither wanted to appear to give in. While many thought a one-on-one meeting between the two was necessary, Johnson did not want to go to the UN, which he perceived as Kosygin's territory. And Kosygin did not want to go to Washington.

Into this impasse stepped Hughes. He is quoted as saying, "President Johnson and Premier Kosygin could not see their way to meet, and the Prime Minister was scheduled to leave the United States in a few days. I became upset about this and thought how tragic it would be if these leaders of the two great nuclear powers, mixed up in world tensions we have today, could not meet. I knew that millions of Americans devoutly hoped they could get together, for all rational people know these men are dealing with inflammable subjects. The whole world is in a dangerous situation now. If those who lead the two greatest powers cannot meet when they are a short distance from each other, the future of the world, particularly of my children and theirs, looks bleak. I had no idea then what could be accomplished, but at least to clear my conscience I resolved to offer New Jersey as a meeting place."[4]

Stephen Farber, administrative assistant to Hughes, said that Hughes called Marvin Watson, President Johnson's appointments secretary, who was unavailable. He then spoke with Walter Rostow, a presidential assistant, who said he would discuss Hughes's offer with the president. They wanted a place that was convenient to a jet airport, and several locations were discussed. Hughes suggested Glassboro State College. He explained, "The reason we picked it was kind of an odd one. We could have done it at Morven, Princeton. They thought it was too small. Charles Englehard's estate would have been available. That was too ornate, to offend a Russian who'd come up from the labor ranks, you know might have been too much style for him . . . but we finally decided on Glassboro. And I picked that because it would have been available and because not that it's in disarray or decaying or anything, but there's cracks in the sidewalk, it looks like the ordinary town. And it turns out that Kosygin was just delighted that we picked that. He says, 'You picked a fine place for this meeting.'"[5] President Johnson, in his memoirs, said, "My old friend Governor Richard J. Hughes of New Jersey had called the White House and talked to Walt Rostow. Hughes had been reading about the problems of arranging a Johnson-Kosygin meeting. Why not agree on some site in New Jersey? He asked. Then he suggested such possible places as Rutgers and Princeton Universities. Rostow promised him we would give his suggestion serious thought and would be back in touch. . . . I asked Marvin Watson to call Hughes and tell him we were interested if he could suggest a good site—not a big city, but one close to an airport, and in a quiet setting. Hughes had been thinking hard during the night and had decided that Glassboro would be ideal."[6]

Hughes recalled being told that President Johnson was actually looking at a map to find the location of Glassboro, but the map he had did not show it. Hughes said, "I always laughed to think of the president of the United States trying to read the map."[7] Johnson's memoirs say that eventually Johnson found Glasssboro on the map. As Johnson wrote, "Colonel James U. Cross, my military aide and chief pilot, was with me in my bedroom along with Rostow. That able pilot and navigator sat on the bed beside me and pored over a New Jersey road map trying to locate Glassboro. Finally, he said: 'Here it is.' I thought to myself: 'That little town doesn't know what it's in for; it will really be on the map in twenty-four hours.' "[8]

The president and Kosygin agreed to meet in Glassboro. Johnson, however, did not immediately notify Hughes of the decision. He wanted to make the announcement himself and did not want the news to slip out. In the meantime, Hughes had called the president of Glassboro to tell him that he wanted to have a meeting there with, as he put it, a number of legislators. Hughes asked the president to be prepared for an event at the campus that would be announced at the last minute. Farber recalled that even before the White House officially notified them that the event would be held there, he and Hughes started down to Glassboro, while Larry Bilder, Hughes's counsel, waited for the official notification. After a call from President Johnson, Bilder followed them down to Glassboro.[9]

It was a chaotic couple of days. Bilder claimed that the real heroes of the summit were the telephone company employees and Colonel David B. Kelly of the state police, who worked hard to provide the necessary communications capability and security. Hughes said, "The state police of New Jersey acted beautifully under the direction of Attorney General Arthur Sills and Colonel David Kelly. They impressed the President again, as they had in 1964, showing that this was one of the best police forces, if not the best in the United States."[10]

Naturally, the White House immediately sent its own advance team to Glassboro. When the team arrived, its members basically took charge and decided that Holly Bush was the best place on the campus for the actual meeting. Holly Bush was a twenty-one-room Georgian mansion built in 1849, described by Hughes as a "modest estate." After the decision was made, the advance team, led by Sherwin Markman, began preparing Holly Bush for the meeting. Hughes said later, "At the height of preparations, the Holly Bush interior took on the appearance of 220 men frantically preparing a Hollywood set for a production expected to be staged in eleven hours. The stage hands directed by Mr. Markman were Glassboro's maintenance men, Bell telephone installers, Atlantic City Electric workers, a local drapery merchant, a crew of electricians and college carpenters and painters."[11] Holly Bush was not air-conditioned, so an air-conditioning system was installed. The advance team even did some redecorating to make it more accommodating to the perceived tastes of Premier Kosygin. Making provisions for the premier and the president was simple compared to providing for the hundreds of news reporters expected to converge on the town. Here, New Jersey Bell came to the rescue: "Four of New Jersey Bell Telephone's top managerial officials arrived in Glassboro to accomplish in twelve hours a job which ordinarily would take three weeks. Their three-pronged task was to provide telephonic facilities and service for: (1) the working press, (2) summit conference governmental officials, and (3) radio and television companies. To complete this assignment, 555 Bell telephone employees worked throughout the night."[12]

Additionally, hundreds of government agents were present to provide tight security. "Mobilized were 330 New Jersey State Policemen, about 400 Secret Servicemen and Federal Bureau of Investigation agents and 150 local policemen."[13]

The conference began on June 23, 1967. Johnson arrived at Philadelphia Airport, where Hughes met him, and together they took a helicopter to the athletic field at Glassboro. President Johnson and Governor Hughes then got into a limousine for the ride to Holly Bush. President Johnson's advisors, including Robert McNamara, McGeorge Bundy, and Walter Rostow, followed in a car marked "staff."[14] President Johnson tended to treat even his high-level advisors like staff.[15]

The people of Glassboro were excited to be part of an international event and gave both leaders a great welcome. The crowd's enthusiasm was a welcome change for Johnson, who had been facing increasingly bitter crowds that objected to his policy in Vietnam. The warm welcome also pleased Premier Kosygin.

Mrs. Kosygin had died just two months before this trip, and the talk of the two leaders turned to wives and family and the importance of family support when dealing with global issues. Momentarily saddened by the reference to the death of Kosygin's wife, the two world leaders turned to happier topics as they began talking about grandchildren. Johnson had just had his first grandchild, and Kosygin was a grandfather. Talking about grandchildren started the meeting off on the right note. Kosygin even presented Johnson with a cup for his grandchild. Johnson said, "We spoke of our grandchildren and of our hopes that they would grow up in a world of peace."[16]

They also discussed other points of mutual concern and interest but did so in relatively general terms. While there was clearly some tension, both leaders attempted to maintain a harmonious atmosphere. When Johnson learned that Kosygin wanted to see Niagara Falls, he immediately set his people to work arranging the trip.

The meeting lasted longer than most had expected. Although it produced no specific agreements on major issues, the two agreed to meet again two days later. In between, Kosygin was treated to a sightseeing trip to Niagara Falls, courtesy of the president. Meanwhile, the president flew to Los Angeles for a speech, then to Texas to visit his new grandson, all while his aides were preparing strategy for the next meeting.

In Glassboro, the advance team from the White House, with the help of many from the college and the state, continued to prepare for the next day. Further changes were made to Holly Bush. Additionally, Betty Hughes had decided to invite her good friend, Lady Bird Johnson, her daughter, Lynda Bird, and Lyudmila Gvishiani, Kosygin's daughter, to the Hughes's summer home at Island Beach State Park. In her autobiography, Mrs. Johnson said, "Betty Hughes, with perception, had suggested a delightful day for us—lunch at the Governor's beach home in a New Jersey State Park on the Atlantic seashore."[17] Arrangements had to be made for that event; in particular, communications facilities had to be prepared for the site. This was especially difficult because the decision to have the Sunday party at the beach was not made until Saturday evening. Betty described that evening: "So we went back to the beach, and then about seven o'clock on Saturday evening—I still had not heard whether Lady Bird was coming—I got a call. We had about seven teenagers, and you know with teenagers of your own, seven o'clock on Saturday night is the zero hour. That's when they are all making their deals, who's got the car and got a blind date, this and that, and I don't even answer the phone because it's never for me. There is only one phone line coming into the beach house. So our Timmy answered the phone and he said, 'The White House?'[18] We had a few friends around in slacks and shorts, all with a martini, and everybody put down their glass real quietly and Dick started across the floor. 'I'm sorry Pop, it's for Mom.' Father was rather deflated, and I went over. It was Marvin Watson telling me that Lady Bird was in Texas at the Ranch and was very anxious to come the next day. . . . Lady Bird had been calling me for over an hour from

Texas and Lady Bird just couldn't get through."[19] Betty quickly realized that she had to have everything ready by the next day. What would she do? There was no good china or silver at the summerhouse. She convinced her friends, who had been sitting sipping martinis, to cook the lunch. She assigned each of them a job, while she rushed around getting the children organized for the next day. She called her mother to come down and help with the children in the morning. She also said that she did not want the children all dressed up and did not want her mother bringing down good china and silverware. Betty wanted the day to be informal and relaxed. Her mother, who was much more formal, reluctantly agreed to the conditions.

Back in Glassboro, the security forces multiplied. Since the second day of the summit was a Sunday, there was concern that there would be even larger crowds, and further concern that antiwar protesters might take the opportunity to demonstrate against Johnson. Colonel Kelly added an additional 215 state troopers.

Johnson, his wife, and daughter were greeted by Hughes and Betty upon their return. When Kosygin arrived by limousine from New York, he was accompanied by his daughter, Lyudmila. They greeted the Johnsons warmly. "Newsmen noted that the second summit meeting was beginning on the same high note of cordiality and good humor that had ended Friday's conference."[20]

While Johnson and Kosygin were meeting, Betty took the Johnson women and Kosygin's daughter on a sightseeing helicopter ride over the beautiful New Jersey shore, and then to lunch at the governor's summer home. Betty was amazed that Kosygin's daughter traveled with them without any security from her own country—just two American secret service agents.[21] Mrs. Johnson wrote, "Betty Hughes was the tour guide—no better one could have been found."[22] Mrs. Johnson described her pleasure at the whole atmosphere created by Betty Hughes. "Then the weathered, gray clapboard house right on the shore of the Atlantic came into view. This house had been the New Jersey Governor's summer residence for a number of years and at present it housed the Governor and Mrs. Hughes and about seven of their ten children, not to mention the numerous visitors that are always in tow with children. With weeks of preparation we could not have provided a better presentation of the American home than this. We were met by all seven children in residence, ranging from Tommy, aged six, who was wearing a shirt with Peanuts characters on it . . . to the eighteen year old son (who had his surfboard handy and was ready to give a demonstration with his friends). . . ."[23] Betty's friend, Emmy Acuff, used one of Betty's recipes to make "a remarkably delicious chicken dish made with such unassuming products as Lipton Onion Soup Mix and Campbell's chicken and celery soups."[24]

Betty commented, "Lady Bird was just in rare form that day. She was just happy. You could see her glow. She was thrilled to be part of all this."[25] The women walked on the beach and, before leaving, the American hostesses gave Lyudmila gifts. Lady Bird Johnson said, "I presented Mrs. Gvishiani with several books—*The Living White House* and the book on the art treasures of our National Gallery."[26]

At the end of the day, when the women were preparing to return to Glassboro, Hughes's youngest child, Thomas, announced to Kosygin's daughter, "Good bye and don't come back." Betty said, "I was mortified. I could feel my blood turning to ice water, and I knew her English was good enough that I could not hope that she hadn't understood."[27] Betty then explained that he was just upset that his day of play at the shore had been disturbed. Lyudmila took it with good grace, understanding the things children sometimes say. Later, Betty said, "Unless Mrs. Gvishiani was a mighty good actress, this was the day she enjoyed most in the United States."[28]

Johnson and Kosygin held a press conference after their meeting, and they were very well-received by the crowd. Betty said that as Kosygin was leaving, "he shook my hands with his two hands and said something in Russian, and the interpreter said, 'he says thank you for being so nice to his daughter.' He could say thank you in English, and he said to me, 'Thank you, thank you.' "[29]

Despite the great hospitality and friendship that had developed among the parties, the president and the premier were unable to announce any major achievements that resulted from the summit. They did acknowledge, however, that the opportunity to meet privately and at length had given each a better understanding of the other. The premier was impressed with his reception. In his press conference, he said, "I would first of all wish to thank all the citizens of Glassboro and the Governor and the President of the College for having created a very good atmosphere for the talks that we were able to have here with the President. I think altogether we've spent and worked here for about eight or nine hours and we've become accustomed to this place and we like the town and we think the people of Glassboro are very good people—and we've been favorably impressed with the time we've spent here."[30]

The state and its governor had done everything possible to give the president and the premier a favorable atmosphere in which to discuss their differences. While no resolution occurred, Johnson could point to some movement on nuclear nonproliferation that would come to fruition some years later.[31] Mrs. Johnson concluded, "Well, the day was one great try! And even if little headway was made, the thirst of the country for a meeting, a face-to-face confrontation, was somewhat assuaged."[32] One result of the meeting was some repairing of the damaged image of President Johnson. Theodore White, the historian and chronicler of national political conventions, said, "Nothing had so raised the prestige of President Johnson in the years of the war in Vietnam as his meeting in June, 1967, with Soviet Premier Kosygin at Glassboro, New Jersey."[33]

The president's gratitude was demonstrated when he returned one year later to Glassboro to serve as the graduation speaker. Again, this was a well-kept secret. The president was under such stress at that time that it was unclear, until the last moment, whether he would be able to attend. It was publicly announced that Hughes was to be the speaker. Only a few people knew that the president might show up. Johnson did return to Glassboro on that occasion, and was welcomed with great friendliness. This, again, was counter to the reception he was getting in many other places. In his speech, a major policy address, he explained his reasoning for returning to Glassboro, stating, "I shall always remember this town as a place of warm friendship and hospitable people."[34] He called for further cooperation with the Soviet Union and urged Americans to reject isolationism. He also defended his position on Vietnam and spoke in favor of various proposals he was making on behalf of peace in the Middle East.

Domestic Disturbances

In July 1967, just a month after the summit at Holly Bush, a much more local problem erupted for the governor. Disturbances broke out in Newark and expanded into Plainfield and Englewood. The disturbances led to some of the darkest days of the Hughes governorship.

The Newark riots were preceded by a series of major riots over issues of civil rights in various places across the United States. The tensions in Newark were exacerbated by the fact that the city had insufficient funds to provide necessary services to its population, including a large number of poor African American families who had migrated to Newark from the South. As the city's finances declined, the conditions in the schools began to deteriorate and more people left the city to live in the suburbs. Additionally, the decision to place a new teaching hospital in Newark, and the related need to relocate hundreds of families, antagonized many low-income residents.

Although the city's population was 52 percent African American, political power remained in the hands of whites. Mayor Hugh Addonizzio, who was white, appointed some African Americans, but most of the important positions in city government were held by whites. The police department was primarily white as well. The police were perceived as brutal, and the municipal courts were seen as unsympathetic to the situation of African Americans. In his book on the Newark riots, Ron Porambo argued that there was a critical housing shortage and that government officials failed to enforce the codes that could have improved housing conditions.[35] He further argued that as a result of the large number (100,000) of rural, poor, and uneducated black families that had migrated to Newark, quadrupling the African American population, jobs for unskilled workers became scarce.[36] Additionally, good medical care was not available for many Newark residents and, ironically, the plan for a new medical school and hospital in the heart of the city had increased the concern of city residents over the lack of housing.[37]

The school system was abysmal. For years the schools in the inner-cities throughout New Jersey and, in fact, throughout the country had been declining. Porambo said: "Thousands of the city's pupils graduate from grade to grade as semi-literates. Only six out of a hundred pupils are above the normal reading level."[38] Since the schools were primarily funded by local property taxes, this created what would later become known as "municipal overload." In a self-perpetuating cycle, as the schools declined, more tax-paying citizens fled the city, increasing the problems. Hughes had tried to increase educational funding for the cities, but because of the local aspect of taxation, and because suburban interests controlled the legislature, there was no significant increase.[39]

All these problems, joined with the pervasive feeling among African Americans that they were being discriminated against, led to a situation in which protests over acts of injustice or perceived injustice could easily escalate into violence. Such a perceived act of injustice occurred on July 12, 1967, when an African American taxi driver was arrested in Newark for tailgating a police car and driving with an expired license. Rumors of a beating and mistreatment of the driver led to five days of rioting, resulting in twenty-six deaths, thousands arrested, and millions of dollars worth of damage done.[40]

Hughes was kept informed about the riots during the first two days. During that time, Mayor Addonizio and the Newark police were handling the situation. On the second day, while officials were trying to calm the tensions, groups started to mobilize for a march against police brutality. That evening, looting and rock-throwing increased. When things got out of hand in the morning hours of the third day, Addonizio called upon Hughes.

Hughes described how he learned that the riot in Newark had gotten out of control early on the third morning. "I had been in touch with our Attorney General and some police authorities during the evening. I went to bed about midnight, leaving word that if anything happened to call me. I did get an almost hysterical call from the mayor of Newark [Hugh Addonizio] about 2:20 A.M. [Friday morning]. He told me that his city was burning down and he would have to have state police and National Guard assistance to quell the riot."[41] Hughes activated the state police and consulted with the chief of defense, who activated the National Guard. Hughes went to Newark immediately in an attempt to work with community leaders and others to ease the tensions.

The riots received major media coverage. President Johnson was concerned. Johnson had been responsible for major civil rights legislation to aid the African American community. Joseph A. Califano, Jr., Johnson's senior domestic advisor, wrote, "The President wanted to stay out of Newark, but Hughes was one of his strongest supporters."[42] Johnson checked with Hughes on July 14, by which time there had been looting and violence, people had been killed, and hundreds of people were in custody. Johnson told Hughes that he was prepared to support him in any way Hughes wanted. He told Hughes that if he needed anything, to contact Ramsey Clark, the attorney general, or J. Edgar Hoover, the head of the FBI. "Hughes told the President he intended to restore order with his own resources."[43] Johnson was pleased that he did not have to intervene. In a letter written years later, Hughes expanded upon his thinking at that time, ". . . I told him [LBJ] frankly that I thought the matter was best managed locally. He accepted this and I did not have to tell him what was in the back of my mind. That an Army Commander taking charge would likely be a guy from Arkansas or Georgia, not having the faintest knowledge of underlying problems in Newark, whereas I did as Governor. A mistake, even an honest one, in that electrified tension, could have been catastrophic."[44]

But not even the New Jersey National Guard was adequately prepared to deal with the situation in Newark.

When Hughes arrived in Newark at 4:30 A.M. early Friday morning, Colonel Kelly of the state police was already at the scene, having arrived ninety minutes before. General James F. Cantwell of the National Guard arrived five minutes after Hughes. Other members of Hughes's staff, including Larry Bilder and Stanley Van Ness, also came. After meeting with them, and officials from Newark, Hughes determined that Kelly, the head of the state police, should be in charge of the National Guard troops as well as the state and local police officers. The presence of the Guard and the state police appeared to increase tension. The Guard had not been adequately trained for riot control, and there was a great deal of confusion. There were numerous reports of snipers—rioters who were shooting at the police and non-rioting citizens—although it appeared in retrospect that many were unfounded rumors. These rumors made the soldiers and the police nervous, and there were instances of overreaction on the part of law enforcement authorities. Porambo's book and a book by Tom Hayden[45] blame most of the deaths in Newark on the activities of the Newark police, the state police, and the National Guard. The Select Commission that studied the riots also pointed to excessive action taken by these authorities.[46]

During the earlier looting, stores that had the words "soul brother" written on them were not targeted by the looters. There were repeated stories, which appeared to be accurate, that in retaliation for the destruction of the white stores, some state police in turn destroyed the "soul brother"-labeled stores.

Brendan Byrne, who later became governor, was then the prosecutor of Essex County. He recalled that Hughes had been "marvelous" in handling the riots—blending firmness and flexibility. Hughes, while liberal on civil rights issues, was a firm believer in law and order. He was determined that the criminal activities of the looters be stopped.

In stating his strong law and order position, however, Hughes made the mistake of referring to the jungle. He said, "The line between the jungle and the law might as well be drawn here as any place in America."[47] His choice of words inflamed feelings. Hughes's other actions, however, proved to be salutary. He toured the city and met with a variety of groups as he attempted to broker a peace. He met with a number of black leaders, including the noted African American criminal defense attorney Raymond Brown. Brown was also a colonel in the National Guard, and Hughes activated him for the duration of the riots. Brown vividly recalled a meeting with a number of the young radicals whom Brown described as "tough guys," many of whom he had represented in criminal cases. Hughes, accompanied only by his counsel, Bilder, a state trooper, and Brown, met with these "tough guys."[48] The meeting lasted so long that the state police worried that Hughes had been kidnapped. Brown was impressed by Hughes's personal bravery in going into the heart of the city and directing events himself. That meeting, as well as meetings with other black leaders, led to agreements to work together to stem the violence. Hughes reported that at one point Martin Luther King, Jr. contacted him and offered to come to Newark. In the aftermath of the assassination of John F. Kennedy, Hughes feared for King's safety and counseled against his coming.[49]

Two days after the riots began, Hughes issued an emergency proclamation. Regulations accompanying the proclamation imposed a curfew from 11 P.M. to 6 A.M. and prohibited the sale or possession of alcoholic beverages as well as the possession of narcotics, firearms, or explosives. By this time there were thousands of National Guard members and hundreds of state troopers in the city. The riots continued for two more days and finally started to taper off on Sunday, in their fifth day. By then there were problems with food supply. Many of the food stores had either been looted or their owners were afraid to open. Hughes realized food sources had to be found. "Colonel Kelly and Stanley Van Ness, the Governor's Counsel (who was African-American) toured the riot area looking for grocery stores that might open. When owners were found to be either unable or unwilling to open, Commissioner Paul N. Ylvisaker arranged for delivery of emergency food supplies."[50] Hughes also asked Ylvisaker to work with Attorney General Ramsey Clark to organize federal assistance, including the help of the Red Cross.[51] Bilder remembered that as early as Saturday he began urging the removal of the troops, but that Colonel Kelly of the state police was opposed.[52]

All day Sunday, Hughes continued his meetings in Newark, including many with local African American leaders. The community leaders pushed for the removal of the troops, and by Monday morning an announcement was made that the troops were leaving Newark. Rioting had begun in Plainfield shortly after it began in Newark, and just as the Newark riots were starting to peter out, those in Plainfield seemed to escalate. Some of the governor's staff, including Bilder and Ylvisaker, immediately went there and found a show of force they considered excessive. At one point, when armored personnel carriers were about to enter the area where the riots were taking place, Ylvisaker jumped in front of the carriers and ordered them

Governor Hughes with Thomas E. Dewey, former governor of New York and Republican nominee for president, during a major trial on which the two served as counsel. *Hughes family collection.*

President John F. Kennedy, who campaigned for Hughes in the waning days of the 1961 gubernatorial campaign, shakes hands with candidate Richard J. Hughes. *Seton Hall University Archives & Special Collections.*

President John F. Kennedy with many members of the Hughes family, on the day when Kennedy campaigned for Hughes in his first campaign. Pictured is President Kennedy with Mary Hughes to his left and in the front to his right Helen (Honey) Hughes, Brian Hughes, Michael Murphy, Timothy Murphy; in the second row Patrick Murphy, Betty Hughes, Richard Hughes; and in the background Maurice McQuade, Betty's sister's husband, and Father Joseph Hughes, brother of the governor. *Pro-Photo Service, Trenton, N.J. Hughes family collection.*

Shortly after the large Hughes family, with its many young children, moved into the governor's mansion, Morven, cartoonist Bil Canfield envisioned some possible consequences. The cartoon is printed with the permission of Bil Canfield and the Scudder Foundation, which holds the rights to items that appeared in the *Newark News*.

Hughes marches in a parade with Colonel David Kelly, the head of the New Jersey State Police, on the left and General James Cantwell, the head of the New Jersey National Guard, on the right. *Ace Alagna Photos permission granted by family of Ace Alagna. Hughes family collection.*

Lady Bird Johnson with Hughes at an event at Morven, the governor's home in Princeton. *Pro-Photo Service, Trenton, N.J. Hughes family collection.*

Governor and Mrs. Hughes with President and Mrs. Lyndon Baines Johnson. The Johnsons are holding and admiring Boehm porcelain birds. The renowned Boehm Company, situated in New Jersey, crafted beautiful creations often used as presents for visiting dignitaries. *Will Gainfort Commercial Photography. Permission given by Mrs. Barbara Gainfort, widow of Will Gainfort. Hughes family collection.*

During the summit at Glassboro between Premier Alexei Kosygin and President Johnson, Betty Hughes invited Lady Bird Johnson and Mrs. Lyudmila Gvishiani, Kosygin's daughter, to the summer residence of the governor. Pictured left to right are Brian Hughes, Helen Sullivan, Betty's mother, and behind her W. Michael Murphy, Betty Hughes, Helen (Honey) Hughes Patterson and behind her John Hughes, Mrs. Gvishiani, Thomas More Hughes, Lady Bird Johnson, and Lynda Bird Johnson. *Kevin S. Smith, photographer. Hughes family collection.*

Hughes was honored at a large testimonial dinner in August 1979 following his retirement from the New Jersey Supreme Court. The entire family was gathered together for one of the few times. Seated in the center, surrounded by their family, are Hughes and his wife Betty. From left, grandchildren Brian, Robert, and Jennifer Hughes, Robert F. Hughes and his wife Betty, W. Michael Murphy Jr. and his former wife Marianne, Patrick Murphy, Helen (Honey) Hughes Patterson, Claudia Salvatore Hughes (John's wife), Thomas More Hughes, Betsy Burge Murphy, (Tim's wife), Brian Murphy Hughes, Mary Elizabeth Hughes, Timothy J. Murphy, and next to him John J. Hughes. Seated on the far right are Richard P. Hughes and his former wife, Marcia. *Hughes family collection.*

to stop. He said he was acting on the governor's orders. The reduction in the appearance of force apparently worked, because the riot began to lose momentum around the same time.[53] Some questioned Ylvisaker's actions, saying he had usurped the authority of Colonel Kelly. Some months later, Ylvisaker defended his role before a United States Senate Investigating Committee. He said, "After we arrived there was no further loss of life and little property damage."[54] He also said that Hughes had given him authority to try to restore normalcy to Plainfield. His actions won the admiration of many community activists. Their assistance would help him later as he tried to develop more programs for the poor communities in the state.

At one point during the riots in Plainfield, Hughes issued a proclamation of emergency, permitting warrantless searches for guns in a section of Plainfield. This search only lasted for two hours, but it raised significant questions. The American Civil Liberties Union argued that no governor had the right to suspend the protections of the United States Constitution.[55] The search turned up five semi-automatic carbines as well as eighteen other weapons, including shotguns, rifles, and sawed-off shotguns.[56]

The Lilley Commission

After the riots ended, the governor appointed a commission to study them. He charged the commission, called the Lilley Commission, with studying the "causes, the incidents and the remedies for the civil disorders."[57] The executive director of the commission, Sanford Jaffee, recalled that when he met with the governor when he was being considered for the post, Hughes seemed to think the report could be put together quickly and inexpensively. But when Jaffee, a New Jersey lawyer then serving as a special assistant to the United States Attorney General, suggested a more extensive study, the governor was quick to agree.[58] Jaffee was impressed by the high quality of the commission that Hughes put together. Two former governors, Alfred E. Driscoll and Robert B. Meyner, were members, and it was chaired by Robert Lilley, the president of New Jersey Bell Telephone Company and later president of A.T. & T., and the vice chairman was Raymond Brown. When asked years later how he selected the members, Hughes said, "My criteria for selecting members of the Lilley Commission were integrity, credibility, objectivity, such prominence in the public domain as to inspire trust, a proven devotion to the State such as to guarantee an objective review of the problem, its causes and the things needed for rectification, to prevent any future repetition of the disaster."[59] John Gibbons, who was a member, recalled that there was never any pressure put on the commission by Hughes to do a whitewash.[60]

In a statement introducing the commission, Hughes said, "It is important that the people of New Jersey be given a full, impartial report on the events in Newark and other communities in our State. It is necessary that the causes of these disorders, as seen by the Commission, be fully and objectively explored. But it is most important that the Commission in its maturity and wisdom and with all the generous devotion which its members have so often given the well-being of New Jersey shall point the way to the remedies which must be adopted by New Jersey and the nation to immunize our society from a repetition of these disasters."[61]

The commission's report cited eleven specific sources of tension: the political framework, the police-citizen relationship, the municipal court, the economic framework, housing, employment, public schools, welfare, antipoverty programs, health, and the growth and problems of the Spanish-speaking community. Additionally, the commission also cited the "pervasive feeling of corruption."[62] The report, and particularly the section discussing corruption, was strongly denounced by officials from Newark who argued that it failed to emphasize the real issues of better housing, job programs, and education.[63] Newark officials also criticized the report for its failure to discuss in detail the activities of the governor and his unfortunate remark about the "jungle."[64] The report's allegation of municipal corruption appeared to be borne out three years later when Mayor Addonizio was convicted for conspiracy and extortion for "sharing in the proceeds of extorted kickbacks totaling $1.5 million from contractors on city water and sewer lines."[65] Addonizio was sentenced to ten years in prison; in imposing sentence the judge said he considered the crimes to be monumental in nature and harmful to society.[66]

The Lilley report expressed concern about inadequate housing, Newark's failing education system, and the high level of unemployment within the city. "In seeking jobs, the Negro carries with him a severe educational disadvantage. At a time when many firms consider a high school diploma a prerequisite for employment, 65.1% of men in Newark above 25 years of age, have not completed 12 years of school."[67]

The schools were old and many of them were dilapidated. The students often had difficult home lives, and little was being done to deal with the numerous problems. As to welfare, the report argued that the system had not adequately changed to meet the growing demands of a poorer and less educated society. Even the best-intentioned administrators were unable to keep up with the growing demands that further exacerbated the tensions in the community.[68] Antipoverty programs, which had insufficient resources and suffered from some perceived administrative bungling, were, ironically, listed among the causes of tension. The health program within Newark was called critical, with extremely high rates of many diseases being reported, as well as complaints about the quality of care in the hospitals.[69]

After the Riots

Shortly after the riots, Hughes announced a program to expand police training to deal with riot situations. The training would involve both state and local police officers.[70] He also announced a program to seek more state jobs for unskilled African Americans. He suggested the possibility of dropping some employment qualifications to make jobs available to these individuals—particularly highway maintenance workers, hospital aides, and other similar positions.[71] At about the same time, Paul Ylvisaker proposed that a model urban complex, including low-income housing, child care centers, and health centers, be built in conjunction with the new New Jersey Medical School in Newark.

A few weeks later, Hughes announced a program to increase the number of African Americans in the National Guard. The establishment of that program resulted from a recommendation by President Johnson's Advisory Commission on Civil Disorders. It had become clear during the riots that virtually all the members of the National Guard were white, thus further exacerbating confrontations during the inner-city riots. The president's commission had reported that only 1.15 percent of all National Guard members across the country were African American.[72] The National Guard was to be increased in New Jersey by 5 percent, and all five percent of the new members were to be African Americans. If successful, the increase would raise the percentage of African Americans in the New Jersey National Guard to 6.84 percent.

One result of the riot was Hughes's dramatic realization of the critical nature of the problems of the inner-cities. That realization led directly to new proposals and measures to help the inner-city and deal with racial concerns. It precipitated the moral recommitment speech given by Hughes on April 25, 1968. He timed the speech to support the launch of new legislation aimed at improving the lives of New Jersey's poor. In the speech, Hughes acknowledged that the riots had influenced his thinking about the need for swift action. "I have in mind the grave social problems of our hard-pressed older suburbs and our struggling rural communities, but above all the overwhelming problems of our cities, large and small alike, and of the people who live in them. Today, I propose that we face—and face four-square—the nagging problems of the urban communities."[73] Hughes focused particularly on education, housing, employment, and welfare. For education he wanted $25 million for an emergency state aid program for the poorest schools, a tripling of the emergency school building aid program. He also called for the creation of a network of neighborhood education centers to deal with the high dropout rate in urban schools, the transfer of control over the Newark schools to the state, and the expansion of a school lunch program in conjunction with the federal government. He also proposed a $25 million fund for the creation of housing for low-income families, an interest subsidy program to increase private investment in new housing construction, a tax abatement program to reduce the cost of rentals, promotion of home ownership by state guarantees for mortgage loans, a rehabilitation loan and grant program and other programs that would stimulate the provision of low- and moderate-income housing in the cities. For employment he suggested programs to increase jobs in both the public and private sector.

Another program Hughes supported involved the state takeover of the costs of municipal and county welfare expenses. Hughes wanted the state to take over 100 percent of the costs. Ultimately, he accepted a compromise proposal by Assemblyman Thomas Kean, who would later serve as Republican governor of the state, and Senator Matturi, another Republican, to have the state take over 75 percent of the costs. "Too shrewd a politician to turn down three-fourths of the loaf the two Republicans wanted to hand him, Hughes accepted their offer."[74]

One more program that grew out of these difficult times was the Educational Opportunity Fund. Ralph Dungan, the Commissioner of Higher Education who had been recruited by Hughes, had a plan to get state colleges to help educate disadvantaged minority students. Dungan worked with the legislature to develop a program that would provide money for tuition as well as remedial programs.[75] The act establishing the program provided for $2 million for direct student aid and support programs. That program has operated for many years and continues to provide opportunities for underprivileged individuals. A study of the program said, "EOF set the pace for many initiatives which today are widely incorporated into college life."[76]

Shortly after the Lilley Report, The Kerner Commission (the President's Advisory Commission on Civil Disorders), issued its report. The Kerner

Commission cited white racism as the primary cause of the disturbances that had erupted in Detroit, Newark, and elsewhere. It warned that the nation was "moving toward two societies, one black, one white—separate and unequal," and that economic and social disparities would worsen unless immediate action was taken.[77] Hughes, who had chaired a subcommittee of the Kerner Commission, strongly supported its work. As chairman of the subcommittee, President's Advisory Panel on Insurance in Riot-Affected Areas, he advocated that insurance companies be prevented from arbitrarily denying coverage to businesses and residents in slum areas. Hughes and the panel brought to public scrutiny the unseemly practice of red-lining, the refusal by insurance companies to insure any commercial or residential properties within certain designated areas, generally inner-city slum areas.

Discrimination remained a fact of life in Newark. As the construction of the medical school began, most of the union workers employed on the job were white. Millicent Fenwick, the courageous congresswoman from New Jersey, said, "Not only did this Newark project [the medical school] force thousands of people to relocate, it deprived skilled minority workers of the opportunity to benefit from the construction."[78] Many unions at the time were often discriminatory and the United States Department of Labor investigated to see if there were violations of the Civil Rights Act in Newark. Fenwick appeared at the hearings and testified "that she personally escorted blacks or Puerto Ricans to apprenticeship programs only to see them rejected."[79] As a result, Hughes joined with leaders of the African American community and his chancellor of higher education, Ralph Dungan, who was in charge of the medical school, to halt federal funding for the medical school until changes were made. Ultimately, a training program for poor and minority residents was set up at the construction site.[80]

In the wake of the riots, some of the corporations in Newark made commitments to the city. Prudential Insurance Company announced a multimillion dollar project in Newark near Penn Station that would include office buildings and a hotel. Additionally, Charles Engelhard provided funds for the New City Corporation, which was devoted to improving the quality of life in Newark. At about the same time "the Newark business, clerical, and philanthropic communities established the Greater Newark Urban Coalition."[81]

Years later, when Hughes was asked what he would have done differently during the riots, he said, "What I would do, or order done, differently, as a matter of hindsight, has often been in my thoughts. Many people believe that my initial talk was too tough. But I believe tough talk and firmness was called for at the time, especially in Newark, for the city was entirely out of control. I met with riot leaders to try to cool the strife, but the shooting finally ended when I ordered the withdrawal of the armor from the city, to prevent the continued inflammatory confrontation it caused."[82] Hughes also pointed out: "When Detroit exploded a few weeks later, I reported that experience to LBJ. He asked me to pass that advice on to Cyrus Vance, who represented the President in charge of armed units outside Detroit. On that advice, Vance kept armored units outside the city, which I believe had the effect of saving lives."[83]

Vietnam

Hughes was a strong supporter of President Johnson's policies on the Vietnam War. At the 1965 Governors' Conference in Minneapolis, Hughes and nearly all the other governors backed Johnson. Years later Hughes would say, "We passed a resolution to endorse his [Johnson's] sending of one hundred and sixty-thousand more troops to Vietnam. I think there was only one abstention, and that was Governor Mark Hatfield, who was very much opposed to the war."[84] David Broder of the *New York Times* confirmed that Hatfield was the only governor who did not support the president. Broder interpreted the strong support as a sign of the "respect the Governors themselves feel for Mr. Johnson's political strength"[85] In March 1966, President Johnson invited all the governors to a meeting in Washington. All but twelve attended. Again the governors were strongly in support of the president's policies in Vietnam. The thirty-eight attending governors, along with the governors of Puerto Rico, Guam, and the Virgin Islands, unanimously supported a resolution backing the president.

By the time of the governors' meeting four months later, in July 1966, opposition to the war was increasing. George Romney, Michigan's Republican governor, for example, challenged the assumptions of the administration's Vietnam policy.[86] By late 1966, the tide was turning against Johnson. Hughes saw a dramatic turnaround when he attended the meeting of the Democratic governors' conference late that year. This was after the 1966 elections when the Republicans made substantial gains in both houses of Congress as well as in governorships. Many of the speakers at the conference were now opposed to the war. The *New York Times* reported that there was significant resentment against the political leadership of President Johnson among the nation's Democratic governors.[87] Hughes, always a strong supporter of Johnson, was angry at his colleagues for not continuing to support the president. In talking about the conference years later, he indicated his strong support for the president. "I always loved him, and I guess I was, that was to reciprocate the fact that he loved me. I guess I was about his favorite governor."[88] He felt that the governors' opposition sprang not from any belief that the war was wrong, but as a response to the negative results in the election. He remembered using strong words and antagonizing some of the other governors when he told them that they had campaigned on the president's "coattails" in 1964 and after "a bad election . . . you stab the man [Johnson] in the back and you criticize him."[89] He added that he was back on good terms with his fellow Democrats by 1968 when they were all out campaigning for Hubert Humphrey.

In 1967, Hughes was asked by President Johnson to serve as an observer at the elections to be held in South Vietnam. He agreed. President Johnson said, "I invited a group of twenty-two distinguished Americans to go to Vietnam to witness the election, which was held on September 3, 1967. These observers were a cross-section of our national leadership, both Democratic and Republican."[90] The president said the observers were universally impressed by what they saw. "Governor Richard Hughes of New Jersey was the first to speak after I had welcomed them and thanked them, 'These were clean elections,' Hughes said. He had talked with about two hundred election officials, peasants, village chiefs, and other Vietnamese citizens. He had found great enthusiasm among them, more he said, than in his own state at election time."[91]

Robert Hughes recalled a story his father told upon his return, of an explosion at one of the polling places that was so powerful that it blew a man out of the building. What his father found amazing was that that the man went back into the polling place to finish casting his ballot.[92] Another of the observers, Governor William Guy of North Dakota, was probably describing the same incident. "We visited a precinct at which a bomb went off and killed three and wounded six during the voting. They closed it for forty-five minutes and then reopened it for more voting."[93]

Some of Hughes's associates in New Jersey, who were less supportive of the war, feared that Hughes might let his usual enthusiasm and support for the president cloud his judgment.[94] They worried that he would go overboard in his normal exuberant way. Before the governor left on the trip, Stephen Farber, his policy advisor, had prepared a memo pointing out that some factions in the South Vietnam community were not permitted to vote in the election and that it might be difficult in a short visit to adequately assess the entire situation. He even suggested to Hughes that if outside observers arrived in Hudson County (a county in New Jersey historically noted for its corrupt elections) a few days before an election, they would not be able to catch the true essence of what was happening. Hughes seemed to agree. In spite of having been forewarned, Hughes reacted very positively to the South Vietnamese election. When Farber picked him up at the Mercer County Airport after the trip, Hughes said, "I guess you're not talking to me," to which Farber replied, "What happened to my memo?" Hughes responded, "It was a great memo. I showed it to Senator Muskie and he thought it was great too." Farber then repeated, "What happened?" and Hughes just smiled.[95] But while Farber thought that Hughes had, in fact, gone overboard, Hughes was not by any means the only member of the team who came away impressed by the fairness of the elections. There appeared to be no dissenters. Senator Bourke Hickenlooper of Iowa, for example said, "I agree completely with Governor Hughes."[96] The *New York Times* reported, "Whitney M. Young, executive director of the National Urban League, said he had overcome his skepticism about the electoral procedures and left 'terribly impressed.' "[97] The *Times* quoted a colorful statement from Hughes. "If there was skullduggery with so many observers moving unannounced around the country, it would have taken 15,000 character actors and 15,000 stagehands to put on that show."[98] Hughes said, "On the way out there I would say out of this group of twenty or twenty-two there might be six or seven who were definitely and unalterably opposed to the war. All of us were of one mind coming back: That we belonged there, that it was a fair election, that we hoped to get out of the war sometime, but that as far as the election went, it was a fair one."[99]

Professor Howard Penniman, who traveled with the team of observers, wrote a book on the elections. He concluded, "Overall, the election was administered in a remarkably efficient manner. While engaged in a war with the armies of North Vietnam and the rebel forces of the South, the government managed to register 5,853,384 voters and to conduct an election in which 4,902,748 cast ballots."[100] Penniman also noted that the rules governing the campaign had provided for fourteen public meetings for the presidential candidates, two press conferences, and three radio and television broadcasts for all the candidates. Richard M. Scammon, director of the Elections Research Center, summed up the elections as "reasonably efficient, reasonably honest, and reasonably free."[101] While some of the members of the president's observation team had gone to Vietnam expecting to see corruption, "all 25 came back with the view that this had been in fact, a well and fairly and honestly run election."[102] Not all election observers were so sanguine. Robert Shaplen, an observer quoted in Penniman's book, argued "that the election, particularly the Senate election in the opinion of many Vietnamese—in contrast to that of American and foreign observers who briefly watched and hastily praised it—was less free and fair than the election last year for the Constituent Assembly."[103]

Penniman pointed out that there was a continuing debate between members of the press and some of the observers. "In retrospect," he wrote, "an interesting aspect of the whole situation was the running debate carried on between newsmen and some observers. Governor Richard Hughes of New Jersey was involved in continuing arguments with journalists who attacked his defense of the elections. The debates also involved Governor Thomas McCall of Oregon and the three senators on the team—Edmund Muskie, Bourke Hickenlooper, and George Murphy."[104] Hughes sounded the same theme. "There was great disharmony among the press there, cleavage, strife between the press out there. The so-called liberal press, like *The New York Times*, was highly critical of American armed forces and statistics and everything else, and some of the papers were, you might say, hawks on the thing."[105]

While in Vietnam, Hughes found some time to visit with several soldiers from New Jersey. He also responded to a request that Betty had received from Sergeant Walter C. Knauss, who had written asking for a New Jersey flag, since many of the other soldiers had flags from their states. Betty forwarded the request to Hughes while he was in Vietnam and he arranged to have a New Jersey flag sent to Knauss.

```
┌─────────────────────────────────────────────┐
│                                             │
│                 Chapter 14                  │
│                                             │
│               1967–1968                     │
│                                             │
│                                             │
└─────────────────────────────────────────────┘
```

H UGHES'S GREAT VICTORY IN 1965, when he was reelected and brought in Democratic majorities in both the Assembly and Senate, and the tremendous success he had in the early days of his second term, led him to become even more ambitious in pushing his progressive liberal agenda. However, a number of the reforms he backed proved unpopular. The legislation Hughes supported to make it more difficult to own a gun, and especially difficult to obtain a permit to carry a handgun, met with opposition from hunters and the gun lobby. Hughes argued that the law would strengthen the hand of law enforcement without interfering with the rights of hunters. He said the state would remain a "sportsman's state."[1] Nonetheless, after the legislation passed, there was a backlash from the opponents.

Another legislative initiative, this one dealing with benefits for strikers, drew even harsher criticism. For years, the Democratic platform included the enactment of laws providing for unemployment benefits for strikers. Businesses feared that such benefits would unbalance the bargaining process, and thus strongly opposed the proposed legislation. It seemed as if everyone other than strong union sympathizers were against this legislation. Newspapers editorialized against it. The Republicans called the proposed law an incentive for workers to strike. It was decried as an attempt to buy union support for the 1967 elections.[2] But the Democrats pushed the issue through the legislature and became only the third state in the country to have such a law. The governor signed the legislation on April 24, 1967, to take effect in 1968. The law would never be used, however, because the Republicans capitalized on that and other issues in the 1967 elections, and as a result, gained control of the Assembly and the Senate. When they took office in 1968, one of the first things they did was eliminate the strikers' benefit law.

There were other reasons for the Democrats' legislative losses in those midterm elections. Many voters were dissatisfied with Democrats at the national level because of frustration with Lyndon Johnson's policy on the Vietnam War. Within New Jersey there was a backlash in response to the recent urban riots, and "to a speech made by Education Commissioner Carl L. Marburger that was interpreted as proposing busing of school children between communities."[3] Busing was a very controversial issue and a cause of great concern to many parents. The Republicans took advantage of these factors to gain control of the legislature.

The day after the Democrats lost control of the legislature in 1967, Hughes was in Washington for a meeting of a subcommittee of the Kerner Commission. President Johnson had asked him to stop by and see him. Hughes told the president about the beating the Democrats had taken and suggested it was the result of the many "reforms" they had pushed through. The president responded, "That happens sometimes when you do things that you know are right."[4] Later, Hughes recounted a comment Johnson made at that meeting suggesting that he was already considering whether he would run again. "I don't know what I am going to do next year, but whatever I do, I am going to consider it sort of in this order: first of all, the interests of the United States of America; and second, I am concerned a little about my place in history as a president; and third the interests of the Democratic Party."[5] While this may have been a hint that Johnson might not run again, Hughes said he was "as surprised as anybody in the country" when the president announced his decision on March 31, 1968.[6]

Another program that had its genesis while the Democrats still controlled the legislature in 1967 was the Medicaid program. The federal government had proposed the creation of a Medicaid program to provide medical benefits to low-income families. To participate in the program, a state had to enact a program by January 1, 1970. Hughes, ever eager to take part in federal programs that would help citizens of New Jersey, was a supporter. If New Jersey got involved, it would receive approximately half the necessary funding for the program from the federal government. It was estimated at the time that the program would cover 1.4 million people in New Jersey. The Medicaid program was generally well received, and did not become an issue in the 1967 elections.

Around the same time, Hughes was supporting efforts to improve the living conditions of migrant laborers. He had appointed a task force to examine conditions in the migrant labor camps, of which there were more than 1,000 in New Jersey, most of them in southern Jersey. The task force issued a report condemning the conditions at a number of the camps, citing overcrowding, polluted water supplies, and inadequate garbage and sanitation systems. The task force urged their immediate closure. Hughes criticized the camps as "inhuman," but gave the operators the opportunity to improve conditions, threatening to close the camps if they did not act.[7] Some members of the task force were upset that Hughes did not act more quickly and forcefully and immediately close the camps. Hughes responded that he had to follow the appropriate legal procedures, and had instructed Attorney General Arthur Sills to order the farmers to improve the conditions within five days or be closed.[8] Subsequently, state officials representing Raymond Male, the state commissioner of labor and industry, carried official notices to a number of the camp operators ordering them to make improvements.[9] A few days later, inspectors made predawn examinations of the offending camps and found that the operators had complied with the orders.[10] Members of the task force, however, followed up with their own inspections and found the conditions to still be intolerable.[11]

Hughes then took additional steps to improve the conditions at those camps. He mandated that flush toilets be installed and that more space be provided for each person as well as other measures to improve the situation. On December 21, 1967, the legislature approved a bill that codified those reforms. The legislation was approved over the strong objection of farmers, who cited the economic hardship of offering better conditions for the migrants.

Hughes ended perhaps the busiest year in his governorship (1967) with a series of eye operations to remove cataracts, which kept him in the hospital for three weeks before Christmas. Christmas that year was even more special, as he arrived home to spend the holidays with his family.

Morven had become more than an official residence to the Hughes family. The atmosphere was joyful and rambunctious, and clearly created by a fun-loving family. Claire McQuade, Betty's sister, recalled that many parties took place at Morven. Betty and Dick had even thrown her a surprise birthday party there.[12] But Christmas was a special time. In one of her columns, Betty described the Christmas of 1967. She wrote about how beautiful Morven looked, adorned with holiday decorations, and the excitement of welcoming Hughes back from the hospital. She went on to list the many visitors that would arrive. "My first husband's mother, Mrs. Martha R. Murphy, was another Christmas caller we all enjoyed. Actually

'Nana' Murphy is grandmother only to the three Murphy boys, but she has adopted all the children as her own grandchildren. She came down Friday, laden with gifts for everyone, from a 21 year old John to 5 year old Tommy." Betty's own mother lived with the family at Morven. Betty wrote, "Nana Sullivan, my mother, who makes her home with us hopped in her car and drove to Buckingham, Pa. to visit an 87 year old relative who is in a nursing home, then doubled back to Trenton to visit another friend in her 80's who is also bedridden. We sent the three older children out on the highways and byways to deliver flowers and gifts and to make their annual Christmas calls on older relatives and friends."[13]

Betty wrote about the many other friends and relatives who stopped by to visit during the holidays. She described the older children and their friends putting together toys for the younger children. The religious significance of the day was not forgotten. "Highlight of Christmas Day was a private Mass here in the Red Room at Morven. The House is 266 years old and as far as we know, there's never been a Mass said here before. Because my husband was unable to get out as a result of the operation on his eyes, his brother, Rev. Joseph R. Hughes, had volunteered to say a private Mass for us at 4 P.M."[14] In later years, when many of the children were married, Betty decided to create what became known as the arbitrary Christmas. The name was chosen because Betty said that the date of December 25 had been arbitrarily created for the birth of Christ, and therefore, they could celebrate the holiday on a date of their own choosing. She realized that most of her sons would have mothers-in-law who would want to have Christmas with their daughters, so Betty arbitrarily selected a day around Christmas for the Hughes/Murphy family to celebrate, enabling each of the children to spend Christmas day with their in-laws. That tradition continues today.[15]

Eartha Kitt and Lady Bird

In 1968, Lady Bird Johnson invited Betty Hughes to attend a "Women Doers' Luncheon" at the White House. The luncheon program had been developed in 1964 to focus on women activists involved in local, state, and national causes. The "women doers" were a blend of professionals and volunteers. The topic for this particular luncheon was crime, specifically, "What Citizens Can Do to Help Insure Safe Streets."[16] Betty asked if her mother, Helen Sullivan, could also join the group. Lady Bird had met her mother when Helen was serving as an auxiliary hostess during the 1964 convention in Atlantic City. She readily agreed. In an oral history for the

Johnson library, Betty described her mother's preparations. "She had new clothes; she had, I suppose like everybody would do, her hair done special, and she has this mink coat but she wouldn't wear it down. She had it in the car with her. I said, 'Mom, no one will see it. You check your coat downstairs.' Well, I just think if you have one, you should wear it.' We stopped at some gas station outside of Washington, and Mother I guess at that time was seventy, and she put this blue eye shadow on. She was really going all the way."[17]

Three distinguished women who worked in the area of crime prevention were asked to speak.[18] The White House also wanted a well-known Hollywood personality who had made contributions in the area of crime prevention to be present as a guest. Eartha Kitt, a well-known African American entertainer who had performed on Broadway and in films, was invited, based on her work helping underprivileged youth.[19]

Fifty women attended the luncheon in the family dining room of the White House. Betty and her mother were seated with Dr. Bennetta Washington, the wife of then mayor of the District of Columbia who was a good friend of Hughes. After opening remarks by the First Lady, one of the scheduled speakers began to talk. The First Lady politely interrupted and introduced a surprise guest, her husband, President Johnson. He spoke briefly on the issue of crime, thanked the women, and prepared to leave. At this point, Eartha Kitt stood up and asked him a question about crime. Mrs. Johnson described what happened. "As Lyndon turned to leave Miss Eartha Kitt, who had been seated at a table close to the podium, rose in his path and said, 'Mr. President, what do you do about delinquent parents—those who have to work and are too busy to look after their children?' Lyndon told her, 'We have just passed a Social Security Bill that allots millions of dollars for day-care centers.' She moved, I think, a step more in front of him. 'But what are we going to do?' she said. 'That's something for you women to discuss here.' Lyndon replied; then turned briefly and walked briskly out."[20]

After the three scheduled speakers finished their remarks, Lady Bird opened the floor to questions and discussion. Eartha Kitt was recognized and went on at some length about the problems of youth, speaking from the perception of a mother and a person who had grown up in poverty. She ultimately strongly denounced the war in Vietnam, directing many of her criticisms to the First Lady. "You take the best of the country and send them off to a war and they get shot. They don't want that . . . they rebel in the streets, they will take pot."[21]

Betty described the scene, "She [Eartha Kitt] was getting closer and closer to Lady Bird until, finally I am guessing that her finger, which was a nagging finger under Lady Bird's nose, wouldn't have been ten inches away. Well, the whole room was just appalled. We were stunned. Nobody said anything. . . . Then I could see that Lady Bird was flushed, and her face was just getting redder right up to her hairline."[22] Johnson later described her own feelings at that moment. "What do you feel in a situation like this? First, a wave of mounting disbelief. Can this be true? Is this a nightmare? Then a sort of surge of adrenalin into the blood, knowing that you are going to answer, that you've got to answer, that you want to answer and at the same time somewhere in the back of your mind a voice that says, 'Be calm, be dignified.' "[23]

Before Johnson had a chance to respond, Betty got into the act. Janet Mezzack, in a dissertation on First Ladies as political women, described what happened next. "Kitt's remarks about children not wanting to go off to war and getting high to avoid it aroused the emotions of Betty Hughes, wife of then Governor Richard Hughes of New Jersey. Not to be outmothered, she immediately rose to her feet and asked to respond to Kitt's remarks. Mrs. Johnson gave her the floor. Betty said that she, too, felt 'morally obligated' to speak. She had eight sons, one of whom had already served in the Air Force. None of her sons wanted to go to Vietnam, but if deferments did not come for each of them, they would go. Her first husband had been killed in World War II. Mrs. Hughes concluded that 'anybody who's taking pot because there is a war in Vietnam is some kind of kook.' "[24]

The crowd reacted by applauding for Betty. Then Mayor Washington's wife, Bennetta, who was African American, stood up. In Betty's words, "She stood up and said, 'May I apologize?' She said, 'I do not apologize for Miss Kitt, that is not my place,'–or, I don't know if she called her by name or 'the other panelist.' She said, 'I wish you all who have been kind enough to come here to know that all of us are honored to be in this house, and that the other speaker's opinions are not mine and are not shared totally by her people.' This must have been difficult for her. In effect, she was apologizing for another member of her race."[25] Johnson then spoke in response. She subsequently commented on the scene, "One paper said that I was pale and that my voice trembled slightly as I replied to Miss Kitt. I think that is correct. I did not have tears in my eyes, as another paper reported. 'Because there is a war on,' I said, 'and I pray that there will be a just and honest peace—that still doesn't give us a free ticket not to try to work for better things—against crime in the streets, and for better education and better health for our people. I cannot identify as much as I should. I have not lived the background that you have, nor can I speak as passionately or as well, but we must keep our eyes and our hearts and our energies fixed on constructive areas and try to do something that will make this a happier, better-educated land.' Once more there was thunderous applause."[26]

After the event Betty was shaken: "I was so frightened. I looked at my mother, and I could see her ready to kill me. You know, the big day that she finally gets to the White House, and then her daughter gets involved in a donnybrook. She was mortified."[27]

Betty was worried that the governor would be angry, especially since he was such a strong supporter of civil rights. She knew her husband was still concerned about his standing with the African American community after the riots in New Jersey in 1967. Hughes described the situation, "She was afraid to call me because . . . she thought I would be mad, that . . . she would be getting me in trouble with black people or civil rights people."[28] President Johnson called him at Morven looking for Betty so he could thank her for supporting his wife. He said, "You've got some wife."[29] Hughes then told the president that Betty was visiting her brother and gave him the number. Betty picks up the story. "A little while later the president called, and my nieces were so impressed. They lived in a large ranch-style home in suburban Washington, and the President just never calls that house."[30] Betty's actions further cemented the close relationship between Hughes and Johnson.

The reaction in the media was significant, and included both support and condemnation of Eartha Kitt. Betty received many letters. She said, "I think it was two-thirds my favor, and the other one-third, oh, they were frightening. Letters saying, 'I hope you and every one of your damn sons comes home from Vietnam in a box,' and, oh, bad. Sometimes even the ones that said they approved of what we had done, I didn't like those either. Because they said, Good for you, Mrs. Hughes, it's high time that somebody put those uppity n——in their place.' Well, I didn't do it for that. I would have done it, any color or any profession, if somebody was that insulting."[31]

Presidential Difficulties

1968 was a difficult year for President Johnson. He had to deal with the turmoil over Vietnam and a number of other difficult foreign policy issues. Johnson said, "If I had to pick a date that symbolized the turmoil we experienced throughout 1968, I think January 23 would be the day—the morning the USS *Pueblo* was seized. The *Pueblo* incident formed the first link in a chain of events—of crisis, tragedy, and disappointment—that added up to one of the most agonizing years any President has ever spent in the White House."[32] The *Pueblo* incident involved North Korea's seizure of an American intelligence monitoring ship off the North Korean coast. The ship reported that it was outside the territorial limits of North Korea. North Korea claimed it was within the territorial waters. Johnson believed that the seizure of the ship was premeditated, but decided to take a measured stance despite some demands for immediate military action. Johnson said later, "In spite of every effort we could make, in spite of our patient attempts to balance firmness with reason, and in spite of our innumerable diplomatic moves, eleven miserable months went by before the men of the *Pueblo* were given their freedom."[33]

During the tough days immediately following the *Pueblo* seizure,[34] Richard and Betty Hughes were guests of the president and Mrs. Johnson at the White House. Hughes recalled: "Betty and I spent an evening [at the White House] one time three or four days after the *Pueblo* seizure. We had been invited to dinner, and Mrs. Johnson had called Betty and asked her if we would do them the favor of staying overnight. It was a great thrill for us."[35] It was a chance for the president to relax with good friends and people who were still supporting him. Mrs. Johnson asked them which room they would prefer—the Lincoln Room or the Queen's Room. Betty, in her usual quick and easy manner, responded: "We would sleep on the carpet in the East Room, we would be so thrilled."[36] They ended up having both rooms. Hughes offered this description of the evening. "It was a wonderful visit, and we sat up with the President. Saying good-bye to his guests, he said, 'Why don't you go on upstairs and have a drink. I will join you later.' Then she [Lady Bird Johnson] came up first, and he came, and when he came we did sit around and had a nightcap. He called the situation room, I guess, in the Pentagon or wherever it is, a couple of times during that conversation about that Pueblo thing. His best information was that ship was sixteen miles out at least [outside the territorial waters of Korea], and that the Communists were lying about where they seized it. But he was drawn and worried that night. I don't think he had been asleep for a couple of days. He didn't look it."[37] Betty, who was with Hughes when he was telling the story, chimed in: "He looked very tired. He looked an awful lot better two weeks ago out at the ranch."[38]

Betty was referring to a trip that she and Hughes had taken to the LBJ ranch shortly before their stay at the White House. Hughes and Betty were often invited to the Texas ranch. Years later, Hughes recalled how frightened he was during a drive around the ranch: "They took us for a ride around to see the turkeys and cows and everything. And he went like hell. Oh what a wild drive. I was real frightened."[39]

Toward the end of 1967 and in early 1968, Johnson was beginning to seriously consider not running for reelection. The problems of Vietnam and many other difficulties, including the stalemate with the North Koreans over the *Pueblo*, were weighing on the president. He had lost popularity despite his great legislative accomplishments.

Hughes's son, Michael, remembered a party he attended in February 1968. His parents were in Washington at a meeting, while he was at Georgetown University and his sister Mary was at Marymount College in Virginia. Hughes, who tried to combine work with family visits, invited Michael and Mary to join him and Betty for dinner. A number of prominent individuals, including Senator Albert Gore Sr., the father of the future vice president and candidate for president, and Marvin Watson, a close associate of President Johnson, were there. After dinner, Watson invited them to his home for dessert. Michael was playing pool in the basement of Watson's home when he heard a commotion upstairs and heard someone say, "Mr. President." He realized President Johnson had arrived. When he met the president, he was asked to sit next to him. Michael was overwhelmed. Johnson began by telling some of his famous stories, but after a while the talk turned almost inevitably to the war in Vietnam. For two and a half hours, Michael listened to the president and the others discussing the war. Michael, who was himself opposed to the war, was impressed by the personal concern that Johnson showed about the soldiers dying in battle and his efforts to reach a diplomatic solution. Eventually, the president turned to Michael and asked him about the reaction to the war at Georgetown. Michael had to admit that there was widespread opposition on campus to the war.[40]

The governor's own attitude toward the war had slowly begun to change, partly as a result of the influence of some of his young staff members. Stephen Farber, a policy advisor, was living at Morven and driving back and forth to Trenton with the governor each day. Farber was constantly pushing Hughes to be more opposed to the war. In early 1968, he convinced Hughes to write a letter to President Johnson suggesting that the United States stop bombing, at least in North Vietnam. They arranged to have the letter hand-delivered to the White House. According to Farber, Hughes was at a political function that evening in Bergen County when he received a call from the president. The president said something to the effect, "My last best friend, how could you do this to me?"[41] When Hughes got off the phone he turned to Farber and said, "Thanks a lot, Steve."[42] In his oral history for the Johnson library, Hughes described the same situation but it differs some-what from the description given by Farber: "I think that I was completely loyal to President Johnson, always would have been, but even I wrote him a letter long before he decided to get out [of the presidential race] asking him to stop the bombing in North Vietnam. I wrote a two page letter to him, as I recall, suggesting that we were being falsely portrayed in the world as the war-makers when we were really helping to be peacemakers, and that the only way to dramatize this was to publicize it. We could publicize it by a dramatic halt in the bombing and by a tripling of the bombing in South Vietnam, if necessary, to stop the infiltration routes, and sending Rusk and McNamara to sit at Geneva until some Russian showed up. Then the whole world would know who were the peacemakers."[43]

Hughes had not expected any response to his letter, but he did receive a response. "He [Johnson] took the trouble a week later to telephone me. He talked to me ten or twelve minutes on the phone and told me that his military commanders had convinced him that if he suspended bombing staging areas of North Vietnamese forces and supplies in North Vietnam that he would, in effect, be killing thousands of American men. He said, 'I am not going to do that. I don't care anything about an election or about a convention or anything, the only thing I care about is the United States of America and American lives.' "[44]

Despite his letter, Hughes remained strongly committed to Johnson in 1968, and despite his friendship with Robert Kennedy, he did not want Kennedy to oppose Johnson in the presidential primary. In March 1968, Hughes predicted that the Democratic Party would be "torn apart and disruptively split" if Kennedy entered the race.[45] The *New York Times* reported, "The Governor, who has never avoided a chance to praise the political support given him in the past by the late President Kennedy and the New York Senator, recommitted the regular party organization in New Jersey firmly behind Mr. Johnson."[46]

Riots and Responses

On April 4, 1968, Martin Luther King, Jr. was assassinated by James Earl Ray. This brought to a head many of the nation's festering racial and societal problems, and many cities went up in flames. Betty, who was being treated for weight problems at Duke University in North Carolina, reported, "My husband called me to say that things were comparatively calm in New

Jersey."[47] His reassuring words, however, belied the fact that there was rioting in Trenton and Newark. Hughes had feared for the safety of Martin Luther King, Jr. when the civil rights leader had offered to come to Newark during the previous summer's disturbances. King had been in Newark just a few days prior to the assassination to gather support for a planned march in Washington.[48] Betty wrote shortly after the assassination, "Somehow it seems that a man who is great enough to win the Nobel Peace Prize at 35 just shouldn't and couldn't be gunned down in an American city. I remembered having heard his wife, Mrs. Martin Luther King, give a verse recital at the War Memorial Building in Trenton, New Jersey. She was well dressed, good looking, and had both heart and intellect. We all thought her such a fitting companion for a great leader."[49]

While the riots in Trenton and Newark were not as severe as those in Newark, Englewood, and Plainfield the prior summer, they were serious. In downtown Trenton there were fires and looting. A nineteen-year-old African American college student was shot to death by a police officer when the officer attempted to arrest him in connection with a looting incident, and major fires wrecked a furniture store, a furniture warehouse, and a grocery store. Police arrested 109 persons, mostly teenagers, and the mayor of Trenton declared a state of emergency.[50]

On April 7, 1968, shortly after the riots began, Hughes announced that he would deliver a special message to the legislature. He intended to propose the need for serious action to deal with the concerns of African Americans in the urban centers. In addition to urging the legislature to act, Hughes closely monitored the situation throughout the state and worked with mayors to restore order. On April 11, 1968, he issued a statement praising leaders of both the African American community and the white community for their efforts at restoring peace.[51] He emphasized that he would not succumb to threats and that he would enforce the laws strictly, but agreed to meet with members of the African American community to listen to their concerns. After the meeting, one of the African American leaders indicated that the conciliatory efforts of the governor were helpful and caused "more people to work constructively rather than destructively."[52] On April 12, 1968, in a continuing effort to defuse the situation, Hughes met with the mother of the college student who had been killed and took a walking tour through the troubled section of Trenton.

The new riots bolstered Hughes's determination to propose new programs to get at the causes of unrest in the cities. But in his typical two-handed approach, he also urged strong law enforcement. A newspaper article reported, "The Governor declared that those who say that [riots] can be controlled solely by sterner police measures are as wrong as those who say they can only be controlled by social programs 'without a community keeping its guard up.' The two approaches, he said, must go hand in hand. 'You can't advocate stronger suppression of riots—keeping the lid on tighter—without also advocating an attack on the causes of the explosions that keep blowing the lid off.' "[53]

On April 25, 1968, Hughes presented his plan to deal with the riots and the underlying urban and racial problems to the legislature, in what is called his Moral Recommitment speech. The proposal carried a price tag of $126.1 million. "We have reached the day of reckoning. . . . And I tell you very seriously and respectfully that we must act in these two months before us or the state in the next six years will sink into stagnation and despair that will take a quarter of a century to overcome."[54] He acknowledged that the big budget increase would require additional taxes, and he again expressed his support for a state income tax. But he said it might be necessary to pursue other tax alternatives since the Republican legislative majority was adamantly opposed to an income tax.

Hughes's proposals to help the inner-cities included a state takeover of welfare costs from the counties and municipalities, state takeover of the Newark school system, a large expansion in urban and law enforcement programs, a multimillion dollar plan for aiding all poor urban schools, and an expansion of low-income housing opportunities.[55]

Shortly after Hughes made those proposals, a bipartisan commission, created by Hughes, recommended that New Jersey issue $2 billion in bonds to make long overdue capital improvements. The commission also endorsed a state income tax.

The governor found himself fighting both for a tax increase to fund his legislative program and for the big bond issue. By early May, Hughes was beginning to compromise on the bond issue. Recognizing that he was not going to get the entire package, he suggested a bond issue of $1.75 billion.[56] Shortly after that, the Republicans, who controlled the legislature, announced that they would not consider the bond issue until they dealt with the budget issues growing out of the moral recommitment speech. By mid-May, Hughes was suggesting that a 1 percent increase in the sales tax, from 3 to 4 percent, and increases in a number of excise taxes, could finance his proposals. Later in May, the Republicans set forth their plan. It called for an $890 million dollar bond issue and a $58.4 million dollar urban aid package. The Republicans planned to pay for the increases with a number of small tax increases, without any increase in the sales tax. After hearing the Republican proposal, which he considered inadequate, Hughes declared his intention to take the battle to the people. He threatened that cuts in his programs could result in more civil disturbances during the coming summer.[57] Republicans retaliated by accusing the governor of "unduly provocative denunciations of the Republican position."[58] At the same time, nonetheless, a number of Republican senators seemed to be moving away from their leadership's position. In June, the Republicans passed, and the governor signed, bills that increased the cigarette tax by three cents, the gasoline tax by one cent, and the corporate income tax by one cent.

Later, Hughes further compromised on his $2 billion bond issue and accepted one of slightly less than $1 billion. Senator Raymond Bateman recalled that at one point the Republicans had agreed on a $950 million bond issue. At that point Senator Frank "Hap" Farley, a powerful Republican senator from Atlantic County, objected, demanding that $20 million be added to finance the building of a state college in his county. At that, Senator Joseph Woodcock responded, saying that Bergen County needed a county college more than did Atlantic County. Farley reportedly told Woodcock that he had a deal. Thus, Stockton State College (now Stockton University) in Atlantic County and Ramapo State College (now Ramapo University) in Bergen County were approved and the bond issue went up to $990 million.[59] The bond issue provided for $640 million for transportation purposes, $337.5 million for public buildings, and $12.5 million for housing assistance.[60] The governor was quoted as saying that the compromise was reached after a good day's arguing.[61] The bonds were all subsequently approved by the voters by substantial majorities.[62]

While the governor was having some success dealing with the underlying issues of urban violence in New Jersey, he had less success convincing his fellow governors of the need for action. At the annual governors' conference held in Cincinnati in July 1968, John W. Gardner, chairman of the Urban Coalition, recognized that "curing social ills will cost enormous sums of money that can be raised only by more taxation."[63] But that proposal for massive additional spending supported by new taxes was sharply criticized by many of the governors.[64] Prior to the conference, Hughes had announced that he did not intend to make a splash. He could not, however, contain himself after listening to his fellow governors. He jumped to the support of Gardner. He attempted to get the governors to consider the needs of the urban areas. He utilized themes from his moral recommitment speech to guide his presentation. Hughes was appealing to a group of predominantly Republican governors. Governor Spiro Agnew, who would soon become vice president of the United States when Richard Nixon was elected president, also spoke at the convention. Agnew, who had dealt with riots in Baltimore, emphasized the need for law and order, suggesting that everyone was blaming everyone but the rioters. Agnew's theme was popular with the governors, and he received a standing ovation. Meanwhile, Hughes's efforts to emphasize the underlying problems of the cities gained little support.[65]

Betty Hughes, who had just returned from Duke, where she lost more than seventy pounds as part of her fight against diabetes, enjoyed the festive portion of that year's conference. "The governors' state dinner and ball seems to me the real top in American pageantry, excepting possibly a state dinner in the White House itself. This is our seventh year, and I never get completely used to it. Each year the cast changes slightly, but the principle is the same. This year was a show stopper. The governors, wives, and the host committee gathered for a sumptuous feast in the roof garden of the Sheraton Gibson Hotel. Later we motored over to the city's beautiful convention hall, where several thousand Ohioans were assembled. We lined up in a large side room, each governor and wife under their own state insignia. Our appearance, interestingly enough, is determined by when our state ratified the Constitution. This makes New Jersey's governor third in line after Delaware and Connecticut."[66]

These busy days would be followed by more excitement in the form of the 1968 Democratic National Convention. It would be the second consecutive convention in which Hughes played a central role, and would prove to be an eventful and exhausting few weeks for the governor.

Chapter 15

The 1968 Democratic National Convention

T HE PERIOD LEADING UP to the 1968 Democratic National Conven-
        tion was a time of turmoil. The plight of the cities—the underlying
        racial tensions—and the war in Vietnam dominated the news.
President Johnson's handling of the war was under attack around the
country. Theodore White, who chronicled the national political conventions, said Johnson had failed to rally the country. "As a politician, leader
of a nation at war, Johnson could not lead. The greatness of the chain of
Democratic politicians that ran from Wilson through Roosevelt through
Truman was that each, as President, when faced with reality abroad,
could explain it politically to Americans at home and carry into combat
a unified nation, willing to offer sons in death for the cause the President
proclaimed."[1] The president's perceived weakness inspired a number of
challengers for the Democratic nomination in 1968. Senator Eugene
McCarthy had begun to oppose Johnson a year earlier, presenting himself
as a candidate with only one issue—the Vietnam War. At first, most of his
support came from students and professors. But a number of Democratic
officials in New Jersey eventually joined the McCarthy campaign. One of
them was Daniel M. Gaby, a member of the Democratic county committee
in Somerset County. Gaby became disillusioned with Johnson's policies on
Vietnam and decided to support McCarthy. He even considered leaving his
county position because of the Democratic Party's support for Johnson.

Much to Gaby's surprise, he and another member of the county
committee were invited to the governor's office. Gaby had never met the
governor before. As leader of the party, Hughes was apparently determined
to keep the Democrats unified behind his friend, the president. At the

meeting, the governor was joined by Bob Burkhardt, the party chairman; William Brown, the executive director; and David Wilentz, the Democratic leader of Middlesex County. Hughes presented his arguments in favor of Johnson's position on the war. His primary argument according to Gaby was the domino theory, which postulated that if Vietnam fell into the Communist camp, many other countries would follow. Gaby, who had studied the issues carefully before deciding to support McCarthy, was not impressed by the arguments. He politely disagreed with the governor and indicated that he still intended to support McCarthy. As Gaby was leaving the meeting, Wilentz caught up with him, put his arm around his shoulder, and said that he had a future in the party and should be on the team. But Gaby remained resolute in his determination to support McCarthy.[2]

In the Democratic primary, Gaby defeated Charles Engelhard in Somerset County to become a delegate to the convention. Approximately 25 percent of the New Jersey delegates were pledged to McCarthy. Gaby and like-minded delegates sought to win over the other delegates, but Hughes was able to keep the rest of the delegation in line behind Johnson.

While McCarthy was the first antiwar Democrat to present himself as a candidate, George McGovern and Robert Kennedy would soon follow. At the time, Johnson was privately considering not running, but these prospective candidates were not aware of that fact. Robert Kennedy had agonized for months over his decision. In part, that agony was caused by the widespread knowledge of the animosity between him and Johnson and that many would see his candidacy as a personal attack on the president. When he finally announced his decision to run, in mid-March of 1968, he tried to play down any animosity, saying: "My decision reflects no personal animosity or disrespect toward President Johnson. He served President Kennedy with the utmost loyalty and was extremely kind to me and members of my family in the difficult months which followed the events of November, 1963."[3] He went on to say that he approved of many of Johnson's efforts in health and education but indicated his profound disagreement with him concerning the war in Vietnam.

Shortly thereafter, on March 31, 1968, President Johnson shocked the nation with his announcement that he would not seek a second full term as president. Johnson emphasized that with the country at war he "should [not] devote an hour or a day of my time to any personal partisan causes or to any duties other than the awesome duties of this office—the Presidency of your country."[4] The night Johnson delivered that speech, Hughes was at the home of the attorney general of New Jersey, Arthur Sills. He received a call from Marvin Watson, who was on the president's staff, alerting him to the fact that at the end of the speech the president would announce his decision not to run. Johnson had said he would let his good friends know in advance, so they could be prepared if they were asked to comment.

After the announcement, Hughes sent Johnson a wire. It said: "In your noble words tonight, I heard the voices of Washington and those who supported him at Valley Forge, of Lincoln at Gettysburg, and of Americans without number who have always put their country first. God bless you, Mr. President."[5] Hughes believed that it was a supreme sacrifice for President Johnson because he understood that Johnson enjoyed power and took his responsibilities as president very seriously.

With the president's announcement, the Democratic nomination became a free-for-all. Kennedy, McCarthy, and McGovern were now joined by Vice President Hubert Humphrey, who was no longer constrained by loyalty to his president. Many Democrats believed there would be a mad dash for the Kennedy camp. In the aftermath of the Johnson decision, however, many Democrats were hesitant to jump on any bandwagon. Hughes said, "There should be no headlong rush to anyone's bandwagon." Most politicians followed his lead.[6] Hughes had received calls immediately after Johnson's announcement from both Robert Kennedy and Senator Ted Kennedy urging him to support Robert's candidacy. He also received a call from McCarthy but he stuck to his position and would not rush to judgment.[7]

Although Hughes had some advance warning about the president's thinking when Johnson openly worried about the war in Vietnam at an earlier meeting at Marvin Watson's house, he was still surprised by Johnson's decision. "I guess I was as surprised as anybody in the country when he made his speech on March 31 [1968]."[8]

Humphrey had hoped to receive the president's endorsement. But Johnson let the players vie for the position, perhaps with the hope that, in the end, the party would turn back to him. Hughes had long-time relationships with both Kennedy and Humphrey. President John Kennedy had campaigned for Hughes at a crucial time in his first gubernatorial campaign and may have turned the tide in that very close election. In his second run, Robert Kennedy had campaigned for him and given him a rousing tribute. In a book about Humphrey, Carl Solberg quoted Johnson saying to Humphrey, "In the end Daley [Mayor Richard J. Daley of Chicago] and Hughes would go with Kennedy."[9] Hughes also had a close relationship with Humphrey, so it was really anyone's guess whom he would support.

Robert Kennedy evoked strong emotions. Many people loved him. Many considered him ruthless. Theodore White described Kennedy: "Wistful and pugnacious, fearless and tender, gay and rueful, profound and antic, strong yet indecisive."[10] His campaign started late, but he had the support of many who were enthralled by the mystique of the Kennedy name. White recognized the power of what became known as the "Kennedy movement." Whether he could have won the nomination and eventually become president can now only be conjecture, because on June 5, 1968, shortly after winning the California primary, Robert Kennedy was fatally shot by Sirhan B. Sirhan.

President Johnson declared an official day of national mourning. In his eulogy, Senator Ted Kennedy said, "My brother need not be idealized, or enlarged in death beyond what he was in life, to be remembered simply as a good and decent man, who saw wrong and tried to right it, saw suffering and tried to heal it, saw war and tried to stop it."[11]

Hughes, shocked by the tragedy, hoped Kennedy's assassination would lead to a new national resolve. He said, "Let us resolve anew to attend to the business of America. Let us turn from hate to reconciliation—from violence to order—with new dedication to seek a newer world as Bob Kennedy was urging when he left our world. Let us persist in the new pursuit of righteousness with a new sense of urgency. Let us keep alive the new hope which Bob Kennedy offered to the young and the poor and the victims of injustice—so that once again we shall be one nation under God, indivisible, with liberty and justice for all."[12] Hughes declared a day of mourning in New Jersey and he attended the requiem Mass for Kennedy at Saint Patrick's Cathedral in New York.

With the assassination of Robert Kennedy, the Democratic presidential picture became even more confused. Leading up to the convention most believed Humphrey would receive the nomination; nevertheless, Johnson continued to jockey behind the scenes for a draft. In a book on Johnson, Robert Dallek quotes John Connally, then governor of Texas, as saying, "Notwithstanding his statement of withdrawal, [Johnson] very much hoped he would be drafted by the convention in 1968."[13] At the same time, some of the Kennedy loyalists were trying to organize a "draft Senator Ted Kennedy" movement.

Prior to the 1968 Democratic National Convention, Hughes was appointed chairman of a Special Democratic Equal Rights Committee. Hughes would also be chairman of the Convention Credentials Committee. The equal rights committee was created in response to the disputes at the 1964 National Convention in Atlantic City over the seating of the Mississippi and Alabama delegations. In October 1967, Hughes announced that forty-eight out of fifty states had given him assurances that their delegations would meet the broad antidiscrimination standards set down by his committee. The only states that did not give such assurances were Alabama and Mississippi. Hughes warned those states that if they did not meet the standards, the Credentials Committee would not accept their delegations.

Prior to the convention there was a good deal of talk about the possible vice presidential candidates. On July 21, 1968, at the governors' convention in Cincinnati, Hughes and another Democratic governor, Samuel H. Shapiro of Illinois, came out "strongly for the Massachusetts Senator [Ted Kennedy]" for vice president.[14] Hughes said he would like to see Kennedy on the ticket "not only because he is the surviving brother in that wonderful family that has done so much for this country but on his own merits."[15] He went on to say, in what may or may not have been a slip of the tongue, that although Kennedy was his personal preference, "it would be up to the Vice President to pick his running mate."[16] Obviously he was referring to Humphrey as the candidate even though Humphrey had not yet been selected. Hughes's wording might have been deliberate—an effort to undermine the idea of Ted Kennedy receiving the nod for the presidential nomination. Hughes's mention of a potential vice presidential candidate was also notable because his own name had already been raised as a possibility. Hughes continued to maintain that he neither "wants nor expects to get an offer to be the vice presidential nominee."[17] On July 26, Senator Kennedy announced that he would not be a candidate for the vice presidential position. On August 10, 1968, Hughes indicated that although he was not campaigning for the position, he would accept it if it were offered.[18]

The whole Democratic National Convention was caught up in the battles over the war in Vietnam and civil rights. Protesters were out in force, and there were terrible clashes between them and the police. Many were arrested. Much of the television coverage focused on the protests, rather than on the convention itself. One commentator described the convention this way: "The Democratic Convention of 1968 is as famous for what occurred in the streets of Chicago during late August as for the events inside the hall that ended with the nomination of Hubert Humphrey. As police and antiwar protesters confronted each other, passions over the war in Vietnam reshaped national politics with explosive impact. Television cameras carried the anger of the demonstrators and the response of the

Chicago police into living rooms across the country. In a year of social unrest, the violence in Chicago symbolized the tensions that threatened to shatter the social order."[19]

Hughes had a tremendous responsibility as chairman of the Credentials Committee. There were challenges at the 1964 convention, but nothing compared to what would occur in 1968.[20] More than one thousand challenges were voiced regarding the seating of various delegations—particularly the Southern delegations. There were nineteen contests involving sixteen states.[21] The fact that Hughes's name was being mentioned for the vice presidency made the chairmanship even more difficult. Shortly before the convention, during a visit to New Jersey, Humphrey referred to Hughes as "the greatest governor in the country" and included him on a list of vice presidential candidates.[22]

As chair of the Credentials Committee, Hughes's decisions were bound to offend some groups. One decision, which was meant to be fair to both competing groups, ended up displeasing both sides. Two Georgia delegations were competing for seating and the Credentials Committee gave seats to both and split the votes evenly between them. "The decision pleased no one."[23] It was, of course, vintage Hughes, trying to create a compromise which would satisfy both sides even though in this case it did not work. The convention concurred with Hughes and voted to divide the delegates between the competing groups. Hughes's chairmanship of the Credentials Committee made his vice presidential nomination virtually impossible because some groups would be offended by whatever decisions the committee made. Angelo Baglivo, a reporter for the *Newark Evening News*, was covering Hughes at the convention. When asked why Hughes accepted the chair, Baglivo said, "He knew it would doom his chances but he did it out of loyalty to the president and the Democratic Party."[24]

Hughes's work as chairman was widely praised.[25] In *The Making of the President, 1968*, Theodore White, after recognizing that the Credentials Committee's deliberations could have degenerated into a succession of brawls, said, "Fortunately, the Party's National Committee had chosen as its chairman Governor Richard Hughes of New Jersey, and they could have made no better choice. Hughes, a man of the old politics, a stern commitment man on the war, was a judge by profession and instinct, a man of absolute fairness whose honor insisted on review of facts."[26] The committee had 110 members, making the role of the chair particularly difficult. Hughes was very proud of his accomplishments as credentials chairman. In a letter written many years later, he said, "By a large majority, we ousted the complete

Mississippi Delegation for having ignored the presence of black Democratic Citizens. And replaced it with a fairly elected mixed delegation . . . our Committee ousted half of the Georgia Delegation, handpicked by then Governor Lester Mattox, of ax handle fame.[27] Mattox left the convention and in an Airport news conference described me as a 'wildeyed liberal socialist.' Also one of our important decisions was to oust the Texas 'unit rule,' used to disenfranchise black voters."[28] White said, "Where the clear issue of race could be defined in the jiggering of delegations, Hughes, with a combined Humphrey-McCarthy majority behind him, could act. The convention of 1964 had forbidden racial discrimination in the selection process; under this authority, the Credentials Committee could recommend the barring of the regular Mississippi delegation and the splitting of the Georgia vote, half to the regulars, half to the McCarthy insurgents."[29]

Running the Credentials Committee was a grueling job. The heat and the bright lights in the committee room exacerbated eye problems that Hughes had been experiencing. Protesters had destroyed the air-conditioning system, leaving the room incredibly hot. Dealing with so many challenges was difficult. Betty Hughes would write, in her signature succinct style, "Proud of husband. Long hard work on credentials committee. Physically and mentally exhausting. Very controversial. Ten years experience as a judge in New Jersey helped him control warring factions. Talk about him as vice presidential candidate receding. The more controversy the less talk. Hear about man who would rather be right than president. Now married to one who would rather be right than be vice-president."[30]

Other decisions made by the Hughes Credentials Committee would have great influence into the future. The committee created a subcommittee to investigate how delegates were selected and how to improve the process. Another subcommittee was authorized to investigate the best methods for increasing participation of all Democrats regardless of religion, race, gender, or national origin. The full convention approved of those initiatives.[31] The convention adopted a resolution assuring that all delegates in the future be selected through a "process in which all Democratic voters have had full and timely opportunity to participate." The resolution prohibited the use of the unit rule in any stage of the delegate selection process; it directed that all feasible efforts should be made to assure that delegates are selected through party primary, convention, or committee procedures open to public participation.[32] These new rules transformed the system the Democrats used to choose their presidential nominee.[33]

Meanwhile, Humphrey was still trying to consolidate his position as the Democratic candidate. There was no clear signal or endorsement from President Johnson. Johnson, who may still have been hoping for a draft, was trying to organize a summit with Premier Kosygin. His prestige had risen as a result of his meeting with Kosygin at Glassboro and he hoped another meeting with the Soviet leader might help restore his popularity.[34] But just as Johnson's people were negotiating to set up a summit, the Russian army invaded Czechoslovakia. This doomed any chances for another summit and further militated against there being a "draft Johnson" movement at the convention.

Humphrey had supported the abolition of the unit rule to appease the northern liberals. As a result, he antagonized the southern delegates, who again began talking about supporting Johnson. To keep southern support, Humphrey had to accept stronger language in the platform about Vietnam than he had wanted.[35] Just as Humphrey was warding off the threat from the Johnson supporters, a movement developed in favor of Senator Edward M. Kennedy.

Since the days of Camelot, the name given to the administration of John F. Kennedy, the Kennedy mystique held great sway in this country. His assassination, and the subsequent assassination of Senator Robert F. Kennedy, shocked the nation and created a great following for the political family. When Senator Ted Kennedy's brother-in-law, Stephen Smith, arrived at the convention, the notion of a "draft Kennedy" movement started. Theodore White described the scene. "By Monday morning what is happening is a Kennedy boom, leaderless, incohesive, a strange, insubstantial, yet inescapably romantic combination among peace delegates and hardened politicians alike."[36] The convention continued in an almost chaotic mode. Johnson began talking up Humphrey when he thought Kennedy might be drafted. Ultimately, Senator Kennedy decided that he would accept the nomination only if there was a genuine draft. The southern delegations got back in line behind Humphrey, the boom for Kennedy died, and Humphrey was chosen as the nominee of the Democratic Party. But as the confusion among the delegates started to abate, the confusion in the streets around the convention continued.

Vice Presidential Hopes

Once Humphrey was selected as the nominee, the serious business of choosing a vice president became paramount. White wrote, "In Humphrey's mind, the three chief contenders for his running mate had for weeks been

Senator [Fred] Harris of Oklahoma, Senator [Edmund] Muskie of Maine and Governor Richard Hughes of New Jersey."[37]

Hughes was ambivalent about running for vice president. In later years he said that he would have loved campaigning for the position but would not have loved the position itself. He often joked that he did not even know where Rwanda was—referring to his lack of knowledge of foreign affairs. At the time, however, he indicated clearly that after discussing the matter with Betty, he would have accepted the nomination. Many of his regular supporters like Bob Burkhardt, the New Jersey State Democratic Chairman, were touting his chances. Joseph Katz, another Hughes supporter who was with him at the convention, said, "We were shooting for the vice presidency."[38] Ira Berkeley, a New Jersey delegate and president of the local AFL-CIO for Retail Clerks, urged support for Hughes. He said Hughes had been "the best friend the working people have ever had in the governor's chair."[39]

The forces loyal to Eugene McCarthy, the early antiwar candidate, were opposed to Hughes. A newspaper reporting on the convention said, "Daniel M. Gaby, cochairman of the McCarthy delegation [from New Jersey], said that 'despite the fact that the governor has excellent qualifications in almost every respect' his strong support of the Johnson Administration on Vietnam would be a liability on a Humphrey ticket."[40] At the same time there was some concern among other New Jersey Democrats about the selection of Hughes. The New Jersey Constitution then provided that, if the governor steps down, the president of the state senate would become the acting governor. At that time in New Jersey, the president of the Senate was a Republican. If Hughes became vice president or stepped down while running for the vice presidency, the governorship in New Jersey would have gone to a Republican.[41]

In his autobiography, Humphrey described his process for selecting the vice president. "Thursday morning. I had to make the final decision on a vice presidential running mate. As early as April, I had thought that Ed Muskie would be my choice, but that morning I was still considering Governor Richard Hughes of New Jersey, Terry Sanford of North Carolina, and Fred Harris of Oklahoma. Each man had some excellent qualifications—some political, some in terms of potential contribution to the country."[42] In a statement describing Hughes, he said, "Richard Hughes was another friend who had been frequently urged on me, more than either Fred or Ed Muskie. He was less glittering than Fred, but a substantial, though frequently underestimated, governor of a state I would need to carry if I would become President. I seriously considered him not simply for his state and for other political values, but for personal qualities I found attractive: political courage, a liberal humane view of government. Once again, as with the Harrises, he and his wife, Betty, had been kind and close to me."[43]

Humphrey also checked with Johnson. "He was for Terry Sanford of North Carolina or if not Sanford, Carl Sanders of Georgia or Richard Hughes."[44] It is not clear if Johnson was listing his choices in order of preference, but if he was, Hughes's third-place position was likely based, at least in part, on political considerations and the need to carry the South.

In his autobiography, Humphrey does not mention the visit from Governor John Connally, which may have doomed Hughes's chances. White describes the scene. "[T]he first of the claimants for participation in his choice came at about 1:30 in the morning—a delegation of Southern governors led by John Connally of Texas. When they left after an hour, Hughes' name had been eliminated; some consolation had to be given to the Southerners for their defeat on unit rule and credentials, and Hughes was the sacrifice. . . . In a twenty-minute meeting with Hughes immediately after the departure of the Southerners, the Vice President broke the news to New Jersey's Governor, a great gentleman who took it well."[45] Hughes confirmed that it happened that way, but added that Humphrey told him to be ready to come to Washington for a high-level position if he were elected. In another version of the same story, Carl Solberg, a biographer of Humphrey, said, "At 2:30 New Jersey's Dick Hughes was called in. Instead of asking Hughes to go on the ticket, however, Humphrey asked his advice on the Muskie problem. [The Muskie "problem" was that his unwed daughter was pregnant.][46] Forthrightly, Hughes replied that he would have no compunction over it. As Hughes left, Humphrey came out with tears in his eyes, exclaiming what a wonderful man the Governor was and how thankful he was for his counsel."[47] It is not surprising that Hughes would have supported Muskie after learning that he would not be the candidate. In one of her columns about the convention, Betty wrote, "Met Senator Muskie first time Sunday night. Both Hughes and Muskie are mentioned as vice presidential possibilities. They have always known and respected one another, but were never close friends until last summer when they made a trip to Vietnam at the request of the President. Now Hughes loves Muskie, Muskie loves Hughes."[48]

It is an intriguing question as to whether Hughes, the great campaigner, could have helped Humphrey win the general election. It was probably unlikely. While Humphrey came relatively close in the popular vote

(31,785,480 to 31,275,166), he was soundly defeated in the Electoral College (301 to 191). Even if he had picked up New Jersey, which he lost, that would not have begun to make up the Electoral College difference. Additionally, Hughes's great strength was his ability to persuade individuals to support him by dint of his personality. It is questionable whether those abilities would have translated successfully to a national campaign. The chosen candidate, Edmund Muskie, was himself a good campaigner and an asset to the campaign.[49] He particularly seemed to shine in comparison to Spiro Agnew, the Republican vice presidential candidate. Muskie was an effective speaker in the New England style, and "had made trust—trust of people for government, trust of black for white and white for black, trust of Americans in Americans—his keynote."[50] Eventually Humphrey adopted that theme and "Humphrey could make it sing."[51]

Hughes never appeared disconsolate over not having been chosen. Any disappointment he might have felt at the time would have been eased by the fact that Humphrey lost and that Hughes had a subsequent career as chief justice of the New Jersey Supreme Court—a position he truly loved. His son, John Hughes, believed that whatever disappointment he felt was caused by the fact that the charge against him was led by his good friend, John Connally. Nevertheless, in later years, Hughes would still refer to Connally as a friend. They were very close during the years they both attended governors' meetings, often ending the day's activities in one or the other's suite for drinks. Betty was also friendly with Connally's wife, Nellie. In one of her earlier columns, Betty described Nellie. "Nellie Connally of Texas is a wonderful girl. Every time I look at her I'm reminded that she was on the spot on that tragic day in Dallas, November 22, 1963, when President Kennedy was assassinated."[52]

Hughes may have felt some disappointment over having been rejected, in part, because of his work as chairman of the Credential Committee. He valued that work highly. But as Angelo Baglivo, the newspaper reporter, said, he must have known the chairmanship would ruin his chances. Betty often told the story of the Connallys' stopping by their suite. Hughes commented that it was nice of them to stop by to say hello. Betty, an astute political observer, had a different interpretation. She said they did not stop by to say hello, they stopped by to say good bye.[53]

Sometime later, Michael Murphy suggested to his father that if he had been a little more circumspect in his dealings as credentials chairman, he might have had the chance to be vice president. Hughes responded that if he could do it all over again, he would have done exactly the same thing. He believed he had done the right thing.[54]

Hughes and Betty actively campaigned across the country for Humphrey. In one of her columns Betty described the campaign. "This is incredible. Dick and I have often been table hopping. Once we even went island hopping down in the Caribbean. This time we're city and state hopping. In less than 48 hours I've been in Princeton, Newark, Washington, Evanston, Illinois and both Kansas City and St. Louis. We're headed for New York, Detroit, Connecticut and back to New York. It's exciting and confusing at the same time. It's a cross between a dream and a nightmare. I've always wanted to be where the action is. Now I've got my wish and I'm wondering if I'll have the stamina to last until Friday."[55] She frequently said years later, "I've been where it's at, now I want to be where it ain't." Later, Hughes would say that he felt that the Humphrey campaign was disorganized. He quoted the always-irrepressible Betty as saying, "Look, if you can't run a campaign trip, a simple thing, how are you going to run a country?"[56] Hughes said that if Humphrey had Bob Burkhardt running his campaign, he would have won. Hughes was not overestimating Burkhardt's abilities. Not only had Burkhardt directed the successful campaigns for Meyner, Hughes, and Senator Harrison Williams in New Jersey, he had also been the executive director of the National Voters' Registration Committee during the successful presidential campaign of President Kennedy. In 1964, he served as executive director of Citizens for Johnson and Humphrey.

Humphrey said, "Dick and Betty worked their hearts out for us. Dick wanted that vice presidency so badly. He's a good trooper. Disappointment and all, he really put out for us."[57] But Hughes did not hesitate to express his negative opinion to Humphrey about the campaign. Hughes said, "I was on the campaign plane with Humphrey and Humphrey's doctor from Baltimore, a fellow named Berman, I think Berman, and a guy Ted Van Dyke, was technical head of the campaign and he was a disaster. He was awful. I mentioned it to Humphrey, he was reading a speech, getting his speech in line and I said, 'Mr. Vice-President, you know this campaign has gone to hell.' He was a little irritated he said, 'Gee, I can't take care of everything. I'm making these speeches, I'm, thinking about policy.' I said, 'yes, but, details are going crazy, people are being affronted, the press is being turned off, we're losing bags, reservations aren't in order, why doesn't somebody take charge.' And he says, 'Well I can't handle everything.' And these dreamy guys around, they weren't Burkhardt, in other words. Or they weren't Kenny O'Donnell. Either of those two men would have made him President of the United States."[58]

Hughes also described an event in St. Louis, where a large crowd was gathered to hear Humphrey. Humphrey was called away to participate in an important conference call with President Johnson. Meanwhile the crowd was getting impatient. Betty suggested that there were a number of prominent women on the stage who could have entertained the crowd while they were waiting for the vice president. She was quoted as telling the event organizer, "Mr. Chairman, these people are leaving. These people have no refreshments, not even a glass of water. These women are leaving and if the Vice President is going to be delayed here you have Inger Stevens, a great singer, I have a talk show, I entertain tens of thousands of people on a daily show."[59] The chairman responded "Oh that's not on the schedule Mrs. Hughes. You go sit with the mayor's wife, she has a gardenia for you."[60] Hughes then said, "I would think when people relayed this disappointment to their neighbors and so forth I would say the Vice-President lost 10,000 votes, because of that stupidity. I told him about that too. He said, 'I can't handle everything.' "[61]

Some supporters of Humphrey were urging him to disassociate himself from the policies of Johnson. Humphrey was hesitant to do so because he did not want to antagonize the president. As the campaign continued, Hughes became more disturbed about the war. Although he continued to support Johnson, he began to believe that Humphrey should take a different tone. His close political confidant, Burkhardt, had changed his position and he now opposed the war.[62] Some of those in the Hughes administration began to urge Hughes to suggest to Humphrey a position that would partially disassociate him from Johnson. Hughes's policy advisor, Stephen Farber, wrote a speech he hoped Humphrey would give. He presented it to Hughes. After some consideration, Hughes decided to recommend it to Humphrey. Hughes called Humphrey and, after some discussion, dictated the speech. He wanted Humphrey to say something like, "I'll stop bombing to give peace a chance."[63] But the vice president declined to use the speech, and he did not use that line, even in the final days of the campaign. He was thus unable to overcome the perception that he supported Johnson's war policies.

Race was another issue in the campaign. One commentator said, "The major underlying issue in 1968 was race. It established the context in which the presidential election was played out."[64] George Wallace, former governor of Alabama and an arch-segregationist, was running as an Independent. He was able to draw a good number of voters, particularly southern Democrats, away from the Democratic candidate. According to one observer, "Richard Nixon and the Republicans were the direct beneficiaries of the wedge driven into the Democratic coalition after 1965 by race."[65]

In addition to campaigning diligently for Humphrey, Hughes worked hard to reunite the Democratic Party in New Jersey. Shortly after returning from Chicago, Dan Gaby, who led the dissident group within the New Jersey delegation, received an invitation to dinner with Hughes at Morven. Gaby was expecting to be part of a large group. When he arrived, he discovered that he and his wife were dining alone with Hughes and Betty. After dinner he and Hughes had a private conversation in the library. During the meeting Hughes convinced Gaby that since Humphrey had prevailed over Gaby's choices he should support the Democratic Party's candidate over Richard Nixon. Gaby agreed, and campaigned for Humphrey against Nixon.[66]

After the convention, the group that had been supporting McCarthy and McGovern coalesced into a new group called the New Democratic Coalition. Gaby was elected the first state chairman of that group. In typical Hughes fashion, trying to keep everyone happy, he would insure that at major political events, Gaby would be invited to sit on the dais and be introduced.[67]

A Republican President

All governors are invited to the inauguration of the president, whether they belong to the president's party or not. Hughes and Betty attended the inauguration of President Nixon in 1969. They wanted to be observers at the changing of the guard. Betty wrote, "I had no idea what to expect. My only previous inauguration had been a Democratic affair four years ago. I suspected that our party of four, which included my husband, myself and Secretary of State and Mrs. Robert Burkhardt, would be the only Jersey Democrats in town. Right. I further suspected we'd feel like Cinderella. Wrong. The Republicans were as hospitable as could be."[68] Three of their sons joined them. They attended the New Jersey Ball sponsored by the Republican State Committee. The Republicans gave Betty an orchid and Hughes an elephant.[69] The elephant, of course, is the symbol of the Republican Party.

In June 1969, Betty and Hughes traveled to Rome for the elevation of newly elected cardinals, four of whom were from the United States. One of the new cardinals was Terence Cardinal Cooke from New York, whose jurisdiction included New Jersey. A large contingent from New Jersey attended. Betty described the elevation: "The church ceremonies were breathtakingly beautiful. What a sight; Cardinals in striking red cassocks and hats in the center nave of St. Peter's. It was like looking at a sea of red."[70] The Hugheses attended a number of events in honor of the various cardinals from the United States. They also enjoyed the usual tourist attractions of Rome. Betty, who usually handled travel arrangements, had assumed that even though they did not have hotel reservations, they would be able to find accommodations when they arrived. However, Rome was very busy in that early summer month and they were unable to find a place to stay. Betty wrote: "Friends of ours had an apartment in Rome, and had told us to feel free to use it. We used it, and gladly."[71] It was most likely the Engelhard apartment. Helen Hughes recalled staying in the Engelhard apartment on a trip with her parents. The Engelhards maintained an apartment in Rome for the use of friends. They themselves stayed in a suite at one of the grand hotels.[72]

Back in the United States, the Hugheses attended a dinner billed as a farewell dinner to the Great Society, the name used by the Johnson administration for its programs. Betty reported on the changing of the guard. "On Monday night in New York, it was fascinating to be part of the final phases of the Great Society. There were more than a dozen hosts and hostesses for a farewell-to-arms party at the Plaza. President and Mrs. Johnson were guests of honor. Five hundred guests dined and danced." She said, "I actually saw some misty eyes as the women of the press corps said 'goodbye' to Lady Bird. Most of them had known her for half their lives. They followed her to Dallas, to the ranch, around the world. They love her."[73]

Dueling Space Programs

During Hughes's tenure as governor and for some time before, the United States was involved in a competition with the Soviet Union to see who could be most successful in their respective space programs. In 1957, the United States was shocked when the Soviet Union launched the *Sputnik* satellite into space. With the launch of *Sputnik*, the United States realized it was vulnerable and that the Soviet Union had the potential to deliver a nuclear warhead any place in the world. This set off a frantic effort in the United States to regain leadership in the exploration of space. In 1961, President Kennedy announced an ambitious plan to put a man on the moon by 1970.[74]

The United States achieved the goal. In July 1969, the Hughes family watched the liftoff of the Apollo 11 spaceship on the country's first manned mission to the moon. Betty described it. "The sky was a beautiful blue, a still and expectant medium for the rocket that carried Neil Armstrong, Mike Collins and New Jersey's own Buzz Aldrin toward the moon, a quarter of a million miles away. Armstrong and Aldrin will stand on it early Monday morning."[75] And on July 20, 1969, Neil Armstrong became the first person to walk on the moon and uttered those now-famous words "That's one small step for man, one giant leap for mankind." The Hugheses were particularly proud of the fact that one of the astronauts was from New Jersey. The Johnsons had also been invited to the lift-off, and the Hugheses were happy to see them.

Sometime later, they had the opportunity to attend a dinner in Los Angeles where President Nixon and 1,400 world and national leaders honored the success of the moon landing. In addition to attending the dinner, Hughes met with Aldrin, who was accompanied by his father, Colonel Edwin Aldrin. Betty said, "It's a nice quirk of fate that gives us in New Jersey two Aldrins to claim."[76] They would also attend a special event a few weeks later in honor of Buzz Aldrin in Montclair, New Jersey, where Aldrin had grown up. Betty described the scene. "Colonel and Mrs Aldrin and their children are a credit to all of us. The rally in Montclair was, I think, more heartwarming than any of the big city parades. This was home town stuff. Little children waved little American flags in chubby fists. The parade ended up in the football field where Colonel 'Buzz' had played for the Montclair eleven just 20 years ago. The Essex Mounted Troop was there. The high school bands and the civic groups. Col. Aldrin came to the microphone, modest, unassuming, but appreciative."[77] The astronaut recalled in his autobiography that Hughes "announced that a scholarship had been funded in my name. It was for students who have desire but not the money and I was delighted to be the cause of it."[78]

Betty and Richard Hughes continued their frenetic domestic activity. One day, impulsively, they decided to throw a birthday party for Betty's sister, Claire McQuade. The cook was on vacation. They had been invited on the same day to the opening of Merv Griffin's new television show. They began their day by shopping for food at a supermarket, where surprised employees recognized the governor. Betty said they "lugged home a station wagon full of groceries, stored it away, and headed for New York and the opening of Merv's new show."[79] Griffin had just moved to a different network. He had helped launch Betty's talk show career and they had become good friends. At the party celebrating the opening, Betty and the governor enjoyed meeting many show business people including Leslie Uggams, Moms Mabley, and Hedy Lamarr, who were among the 500 guests. The next day they hosted the birthday party for Claire with a guest list of close to sixty.

Later that same year they gave one of the largest parties ever at Morven. They invited all the judges in the state, and their wives. Hughes, himself a former judge, had long planned to invite all of the New Jersey judges to a party, and at the time there were about 200 in all. After the reception, Richard and Betty and their guests all traveled to the Cultural Center in Trenton for a catered dinner and a preview of a museum show featuring artist Ben Shahn.[80]

Chapter 16

An Education Governor

Throughout his governorship and his life, education was important to Hughes. Many governors in New Jersey have focused on education, but Hughes may have been one of the most important, particularly in the area of higher education. In New Jersey, primary and secondary education is largely handled by local municipalities. Before and during Hughes's governorship, the state paid a relatively small percentage of the costs, with most of the money coming from local property taxes. Thus, there was a noticeable disparity in quality between schools in affluent districts and those in poorer areas. The poorer districts were generally those located in inner-cities, where the population was becoming increasingly African American. Overall, local governments in New Jersey spent a great deal on elementary and high school education, but most of that money was being spent in the affluent districts. Hughes made significant efforts to increase state funding for primary and secondary schools, but the issue of adequate funding for schools in poorer districts would continue to perplex governors of New Jersey for many years. Hughes would have more influence when he became chief justice, however, as decisions made by his court significantly increased state funding for those schools.

Higher education, on the other hand, had been consistently and dramatically shortchanged by the state. When Hughes became governor, "almost two-thirds of high school graduates left the state"[1] to attend college. While New Jersey was home to a prestigious Ivy League school, Princeton, and a number of respected private schools, including Seton Hall, St. Peter's, Fairleigh Dickinson, Rider, Drew, Caldwell, Georgian Court, St. Elizabeth's, and Monmouth, it was significantly lacking in state-funded colleges. It had a good state university in Rutgers, an engineering school, the Newark College of Engineering, and it did have a number of other state colleges, but New Jersey's facilities were grossly insufficient for the majority of in-state students seeking higher education. Not only were there not enough seats available, but most of the state colleges, other than Rutgers and the Newark College of Engineering, were primarily focused on teacher education. There was a dearth of opportunities for students who wanted a state education but did not want to be teachers.

At the time, there was no county college system. During Hughes's first year in office, he supported the creation of a whole new county college system and the expansion of the state colleges.[2] These county colleges were to be two-year colleges—"established by one or more counties, offering programs of instruction, extending not more than two years beyond the high school, which may include but need not be limited to specialized or comprehensive curriculums, including college credit transfer courses, terminal courses in the liberal arts and sciences, and technical institute type programs."[3] These county colleges would be under the control of the Board of Education, which also ran the primary and secondary schools, and the commissioner of education was to assess the educational needs of any county that deemed it appropriate to create a county college. "If the State board finds such a need [educational] to exist and further finds that establishing and maintaining such college is financially feasible, it shall approve the petition and shall so notify the board or boards of chosen freeholders."[4] The county college system was to be funded by the county, the state, and the students. They would pick up some of the slack created by the absence of a larger state college system and enable many students to attend college without great expense. Many people still see this contribution to New Jersey's higher education infrastructure as one of the great accomplishments of the Hughes governorship. Senator Richard J. Coffee, who served in the Senate while Hughes was governor and also helped to establish Mercer County College, stressed the importance of the creation of the county college system in permitting more New Jersey residents to at least begin their higher educational experiences in New Jersey.[5]

Despite the importance of the county college system, it was not a substitute for a larger state college system. Students who wanted a complete educational experience with the possibility of advanced degrees had very few opportunities within the state system in New Jersey. At this point there was still no public medical school and very little opportunity to obtain a doctoral degree at any state school other than Rutgers. Hughes continued to work to expand higher education opportunities in New Jersey. Richard McCormick, a well-regarded historian at Rutgers University, commented on how important it was for Rutgers when the state chose Hughes as governor because Hughes was "very sympathetic to higher education."[6] McCormick noted the difference between Meyner and Hughes, indicating that Meyner was so concerned about spending money that he would question the expansion of any educational program. Hughes, in contrast, had a natural tendency to support any reasonable proposal.[7]

Perhaps most important, Hughes created a separate department within state government focused on higher education. Prior to the Hughes administration, the management of higher education was incorporated within the education department, which mainly focused on primary and secondary education. A significant battle took place in order for Hughes to wrest control of higher education away from the Department of Education, and create a separate department focusing exclusively on it.[8]

Prior to the 1960s, there were six schools in New Jersey called normal schools, whose major function was to prepare students to become teachers. In 1945, these schools were placed under the control of the Board of Education. Rutgers University, which functioned for many years as a private university, became a fully public university in 1956 and when it did, it, too, was controlled by the Board of Education. There was another publicly funded college at the time, Newark College of Engineering (later New Jersey Institute of Technology).

In his first Inaugural Address Hughes stressed the need for improving higher education. "A new emphasis must be given to higher education. There is a pressing need for additional facilities, a pressure which fortunately has sparked a renewed quest for excellence. Our youth should be encouraged to seek the best education from which they, as individuals, can profit. And this profit not only accrues to the individual, but also to the State and to the Nation."[9]

Many members of Hughes's staff wanted to create a separate Board of Higher Education with its own commissioner. This issue was sensitive, however, because the then-commissioner of education was a powerful figure in his own right. In a Princeton University dissertation, Richard Leone described the political battle that eventually led to the creation of a separate Department of Higher Education. He noted, "The recent history of public higher education in New Jersey parallels other states of the Northeast. State colleges in this region traditionally have been normal schools with perhaps one or two universities with broader roles. After years of state reliance on private institutions to provide liberal arts and professional training, growing public demands and expectations forced these states to expand rapidly both in enrollment and curriculum at public institutions."[10] He pointed out that the existing commissioner of education was primarily focused on primary and secondary schools, and the state colleges, at the time, were devoted to producing teachers. This situation did not serve students who wanted to pursue non-teaching careers. The result was that, by 1965, New Jersey "ranked 49 in per capita state expenditures for public higher education though the state was the sixth richest in per capita income."[11] New Jersey led the nation in the number of high school graduates exiting the state because of the lack of space in public institutions. Industries desiring college-educated employees and parents supporting college students were very unhappy about the situation and they expressed their dissatisfaction loudly.[12] In a later article, Leone said, "In education circles, it [New Jersey] was known as the 'cuckoo' state—after the bird that lays eggs in someone else's nest."[13]

In 1962, shortly after the election of Hughes, the Strayer Report was published. The report was prepared for the State Board of Education and it detailed the problems with higher education in New Jersey. It stressed the need to expand the state colleges from merely teachers' colleges to more diversified institutions. It recommended programs that provided arts and sciences education, preparation for graduate work and university research, pre-professional courses "in such fields as nursing, home economics, business practice and management, journalism, physical therapy and the like."[14] The Strayer Report recognized that in order to increase enrollment, it would be necessary to make major capital additions, including more classrooms, laboratories, residence halls, physical education facilities, dining halls, and student centers.[15] In response to the report, Hughes presented a special message to the legislature.[16] He recommended a bond issue of $750 million, much of which would finance improvements of college and county college facilities. That bond issue, which was considered massive at the time, was defeated, and was at least partially responsible for the Democrats losing control of the legislature.

The following year, sparked by suggestions from C. Charles Stephano, one of his speechwriters, Hughes created a Governor's Committee to study the problems facing higher education. In his charge to the committee, Hughes said, "The Committee should review the higher education facilities of the State of New Jersey with a view to making recommendations as to the overall policy and structure which the State should adopt to: 1) Provide educational opportunities for the qualified youth seeking admittance to

New Jersey's institutions of higher learning; and 2) provide the programs and facilities to produce the trained personnel required for New Jersey's business, industrial technological, scientific and cultural development, and for the public services demanded of a progressive, urban State."[17]

The committee found that the existing higher education offerings were gravely inadequate to meet the needs of New Jersey's citizens, and to satisfy the demands of a rapidly growing industrial state. There was an insufficient variety of educational curricula, little opportunity for professional study, and limited prospects for specialization in advanced fields of knowledge.[18] The committee also noted the need for a different structure of governance, stating that the existing system of control was outmoded, and that a single board for all public education could not handle the growing complexities of higher education.[19] Undoubtedly, this is the report that Hughes expected and wanted, as the committee's work supported the governor's ultimate desire to create a separate Board of Higher Education. But Hughes, realizing that he did not have the power to move on the recommendations, reacted cautiously to the report. He thanked the members for their labors, calling their report challenging and provocative, but he concluded that more study and discussion was necessary. The governor specifically noted that he discussed the report with Commissioner Frederick M. Raubinger and the chairman of the State Board of Education, George Smith, and informed them that he would be most interested in the response of the State Board and the State Department of Education.[20] Hughes's lukewarm response to the work of that committee would make it difficult some years later for him to convince the education establishment that he was really serious about education change and reform. Richard Leone noted that the governor's failure to be more proactive on the issue disappointed the original proponents of reform, and some of them even felt betrayed. When the governor was ready to lead a reform movement, he had to convince these potential allies that he was sincere.[21] Leone defended the approach of Hughes, saying that those who were disillusioned by his response did not understand that Hughes, the former judge, viewed his responsibilities in education as quasi-judicial. He needed evidence to support his vision of the best structure for higher education.[22]

While there was general agreement that the state's higher education system needed improvement, there was disagreement over means. Two options existed. The first was to give the existing Board of Education additional staff to focus particularly on the problems of higher education. The second was to create a new department charged solely with the responsibility of delivering and managing higher education. The commissioner and the board favored the first approach; Hughes and the committee favored the second.

The existing circumstances prompted Hughes to show restraint as he advocated for the approach he supported. Commissioner Raubinger was a strong personality who felt little need to consult with Hughes. Raubinger had been commissioner under Governor Meyner and was retained in that position by Hughes. He had no direct loyalty to Hughes and seldom consulted the governor on policy matters. Consequently, the governor looked first to his personal staff for advice on education policy.[23] Many members of Hughes's staff were disappointed by the Department of Education's lack of responsiveness, and their feelings eventually developed into "real resentment."[24] Raubinger, however, apparently did not feel the need to appease the governor. Leone wrote, "During his first term, Governor Hughes' reputation as a 'lucky' victor in 1961 with no pretensions to mastery of public affairs, significantly contributed to the general feeling that cabinet members could ignore his requests with impunity."[25] The defeat of the bond issue in 1963, and the general feeling that Hughes would have a hard time winning reelection, only added to the cabinet members' confidence that they need not answer to the governor. Leone further noted: "Richard J. Hughes had no illusions about his own effectiveness as an administrator. Once in a discussion of the merits of a potential appointee, a staff member pointed out to the Governor that the man in question was 'not a very good administrator.' The Governor, with a sly smile (and, no doubt, somewhat tongue in cheek), quietly replied that a man could make a contribution to government and politics without being a good administrator."[26]

In early 1965, initiatives aimed at improving higher education were underway. A Citizens Committee on New Jersey Higher Education chaired by Princeton University President Robert Goheen had begun functioning independently. In May 1965, Goheen wrote to the governor indicating the concern of leading industrialists about the conditions of higher education in the state. At approximately the same time, the Lord Committee was reinvigorated and began studying education issues. Ultimately, these two committees would have a significant impact in gathering support for future initiatives to reform higher education. The Citizens Committee would eventually consist of more than 100 prominent New Jerseyans representing all sectors of society. The committee consulted experts with impeccable credentials who were not controlled by the education establishment.[27] At the same time, the Lord Committee began its own study and ultimately concluded that a new structure was necessary.[28]

While this was happening, the governor continued to meet with Raubinger and others within the education community. As Leone said, "One of the characteristics of the 'Hughes' style' was that those who met with him almost always believed him sympathetic to their viewpoint or perhaps even won over. Visitors frequently emerged from the Governor's inner office convinced of gubernatorial commitment, only to realize later that the governor carefully had preserved his options."[29] Larry Bilder, who worked closely with the governor during that time, recalled that Hughes would meet with groups of educators, who, on occasion, would talk down to the governor and to him, suggesting that they thought he and Hughes had no understanding of the issues. But even though Hughes fully understood many of the ideas suggested, the governor would listen politely, pretend to be impressed, and the others would leave happy.[30] During this time, plans took shape to host a governor's conference on education in 1966.

Hughes swept to victory in the 1965 election, bringing in large Democratic majorities in both the Senate and the Assembly. The controversy over Rutgers Professor Genovese and his strong antiwar sentiments, and the governor's handling of the case, had the unintended result of elevating the view of Hughes among the education elite.[31] After his resounding victory, Hughes felt that he could push through an ambitious legislative agenda including education reform. In his second Inaugural Address on January 18, 1966, Hughes argued for education reform. "The very first order of public greatness must be education. . . . I want this Legislature to be remembered for generations to come as the 'Education Legislature'—the Legislature that built the foundation of New Jersey's greatness."[32] In his annual message he further described his plans. "New Jersey must begin to erase the shameful statistic which shows us, the sixth wealthiest state per capita in the Nation, in forty-eighth place in our support of higher education."[33] In that message, Hughes proposed a major increase in spending for capital construction, increased scholarship and financial aid, and legislation to create a New Jersey College Dormitory and Building Authority.

The planning for a major education conference was soon in full swing. Richard Leone, a staff member for the governor, selected Stephen Farber as the conference's executive director. Members of the governor's staff intended the program to be national in scope, but Farber recalled that Raubinger only wanted New Jersey people on the panels. With Hughes's blessing, Farber dismissed Raubinger's idea and insisted on inviting a broad-based group of people from all across the country. When his actions met with objections, Hughes called in the members of the Board of Education and Raubinger, and insisted on the need to include different viewpoints.[34] The conference was supported by grants from a number of foundations, including the Carnegie Foundation. The securing of private funding permitted the Governor's Office to keep control of the process and avoid having to obtain funding from the Department of Education. Joseph Katz, a former special assistant to the governor, was brought in to handle publicity. Katz, then a lobbyist, kept the newspapers filled with stories about the conference.

The conference attracted an audience of more than two thousand and "brought together the most notable group of educators ever assembled in New Jersey on a single day."[35] Harold Howe, the United States Commissioner of Higher Education, opened the meeting. Many prominent educators were among the speakers. They included James Conant, president-emeritus of Harvard University; Terry Sanford, former governor of North Carolina and president of Duke University; Allan M. Cartter, vice president of the American Council on Education, and Henry Chauncey, president of Educational Testing Service. Also participating was James Farmer, founder of the Congress of Racial Equality (CORE).[36] A number of the prominent speakers, including Howe, endorsed the creation of a separate board and leader to run the state's higher education.[37]

The Board of Education made plans to issue a statement criticizing the conference. Hearing about the plans, Hughes called in the commissioner and the chairman of the board, asking that any response to the conference be temperate. The two education officials promised the governor instead that there would be no statement on their part. The staff of the department, however, issued a statement that was strongly critical of the conference and that endorsed the existing structure of higher education governance. Leone said that the unanimous reaction of the governor's staff was that the governor had been betrayed. Hughes personally dictated a response. "I feel it necessary to state that, so long as I am Governor of New Jersey, there shall be free and open public discussion on all matters affecting the well-being of the people. This includes public education. . . . I . . . assume that those . . . with the responsibility for public education would not resent public discussion. . . . To do otherwise is to defend a status quo with the contention that it represents the best of all possible worlds. And this attitude has an element of hysteria which does not bode well for the attainment of the goals of excellence which we seek, or should be seeking. . . . It seems to me that this wish to muffle public discussion is not in the best interest of the state. . . . It should be emphasized that no one group controls public education. No one should consider public education to be a private preserve."[38] Much of the press response was supportive of the governor and critical of the education establishment.

In an effort to forestall criticism of the Division of Higher Education within the Department of Education, Raubinger dismissed the head of the division, replacing him with Michael Gilligan, the president of Jersey City State College. While Gilligan had a reputation as a strong administrator, the main reason for his selection appeared to be that he was an Irish-Catholic who was well-connected with the powerful Democratic organization in Hudson County. He was perceived as someone who could develop a strong rapport with the governor and strengthen the political defenses of the department.[39] The strategy backfired. The governor and his staff believed the appointment was a signal that Raubinger would not reform the existing structure. In Leone's words, "The Governor, upon hearing reports of the 'political' reasons for Gilligan's selection, considered them demeaning to him and unworthy of the Commissioner. The incident suggests the schoolmen's continuing misjudgments of the Governor."[40]

The New Jersey Education Association, which represents the state's teachers, originally rejected the idea of a separate board. Proponents of reform were concerned about the association's political clout. As the debate continued, however, the association's members began to recognize that the commissioner and the board were not working for reform.[41] Also recognizing that Hughes was taking an aggressive stance, the educators' association did not want to antagonize a governor who had been recently reelected and had a Democratic majority in the legislature. The association ended up taking a neutral position.

On May 14, 1966, the Citizens' Committee recommended to the governor the creation of a separate Department of Higher Education with its own board "to establish general policy and for the planning and over-sight of higher education in New Jersey."[42] The commissioner of education and the State Board of Education responded with a lengthy defense of the status quo. While the board agreed that there was "a pressing need to expand facilities for higher education," and further agreed that there were "inadequate State funds available," it did not agree that a new structure of governance was necessary. The board dismissed the idea that the existing system was outmoded, and despite the "rapidly growing complexity of demands being made upon the single board," it remained adamant that it could still handle the state's entire educational system.[43] The Board of Education argued that it "would be more efficient to make judicious additions to the present staff, rather than to create additional and separate staffs, as recommended by the Governor's Committee."[44]

Shortly after the Citizens' Committee made its recommendation, stories appeared in the newspapers that Commissioner Raubinger had accepted a teaching post at the University of Illinois.[45] Hughes immediately issued a statement praising the accomplishments of Raubinger and expressing regrets over his departure. There was some speculation that Raubinger would have stayed, if asked, but the manner in which Hughes responded indicated that there would be no such request.[46] There were some efforts to get Hughes to try to dissuade Raubinger, but the governor refused.

On May 25, 1966, Hughes presented a special message to the legislature proposing the Higher Education Act of 1966. In his address, he said, "We must design a system of higher education which both quantitatively and qualitatively represents a response to the often stated but still unfulfilled needs of our college age students."[47] He said the legislation would provide thousands of additional spaces so that fewer students would have to leave the state to pursue a higher education. The Department of Higher Education "was given power to exercise all powers and duties formerly exercised by the state board of education concerning higher education, coordinate higher education related activities between the state and federal government, and serve as an advisor to the governor."[48] The legislation created a Chancellor of Higher Education, who would function under a Board of Higher Education, whose members would include representatives of the education community and other citizens.

The next step for Hughes was to convince the legislature to support the proposal. Because Hughes had carefully kept his intentions unclear during the preliminary stages of the process, the education community, which opposed the change, "had devoted little effort to early lobbying with legislators."[49] Meanwhile, the reform coalition had extensively lobbied influential legislators concerning the substantive issues involved in the legislation.[50] The governor's staff and others rounded up influential members of the legislature to sponsor the legislation. Senator Matthew Feldman from Bergen County agreed to be the chief sponsor. The entire delegation from Bergen County was supportive of the bill, convinced that its suburban upscale constituents would enthusiastically support a program to improve higher education. Senator Anthony Grossi of Passaic, who was one of the party leaders who first proposed Hughes for governor, was also on board. Senator Si Ridolfi, the majority leader and long-time friend of Hughes, also acceded to the request of Hughes to be a sponsor. Hughes, who had always worked well with Republicans, was aided by the decision of William Ozzard, the minority leader, to support the legislation. Ten senators sponsored the bill, leaving only five more needed for Senate passage.[51] (At that time twenty-nine senators comprised the changing complexion of the Senate brought about by the decisions of the United States Supreme Court requiring proportional representation.) In the Assembly, Robert Wilentz, whose father was the first to call Hughes to suggest that he run for the governorship, was highly supportive. Additionally, the media was generally in favor of the proposed legislation, with the *New York Times*, the *Daily Home News of New Brunswick*, and the *Trenton Evening News* voicing support. The *Newark Evening News* and the *Bergen Record* initially opposed the legislation, but after some lobbying by members of the Citizens' Committee, they gave mildly favorable reviews.

The legislative session was drawing to a close and there was a debate as to whether there should be a push for immediate passage, or whether the matter should be put off until the next session, when hearings could be held. Hughes decided that it was inappropriate to push such important legislation through quickly and, even though the votes seemed to be there, he decided to wait and go through the full legislative process.

George Smith, chairman of the State Board of Education, worked actively against the legislation. He restated his argument that there was no reason to believe that two boards would be better than one. He insisted that substantial strides had been made in the past few years, under the existing structure, to improve conditions for higher education in the state. In response, proponents of the legislation pointed out that all major states except New Jersey and Pennsylvania had two boards. In July 1966, the Board of Education released a *Report on New Jersey Higher Education* presenting arguments in opposition to the new proposal. It argued that the single coordinated system had grown out of an earlier bifurcated system that had not worked well. It said the combined approach worked well and that the proposed new set-up would add unnecessary overhead expenses and wrongly separate higher education from elementary and secondary school education.[52]

Another factor in the debate was the concern of Rutgers officials that the flexibility and autonomy that the state university enjoyed might be compromised by the new legislation. According to Leone, "Eventually language was inserted in the legislation which made it clear that Rutgers' status would be unchanged. Similar language was developed for Newark College of Engineering."[53]

Every member of the legislature was wooed by the reform coalition. "If a legislator was in doubt concerning the substantive issues, he was contacted by a reform educator from his district—if one could be located—otherwise by an expert from the Citizens' Committee."[54] The governor invited Democrats to his office for consultations. Many prominent members of the Citizens' Committee were tapped to make appeals to other legislators. Supporters of reform such as Bishop John J. Dougherty, the president of Seton Hall University, Mrs. Katherine Kruberger, the Republican National committeewoman for New Jersey, and Joel Jacobson, the president of the Industrial Union Council, aided the effort.

Just as the legislation was coming up for a vote, the national elections of November 1966 took place. The Democrats lost two congressional seats in New Jersey, and Clifford Case, the Republican senator, won overwhelmingly. Hughes pressed forward despite the election results. The New Jersey legislature, whose members were not up for election at that time, retained its Democratic majorities. Leone said, "The Governor's power was great because his reputation with all parties was at its peak. He had demonstrated that this year he would employ all his influence to obtain what he wanted. Those with legislative desires of their own would weigh their priorities carefully before risking the Governor's ire."[55] In December 1966 the Higher Education Act passed the legislature easily.

With Raubinger now out of the picture, Hughes was in a position to completely restructure the education community with his appointments of the next commissioner of education as well as the new chancellor of higher education. For both positions he reached beyond the borders of New Jersey. Carl Marburger was chosen as the commissioner of education, and Ralph Dungan was selected as the chancellor. Dungan had served in the administrations of both President Kennedy and President Johnson as a special assistant to the president.[56] At the time he was tapped to serve as the chancellor of higher education in New Jersey, he was serving as the ambassador to Chile. Joel Sterns, who had worked in the Kennedy administration and was then working for Hughes, convinced Dungan to accept the position.

Almost immediately, Dungan became involved in the controversy over the placement of the New Jersey Medical School in Newark. He met with local activists opposing the new medical school. He offered community participation in the governance of the school, and he promised that the new school would provide health care to the surrounding community.[57] Dungan also worked diligently to persuade the state colleges and universities to increase the number of minority students they accepted.[58]

While New Jersey was never able to totally reverse the outward migration of students from New Jersey to other states, in the years after the new governance system was introduced there was a substantial increase in available seats in state schools. The state colleges, which had mainly been in the business of teacher training, were broadened and expanded and other state colleges like Stockton and Ramapo were created. These schools began offering master's and doctoral degrees. In more recent years many of those colleges have become universities offering a multitude of programs in many disciplines. Additionally, the University of Medicine and Dentistry of New Jersey has expanded dramatically, with eight different schools on five campuses across the state and is the largest university of health sciences of its kind in the country.

In 1994, then newly-elected Governor Christine Todd Whitman proposed to eliminate the Board of Higher Education and the chancellor for which Hughes and his peers had fought so hard.[59] She made the proposal as a cost-saving measure, arguing that the state would save $7.4 million.[60] Proponents of abolishing the board and chancellor argued that since the state colleges had been given more independence as a result of a 1986 autonomy law, oversight was no longer necessary. Whitman believed that the responsibility for the colleges and universities could be placed on the individual college presidents and their boards of trustees.[61] Richard Leone, writing in opposition to Whitman's proposal, placed the success of higher education in New Jersey not on the state autonomy act but more directly on the decision of Hughes to create the new structure in 1966. He argued that there was a need for continuing oversight, and that the notion that less government is better was not true.[62] Robert Braun, at the time the education editor for the *Newark Star-Ledger*, also criticized the idea of dismantling the Department of Higher Education, saying the state Higher Education Act "was a thoughtful, considered, debated, tested, and, now, 30 years later, proven idea."[63] Nonetheless, the Whitman proposal became law, and in the following years, various scandals rocked the University of Medicine and Dentistry of New Jersey.[64] The lack of oversight may have contributed to those problems. After the news of the scandals at UMDNJ came out, Braun wrote an article entitled, "Bill comes due for abolishing college oversight."[65]

Years later, Hughes's important efforts in higher education were still being recalled. In 2006, in testimony before the Assembly's Higher Education Committee, Jon Shure, the president of New Jersey Policy Perspective, said, "It was exactly 40 years ago that a visionary Governor, Richard J. Hughes, stood before the state Legislature and said New Jersey was doing an embarrassingly poor job of providing a college education to its young people—and that this had to change. He won passage of the state sales tax and the expansion and improvement of New Jersey's state colleges and universities began in earnest. A lot of good things happened. Capacity increased; quality improved; financial assistance took off-and more New Jersey kids were able to go to college in New Jersey. In short, New Jersey began to rise to its responsibilities."[66] He went on to say, however, that New Jersey was again falling behind in educating many of the young men and women of the state, and that another wake-up call was necessary.[67]

New Jersey has often suffered from the fact that it is tucked between the major cities of New York and Philadelphia. Ben Franklin famously described the state as a barrel tapped at both ends. Many people in northern New Jersey hear more about New York news than they do about New Jersey, and people in southern New Jersey often know more about Philadelphia than they do about their own state. Part of this is attributable to the fact that New Jersey never had a major state television station. That problem was partially solved during the Hughes administration when a statute was passed creating the New Jersey Public Broadcasting Authority to "Establish, own, and operate noncommercial educational television or radio broadcasting stations, one or more public broadcasting and public broadcasting telecommunications networks or systems, and interconnection and program production facilities."[68] About the same time, the voters approved a $7.5 million bond issue to construct four transmitters and a broadcast complex. By 1971 New Jersey Public Television was up and running. This was the result of efforts by the Hughes administration starting in 1967, when the governor created a commission to develop a program for educational television and radio. The commission consisted of five members of the cabinet and twelve representatives from the communications and education field. Again Hughes brought in prominent people to serve. The outside members included such diverse individuals as Edward J. Meade, Jr., who was in charge of public education for the Ford Foundation, and a former Philadelphia Eagles football star, Pete Retzlaff, who had become a sports commentator.[69] Later, other personalities including Merv Griffin were added to the commission. Over the years the Public Broadcasting Network added more stations throughout the state. In 1981, it changed its name to New Jersey Network. The station has been able to make important local news and information available, but despite those efforts, New Jersey residents still obtain much of their news from stations that are focused mainly on New York City and Philadelphia.

Chapter 17

The Hugheses Leaving Morven and Returning to Private Life

BETTY HUGHES WAS AN OUTGOING and vivacious woman, and was a major asset to her husband. Throughout the later part of her life, Betty was engaged in an ongoing battle with her weight. She would eventually deal with a number of illnesses, some of them related to her weight problem, but her occasional bouts of illness did not slow her down. During the years of Hughes's governorship, she was a busy hostess. Her warm and welcoming personality led to lifelong friendships with many visitors including Lady Bird Johnson. She was often asked her opinion and would willingly give it.

Her gift for entertaining led to an invitation to appear on the *Mike Douglas Show*. She was so outgoing and natural during her appearance that she was asked to come back for a number of follow-up visits. Early in 1969, Betty was invited to do her own television talk show on WCAU-TV. Called *Betty Hughes and Friends*, it proved a success, and Betty hosted more than 500 shows over the course of five years. She interviewed many of the important figures of the time, including Walter Cronkite, Lady Bird Johnson, Bishop Fulton J. Sheen, Helen Hayes, Joan Crawford, Rudy Vallee, Hubert Humphrey, Bennett Cerf, and Robert Goulet. Betty became a celebrity in her own right, not just as the wife of the governor. She also did a number of guest spots on other shows. In June 1969, for example, she made a guest appearance on a show called *Della* starring the well-known singer Della Reese.

Betty also wrote a regular column that appeared in a number of newspapers. Called "Memo from Morven," the column covered anything and everything. Subjects ranged from meetings with national and international leaders to how to deal with the problems of raising children. After the governorship ended, the column continued for some time, simply called "Bulletin from Betty."

One of her columns described a visit to Rose Kennedy's home in Palm Beach, Florida. Betty expressed her long-time fascination with the Irish Kennedy family and how excited she was to be able to see Kennedy's home and speak with her. "What's she really like? She is marvelous! She wears a size 8. She does not diet but she does not drink, and does not smoke. She plays golf almost daily. She walks three to four miles a day. She carries her own golf bags. She attends daily Mass at 7:30. Once in a while, she gets really lazy, and lies abed . . . until the 8 A.M. Mass."[1] Betty concluded the column: "This is Mrs. Joseph P. (Rose) Kennedy. A product of this era. A lady by any standards."[2]

In another column written shortly after the assassination of Robert Kennedy, she spoke about her interest in the Kennedy family and her delight as an Irish American when Jack became president. She also described her thrill when she was first invited to the White House as a guest of Jack and Jackie. She expressed deep sympathy over the many tragedies that struck the Kennedy family.[3]

Family life at Morven was another topic close to Betty's heart that became grist for her column. She recounted a day in February 1969, when members of the family made a trip to their summer home at Island Beach, the home Lady Bird Johnson and Mrs. Gvishiani visited during the Glassboro summit. "We brought logs for the fireplace, two Scrabble games, and enough food for Sunday breakfast and lunch. Dick and I and the five youngest children roamed the beach, picked up driftwood, and counted the days till summer. Stopped on Sunday to see an aunt in Asbury Park who's been ill, bearing a quick 'n' easy meat loaf as our hostess present."[4]

One column described a particularly busy few months. She began by explaining that despite a wonderful life she was complaining because she was just plain exhausted. "We have had a great summer and yours truly is just plain exhausted, worn out, dried up, bushed, and very, very tired. In the past four months we've been to Rome for the elevation of the Catholic cardinals. I've had a quick trip to North Carolina to the Duke Clinic. We've been to Denver for an education conference, to the L.B.J. ranch for a two- day visit. We went to Cape Kennedy for the moon launch. Twice to California. Once for a television show and the second time for the state dinner for the astronauts. To Island Beach for a week. To Aspen and Colorado Springs for a governors' conference. In between, three big weddings and three big political teas here at Morven."[5]

Many of her columns and other writings dealt with her weight problem and her weight control program visits to Duke University Hospital. In one article she speculated on why she had difficulty keeping her weight down. She compared herself with other fat women who were unhappy with their lives and often refused to go out because of their weight. She realized that much of her problem was that she was not unhappy with her life. She wrote:

> I was fat and happy. I loved my husband, my children, my life, my friends. I went nearly everyplace I was invited. I was photographed constantly. I swam at Acapulco (size 48 bathing suit), dined at The White House (turquoise brocade tent, custom made). When I thought about it, my rationalization was carefully worked out, and mighty comforting. "After all, I'm 46. A mother. A grandmother. I was slender when it mattered, in my high school and college years. I had a great home life as a child. I was a real prom trotter in those days. I've had two wonderful husbands. I have ten healthy children. I've been to Europe and Mexico and Hawaii and all over this wonderful country. The New Jersey voters elected my husband governor two times, knowing he had a fat wife. To be fat is awful, but to be hungry is worse. Dick is very good natured about it all. Life is short. Why worry?" There you have it. Life is short. Those three little words changed everything. Three good friends and top notch physicians finally convinced me that life was going to be much shorter if I didn't peel off 75 to a hundred pounds."[6]

She was told that she would not live beyond another ten years if she didn't lose weight. She worried that her still young children would not have a mother and wondered, "Where would Dick, already having lost his first wife, ever locate a third wife? True he's bright, good natured, successful and kind. But in ten years he'd be 68, minus a fortune and plus three teenagers. Something would have to be done."[7] The event that finally convinced her to go to Duke was an appearance on the *Mike Douglas Show* together with Bess Meyerson, a former Miss America. She was looking at the tape of the show and realized that while she was only a little older than Meyerson, a viewer could have considered Bess as her daughter. That led her to agree to admit herself to the weight program for the four months that it would take to slim down.[8] So after organizing the family, with the work spread among Hughes, Betty's mother, and Mary "Devey" Abbott, her best friend and personal secretary, she left for Duke. She spent that time eating a special diet consisting primarily of rice, fruit, and other healthy foods. She lost nine and one-half pounds the first week, and then settled into a weekly loss of four or five pounds.[9] She stuck with the regimen, making only one trip back to New Jersey during the four months, for her mother's seventieth birthday party.[10] Many family members did go to Duke to visit her during her stay, however. By the end of the treatment she'd lost seventy-five pounds and was completely off her diabetes medication.

Betty was glad that she lost the weight because the next few months were a whirlwind of major events, including the Democratic National Convention. Another event that occurred during that time involved the christening of the new naval vessel, the S.S. *Trenton.* As the wife of the governor of the state whose capital is Trenton, she was chosen to christen the ship. Her column dealing with that event shows the great pride she had in New Jersey.[11]

In one column she responded to a letter from a citizen who complained that the trips she was taking were costing the state money. The writer specifically alluded to the Apollo 11 liftoff trip and her cross-country driving journey with two station wagons and a gang of children. She explained that because her husband was the official representative from New Jersey, his trip to the lift-off was paid out of the governor's travel allowance, and he had flown economy class to Florida. She had paid for her own trip, and she explained that since she wrote a number of articles during the trip for which she'd been paid, she would take the expense as a business deduction on her income tax. She stressed that the money for the trip to California with the children came primarily from compensation she received from *McCall's* magazine for writing an article about the cross-country journey.[12] Betty also took the opportunity to explain that when a commission recommended increases in state salaries and such increases were authorized, her husband approved all the raises except the raise for himself. She admitted, however, that the governor had declined his raise over her strong objection.[13] Kenneth Kunzman, a close friend and later partner of Hughes in private practice, confirmed the care that the Hugheses took in spending state money, noting that there was a very limited budget for entertainment while Hughes was governor, and when that budget was exhausted, Richard and Betty would pay for entertainment out of their own pockets.[14]

Through the columns and her talk show, Betty got to know many people outside New Jersey. One of them was Bennett Cerf, an author and book publisher, perhaps best known for his long-time role as a panelist on the television show *What's My Line?* His wife Phyllis was known as Thruppie.

Hughes recalled, "After Bennett Cerf died Betty used to talk to his widow Thruppie. Once she called and asked Thruppie what she was doing. Thruppie said, 'I'm sitting in my kitchen, drinking whiskey and playing poker with a real nice guy, Bob Wagner.' A few months later they were married."[15] Bob Wagner was the mayor of New York, Robert F. Wagner.

Under the Constitution of New Jersey, the governor can have two terms in succession. A former governor can run again after he or she has been out of office for a term. Therefore, in 1969, Richard Hughes could not be a candidate. The Republican candidate who won the primary on June 3, 1969, was William Cahill. Cahill came from the more moderate wing of the Republican Party and he ran as a moderate in a field with four other candidates.[16] He had certain advantages. He was a Catholic in a state with a large Catholic population. He had credentials as a former agent of the Federal Bureau of Investigation, a first assistant Camden County prosecutor, and a former special deputy attorney general of the state. Those credentials suggested he would give priority to the fight against organized crime. Additionally, as a result of reapportionment, he had served in two fairly different congressional districts in the southern part of the state. As a result he was well-known by many voters in that region.

The early favorite in the Republican primary, however, appeared to be Charles Sandman, the most conservative candidate.[17] It was dogma among New Jersey politicians that when the Republicans choose a conservative candidate, the Democrat will win, and when they choose a moderate, the Republican will win. Nelson Gross, the Bergen County Republican leader at the time, believing in the prevailing wisdom that it was necessary to pick a moderate to win, decided to swing the support of Bergen County to one of the moderates, William Cahill. With the support of Bergen County, Cahill won the nomination.[18]

The Democratic candidate was Robert Meyner, who had served two terms as governor before Hughes. While the state constitution barred more than two successive terms, a person may be elected to a third term after another governor has served. Meyner had remained active in politics through the chairmanship of many commissions and other activities. By the end of his two terms, however, Meyner had alienated some of the party leaders. Nevertheless, he had sufficient continuing popularity to win the primary. The fact that five different candidates vied for the Democratic nomination contributed to his win.[19] In spite of his primary win, Meyner had lukewarm support throughout the general campaign, which was not run very effectively. Additionally, John Kenny, the Hudson County leader, still disliked Meyner because of his unwillingness to support Kennedy in 1960 and his unwillingness to accept the recommendations of Kenny on appointments and other issues. Kenny actively campaigned against Meyner, and Hudson County, a traditionally Democratic County, went for Cahill.[20] Cahill soundly defeated Meyner (1,411,905 to 911,003).

As the incumbent governor and long-time Democratic loyalist, Hughes would naturally support Meyner. However, Cahill was philosophically more in tune with Hughes than the more fiscally conservative Meyner. While his support for the Democratic Party would not let him admit it, Hughes was probably happy that Cahill won, and when some years later he was tapped by Cahill to be the chief justice of the New Jersey Supreme Court, he probably was even happier about Cahill's victory.

Shortly before a new governor is inaugurated, the outgoing governor gives a final legislative address. Hughes's message epitomized his concerns. "Let history record that we who have governed during these past eight years set as our goal the protection and uplifting of those New Jerseyans who are truly forgotten—who are least able to speak for themselves. . . . For government will always hear those who speak most loudly—those with long membership lists and heavy treasure chests. But government must have a special sense of mission, and make a special effort, to hear the ignored and the neglected."[21] This sentiment epitomized some of the things he did as governor. He would often tour state facilities, and react forcefully when he saw intolerable conditions. In a letter to Governor Kean, Hughes wrote, "One of the chief happy memories of my time as Governor involves my constant visits to institutions, for the blind, the retarded and elderly handicapped. . . . I saw some pitiful physical conditions and raised hell about them for eight years. I like to think I left them a little better by the time I was deposed in 1970."[22] In a letter to George Amick, a reporter, Hughes wrote about a visit to an institution in Totowa. "Seeing pitiful sights like kids suffering elephantiasis, with heads as big as watermelons. The Nursery was not air conditioned, the cost of $65,000 being too rich for legislative blood. I put some feet to the fire when I returned to Trenton, and soon got an appropriation."[23] He continued, "The conditions we saw on one of the visits, at the then 'feeble-minded colony' at New Lisbon, caused the late Senator Tony Grossi to weep, and even the late Charlie Sandman, the Senate President, to unbend and give me support on a corrective bond issue.[24] In another reference he cited a visit to the Children's Unit of Trenton Psychiatric Hospital that resulted in improvements being made shortly thereafter.

There were many assessments of Hughes after he completed his term. In an article entitled "Label Him Unlabelable," Earl Josephson pointed out many of the successes of Hughes but also some of the problems he had failed to solve effectively.[25] He recognized that Hughes could talk the talk with the bosses, but simultaneously gain the respect of intellectuals and college professors whose ideas helped improve the state. Josephson suggested that Hughes had neglected some state problems, but recognized that Hughes believed "you could fight just so many battles at one time."[26]

Allegations of Mob Influence

One of the battles that Hughes was criticized for not fighting rigorously enough had to do with mob influence in New Jersey politics. Hughes turned his attention to this issue late in 1968, when William J. Brennan III (the son of Justice Brennan of the United States Supreme Court) was directing a special investigation of organized crime for the New Jersey Attorney General's Office. On December 11, 1968, Brennan charged that some state legislators were "too comfortable" with the mob. His allegations created a firestorm within New Jersey political circles. Hughes demanded that Brennan give the names of those legislators to a select group of legislative leaders made up of both Republicans and Democrats. Brennan refused. On December 16, Hughes directed Attorney General Sills to convene a statewide grand jury to take testimony in the matter. Because of the rules of the grand jury, the information would be kept confidential. At the same time, there was a continuing effort by the governor to require Brennan to disclose the names to a select number of legislators. The legislature, however, balked at the idea that only a small number of legislators should hear the names, and demanded public disclosure. Hughes believed that it was inappropriate to present the names in public because of the potential injury to reputations of innocent parties, and he said that a public disclosure would be "unconscionable."[27] While all of this was brewing, Hughes appointed two individuals to the newly created State Commission of Investigation (SCI), which was created to investigate organized crime and official corruption in New Jersey. The commission was to include four members—two Democrats and two Republicans. Two were to be appointed by the governor and one each by the speaker of the Assembly and the president of the Senate. The Governor chose William F. Hyland, who had already served as president of the Department of Public Utilities and would later serve as attorney general, and Charles Bertini, the incoming president of the New Jersey Bar Association.

Hyland described how Hughes convinced him to serve as chairman of the SCI. Hyland had six children and had spent many years in public service, both as an elected member of the legislature and as head of the Department of Public Utilities. He decided to leave political life in order to make more money as a lawyer. His plan to return to full-time private practice coincided with Hughes's plan to make him chairman. Hughes and Hyland had become close personal friends. They traveled together with their wives on trips to the Bahamas, Bermuda, and other places. Hughes importuned him to take the chairmanship. Hyland tried to refuse. Finally, after repeated requests, Hughes called him at home on Christmas Eve. Hughes said he was in Hawaii, "sick as a dog," and he was being criticized for failure to appoint a chairman. By the end of the call, Hyland had agreed to serve as chairman of the SCI.[28] Hyland believed that the Brennan allegations, while unfortunate, led to the creation of a number of important methods of dealing with crime, including the statewide grand jury, the witness immunity statute, and wiretap legislation.[29]

Shortly after the Brennan allegations, the legislature created a bipartisan commission to investigate mob corruption within the legislature. The State Commission of Investigation deferred to the Legislative Commission to explore the issue. Eventually, the names of three legislators appeared in newspaper stories describing alleged corruption. They were Sido Ridolfi, John Selecky, and David Friedland. Ridolfi, a state senator, had served for sixteen years in the Senate, and had been president of the Senate for two years. He was also a close friend of Hughes. In fact, he had introduced Hughes to his wife, Betty. Ridolfi and Friedland were Democrats; Selecky was a Republican.

There were apparently two reasons why Hughes wanted Brennan's allegations to be kept private. First, he wanted to protect the legislators' reputations, and second, he hoped to protect the reputation of the young Brennan himself. Hughes was a friend of Justice William Brennan, and believed that the information would end up being embarrassing to the son if he had insufficient support for his allegations. Shortly thereafter, the young Brennan was relieved as prosecutor of the state's investigation of the Mafia and reassigned to other responsibilities. Arthur Sills, the attorney general, then established an organized crime unit. Sills was upset with Brennan because the allegations interfered with his own political ambitions.[30] Sills was hoping to run for governor after Hughes completed his term. Hughes eventually brought Brennan into the office of the Counsel to the Governor. Hughes never wanted to fire anyone.

An article in the *New York Times* concerning the incident showed Hughes's continuing ability to carry two buckets at the same time. He thought Brennan's original charges were a "mistake," because they impugned the reputations of people with insufficient evidence, but he still considered Brennan "an honorable, decent, fine young man."[31] On December 30, 1968, Brennan testified before the Legislative Committee. The general reaction was that there was very little support for the allegations.[32] The *New York Times* reported: "In any event, there was one comment here today that created no controversy. That was when Mr. Brennan told the committee that if he had to do it all over again, he would have kept quiet."[33] The allegations against Ridolfi were that he had represented alleged Mafia members in the purchase of a house and an exterminating business. The complaint against Assemblyman Selecky was that he had written a character reference for the nephew of a top Mafia leader and against Friedland that he attempted to stop a complaint against a Mafia loan shark. Ultimately, the Legislative Committee, led by the independent-minded Alfred N. Beadleston, determined that there was no legitimate basis for any criminal charges. However, the committee did criticize Ridolfi and Selecky for their relationship with mob figures, saying those relationships reflected badly on the legislature. The committee also found that the issue concerning Friedland was too confused for the committee to make a decision. Although no criminal charges were ever brought, the allegations hurt the legislators' political careers.

Some years later Friedland was, in fact, indicted and convicted in connection with other questionable activities. Friedland's history is fascinating. As a young man and lawyer, he was known for "his brilliance, compassion, wit and courage."[34] He was a member of the Assembly from Hudson County for many years. During his time as a legislator he was suspended from the practice of law for six months for "act[ing] improperly in the settling of a loan-sharking case."[35] Despite this, he was reelected and continued to have substantial power within the Assembly. In 1980, he was indicted and convicted for receiving kickbacks in conjunction with his role as general counsel for a pension fund. He was sentenced to seven years in prison but avoided that punishment by agreeing to help the United States Attorney's Office stop other kickback and embezzling schemes in New Jersey. However, during this time he became involved in another illegal scheme. In 1985, when he learned he was about to be indicted for that one, he faked his own death in a scuba diving accident in the Bahamas. He then became a fugitive but was eventually caught in the Maldives, an archipelago in the Indian Ocean, in 1987.[36] He pled guilty to RICO conspiracy charges and was sentenced to almost sixteen years in prison. He again tried to negotiate by offering to serve as an informant, but his offer was turned down.

At the very close of the Hughes governorship there was a public release of tapes recorded by the Federal Bureau of Investigation involving Angelo (Gyp) DeCarlo, a reputed Mafia chief in New Jersey. These tapes mentioned many individuals in New Jersey, including Hughes. As he had done previously when others were named in various reports without sufficient grounds of support, Hughes immediately denounced the dissemination of the tapes as a threat to the reputations of innocent parties and charged that such sensationalism endangered American concepts of personal freedom, injured innocent persons, and did not "put a single hood in jail."[37] At the time, United States Attorney Frederick Lacey, who would later serve as a Federal District Court judge, was aggressively seeking out corruption in New Jersey. A federal judge had released the tapes in conjunction with a case being prosecuted by Lacey. Hughes was mentioned on the tapes by a Mafia leader who bragged that he had met the governor in 1962 and by another who discussed how the mob would operate under the Hughes administration.[38] However, Hughes had no recollection of meeting the person he was alleged to have met. Hughes had met hundreds of thousands of people during his career and even with his tremendous recall for names it would have been difficult for him to be sure. Hughes was particularly incensed by the allegation made by a Mafia member on the tapes that DeCarlo had gotten John Kenny to convince Hughes to choose Colonel David B. Kelly as the head of the state police. Hughes had great respect for Kelly and confidence in his abilities. He had seen the great work he had done to set up the summit meeting at Glassboro. Although he ultimately disagreed on strategy with Kelly during the Newark riots, he had chosen Kelly to coordinate operations during the upheaval. With regard to the appointment of Kelly, Hughes said, "It was my choice alone due to my knowledge of his outstanding record and unimpeachable reputation, and my decision was fully approved by the Attorney General of New Jersey. Colonel Kelly is one of the nation's finest law enforcement officials. That is why Federal authorities respect him so highly and why I appointed him and why Governor-elect Cahill has re-appointed him."[39] Thus, he argued that John Kenny had no role in the appointment process.

Colonel Kelly continued to serve in his position until almost the end of the Cahill administration.

Hughes seemed somewhat vulnerable at this moment because at the same time the bribery trial of Judge Ralph DeVita was going on. The news stories about the DeCarlo tapes often included mention of the DeVita trial and the fact that Hughes had appointed DeVita after being warned of the possibility of mob connections. Additionally, these tapes came out shortly after the controversy caused by William Brennan's charges that some legislators were too close to the mob. These controversies made the last months of the Hughes administration difficult. But most thought that the accomplishments of Hughes and the fact that none of the allegations involved Hughes personally far outweighed any of the difficulties.

On January 18, 1970, shortly before Hughes stepped down as governor, John McLaughlin, a well-known newsman of New Jersey, wrote a lengthy piece about Hughes in which he both praised and criticized Hughes. His piece suggested that Hughes had been too willing to take on faith the goodness of many of those in political life. He said, "Indeed, for Hughes, the Democratic Party is almost a religion. He believes in it. He believes it does stand for the things it says it does. And he thinks the people in it who, from time to time, do good things, are good people. He is a sophisticated man in other areas, but his approach to politics is that of a fundamentalist. He takes a lot on faith."[40] McLaughlin did not accuse Hughes of doing anything inappropriate himself but suggested that the governor could have been more vigilant in seeking to root out corruption. He acknowledged that Hughes tended to accept the situation he inherited and made some deals in order to get the things he wanted most. "He is a man of extraordinary persuasive powers. He gave them [referring to the leaders] their appointments—but he exacted his price. They gave him the votes for his programs and they gave him the Senate confirmations on the appointments he wanted. So Hughes got his new departments of Transportation, Community Affairs and Higher Education. He almost got his income tax and he did get his sales tax. He got his gun control and drunk-driving laws and he got a set of pollution control laws that are among the strongest anywhere. He got a middle-income housing program and he got hundreds of millions of dollars in bond issues, and in the process he built a national reputation as one of the very best governors in America."[41]

An editorial in the *Bergen Record* said, "Sometimes to reporters of the beat, it seemed that wherever they went across the state, there Dick Hughes would be, chatting with a kid on the street, saying his respects to the family of the deceased, toasting the parents of the bride, snipping a ribbon, dedicating a hospital, reaching out to touch human hands. He has borne with quiet fortitude certain personal adversities. He has worn himself thin in the service of the state. Now he goes back to a home of his own, a life of his own, the practice of law he loves, to his family. It is indicated that one reach for his hand and say well done, good and faithful servant. It remains difficult to say goodbye."[42]

In her first column after the governor returned to private life, Betty wrote that throughout her husband's governorship she had avoided commenting on political matters and particularly on her husband as political leader. However, now that Hughes was no longer the governor of New Jersey, Betty wanted to finally express herself with regard to her husband. She wrote, "I say a finer man than Dick Hughes does not walk the earth."[43]

Private Practice Redux

After Hughes completed his eight years as governor, he and Betty and the family bade goodbye to Morven and returned to private life. He joined the firm of Pindar McElroy Connell Foley and Geiser. It was renamed Hughes McElroy Connell Foley and Geiser. The firm was located in Newark, so he would often take the train from Trenton up to Newark.

He had, for many years, been close personal friends with Adrian "Bud" Foley and John Pindar, another partner in the firm. They had become friends while he was a trial judge, and Pindar and Foley had been helpful when Hughes opened his own office in Trenton after leaving the bench. They and Walter Connell, Bill McElroy, and Ted Geiser had, in the waning months of his tenure, invited Hughes to join their firm. Hughes said: "We had always been friends and I wanted to do it. Just before Christmas, to elude the reporters, instead of coming to meet me at the State House, I asked them to meet me at Morven. We talked about it, over a sandwich, in the presence of the Chairman of my board, my beloved wife Betty Hughes. We made our deal, not to be publicized until I left as Governor in January."[44]

Hughes immediately began handling his own cases, taking depositions and willingly shouldering the tasks of a true working lawyer. Ken Kunzman, a partner in the firm, said that Hughes would often say that he thought he was going to be sitting in a big corner office musing about the law and instead found himself hustling around the state representing clients. Kunzman recalled that he did it with zest.[45]

Edward Deutsch, now a partner at McElroy Deutsch Mulvaney and Carpenter, was a first-year associate at the firm when Hughes joined. He was assigned to work with Hughes, and although he was happy about the assignment, he wasn't quite sure how it would go. Hughes gave him a case to work on, and because of his eye difficulties, he wanted Deutsch to read all the case materials and research the issues involved. After a week of research and study Deutsch met with Hughes and briefed him on the case for a number of hours. Hughes asked relatively few questions and Deutsch was a little worried. Later the same day, Deutsch sat in on Hughes's meeting with the client. Hughes had absorbed all that Deutsch had told him and explained it lucidly and succinctly. Deutsch was amazed at Hughes's ability to retain so much information and to present it in such a logical and articulate manner.[46]

Hughes's contacts brought a great deal of business to the firm. The Engelhard Corporation, headed by Charles Engelhard, Hughes's friend, sent business to him. Law firms from New York with whom he had been involved also sent business his way.

For the first time in a long time the governor was making significant amounts of money. His salary as governor would not have covered the expenses for his large family. Betty's position as a writer and television personality actually paid many of the bills while Hughes was in office. Hughes himself noted that Betty had made more money during his last year as governor than he did.[47]

Hughes's reputation and contacts may have occasionally paid dividends. Kunzman recalled one case involving opposing lawyers who were quite aggressive. When the lawyers were called into the chambers of the judge, they saw pictures of the judge with Hughes hanging on the wall. They decided to settle quickly.

Kunzman also recalled Hughes being sensational in mentoring young lawyers in the firm. He was viewed as a team player who would work with all the lawyers in the firm. Additionally, he continued his habit of responding to all correspondence. Kunzman marveled at his determination to answer all correspondence immediately. Occasionally, when Kunzman was leaving the office Hughes would still be busy responding to the many letters on his desk.[48]

Crusading on Corrections

But Hughes would not stay out of the public eye for long. Shortly after his return to private life, the American Bar Association, at the urging of United States Supreme Court Chief Justice Warren Burger, created a Commission on Correctional Facilities and Services. The president of the Bar Association appointed Hughes as its first chair. Hughes explained why he accepted the appointment. "I accepted for two reasons, first (sentimentally) because my beloved father had been warden of the New Jersey State Prison (then and now an ancient and terrible edifice) when I was seven years old, and secondly, because in my eight years as Governor of New Jersey, with all the pressures for tax, educational and other reform, I had never been able to reach that correctional revival so badly needed in New Jersey and practically every other state. And so I seem to be getting a second chance, and I intend to devote a large portion of my professional time to this great work."[49]

In 1970, Hughes attended the meeting of the American Bar Association in St. Louis and heard from Burger about the importance of correctional improvement. He attended the first meeting of the commission in June of that year at the United States Supreme Court in Washington. The commission consisted of many luminaries including Robert McNamara, Karl Menninger, and George Meany.

When a report of the commission's work was finally released in 1975 (after Hughes had already resigned), Robert McKay, the distinguished dean of New York University Law School and the successor to Hughes as chairman, gave much of the credit for the success of the commission to Hughes. He said Hughes "traveled tirelessly to carry the message of correctional reform to the four corners of the country, and was always available to staff for necessary consultations."[50]

The work of the commission was initially supported by the Ford Foundation and later by other federal and state grants. Hughes worked with the staff to develop financial resources to support the commission's wide-ranging plans. Not surprisingly, the commission discovered great problems with the entire system of corrections throughout the country and realized the need for action. The commission proposed a twofold strategy: first, to begin some well-conceived action programs as quickly as possible; second, to develop a major blueprint for future action.[51] The commission chose thirteen new projects to begin their efforts. These projects spanned the gamut of problems inherent in the corrections system. Among them, to cite some examples, was a national volunteer parole aide program in which almost 2,000 lawyers worked one-on-one with parolees; a national clearinghouse on offender employment restrictions that focused on removing unreasonable restrictions; and an educational program for correctional officers.[52]

The work of the commission also stimulated actions by various state bar associations to develop similar programs within their own states.[53] While the commission report recognized that these efforts were not sufficient to solve all the problems of the correctional system, their efforts helped to focus attention on these difficult issues and to begin movement toward improvement.

At the same time Hughes was chairing the commission, he served as a delegate to the United Nations Correctional Reform Conference. This work took him beyond the United States. One meeting he attended was held in Kyoto, Japan. He described the scene: "So began my wonderful week in Japan. Gathering in the great international conference hall (one of the largest in the world), about 1,500 delegates met in exciting grandeur. Rising to receive Their Imperial Highnesses, Prince and Princess Takamatsu (whom I met personally at a cocktail reception later that evening), we then heard the chief legal authorities of Japan and other nations. The assembly hall, very like the UN itself, with six banks of interpreters in Japanese, English, French, Russian, etc. The Babel of many tongues, the courteous bowing of the Japanese, the inspiring opening statements, the interesting workshops, the exchange of programs and techniques—all made for a most interesting conference."[54]

On a more local level, Hughes was appointed by Governor Cahill to serve on an important state committee called the New Jersey Tax Policy Committee. Hughes's work in these areas helped make the transition from governor to private attorney easier. He was able to continue his involvement in public service, while simultaneously building a private practice to help cover the expenses of college education for his large family.

During this time he also served on the board of directors of a publicly owned Real Estate Investment Trust (REIT) sponsored by Beneficial Standard Life Insurance Company of Los Angeles. James Kellogg, a vice president at Walson & Co. in New York City, then the third-largest brokerage house in the country, knew that Beneficial Standard wanted to sell its REIT in the east. The leadership of that company wanted a prominent east coast name for membership on the board. Kellogg recommended Hughes. Kellogg's father had been on the board of the Port Authority during the time that Hughes was governor. Again combining functions, Hughes was delighted to serve on the board in part because the meetings were in California, where one of his children was then living. He could combine the meetings of the board with visits.[55]

Hughes had more time to enjoy his children and engage in their lives. His son Tom was still quite young, and Hughes found himself "eagerly going to a parent teachers meeting and talking to the parents of other small children."[56]

Hughes, however, did not and could not give up his love for politics. He continued to be involved. Governor Byrne remembered him as a great campaigner who worked for him during his gubernatorial run.[57] He was always willing to campaign for Democrats who requested his support. He was elected as Democratic National committeeman from New Jersey. There was even some talk that Hughes might again run for governor. When Hughes accepted the chairmanship of a major fundraising dinner in Essex County, at least one commentator speculated that this was partly to position himself for a future run for office. While recognizing that Hughes was doing so well in private practice that it was unlikely he would return to Trenton, the commentator said, "But the cold facts are there, including his acceptance of the chairmanship of a political dinner. Other indications that his feet are still in the political arena can be seen at his numerous appearances at political dinners."[58] But Hughes so enjoyed those dinners that he may have had no ulterior motives.

He also enjoyed events that celebrated his Irish heritage. One such event was a Saint Patrick's Day dinner in Massachusetts at which he related the history of the governor's mansion to illustrate the irony of his ascent to the position of governor. The historic house was owned by the Stocktons, an old and respected family in New Jersey history. But like most of the old respected families at the time, they were Protestants and they looked down upon the Catholic Irish. In his telling of the history of the house, Hughes included comments from early members of the Stockton family referring to the boisterous drunken activities of the Irish. Hughes further related that the Stocktons would often discipline their Irish servants with whips. He concluded by saying, "The next time there is any record of anything Irish happening at Morven was Saint Patrick's Day, 1962 when the Hughes clan moved in. And now another Governor of Irish lineage is in residence. How does one say 'touche' in Gaelic?"[59]

This more easygoing period of Hughes's life was not without shadows. Shortly after Hughes stepped down from the governorship, two of his trusted associates, Robert Burkhardt and John Kervick, were indicted. This distressed Hughes, who had been well served by both men. In the late 1960s and early 1970s two United States attorneys, Frederick Lacey and Herbert Stern, began to focus on corruption in New Jersey. They indicted and convicted many of the state's important political figures, both Democrats and Republicans. Two of the most notable convictions involved the mayor of Newark, Hugh Addonizio, and the mayor of Jersey City, John V. Kenny. While Hughes knew and worked with both of those men, they were not close friends and associates in the way Burkhardt and Kervick were. Both of them had worked in the Hughes administration—Burkhardt as secretary of state and Kervick as treasurer.

Both men pleaded guilty to conspiracy and bribery.[60] There was some suggestion at the time that Hughes may have been involved in the crimes committed by Burkhardt and Kervick. A vicious rumor was floated that Hughes had escaped indictment by one vote in the grand jury. Herbert Stern, the United States attorney, immediately sought to dispel that rumor. Paul Hoffman, who wrote a book about Stern, recounted, "Stern labeled it 'an unmitigated falsehood.' 'I will proceed against anybody,' he said, 'regardless of position, power or influence, if he's violated the law of the United States. But I'm not going to sit by and let anybody, through whispers, gossip or innuendo, try and destroy another man's reputation.'"[61]

Hughes, who displayed marked loyalty to his friends, had to face the fact that some of his closest friends had disappointed him. Years later, however, in a letter supporting Burkhardt's son for a position, he recalled not the disappointment of Burkhardt's actions, but his respect for what Burkhardt had achieved. He wrote to Governor Mario Cuomo, "No single figure, including myself, is more responsible for the accomplishments of my Administration, conceded, on both sides of the aisle to be the most impressive since the tenure of Woodrow Wilson. . . . One time we visited Bob Kennedy at the Justice Department shortly after the assassination, and Bob Kennedy brought tears to Burkhardt's eyes when he said that John Kennedy had told him to line up Bob Burkhardt to direct his 1964 campaign!"[62]

Despite those difficulties, Hughes's years after his governorship were a rewarding combination of private practice, public service, politics, and family.

Chapter 18

Chief Justice

HUGHES WAS THE ONLY PERSON in New Jersey history to serve as both the state's governor and its chief justice.[1] Hughes's appointment to the position of chief justice of the New Jersey Supreme Court came as a shock to many in the state because he was appointed by Republican Governor William Cahill. In typical Hughes fashion, however, the men were actually good friends and respected each other a great deal, despite their allegiances to different political parties. The two, who were both Irish Catholics, first met when Hughes was a judge and Cahill was a trial lawyer. Hughes described Cahill as "a fine lawyer" who "had tried cases before me."[2] They also worked together while Cahill was a congressman and Hughes was governor.[3]

Cahill's liberal leanings led to problems during his administration. He alienated some of his Republican constituency by supporting an income tax and other liberal positions. In addition, Paul Sherwin, his secretary of state, as well as other party leaders close to Cahill, were indicted.[4] It was not a surprise, therefore, when he lost the 1973 Republican gubernatorial primary to Congressman Charles Sandman, the conservative he had beaten in 1969. Sandman subsequently lost to Brendan Byrne in the general election by a margin of 1,397,613 to 676,235.

Byrne, who served in the Hughes administration as a member of the Public Utilities Commission and, before that, as prosecutor of Essex County, had stepped down from his position as a Superior Court judge to run for governor. The Republicans were suffering from scandals at both the national and state levels and the idea of a governor who was a former prosecutor and judge was very appealing to New Jersey voters.[5]

In August 1973, Joseph Weintraub stepped down as chief justice of the New Jersey Supreme Court after sixteen years. Governor Cahill appointed his chief counsel, Pierre Garvin, to succeed him. Garvin, tragically, died just a few months later. Cahill was already a lame duck and in November, Byrne won the general election. Although Cahill knew the Democrats would never let him appoint a Republican as chief justice, he still wanted to make the appointment. There are varying stories as to who first suggested that he choose Hughes,[6] but eventually Cahill decided to appoint his old friend.

When the opportunity was presented, Hughes had to consider the financial consequences. Serving as chief justice would be a significant financial loss. The salary of the chief justice was not comparable to what he was earning in private practice. Betty nonetheless urged him to accept, arguing that the chief justice post was a perfect finale to a wonderful career.

Richard Leone, who had served in the Hughes administration and was Byrne's director of transition, recalled a meeting with Cahill and Richard DeKorte at Morven to discuss the transition.[7] As the meeting was coming to an end, Cahill said there was one last appointment he wanted to make during the lame duck session—the appointment of the chief justice. Leone said he did not think Byrne would stand for that. Cahill replied, "He'll stand for this—it's Dick Hughes."[8] The next day Leone reported Cahill's intention to appoint the chief justice to Byrne. Leone noticed that, as he initiated the idea, Byrne's shoulders tensed, and he was about to object, but when Leone said that Hughes was the appointee, Byrne immediately relaxed and eventually he acquiesced. While Byrne clearly wanted to choose the chief justice himself, he could not object to the appointment of the man he had happily worked for, and whom he knew to be eminently qualified.[9] Byrne, however, did reach out to Chief Justice Weintraub to ask his opinion of Hughes. Weintraub approved the choice.[10]

In many ways, Hughes was an ideal candidate to serve as chief justice of New Jersey's highest court. He had many years of experience as both a lawyer and a judge. He also had the administrative skills, acquired during his governorship, needed to oversee a large and complex court system. The chief justice in New Jersey, unlike the chief justices in some states, actively manages the judicial system. For example, the chief justice determines who will serve as assignment judges, those judges in each vicinage who are responsible for the management of the courts and judicial personnel within the vicinage. The chief justice designates those judges who will sit on the Appellate Division and also decides the appropriate assignments for all Superior Court judges. The chief justice is also responsible for running the support staff for the entire judiciary. Although there was some question about his ability as an administrator, Justice Morris Pashman, who served on the court with Hughes, said, "Chief Justice Hughes was not only a great jurist, he was also an excellent administrator."[11] Pashman also indicated that Hughes put in place many administrative innovations that greatly improved the justice system.

Hughes's tenure as chief justice represented a sea change from that of his predecessor. For sixteen years Justice Weintraub, a brilliant legal scholar, ran the court and seemed to dominate it. Weintraub had a distinguished legal background, graduating from Cornell University Phi Beta Kappa, and attending Cornell Law School. There he won special honors and was editor-in-chief of the Law Quarterly. Coincidentally, he attended Newark's Barringer High School with future Justice William Brennan of the United States Supreme Court. Justice Daniel O'Hern, a member of the New Jersey Supreme Court, who had served as a clerk to Justice Brennan during his first year on the U.S. Supreme Court, said, "Of the two of them, I suppose that on their high school graduation day in 1924, classmates would have predicted for Joseph Weintraub the greater promise for a career in the law."[12] Weintraub, however, was not adept at dealing with others. Justice O'Hern quoted Governor Brendan Byrne as saying, "Weintraub was so confident of his own powers of reasoning that he could not understand how others might not reach the same conclusion."[13] Hughes, by contrast, was always willing to listen to the other side and, as Stanley Van Ness so nicely put it, "would suffer fools gladly."[14] He also had a great relationship with his own colleagues on the court. Justice Pashman said, "Richard Hughes is a man of great humility, strong character, wide knowledge, and utmost integrity. He has a quality that spells quiet decency, warm friendliness, and simple dignity."[15] Pashman also noted that Hughes gave each of the associate justices ample opportunity to express their views and was willing to tolerate dissent.

Under Weintraub, the bar's relationship with the court deteriorated. The court issued a rule, for example, which drastically reduced contingent fees lawyers could receive. There are three ways attorneys charge for their services: billing for the hours of work performed; a flat fee to be paid regardless of the time required; or a contingent fee. In the latter, the attorney agrees that his or her compensation will depend upon the amount received; if nothing is recovered, the attorney does not earn a fee. The contingent fee agreement permits individuals who might otherwise be unable to do so to retain an attorney. A tradition developed under which attorneys in New Jersey charged one third of a client's recovery as a fee, and some believed this was too high. Under its rule-making power, the New Jersey Supreme Court issued a rule effective in January 1972 which had the effect of severely limiting fees on larger recoveries.[16] While the rule provided for traditional fees on smaller verdicts, it severely limited awards on higher verdicts. Essentially, fees were reduced from one third on all recoveries to 20 percent on amounts from $50,000 to $100,000 and 10 percent on amounts over $100,000. The American Trial Lawyers Association brought suit challenging the constitutionality of the rule and the trial court struck it down.[17] Hughes wrote the opinion for the Supreme Court upholding the court's power to issue the rule, citing New Jersey's constitution, which vests in the Supreme Court "jurisdiction over the admission to the practice of law and the discipline of persons admitted."[18] In the decision, Hughes strongly asserted the court's authority over the lawyers of the state. However, with his desire to please all sides as long as his basic principles were upheld, he stated, "We have no doubt that the power [to control contingent fees] exists. . . . But whether R. 1:21–7 should continue as an ongoing rule of court, whether it should be modified or whether it should be repealed and the problem attacked in some other way are matters to which this decision has not addressed itself."[19] He was thus signaling to the lawyers that he was not intransigent on the issue. Eventually, the court significantly modified the rule to increase the allowable percentages.

New Jersey forbids any member of the judiciary to have any involvement in politics. At one point, that prohibition even extended to spouses, a restriction that was justified as necessary to maintain public confidence in the integrity of the judicial system. Ellen Gaulkin, the wife of Judge Geoffrey Gaulkin, sought permission to run for a seat on the Weehawken Board of Education. In a letter to Judge Gaulkin, the New Jersey Supreme Court refused permission, relying on the presumption that society would believe that when the spouse of a judge is politically active, the judge is also politically active. Ellen Gaulkin then sought a formal review by the court. After that review, the court in a unanimous opinion by Chief Justice Hughes reversed its position and permitted her to run for office. Hughes noted the growing trend in the law to recognize the independence of spouses.[20] He recognized that no other state in the country had such a stringent limitation on the spouse of a judge.[21] Hughes wrote, "While we now see the need and justice of withdrawing the Court's previous disapproval of spousal political involvement, which we do by this opinion, we are equally determined that every precaution shall be taken to assure that the judiciary itself shall continue its careful separation from direct or indirect involvement in politics."[22] Rosemary Higgins Cass, who would later become a judge herself, wrote a brief in the matter on behalf of the New Jersey State Bar Association. She asked the court to consider a hypothetical question: if the vast majority of the judges were women, would the court feel that all the husbands should be barred from all political activity?[23] Judge Cass recalled that Hughes told her afterwards that there was an additional advocate arguing for Judge Cass's position: his wife, Betty.

Two Key Social Issues

The New Jersey Supreme Court before, during, and after the Hughes years dealt with two particularly important social issues. The court basically led the nation in confronting the problems of inadequate urban schools and insufficient provision of low- and moderate-income housing. While some argued that the court was intruding on the role of the legislature, the court found it imperative to deal with these pressing concerns. The two cases—or more properly series of cases—focusing on these issues were *Robinson v. Cahill*[24] and *NAACP v. Mount Laurel*.[25]

As governor, Hughes continually sought to increase spending for education. He was successful in finding money to support the county colleges and the state colleges. Because of the emphasis on home rule and the lack of a large state budget, however, he was never able to increase dramatically state spending for the public schools. By 1973, the state was supplying 27 percent of the funds for the public schools while the local municipalities were providing most of the remainder. The state's percentage contribution was higher than it was when Hughes became governor, but it was still well below the national average.[26]

The heavy emphasis on local funding resulted in significant disparities between the spending on education in poor urban districts and wealthy suburban districts. Additionally, the tax bases of many cities had been drained by the flight of residents and businesses to the suburbs. The cities also faced the financial strains of addressing social problems.

Shortly before Hughes became chief justice, the New Jersey Supreme Court was presented with a case that challenged the existing system of school funding. The plaintiffs in the case, *Robinson v. Cahill*, were students in poor urban districts whose schools were failing to provide an adequate education. The case was argued on a number of grounds. The first was Equal Protection under the United States Constitution. But just as the

Robinson case was progressing through the New Jersey courts, a similar case from Texas was being heard by the United States Supreme Court.[27] In that case, the U.S. Supreme Court held that the Texas system, which was similar to New Jersey's, was not unconstitutional. The New Jersey courts were therefore unable to find the system in New Jersey in violation of the Equal Protection Clause of the United States Constitution.

However, the New Jersey Supreme Court, in an opinion by Chief Justice Weintraub, did find that the existing system of school funding, which relied so heavily on property taxes, was unconstitutional. The decision in *Robinson* rested on a specific provision of New Jersey's constitution that the State has an obligation to provide a thorough and efficient education for all students from age five to eighteen.[28] The court recognized that the poorer urban centers were burdened by what the court referred to as "municipal overload." Cities had so many financial burdens, and had lost so much of their tax base, that they were simply unable to spend sufficient funds on their school systems. The court did not identify any specific remedy. Rather, it ordered the legislature to come up with a solution to the constitutional problem.

By the time Hughes became chief justice, the legislature had not yet devised a solution. Throughout his years as chief justice, the issue of school funding repeatedly came before the court. The court grappled with the difficult legal issues involved in trying to force the executive and legislative branches of the government to provide the necessary funds to improve the schools in urban areas. At first, Hughes moved slowly, trying to reconcile the needs of the schools with the principle of separation of powers. Clearly, the legislature was the appropriate body to determine how to fund this mandated increase in support for the public schools. The legislature, fearing a backlash if it raised taxes, hesitated to act. In *Robinson II*,[29] the court allowed the legislature time to come up with its own plan. In *Robinson III*,[30] it again extended the deadline. Hughes, writing for the court in 1975 in *Robinson IV*,[31] began to insist upon action. He again gave deference to the legislature, saying, "The Court's function is to appraise compliance with the Constitution, not to legislate an educational system,"[32] but restated that the court would step in to act if the legislature defaulted on its obligation. He then set forth a provisional remedy for the 1976–1977 school year in the event that the legislature failed to act. That remedy was to reconfigure school aid to better help the poor urban and rural districts.

In response to this decision, the legislature passed the Public School Education Act of 1975[33] shortly before the court-ordered deadline. This legislation was the product of much debate. Governor Byrne supported an income tax solution to the funding problem, but faced significant antitax sentiment both in the legislature and from the general public. So, at the time of the passage of the Education Act, there was still no means available to fully fund the proposal.

In *Robinson V,*[34] the court upheld the facial validity of the act. That decision, an unsigned *per curiam* opinion for the Court, emphasized the steps the legislature had taken to quantify what constituted a "thorough and efficient education." The legislature had also taken steps to increase the aid to the poorer districts that were suffering from municipal overload. Thus, the court concluded that—assuming the act was fully funded—it was constitutional. However, the court also issued a threat that if the legislature did not enact legislation by April 6, 1976, to fully fund the act, it would take matters into its own hands.

Hughes wrote a concurring opinion. He emphasized his concerns about the "workability" of the new system designed by the legislature. He said that the commissioner of education did not have sufficient powers to ensure a statewide "thorough and efficient system." He argued that the problems of municipal overload were so great that no commissioner of education could ensure the success of the schools in the poorer districts. But ultimately, in deference to the concept of separation of powers, he decided to concur in upholding the constitutionality of the act. However, he concluded by saying, "if perchance in the reasonably near future there should be no effective step toward equalization, and it were to be established by proofs that such failure caused to continue to fester the invidious discordancies of tax resources destructive of the possibility of meeting the constitutional goal, I would feel constrained to then determine the unconstitutionality in application of the 1975 Act."[35] His concerns, joined with the concerns of two fellow justices, foreshadowed the events of the future. Years after Hughes left the court, another chief justice, Robert T. Wilentz, in writing for the court, declared the 1975 act to be unconstitutional in its application.

Despite the clear threat issued in the opinion, the legislature still failed to fund the act. Fear of the antitax backlash was strong. Most of the legislators represented suburban districts where residents were content with the quality of their schools. Many suburbanites, citing the doctrine of home rule, felt that urban residents should support their own schools, just as they supported theirs. Even the Democrats, who usually supported the poorer communities, were divided. The urban Democratic legislators were aligned against the suburban Democratic lawmakers.[36]

When the legislature failed to fund the new act, the court, in *Robinson v. Cahill VI*,[37] ordered that no state education funds could be dispersed to any school district after July 1, 1976. Since every school district was at least partially funded by the state, this meant that the schools could not open. Although closing the schools on July 1 would not have the same impact as closing them during the school year, the decision would affect many students intending to attend summer school and many handicapped students in year-round programs.[38] In response to public pressure, the legislature passed—and Governor Byrne signed—a 2 to 2-1/2 percent income tax. There was great consternation and Byrne was soundly criticized. Based on the acronym for off-track betting that New York was developing at the time, OTB, Byrne gained the nickname "OTB," One Term Byrne.

Added to the income tax was a provision for property tax relief. Some of the money from the tax was set aside to give rebates to all homeowners in the state and rebates for renters. Instead of getting a reduction in the income tax paid, homeowners and renters received rebate checks by mail. Eventually New Jerseyans became accustomed to the small income tax (in later years it was increased significantly). The rebate checks came directly from the governor's office and seemed like windfalls when they were received. Byrne, avoiding the prophecy contained in his nickname, was elected to a second term.

Hughes had finally achieved his long-sought result: an income tax. Robert Braun, for many years the education editor for the *Newark Star-Ledger*, criticized Hughes and the Supreme Court for trying to run the schools. Braun discussed a meeting with Hughes while he was chief justice, arranged to discuss the work he had done for colleges when he was governor. Braun said, ". . . he didn't want to talk about that. He wanted to talk about how the Legislature had refused to give him the state income tax he wanted back in the 1960s. 'They didn't want the income tax then? Well, they'll want one now.' I didn't know what he meant. A few days later, he issued a ruling closing the schools until legislators screamed from pain and passed the tax. So it was more a public relations gimmick than a real threat. So the schools were closed for the summer. Still, the idea that one guy—even so nice a guy as Dick Hughes—had that sort of unrestrained power gave pause."[39] Braun did not believe that the courts should have such power.[40] But the decisions made by the Hughes Court would be considered restrained when compared with the next series of school funding cases decided under the succeeding chief justice.

Later, the New Jersey Supreme Court dealt with a whole new set of cases dealing with school funding entitled *Abbott v. Burke I through XX*.[41] In these cases the court went much further than it had gone in the *Robinson* cases. As predicted by Hughes in his concurring opinion in *Robinson V*, the court determined in *Abbott II*[42] that the statute deemed facially constitutional in *Robinson* V was unconstitutional as applied to the poorest districts in the state.[43] Those districts which were primarily urban became known as Abbott Districts and had to receive funding equal to, or more than, the funding provided in the wealthiest districts in the state.[44] Eventually, the Abbott Districts would receive approximately 80 to 90 percent of their funding from the state, while other districts received the vast proportion of funding from local property taxes.[45] Later, a group of rural schools argued that they, too, should be given added support because they had problems similar to those in the inner-cities.[46]

In later *Abbott* cases, the court went still further and mandated particular programs and new school construction and directed that the state had to provide all the needed funding for the new school construction. The New Jersey Supreme Court, starting with the seminal decisions in *Robinson v. Cahill* was one of the first state courts to become so involved in the issue of school funding.[47] New Jersey, propelled by the Supreme Court, has taken dramatic steps to improve educational opportunities in the poorest areas in the state.

The other broad-reaching case decided during Hughes's tenure, *Mount Laurel*,[48] dealt with the high cost of housing in New Jersey. As a result of rapidly increasing prices, many people with low and moderate incomes were unable to buy homes. Some argued that the increased costs were partially the result of exclusionary zoning. Many towns, in an effort to protect their property tax bases, enacted zoning regulations that had the effect of limiting low- and moderate-income housing. For example, some towns would mandate minimum lot sizes and house sizes and ban mobile trailers. The National Association for the Advancement of Colored People (NAACP) brought the Mount Laurel case on the grounds of racial discrimination, arguing that these exclusionary zoning practices were intentionally designed to keep out African Americans. The court did not decide the case on that basis, but on the basis that police power enactments by local municipalities must adhere to constitutional principles of due process and equal protection. Since many of the exclusionary zoning practices did not promote the general welfare, they were deemed to be unconstitutional.

As a result of the court ruling, many communities had to rewrite their zoning laws to eliminate provisions that restricted the availability of low- and moderate-income housing. Many communities dragged their feet to avoid an influx of poorer people. While the exclusionary zoning may have been based, in part, on race and class considerations, many communities used them as a means of protecting their tax base. More people usually meant more schools, more expenses, and less open space.

This decision, like the decision in *Robinson v. Cahill*, was criticized for interfering with the legislative process and with home rule. The court indicated that it had only stepped in because the legislature and the local communities had failed to act. It left open the opportunity for the legislature to develop a plan to provide for low- and moderate-income housing.

Because of the foot-dragging by the towns who did not want to comply and the failure of the legislature to act, little low- and moderate-income housing was developed while Hughes was chief justice. Years later in *Mount Laurel II*,[49] the court, under Chief Justice Wilentz, would mandate that local communities take affirmative steps to provide for the creation of such housing. This led to an even greater outcry from the suburbs and criticism from the governor and the legislature. It did, however, much like the decision in the *Robinson* case, galvanize the legislature to pass the Fair Housing Act,[50] the constitutionality of which was upheld in *Mount Laurel III*.[51] Although the Robinson and Mount Laurel series of cases are probably the most far-reaching cases decided by the Hughes Court, the most difficult and gut-wrenching case the court faced may have been the right-to-die case of Karen Ann Quinlan.

The Quinlan Case

Karen Ann Quinlan was a young woman from Morristown, New Jersey, who, for undetermined reasons, went into a coma.[52] It eventually became clear that she was in a persistent vegetative state and unaware of what was going on around her. She was kept alive by a respirator and a feeding tube. Her loving parents, who were devout Catholics, agonized over what to do. Finally, they decided to ask that the respirator be removed. The doctors refused their request. They argued that since she was not brain-dead, it was not permissible to remove the respirator. A legal battle ensued that would become one of the most famous cases in recent history. Covered extensively by the news media, the case received national attention and was the cause of much debate. While it was in progress, the *New York Daily News* took a poll that found 59 percent of responders agreeing that Karen

Ann should be permitted to die, 24 percent disagreeing, and 17 percent with no opinion.[53]

One author described the Quinlans in the following way: "Joseph and Julia Quinlan were ordinary Americans who had extraordinary virtues. Thrust into the limelight, they displayed a modest courage and moral sincerity, which the media translated into almost saintly terms. They had given up hope for her recovery, but they still visited her at least once a day. They were seeking permission from the Court to let her die or as Joseph Quinlan said 'to place her in the hands of the Lord.' "[54]

Even before the *Quinlan* case, some patients and their families, in response to new technology that had the ability to prolong life, were demanding the right to forgo or withdraw life-support.[55] The legislatures and the courts had not yet dealt with these issues. It was the Quinlan case that ultimately gave meaning to the term "right to die."[56]

A distinguished group of lawyers gathered in Judge Robert Muir's court-room in Morristown to examine the facts of the case. One of the lawyers, opposing any right to terminate treatment, went so far as to allude to Nazi Germany's extermination of people no longer deemed useful. The state maintained that it would be murder to remove the respirator. Paul Armstrong,[57] representing the Quinlans, argued for their right to remove the respirator. The trial court in New Jersey appointed a guardian. After a trial and hearing, the court determined that the respirator should not be removed. Representatives of the American Medical Association and the American Bar Association applauded the judge for preserving physicians' autonomy.[58]

But the decision by Judge Muir did not end the case or the controversy. The Supreme Court ruled it would hear the appeal directly without the necessity of first having the Appellate Division consider it. This is a route only used in cases of great importance when it is clear that the court will have to consider the case eventually.[59]

Hughes wrote the opinion for the unanimous court. One of the justices originally intended to write a separate opinion, but Hughes pushed hard and ultimately convinced the justice that it was important that the opinion be unanimous. Some years later he wrote to an attorney, "As you perceive, it was a unanimous decision, although the Court, after initial argument, seemed to be going in six different directions. The Justices felt, because of its landmark importance, however, that the opinion should be written by the chief justice rather than by assignment to another Justice.[60] But when I got the opinion on paper, and identified the constitutional right of privacy as the touchstone for decision, all of us came together. Not without a lot of work, interminable circulation of drafts, telephone and personal conferences, etc. But we made it."[61]

Ultimately, the court decided that Karen's father should be her guardian and have the power to decide, in conjunction with the doctors and the ethics committee at the hospital, whether to remove the respirator. Hughes, who always wrote his own opinions, worked on part of the opinion in North Carolina, during one of Betty's visits to Duke University's weight-control program. He had been scheduled to go to Japan for a conference, but Betty, concerned that the parents had waited long enough, said, "Tell the Japanese that they'll have to wait. That girl is dying. Sit down this afternoon and get going."[62] Hughes wrote another part of the decision in Trenton, where his son, Patrick Murphy, remembered hearing him discussing the case on the phone, persuading his colleagues to insure unanimity.[63]

The opinion details the findings of the doctors concerning the condition of Karen Ann, which described the patient as being in a "chronic persistent vegetative state."[64] Dr. Fred Plum, one of the expert witnesses, defined a patient in such a state as a "subject who remains with the capacity to maintain the vegetative parts of neurological function but who no longer has any cognitive function."[65] Hughes further described her condition: "Karen is described as emaciated, having suffered a weight loss of at least 40 pounds, and undergoing a continuing deteriorative process. Her posture is described as fetal-like and grotesque; there is extreme flexion-rigidity of the arms, legs and related muscles and her joints are severely rigid and deformed."[66] The doctors also agreed that she was not brain-dead under the then-existing definitions. The testimony further indicated that removal of the respirator would result in her death, although it was not known how long it would take.

The court looked at a number of theories[67] but turned to the unwritten right to privacy as the determining legal principle. It based its analysis both upon a decision of the United States Supreme Court[68] and the New Jersey Constitution.[69] While the court recognized that the right to privacy was not without limitation, it determined that it did encompass the right of a person to refuse life-sustaining treatment. Writing for the court, Hughes recognized the state's interest in preserving life, but went on to say, "We think that the State's interest *contra* weakens and the individual's right to privacy grows as the degree of bodily invasion increases and the prognosis dims. . . . It is for that reason that we believe Karen's choice, if she were competent to make it would be vindicated by the law. Her prognosis is extremely poor,—she will never resume cognitive life. And the bodily invasion is very great,—she requires 24 hour intensive nursing care, antibiotics, the assistance of a respirator, a catheter and feeding tube."[70] In the conclusion, Hughes summed up the opinion:

> We repeat for the sake of emphasis and clarity that upon the concurrence of the guardian and family of Karen, should the responsible attending physicians conclude that there is no reasonable possibility of Karen's ever emerging from her present comatose condition to a cognitive, sapient state and that the life-support apparatus now being administered to Karen should be discontinued, they shall consult with the hospital 'Ethical Committee' or like body of the institution in which Karen is then hospitalized. If that consultative body agrees that there is no reasonable possibility of Karen's ever emerging from her present comatose condition to a cognitive, sapient state, the present life-support system may be withdrawn and said action shall be without any civil or criminal liability therefore, on the part of any participant, whether guardian, physician, hospital or others.[71]

One of the striking things about the decision is the long description given of the Roman Catholic position on the issue. The court recognized that the Catholic Church would not prohibit the removal of the respirator. Hughes wrote, "The 'Catholic view' of religious neutrality in the circumstances of this case is considered by the Court only in the aspect of its impact upon the conscience, motivation and purpose of the intending guardian, Joseph Quinlan, and not as a precedent in terms of the civil law."[72] As a Catholic, Joseph Quinlan had researched the Catholic position before he decided to request the removal of life support. He would not have made his decision if the Catholic Church prohibited the respirator's removal. Hughes's recitation of the Catholic Church's position was not necessary, however, to determine the propriety of the choice of Joseph Quinlan as guardian for his daughter. It appeared that the chief justice, a devout Catholic, wanted to assure himself of the morality of the decision he was making.

The announcement of the decision was front-page news throughout the country and abroad. Opening the CBS Evening News, Walter Cronkite announced in somber tones, "The Supreme Court of New Jersey ruled today on an issue that has tormented the consciences of the legal and medical professions."[73]

After the opinion, the respirator was removed, and despite the predictions of the doctors, Karen did not die as a result. She lived for more than nine years. In part, her survival was a result of the slow weaning from the respirator performed by the doctors. At first she was able to breathe on her own for only an hour, but that slowly increased, until eventually she was successfully weaned and lived for many years in the continuing vegetative state.[74] Her parents never returned to court to request the removal of the feeding tube. In the end, they created a hospice program in honor of their daughter.

The position of the court, taken as a given today, was viewed at the time as momentous and controversial. Since then, many courts have reached similar results. In the *Cruzan* case,[75] the United States Supreme Court referred to the *Quinlan* case as the "seminal" case in the right-to-die area and assumed the existence of a constitutional right to refuse medical treatment. Many states have now adopted statutes that permit people to draft living wills that set forth their desires should they be in a situation in which they are unable to make medical decisions for themselves.

Mrs. Quinlan, who attended the hearing before the Supreme Court, said that Hughes and the other justices asked many questions but she could not get any impression as to the potential outcome. She was amazed when the decision was unanimous in favor of her and her husband.[76] Mrs. Quinlan indicated that she had never met Chief Justice Hughes before the case, although she and her husband always had a good opinion of him and respected him as a good and caring former governor. But after the case was over, Hughes became friendly with the Quinlans and included them in many family events. Mrs. Quinlan recalled that he was a gracious and charming host. She considered it a privilege to be his friend. The Quinlans even sat with the Hughes family during the governor's funeral.[77]

Other Opinions

The Hughes Court decided a case involving a conflict between two principles to which Hughes was devoted. The case revolved around the newsperson's privilege, which permits a reporter or other member of the news media under certain circumstances to refuse to reveal sources. The law recognized this privilege out of concern that without it reporters would be unable to function effectively.

Hughes had a great deal of fondness for the press and counted many newspaper people among his friends. Betty, for example, wrote a regular column for newspapers. He was dedicated to the Constitution and particularly to the First Amendment, as vividly demonstrated by his defense of the right of Rutgers Professor Genovese to speak against the war in Vietnam. Hughes also had a strong commitment to ensuring that the criminal justice system was fair. He felt strongly that when it came to the rights of criminal defendants, they must be given every consideration. The case in question was one of those situations in which two liberal principles collided—the right of a free press versus the rights of criminal defendants to a fair trial.

In the case, *In the Matter of Myron Farber*,[78] the majority, faced with the conflict between these two rights, determined that when First Amendment freedom interfered with the right of a defendant to receive a fair trial, the constitutional right to a fair trial would control. In that case, the state had subpoenaed records in a criminal case from Myron Farber, a reporter. When he refused to turn over the information, he was held in contempt of court. Farber argued that he had a privilege under a state statute to refuse to disclose the information. The court decided that the decision of the trial court holding Farber in contempt was correct. The court determined that the defendant's right to confront witnesses guaranteed by the Sixth Amendment of the U.S. Constitution and by the New Jersey Constitution trumped the right of the reporter to protect his sources.[79]

In a concurring opinion, Hughes showed his interest in history and his dedication to the principles of a fair trial. One of the issues had to do with whether the court could review the information privately in order to decide whether it should be protected or not. The reporter argued that he, the reporter, should be the one to make that decision. Hughes said, "Their claim to a final adjudication without an *in camera* [in the chambers of the judge] scrutiny by the court upon which to base its decision would project the absurd proposition that the press, and not the courts, should be the final arbiter of the constitutional mandate."[80] He went on to say:

> Such a conclusion would be discordant with the entire history of constitutional adjudication since the foundation of the Republic. It would be destructive of values upon which our constitutional democracy rests, that is to say, on the premise that the Constitution is supreme over the transitory will of any man, or of any group of men, or of the Congress itself, or even of a President, or of the press, or of any special interest,

no matter how worthy. In the perspective of history, given the need for freedom of the press and religion, of free speech and assemblage and other rights of free people, all such rights are diminished if men may be condemned without the right to fair trial and without compulsory process to effectuate that right.[81]

Some years later, Hughes reaffirmed his belief in the correctness of his position. In a letter to Edward Bloustein, president of Rutgers University, Hughes wrote, "I enjoyed your review, in Sunday's New York Times, of Myron Farber's book 'Somebody is Lying.' I have thought, very often, of our decision in Farber's case for, like you, I am a First Amendment loyalist. But the more I ponder, the more I am convinced we were right, if the Sixth Amendment right to fair trial is, in fact to mean anything."[82] Hughes added, "I am far from a constitutional scholar, but I still have no doubt that if the Sixth Amendment is not enforced, other constitutional values are meaningless."[83]

In one of Hughes's dissenting opinions, his law and order approach was very apparent, as was his emphasis on what he perceived as the clear meaning of a statute. The case was a criminal one dealing with the validity of a murder conviction under what is known as the felony murder doctrine. That doctrine, which is used in many states, provides that when a death is caused during the commission of a felony, the person committing the felony is guilty even if the person causing the death did not intend to kill. The New Jersey statute provided: "If any person, in committing or attempting to commit [a serious crime] of which the probable consequences may be bloodshed, kills another, or if the death of anyone ensues from the committing or attempting to commit any such crime or act, then such person so killing is guilty of murder."[84] The facts of the case involved a robbery carried out by four men. The victim of the robbery shot at one of the men and killed him. Another of the culprits shot and killed the victim of the robbery. One of the remaining robbers was charged with the murder of both his companion and the victim. The issue was whether or not the "ensues" clause in this statute would include the killing by others of either victims or companions. The Appellate Division of the New Jersey Superior Court, in a split opinion, decided that the defendant could be convicted for both murders—finding that the ensues clause was broad and intended to cover these very situations.[85]

However, the New Jersey Supreme Court, in a six-to-one opinion with only Hughes dissenting, narrowed the scope of the doctrine to those situations in which the defendant or one of his companions directly caused the death. The majority recognized that most states had not applied that doctrine in cases when one of the felons was killed. It also acknowledged that many other states had utilized the felony murder doctrine in situations dealing with the killing of an innocent party by a third party. Nevertheless, the court held that the legislature could not have intended to expand the scope of the felony murder rule beyond what was generally perceived to be its scope at common law. The court thus held that the felony murder doctrine would not apply in cases where a person other than one of the felons directly caused the death. Hughes, in a short but pointed opinion, simply disagreed. He said:

> I certainly believe that what was there referred to as the "ensues clause" can have no other logical or legislatively intended meaning than to extend criminal liability, in a causative sense to death which ensues or is proximately caused by initiation and furtherance of the felony. Thus on the concept stated by the Appellate Division: The proximate cause theory, simply stated, is that when a felon sets in motion a chain of events which were or should have been within his contemplation when the motion was initiated, the felon, and those acting in concert with him, should be held responsible for any death which by direct and almost inevitable consequences results from the initial criminal act.[86]

Subsequently, the New Jersey legislature rewrote the felony murder statute and split the difference. The law became that a felon could be guilty when a third party killed an innocent party but not when a third party killed a co-felon.[87]

Hughes in his opinion focused on the precise meaning of the words of the statute whereas the majority had emphasized the intent of the legislature. In another case Hughes was more willing to look at the intent of the legislature and ended up dissenting again. That case dealt with the appointment of a member of the New Jersey Supreme Court itself. Stephen Wiley, a state senator, had been nominated by Governor Byrne to be an associate justice of the Supreme Court. The Constitution of New Jersey, in an effort to prevent legislators from profiting from their positions, provided that: "No member of the Senate or General Assembly, during the term for which he shall have been elected, shall be nominated, elected or appointed to any State civil office or position, of profit, which shall have been created by law, or the emoluments whereof shall have been increased by law, during such term."[88] It was undisputed that while Wiley was a senator, the salaries of associate justices had been increased. This would seem to have precluded him from serving on the court. However, the legislature had also provided, while voting on the increase in salaries, "The increase in salary provided for in this act shall not be applicable to any present member of the Senate or General Assembly during the term for which he shall have been elected should such member hereafter be appointed to any of the offices enumerated in section 1 of this act."[89] This provision was obviously intended to get around the provision of the constitution and permit members of the legislature to accept subsequent positions as long as they did not receive the benefit of the raises they voted on. Wiley's nomination was promptly challenged and the question came before the Supreme Court. The validity of the legislation, however, came under scrutiny because of another provision of the constitution that prohibited "special legislation." The majority of the court held that the raises applied to the associate justices of the Supreme Court and the exclusion of one justice from that raise had to be considered arbitrary and thus violated the special legislation provision. Hughes and two other justices dissented. Hughes began his opinion by setting forth his basic concern that the court should be very hesitant to overturn a decision made by the executive and legislative branches of the government. Since the governor nominated and the Senate consented to the appointment of Wiley, it could be said that the court was interfering with the actions of both of those branches of government.

Hughes wrote a long opinion in which he emphasized the legislative intent to give the senator the opportunity to serve. The legislature had attempted to eliminate the concern of the constitutional provision by eliminating the benefit of the increase in salary. Recognizing that the words in the constitutional provision seemed to be against his position, Hughes wrote, "When aid to construction of the meaning of words, as used in the statute, is available, there certainly can be no 'rule of law' which forbids its use, however clear the words may appear on 'superficial examination.'"[90] Hughes went on to quote an earlier New Jersey opinion for the proposition, "Since words are inexact tools at best, resort may freely be had to the pertinent constitutional and legislative history for aid in ascertaining the true sense and meaning of the language used."[91] He ultimately concluded that Senator Wiley had the right to take the position as associate justice.

Judicial Craftsman

In an article written shortly after he left the Supreme Court, Hughes set forth his judicial philosophy.[92] He praised the authors of the 1947 Constitution, which had greatly improved the legal system in New Jersey and given the Supreme Court of New Jersey great powers. He emphasized the importance of judicial independence and praised the system of appointment as opposed to an electoral system for choosing judges. "It is therefore most fortunate," he said, "that in New Jersey, the constitutional method of appointment of judges, the traditional bipartisan division of court membership and absolute freedom from politics assure an independent judiciary, having the respect and support of the people."[93] He praised the prior chief justices and the court's "willingness to cope with new problems and devise new solutions in the name of justice, as the common law unfolds and the Constitution adapts its magnificent basic philosophy to meet new societal problems, as a living organism rather than a dead letter."[94] "We have discarded the chains of *stare decisis*, so far as that ancient principle would bind us to the injustices of the past."[95] One of his clerks said, "He had an instinct for justice, and would not be deterred from reaching the right result even if it meant making new law."[96]

Hughes also approved of the practice of disagreeing on occasion with United States Supreme Court opinions. He believed the New Jersey Constitution could and should be used to reach results the United States Supreme Court would not grant under the United States Constitution. For example, during his tenure on the court, the court applied that doctrine for the first time in a search and seizure case, recognizing the right of the New Jersey Supreme Court to expand the rights in a consent search case beyond that given by the United States Supreme Court. The court did this by relying on the provision of the New Jersey Constitution protecting against unreasonable searches and seizures. The New Jersey Supreme Court decided that although it could not disagree with the U.S. Supreme Court's interpretation of the Fourth Amendment, which had been criticized as being inadequately protective of defendants' right during a consent search,[97] it could grant greater rights under the Search and Seizure provision of the New Jersey Constitution. The New Jersey Court in *State v. Johnson*[98] placed on the prosecution the heavier burden of demonstrating that the suspect knew that he had the right to refuse consent. In this case, the court was striking out in a different direction. But the *Johnson* case was to set a trend that continued into the future, with the New Jersey Supreme Court following its own more defendant-oriented path.

Hughes also praised decisions of the New Jersey Supreme Court that adopted the "fairness and rightness" doctrine. This doctrine was devised to apply even when no specific constitutional right was involved, and was used to prevent arbitrary abuses of power for which there would otherwise be no recourse.[99] Hughes applauded Justice Nathan Jacobs, who was primarily responsible for the evolution of the "rightness and fairness doctrine." Hughes cited other examples of its use, noting that "in New Jersey a school board may not deny reappointment and tenure to a teacher without expressing a reason . . . nor can a prisoner be sentenced without disclosing to his counsel the main points of the pre-sentence probation report upon which his condemnation is based."[100] However, Hughes also recognized that the court was not a "super legislature" and that, when appropriate, it should defer to the legislature. Justice Sidney Schreiber, a colleague of Hughes, said, "The opinions of Chief Justice Hughes . . . reflect what might best be termed a result-oriented approach to judicial decision-making."[101] He went on to characterize that approach as the result of the chief justice's "ringing conscience for fairness and justice."[102]

Some justices and judges have their law clerks draft their opinions. Hughes wrote his own. The clerks would pull all the relevant books for him and place them on a shelf by his desk. He read all the material despite the strain of poor eyesight. When he finished a draft, he would turn it over to the clerks so they could make suggestions and find support for some of the propositions. Most of the input was minor. As one clerk put it, "Generally that was minimal, because he had hit the target head-on."[103] Another of his clerks wrote, "He drafted all his own opinions. Our job was to then edit, beef up, find and check citations and test the bench memo written by other clerks to make sure the law was correct . . . but, he was the author from the 'get go.'"[104] In all, Hughes wrote twenty-seven majority opinions, five concurring opinions, and twelve dissenting opinions. He joined, of course, in many other opinions. He may have written other opinions as well because the court occasionally issues *per curiam* opinions which are not signed. This is particularly true in cases dealing with lawyer discipline.

Hughes believed the court should be respectful of the attorneys who appear before it. Hughes certainly questioned the attorneys, but his manner was not at all suggestive of an interrogation. A letter he wrote many years later emphasized his respect for lawyers and for the court. It was to Marie Garibaldi, who had just been appointed as the first woman member of the New Jersey Supreme Court. It read:

Dear Marie: (henceforth it shall be "Dear Justice")

The news of your appointment was well received in my family. I was content and happy because the Governor recognized a complete professional, able, dedicated, hard-working—an ornament to the law. But my wife Betty was almost hysterical. She has so long suspected me as a male chauvinist—although my leaning toward women is well known. She is on cloud nine because the Governor appointed the first woman to our Supreme Court. I will have to watch her closely—lest she turn Republican. [Governor Kean, who appointed Justice Garibaldi, was a Republican.]

We wish for you a long, happy, productive tenure on a great court. You will have no difficulty in becoming accustomed to its routine, its industry and its dedication to Constitution and law. Beyond this, I picture you as tolerant to the young lawyer, groping his way and making a few mistakes as he confronts a formidable, experienced senior. I know you will keep things reasonably even, and thus fulfill the aphorism of Sir Francis Bacon—"The place of justice is a hallowed place." The attitude of a judge can produce either terror or composure in the advocate. Composure leads to sensible argument and that leads in turn to justice.

My congratulations and best wishes for a totally happy tenure on the court.[105]

Court Administrator

In his administrative role as chief justice, Hughes initiated a system of judicial evaluation—the first in the country. He also appointed nonlawyers to the disciplinary committees dealing with improprieties of attorneys. He worked to reduce sentencing disparities within and between the counties. He announced the first pretrial intervention program in the country in an effort to keep young offenders and first-time offenders out of the criminal process. He took a large group of judges on a tour of Rahway State Prison so that they would understand the consequences of their sentencing decisions. In fact, shortly after his appointment to the Supreme Court he said, "I intend to reinstate the rule we had when I was on the bench prior to 1957, which required judges to give the reasons for imposing sentences in writing. I also will require each judge to visit the institution where he sends a man within 18 months or two years of the sentence, so he'll know what he's doing."[106]

Hughes was not a detail man, but he was concerned about the administration of the courts. Some would say that he did not focus sufficiently on ways to make the judiciary more efficient. When there was an explosion in the number of cases before the courts, his general response was to ask for an increase in the number of judges, rather than to seek greater efficiency. But he was of the old school, and thought more about the system's effectiveness than he did about its efficiency.

He did, however, have the foresight to demand an independent computer system for the judiciary. Earl Josephson remembered, when he was working for the procurement division of state government, an attempt to have the judiciary share a computer with other branches of government. Hughes thought that such sharing might interfere with the independence of the judiciary. In New Jersey, the courts had often debated with the legislature over the independence of the judiciary. When the dispute arose about the separate judicial computer system, Hughes, in his typical understated way, called Josephson and after asking about his family and other appropriate small talk, said that he had been discussing the issue with the Supreme Court justices and they were unanimous in feeling that the court needed its own computer system. He subtly suggested that the court was prepared to decide that the failure to provide such a system would threaten its independence and thus would be unconstitutional. The court ended up with its own computer system.[107]

One of his goals as chief justice was to motivate the judges to be strict in punishing those who engaged in violent crime. On November 17, 1975, he issued a statement essentially urging his judges to avoid leniency in sentencing. "The members of this Court, like most citizens, are not unaware of the social ills of our times,—the broken family, the deprived childhood, the brutal parent, the insufficiency of police patrols, educational deficiencies, drug addiction, discrimination, poverty, the urban waste,—who can count the problems of twentieth century America? Yet I now affirm that not one of these factors, not all of them in combination, can justify or excuse in the slightest degree laying so much as a finger on a non-offending citizen."[108] He went on to indicate that the court was aware of instances in which judges had granted "excessive leniency" to violent criminals. He therefore set up a number of procedures that would limit the situations in which individuals who had engaged in violent crimes could receive a lesser sentence. Among others things, he wanted the prosecutors and judges to be aware of the entire criminal history of the defendant before agreeing to downgrade charges. He recognized that this could result in significant delay as more information would have to be gathered and more cases would have to be tried, but he argued that the need to deal with violence in society was worth the price.

Hughes gave a State of the Judiciary Address to the legislature in 1977. In that address he said, "So far as I can determine, this is the first time our branches of government have come together in the chambers of the Legislature to consider together the public interest in the administration of justice."[109] It would also be the last time such an event occurred. As part of his remarks, Hughes urged the legislature to place on the ballot a constitutional amendment to merge county courts, which had limited jurisdiction, into one statewide Superior Court. Many years later such an amendment was adopted. Another reason for Hughes's appearance before the legislature was his concern over judicial attrition. In New Jersey, the legislature determines the salaries of the judges. There are no automatic cost-of-living raises or any authority for the judicial system to increase the salaries of judges. At the time of the address, there had been no pay raise for many years. Hughes was well aware of the difficulty of living on a judicial salary since he had resigned from the judiciary many years earlier because the salary was not sufficient for him to raise his children. After discussing at length all the new initiatives and programs the judiciary had developed, Hughes said, "The subject I am about to discuss, however, is so serious and urgent that a failure to act in this session of the Legislature could foreshadow, indeed almost invite, a beginning deterioration in the New Jersey court system. I do not want to see this happen—I do not believe either you or the people want it to happen. But ominous signs of change are apparent, none of which are in the interest of the state. Several of our finest and most experienced judges have been forced to resign to adequately support their families. The greatest difficulty has been encountered by the Governor in persuading able and experienced lawyers with children in college, for instance, to accept appointment to the bench."[110]

While Hughes was chief justice the state began work on a new Justice Center in Trenton, which would later become the Richard J. Hughes Justice Center. When construction began, it was still unnamed. Hughes wrote to Governor Brendan Byrne suggesting that there be a statue erected there to Woodrow Wilson, whom Hughes still considered a political hero. In the course of the letter Hughes said that he had been reading some of the Wilson papers and the Wilson biography, *When the Cheering Stopped*.

He wrote, "All of this makes me think that Wilson and his ideals are the epitome of 'law' in its finest sense. This in broad context, not our traditional 'common Law' or our respected 'constitutional law' but the 'law' of poor men, of little nations, of democracy, of the powerless and forgotten, the law of which Alfred Lord Tennyson dreamed when he wrote: 'Ah! When shall all men's good be each man's rule, and universal Peace lie like a shaft of light across the land.' "[111] Hughes concluded with a combination of his pragmatism and his idealism. "We don't have a Lincoln in New Jersey but we do have a Wilson. He was indeed an awful politician. LBJ or Eisenhower or even Nixon could have put over the League of Nations by including Lodge and a few Republicans in the trip to Europe, hence avoiding the 'Holocaust' and probably World War II. But politician or not, Wilson reached for something fine in the human soul, and this should be somehow preserved."[112] Hughes's suggestion was not acted on; instead the Justice Center became a memorial to him.

In addition to the usual responsibilities, the chief justice in New Jersey has some additional and unusual functions. In the 1950s, a dispute arose concerning the Board of Prudential Insurance Company, one of the largest companies headquartered in New Jersey. The legislature decided to restructure the board. In that restructuring, the legislature decided that the board should consist of twenty-three directors and that the chief justice should choose six of its members.[113] Appointment to the board was a choice assignment because members received a stipend, and they got to mingle with other influential members of the business community.

Hughes's first appointment to the Prudential Board was his good friend and the person who had appointed him to the chief justice position, William Cahill. An old adversary of Cahill argued that the appointment smacked of political cronyism.[114] Cahill, a lawyer, former congressman, and former governor, was well qualified to serve on the board. And there was clear precedent for the appointment. Governor Meyner had appointed Joseph Weintraub as chief justice of the Supreme Court. Chief Justice Weintraub then appointed Governor Meyner to serve on the board after he had completed his governorship. In later years Governor Byrne would also be appointed to the Prudential Board.

The Constitution of New Jersey provides for mandatory retirement for judges at age seventy. Hughes often referred to this as "mandatory senility." When Hughes turned seventy he had no choice but to step down from his position, even though he would have preferred to continue. Numerous tributes honoring his many years of public service followed. Bolton Schwartz, a long-time reporter and the person who regularly ran the Correspondents' Dinner, wrote an article about Hughes's having created the sales and income taxes but then said:

> But they give us grounds for marveling how come you are to most of us the most beloved chief executive the state has ever had. Recalling the old days brings back memories of the arguments we used to have, with me complaining about left wing things you were doing (insisting you were the state's number one communist) and you calling me "the Jewish Archie Bunker." We were both right, of course. When I complained about taxes you used to say, "Would you like to take the bread out of the mouths of poor orphans?" And I found myself without response. When it appeared the press was likely to take my view you arranged tours to the various state homes for troubled kids and shamed reporters into going along. . . . Throughout your governorship, you never failed to attend and speak at the annual State House Correspondents' Dinner. When former Judge Van Riper, who had been the speaker for many years, died you automatically took over the chore. When you became Chief Justice, you told me you weren't sure you should continue, but I convinced you and you delivered what you said was a non-controversial address about your cat that was absolutely hilarious.[115]

In fact, Hughes's ability as an after-dinner speaker was legendary and he was called on repeatedly to speak at affairs of all kinds. This continued well into his retirement.

Chapter 19

The Later Years

A FTER HUGHES RETIRED AS CHIEF JUSTICE, the New Jersey
legislature created the Richard J. Hughes Chair in Constitutional
and Public Law and Service at Seton Hall University School of
Law. Seton Hall was probably chosen for a number of reasons: his son,
Michael Murphy, had graduated from the law school; his son, Thomas More
Hughes, was a student at the undergraduate school; and Hughes had hired a
number of outstanding Seton Hall Law School graduates as clerks. Hughes
filled the chair during its first year. He ran a series of lectures featuring
several prominent officials from New Jersey, including former governors
and administrators. Jane Kelly, who worked with Hughes to prepare the
program and who assisted him on an article he wrote for the law review
entitled "Reflections: A Growing Court,"[1] remembered that the course was
very popular with the students.[2] In the ensuing years, many prominent
jurists and scholars have filled the chair.

Hughes, of course, had never been satisfied with doing just one thing
at any one time, so upon retirement, he also became "of Counsel" to the
firm in Trenton that had been started by Joel Sterns, who had been in
Hughes's administration and was a close friend of the former governor.
Other members of the Hughes administration were also partners in the firm.
In the years after the governorship, the firm prospered and when Hughes
became available, Sterns convinced him to join. Adrian "Bud" Foley, who
was Hughes's partner during the years between the governorship and the
Supreme Court, wanted Hughes to rejoin his firm. Sterns and Foley encouraged Hughes to enthusiastically choose one of the firms and be comfortable
with the decision. Hughes enjoyed his partnership with Connell and Foley

but the Sterns firm was in Trenton and thus much more convenient. Foley and Sterns met and devised a financial package that would be the same for both firms. That made it possible for Hughes to make a decision based on convenience factors.[3] He chose the Sterns firm. After he joined, Hughes was asked what it was like to have his former assistant as his boss. Hughes responded, "Not so different as one might imagine. . . . Joel always did think he ran the Governor's office."[4]

During these years Hughes would often be called upon to promote important public projects. Governor Kean, a Republican, asked Hughes to help gather support for a bond issue. Kean chose Hughes because he was "perhaps the most popular Democrat in the state."[5] When the federal government made Martin Luther King Day a national holiday, Governor Kean emphasized its importance by creating a forty-member Commemorative Commission. He chose Hughes as one of its co-chairmen. In describing Kean's reasons for choosing Hughes, Kean's biographer, Alvin Felzenberg, said, "Hughes had been Governor at the height of the civil rights struggles and had personally known King. His recollections of his conversations with the civil rights leader in the aftermath of the Newark riots captured the imagination of a generation that came into political consciousness after King's death."[6] Hughes subsequently had to write to the governor informing him that the legislative appointments to the commission were all Democratic and that the federal statute defining the creation of the Martin Luther King Jr. Federal Holiday Commission provided that "not more than half of the members of the Commission appointed . . . shall be members of the same political party." He urged a revision of the executive order setting up the commission to add an equal number of Republicans, feeling that the commission should be "above politics." He said, "For my part, despite my notorious fervency as a Democrat, I pledge to greet our 4 Republican legislative members effusively, hopefully at our next commission meeting."[7]

Hughes began engaging in other activities as well. Robert O'Brien, the president of Carteret Savings and Loan Association in Newark, invited Hughes to sit on his board of directors and Hughes accepted. O'Brien, highly regarded in the banking industry, had come to know Hughes while he was governor. Their friendship continued after Hughes left the governorship. O'Brien realized that the governor, who had spent so much of his career in public service and had such a large family, was not entirely financially secure. When Hughes was about six months away from mandatory retirement, O'Brien went to Hughes's Supreme Court chambers and asked him whether he would consider joining the board. Hughes told him he couldn't discuss anything like that while he was still on the court and that they could talk about it after he retired. Eventually he accepted the offer.

O'Brien did not make the decision simply to help Hughes. He knew Hughes would be a great addition to the board. O'Brien said Hughes had a great ability to consider an idea and make an excellent judgment about its validity. Usually, if Hughes liked an idea, the whole board would then embrace it. O'Brien noted, however, that Hughes never sought to dominate the board and that he would listen more than speak, simply commenting on proposals in an intelligent and insightful way.

At that time, Carteret had started a campaign to merge with many smaller associations. O'Brien used Hughes to help achieve that goal. He would often take Hughes to meet with the owners of these smaller savings and loans. The owners were impressed by the presence of the former governor and chief justice, and realized that Carteret was not out to cheat them in any way. As a result, many of these institutions agreed to be acquired. O'Brien said Hughes simply wowed the others and he recalled Hughes as a "man of the people" who treated everyone, from janitors to the Duke of Windsor, the same way.[8] Hughes served on the Carteret board for a number of years.

Hughes also served on the board of a company owned by Robert Brennan. Brennan, a broker, had amassed a large fortune buying and selling penny stocks. His company was called First Jersey Securities, and he became famous for commercials that featured him arriving in a helicopter and urging people to "come grow with me." He eventually put together a company called International Thoroughbred Breeders so he could be involved with race tracks and horse breeding. Brennan asked Hughes to serve on the board of International Thoroughbred Breeders. While at the time there was no indication that Brennan would eventually be charged with various counts of fraud, Hughes had reservations. On the one hand, Brennan was a dynamic and charming individual who was very much involved in philanthropy. He sat on the boards of a number of reputable institutions and had given away a good deal of money. On the other hand, his extraordinarily quick rise to power made people nervous. Before joining his board, Hughes asked his friend, Robert O'Brien, to check into Brennan's background. O'Brien contacted a prominent attorney who was usually in the know, who said there was nothing of public record that was negative. Hughes decided to serve on the board, as did a number of other prominent individuals. Eventually, the empire that Brennan had built began to collapse, and ultimately, long after Hughes had left the board, Brennan was convicted of tax fraud.

The Death of Betty

In October 1983, Betty Hughes died in Florida. Hughes said, "My wife Betty passed away peacefully, dozing in her favorite armchair at our home in Boca Raton."[9] Just a few months before, he had written to his good friend Paul Ylvisaker about living in Florida with Betty. "The mild climate, good cardiologists and hospital nearby, no stairs or such aggravations, a great cook (me), are all conducive to her well-being, and God willing, I will have her a few more years."[10] But that was not to be. She died a few months after those words were written. Hughes described her passing. "She was quite miserable, unable to eat, and had a sense of acceptance of impending death, although she hoped to last until Christmas, to see all the kids, etc. On Tuesday night I tried to get her to eat a little, then started our nightly Scrabble game. She conceded and said we would finish later, and she was tired and wanted to read the paper. I established her in her favorite armchair, told her to call me if she wanted anything, and with her encouragement I walked into another room to see a little of the World Series game. In a few minutes, I checked her, and though she appeared to be asleep, I could not see any breathing motion. I took her pulse and it was flat and I knew that she had gone back to God. She had wanted to go just that way."[11]

Betty was a true partner, and her death was extremely traumatic for Hughes. Hughes described his life with her as "30 golden years of marriage."[12] Although Betty assumed the major responsibility for raising the family, she also managed to earn money with her writing and her television show.

She was a gracious hostess and became friendly with many national and state leaders and their spouses. After her death Hughes kept her memory alive. He began a newsletter for the family so that everyone could keep in touch. He often included copies of Betty's columns with the newsletters. He also sent copies of Betty's columns to people about whom she had written. In one poignant letter, Lady Bird Johnson wrote to Hughes, "Dear Dick, I read Betty's columns with a great deal of warmth and nostalgia. She was such a dear and wonderful friend. She related with such grace and style two events in my life that will live in my memory forever. Dick, thank you for sharing these with me. I well know the void you are experiencing, and it is good that you can take comfort from all those happy and cherished times gone by."[13]

Betty had been a heavy smoker throughout her life. Hughes also smoked heavily. When Betty was ordered to quit smoking by her doctors in 1982, Hughes knew that if he continued to smoke, she would never be able to stop. He stopped cold turkey and never smoked again. Betty also stopped but would occasionally cheat. Her son, Tom, remembered catching her smoking in the bathroom. She said, "Please don't tell Dad."[14] Apparently Tom never did tell his father because in another letter that Hughes wrote after Betty's death he described the decision to stop smoking. "After Betty's first attack in November 1981 and four weeks in the hospital, she came home and was soon up to a pack a day. She went back to the hospital January 1, 1982, and this scared the hell out of us. I knew she couldn't quit unless I did. So that month we quit cold turkey and neither of us ever smoked again. My three-pack a day habit lasted 57 years, and her two-pack habit for 45 years. Nothing like the threat of death to scare people into sanity!"[15]

Betty and Dick had a clear love affair. In a letter he wrote to Betty a couple of years before her death, Hughes said, "If you should go first, which I strongly disapprove, your deep throaty voice, your kindness, your laughter, your zip, your caring, will live forever in my memory and will sustain me. If, more likely, I pass on first, I would like you to know, 1) that you made me happier than any man is entitled to expect, 2) that I will willingly (if I get to be where he is) suffer a bolt in the jaw from Bill Murphy (for it was well worth it) [Bill Murphy was Betty's first husband] and 3) that even if I have been selfish and negligent, I love you with all my heart! And always will, even in that other place."[16] Mary (Devey) Abbott, perhaps Betty's best friend and the woman who served as her social secretary during the years when Hughes was governor, recalled Betty saying very near the end of her life, "I don't mind dying but I hate leaving Dick. He was the most wonderful man in the world."[17]

In a letter to very close friends, the Dunnes, Hughes wrote, "Betty's great cardiologist, Dr. Mike Lewis, who was crazy about her, once was present in her room when she asked me to hand her a newspaper, which I did with my usual words of obedience. On his way out of the hospital, he told the Chief Nurse,—'Would you believe this,—he still calls her doll-baby!'[18]

In a letter Hughes wrote to Merv Griffin some years later, he said, "Many friends have told me about your interview with Jimmy Breslin a while ago. You countered his unhappy view of second marriage by a discussion of the joyous love affair of Betty and Dick Hughes for many years, up to their necks in kids and hard work. Of course you were entirely right."[19]

Hughes reminisced about Betty in a letter to a priest who had been a classmate at the seminary. "Two months before Betty and I married in 1954, she was shopping in New York and stopped for confession at the Franciscan Church across from Penn Station. She told the priest she was crazy in love with a Judge, a widower with four children, and since she had three kids she didn't know if she could handle it. She was shocked when he said 'of course you can't!' He continued—'But you and God and this Judge can handle it. You see it takes three. But promise me that you and your husband will pray daily for your kids' vocations in life,' and she promised." Hughes went on to say that they had regularly prayed for the children's true vocations. He also wrote that one of the younger children, after hearing this for some time, finally asked when they would be going on the vacations.[20]

Betty had donated her eyes so that others could have the gift of sight. Hughes was so very proud of that unselfish act that he became a major spokesman in favor of eye donation. He convinced the New Jersey Bar Association to set up a "Sight and Life Committee" in Betty's honor to persuade others to donate organs at their deaths. Hughes's own eyesight had always been bad, and he wore glasses throughout his life. He lost the sight in one eye completely toward the end of his life. His son, Tom, was legally blind. Hughes spent much of the next few years promoting the eye donation program. He wrote innumerable letters and spoke to many people urging them to support the program. His letters always spoke of his devotion to Betty.

In one of those letters, addressed to Mort Pye, the editor of the *Newark Star-Ledger*, Hughes wrote, "Mort, I hope you will beat the drums for this transplant miracle. I cannot tell you how my grief for Betty has been assuaged by thinking of the two blind strangers to whom she gave the gift of sight. I'll never get over her but I know she would want me to hustle this program, and it would please her, and that is important to me."[21]

Hughes, always deeply religious, became even more so after Betty's death. In a letter to his son Tim, he expressed his need for the support he received from his belief in God. "You may not know that since Betty left me I have attended daily Mass and feel comfortable only there. In the Liturgy today, the Communion antiphon reads, 'Blessed are the sorrowing, for they shall be consoled.' And with a sudden intensity, which I never before experienced, I was indeed consoled. My eyes were opened, and I suddenly realized the part these unhappy separations played in the Divine plan for my own salvation and return to the Father, and those of my kids, for which I pray daily. In a sense, it is 'paying my dues' for my 17 happy years with Miriam and then 30 more with your Mom. And this consolation miracle gave meaning to my remaining life, a sense of mission, and is most comforting. For Miriam and Betty having surely left the world in the friendship of Our Lord, are at home and wish us to join them one day. And this pain, which has not lessened, may be the way home. I am convinced of that and will continue with reconciliation and even joy, the mission God intends for me in the twilight."[22]

During the years after Betty's death, Hughes tried to keep the family together. He realized that the one role he might not have carried out as well as he should have, was that of father. His newsletter, which referred to his kids as his olive plants, was designed to keep the family informed of what he was doing and what everyone else was doing. He wrote letters to many of his children telling them of his devotion and offering them support in many ways. He occasionally paid the debts of some of the children, paid for others to travel to Florida for visits, or supported their aspirations. In 1985, he wrote to his son Tim, who was then applying to law school, "Please never hesitate to ask me for any help you need. I think my surviving purpose, in whatever remains of my life, is to be supportive to you kids, my 'olive plants.' "[23]

Hughes was living with Betty in Florida at the time of her death. When she died he decided to purchase a home in the Trenton area to be closer to most of the members of the family. He would spend time in both Florida and Trenton. For a substantial period of time, his daughter Helen and his granddaughter Elizabeth came to live with him in his home near Trenton. This was a great tonic for him and he enjoyed the role of grandfather. He had many other grandchildren whom he enjoyed, but this close relationship with Elizabeth, named after Betty, helped to overcome the sorrow he felt at the loss of Betty. At the same time his daughter Mary was living with him in Florida. These arrangements gave peace of mind to the rest of the family, knowing that a member of the family would be with him wherever he was staying.

But the joys of being a grandfather also became a source of great sorrow when one of his grandchildren died. Robert's son, Brian, died very young. Robert described the comfort his father gave him in this difficult time. "He left the warmth of Florida for the cold of New Jersey—even colder in my grief stricken home. I watched from the doorway as the car that brought him from the Airport came to the front of our home. Getting out of the car, old and unsure of his steps yet not waiting for his children to help him, he walked quickly to me and, putting his arms around me, again without a word, he gave me his warmth."[24]

Hughes apologized to family members for any lack of attention during his public career. Although he often included his brother in activities, he seemed to feel that he had received the lion's share of attention during their lives, and that his brother might have been hurt as a result. He knew that his father loved to brag about him, perhaps excluding other family members from such praise. In a particularly poignant letter he wrote to his brother Joseph, the priest, he said, "Now, while I have time, I would like to tell you something else. Being a selfish and self-centered slob, I was always in a hurry and did not always verbalize many personal things, as I should have done, long since. You won't remember this but when you were a kid, you and I shared a bedroom on the fourth floor of Gran's house at 428. When I would come home from a date or like escapade, I would kneel beside your bed for night prayers. As I looked at you, sleeping so quietly, I prayed God that He would give you a good life, long healthy and rewarding. And He surely did. When I think of your priesthood, the war, your service to God, building your Churches, touching so many thousands of souls, standing by always to console and support and help our family members as life's unhappy events would beat us to the ground from time to time, I think God gave you a most successful life."[25]

In 1985, Hughes wrote a letter to a priest whom he had known from his days in the seminary at St. Charles. In that fascinating letter he reflected on his life. "In looking back on a tumultuous life, which old men are inclined to do, I realize that God generously kept sending me blessings, with some sorrow and grief mixed in for seasoning. Some of its high points, including the two great wives he sent me, are mentioned in the enclosed piece which appeared lately in a N.J. magazine. Not mentioned are some tough times, my oldest son an alcoholic from his Air Force days at 18 to the age of 40 in an Orlando skid row. Then the lord took him by the hand, led him to treatment, and 10 years later he is sober and successful. Another son, Tim Murphy was only 2 when I married his mother. Later in life, he left Georgetown and was 'out to lunch' for 10 years. Four years ago, he recovered his sobriety, has a 3.8 average at Rutgers U, and has already been accepted at five fine law schools."[26]

Battling for Judicial Independence

Governor Hughes was often called upon by subsequent governors. He was a great help to Governor Kean when Kean was trying to reappoint Chief Justice Robert Wilentz to a second term as chief justice. Wilentz had replaced Hughes as chief justice in 1979.[27] Under the Constitution of New Jersey all judges and justices are appointed for seven-year terms. If they are reappointed, they may serve until mandatory retirement at age seventy. During Chief Justice Wilentz's time on the court a number of liberal decisions had inflamed many of New Jersey's citizens. These included the Mount Laurel series of cases that had begun under Hughes but were significantly extended by a major decision written by Wilentz. That decision dramatically expanded the requirements for municipalities to take affirmative steps to provide for low- and moderate- income housing in their communities, and many senators from suburban districts were dismayed by the decision. The school funding cases (the *Abbott v. Burke* cases) requiring the state to spend large amounts of money on the urban schools had also rankled many members of the legislature. Consequently, there was significant opposition when Wilentz came up for reappointment. Governor Kean had been opposed to the Mount Laurel opinions, going so far as to call them communistic. However, in deference to the concept of judicial independence, and enjoying a strong personal relationship with Wilentz, Kean chose to reappoint him. This was a Republican governor reappointing as chief justice a Democrat. Strange as that practice might appear, Kean's action was consistent with the tradition of judicial reappointment barring some strong reason other than opinions that would justify denial.

There was a huge confirmation battle. Many senators were prepared to oppose him. The underlying reasons for their opposition were the decisions Wilentz had handed down. But, in recognition of the strong tradition of judicial independence, the senators relied primarily on the argument that Wilentz was living in New York rather than in New Jersey. He owned a summer home in New Jersey and rented an apartment in Perth Amboy, but he spent most of his time in a New York apartment. He and his wife had originally bought the apartment in New York when his children were attending school there. At the time of the dispute, one of the reasons they continued to live in New York was that his wife was being treated for cancer at a New York hospital.

Wilentz and Hughes were very different. Felzenberg, the Kean biographer, describes Hughes's great ability to compromise, having learned that art prior to becoming chief justice. Felzenberg thought Wilentz lacked that ability, saying he did not "demonstrate Hughes's capacity to 'suffer fools,' his flexibility, his likeability, or his temperament, judicial or otherwise."[28]

Another complaint against Wilentz had to do with his selection of Donald E. Stokes, the dean of the Woodrow Wilson School at Princeton University, as the tie-breaker for legislative redistricting. The process in New Jersey for reapportioning the legislature provides for a commission composed of five members chosen by the Republicans and five members chosen by the Democrats. If those ten members cannot agree, the chief justice chooses a tie-breaker.[29] Many of the Republicans felt that the selection of Stokes by Wilentz was made intentionally to benefit the Democrats.

Hughes worked with Kean to secure the reappointment. He spent hours in the governor's office on the telephone with various members of the Senate urging them to support Wilentz. This was consistent with Hughes's overall philosophy. He was totally committed to the concept of judicial independence and thought that the opposition to Wilentz was an intolerable intrusion upon that doctrine. Furthermore, Hughes was supportive of most of the decisions that were at the heart of the dispute. He had been on the court when the first Mount Laurel opinion was written, and although he did not write the opinion, he joined in the decision.

The night of the voting was a long one for the Senate. The Senate president kept the vote board open as negotiations were taking place.[30] The vote hovered for a while at twenty but twenty-one were needed. Ultimately, Wilentz received the twenty-one votes necessary for reappointment after he agreed to convert his summer home into a winter home and spend more time there. Senator Lee Laskin, a Republican, cast the final vote in favor after a telephone conversation with Governor Kean and others.

Michael Cole, who was chief counsel for Governor Kean, remembers that Hughes was like a superstar arguing the importance of the reappointment to the integrity of the judiciary.[31] In an article for the *New York Times*, Joseph F. Sullivan wrote, "Former Governor and Chief Justice Richard J. Hughes sat in the State Senate chamber Thursday night as the 40-member house agonized over the reappointment of the man who had succeeded him as Chief Justice, Robert N. Wilentz. For three hours, the vote board stood at 20 to 19 for reconfirmation, threatening a tie vote that could have led to Chief Justice Wilentz—after seven years as the head of the New Jersey judiciary—becoming the first justice ever denied reappointment and tenure. 'They're gambling with the best court system in the country' Mr. Hughes said of the senators. 'They're playing Russian roulette with the destiny of the state.'"[32] Michael Cole believes that the reappointment would never have been approved without the aid of Hughes.

The Wilentz matter was also important for limiting the scope of senatorial courtesy. New Jersey has for years had a system of senatorial courtesy that permits any senator from the home district where a nominee resides to block the nomination simply by refusing to sign off on the nomination. These systems are not unique to New Jersey. However, that practice is of particular concern when it relates to reappointment of a justice or judge because of its interference with judicial independence. One of the senators from Wilentz's home district, Peter Garibaldi, had sought to invoke senatorial courtesy to block a vote on the confirmation. The president of the Senate, however, required the Judiciary Committee to take up the issue of the nomination, saying that no sitting chief justice had ever been blocked by senatorial courtesy.[33] As governor and afterwards, Hughes had opposed the use of senatorial courtesy and his distaste for the practice was another reason for his willingness to vigorously defend Wilentz.

In an interesting quirk of fate, some years after the death of Hughes, his daughter-in-law, Marianne Espinosa Murphy, fell victim to senatorial courtesy. She had been appointed as a Superior Court judge in Morris County. Her father-in-law had been one of her supporters and swore her in. Marianne had met Hughes's son, Michael Murphy, when she was clerking for Hughes while he was chief justice. At the time of her reappointment, Michael Murphy was serving as Morris County prosecutor. After she had served seven years on the bench, Governor Florio nominated her for a second term. Her nomination would have also given her tenure. Senator John H. Dorsey, who was one of the senators who tried to block the reappointment of Wilentz, exercised his right of senatorial courtesy to block her reappointment. The reasoning was not clear. Dorsey claimed that she was unfair in her treatment of fathers in divorce cases and did not have good judicial temperament. Others suggested that he had problems with decisions made by her husband in his role as prosecutor.

Unfortunately for Espinosa Murphy, the limit placed by the Senate on the use of senatorial courtesy in the context of the reappointment of Wilentz only applied to reappointment to the Supreme Court and not to reappointments to the Superior Court. A law suit was brought challenging the practice of senatorial courtesy. Wilentz did not participate in the case because he had been actively involved in trying to aid the reappointment of Judge Espinosa Murphy and perhaps in part because of his own difficulties with the issue during the fight over his reappointment. The remaining six members of the court permitted the use of senatorial courtesy in that particular instance because in fact there had been a procedural vote protecting the right of the senator to use the procedure. Some members of the court felt an actual decision on the reappointment had thus been made. On the overriding issue of the constitutionality of senatorial courtesy, the court split three to three, thus affirming the lower court decision that it was not unconstitutional.

Espinosa Murphy returned to the practice of law after she lost her challenge. Senator Dorsey lost his senatorial seat in the next election to Gordon MacInnes. While there were undoubtedly various reasons for that defeat, his actions in blocking her reappointment played a role. One newspaper reported, "MacInnes defeated powerful Senate Majority Leader John H. Dorsey by fewer than 300 votes, results that ran counter to the traditionally heavy Republican registration in the 25th Legislative District. Most observers attributed his victory to the firestorm of protest that developed over Dorsey's blackball of a female judge."[34] The seat was in Morris County, a traditional Republican stronghold, and would usually be a fairly easy victory for an incumbent Republican. In 2005, having moved from Morris County, she was again appointed to the Superior Court but this time in Union County.

The challenge to the Wilentz reappointment was seen by Hughes as an attack on the independence of the judiciary. He reacted very strongly when he perceived a threat to that independence. One of those threats came from Senator Gerald Cardinale, a generally conservative Republican from Bergen County, who often challenged decisions of the New Jersey Supreme Court. He introduced a bill requiring that after a judge had been in office for five years, he or she would have to be considered in a nonpartisan election and would lose the position if not approved by the voters. (Such a system is in place in a number of states.) Hughes considered this a terrible idea. He went on the offensive, criticizing the idea and even discussing it at the Legislative Correspondents' Dinner. When Cardinale objected to Hughes's comments, Hughes wrote to him, "My remarks at the Correspondents' dinner seem to have touched a sensitive nerve. I am sorry if they caused you pain, certainly not intended. Indeed, I harbored the small hope that they might touch the conscience of those who would harm their own State by threatening the integrity of its judicial system."[35] After discussing the history of the United States Constitution, Hughes said, "I am astonished when an educated man, with experience in high office, demonstrates so little understanding, not to speak of respect, for these

Constitutions, [United States and New Jersey] under which we Americans live. You apparently . . . lean toward a pure, rather than a constitutional democracy. Except for the Constitution we would all be going to the same church, some of us riding on the back of the bus and excluded from schools and other freedoms. Of this 'will of the majority,' Jefferson once said, 'Let no more be heard of trust in man—bind him down from mischief with the chains of the Constitution!' "[36] Hughes added that even Republicans in New Jersey supported the independence of the judiciary, citing the views of Governor Alfred Driscoll, who was in office when the 1947 Constitution of New Jersey was established and those of Senator Hap Farley, the long-time Republican power in South Jersey. Hughes again referred to the advice Driscoll had given him when he appointed him to the court about being independent. Hughes sent a copy of the letter to Chief Justice Wilentz. Wilentz responded by thanking him for his support and by indicating how difficult it was for he himself to speak out on the issue because of his position. Wilentz said, "When the defender of the judiciary is you, nothing could be better. Many many thanks."[37]

Hughes was also involved in separation of powers issues. He had dealt with those issues as chief justice. During Governor Byrne's administration, the legislature unanimously passed a law creating a legislative veto that gave the legislature oversight over actions of the state's administrative agencies. The law grew out of concern that some of the administrative agencies were intruding too much on the state's citizens. That legislation was held to be unconstitutional by the New Jersey Supreme Court in 1982.[38] Subsequently the legislature attempted to skirt that decision by putting on the ballot an amendment to the New Jersey Constitution which would authorize the use of a legislative veto. Hughes spoke out forcefully against the veto.[39] He joined with Governor Kean and with other former governors of New Jersey in opposing the amendment. He argued, "The Governor can fulfill his duty to 'take care that the laws be faithfully executed' only through the Executive Departments and agencies of State Government, and their rules and regulations regularly adopted. The 'legislative oversight' amendment, as pretty as it sounds, would make this executive responsibility, read like this—'The Governor shall take care that the laws be faithfully executed—except to the extent that the Legislature, unilaterally, prevents him from doing so.' "[40] The proposed constitutional amendment was soundly defeated—851,883 to 511,115.

Some years later, however, in 1992, the same proposed constitutional amendment was again presented to the voters in New Jersey. It was approved. In the intervening years the perception of the administrative agencies as having too much control increased and was symbolized by a particularly notorious instance: the state Health Department decided that all eggs cooked in any restaurant had to be cooked to a certain degree. Supporters of the constitutional amendment used the "runny egg case" as a rallying cry. The legislation was approved 1,352,099 to 978,991. Hughes was not involved in the 1992 debate. He died a month after the amendment was approved.

In 1987, Hughes took on a battle to protect the United States Constitution. The issue dealt with a proposed constitutional convention for the purpose of imposing a constitutional amendment that would mandate a balanced budget. The United States Constitution had never contained such a provision, but at the time increasing budget deficits had spurred a strong movement to impose such a constitutional restriction. Hughes saw the movement as a threat to the constitutional framework. At the time, thirty-one states had approved such a constitutional convention and thirty-four states were required for approval. Hughes felt that the provision was dangerous in itself and that it would also undermine the Constitution by giving the impression that it could be easily changed for any reason. In a newspaper column, Regina Murray marveled at the willingness of Hughes, at the age of seventy-eight, to wage a vigorous campaign against the constitutional convention. He traversed the state using "his legendary skills of persuasion, honed during a lifetime of politics, to convince lawmakers of the need to preserve the original document which had been created by the country's founding fathers."[41] The proposed legislation was defeated in New Jersey.

Hughes also fought against the dismantling of the Public Advocate's Office.[42] He lost that battle. The Public Defender's Office was created during his administration and in later years that office was expanded into a Public Advocate's Office with increased powers. Those powers, including challenging actions of state agencies, were responsible for important litigation that achieved significant changes in the working of government. The office, however, came under criticism for being activist. Eventually, a successful effort was made to eliminate the expanded powers of the public advocate. The Public Advocate's Office was dismantled, although some of its functions including its public defender role were retained. Many years later the public advocate office was reestablished.

Later in life, Hughes also served as chairman of the Board of Trustees of the Mercer Council on Alcoholism and Drug Abuse. His interest in this area was, undoubtedly, partly the result of the struggles some of his own family had with alcoholism.

Even though Hughes had increasing problems with his eyesight as he aged, he still liked to attend events. Michael Cole, Counsel to Governor Kean, remembered that he and Gerry English, both active political and legal leaders—Cole an Independent who worked in Republican administrations and English a Democrat—would sit with Hughes at functions so that they could identify for him people who would stop by to visit. They said Hughes would immediately recognize the names and greet the people with pleasure and shared memories.[43]

Tributes

Among the many honors Hughes received during his life was one of the Catholic Church's most prestigious. He was named a Knight of St. Gregory. This award is given for "meritorious service which benefits religion and the Holy See."[44] Hughes, the first Catholic governor of New Jersey, was an extremely devout Catholic. It was not surprising that he would receive such an award. Another distinguished honor was the naming of the new justice center in Trenton after him.

Hughes's eightieth birthday was an occasion for a major tribute.[45] Even though he had been out of office for ten years, a large crowd gathered at the Hyatt Regency Hotel in Princeton. Governors Meyner and Byrne were the honorary chairs of the event. Two letters sent to commemorate the occasion were particularly poignant. One was from Lady Bird Johnson and one from Senator Edward Kennedy. Mrs. Johnson wrote, "How delighted I am to add my voice to the chorus of happy birthday wishes you are receiving today and to be counted among the legions of those who hold you in great esteem and affection. I smile to recall memorable times with you and Betty, very especially among them, the landmark visit by Alexei Kosygin to Glassboro and being with you at Morven and meeting your remarkable family, most of all I remember the warmth and strength of your friendship to Lyndon and me. Those are the binds which speak to the heart and for which I am everlastingly grateful, with admiration and a large salute, Lady Bird Johnson."[46] Kennedy wrote, "This is not only a birthday celebration, but a celebration of your life-long commitment to making a difference. With an illustrious career of public and private service behind you, you can surely reflect with a sense of enormous fulfillment on your many and enduring contributions. Like my brothers before me, I have valued your friendship and admired your commitment to the progressive and responsive values of our Democratic Party."[47]

Politics was also involved in the tribute. At that time, Democratic Congressman James J. Florio was running for the governorship. Hughes naturally was supporting him. The official invitation to the birthday party said, "The Hughes Family and Friends cordially invite you to join Congressman James J. Florio at a brunch reception to celebrate the 80th birthday of the Honorable Richard J. Hughes."

In 1992 Hughes also helped his son, Brian, who was running for Congress. One event which was scheduled to aid in the campaign was advertised this way: "Please join us to reminisce with Dick Hughes and help to launch the political career of his son, Brian." Brian, like his father, was unable to win that campaign but years later was elected county executive of Mercer County.

Death at Eighty-three

Hughes died on December 7, 1992. He was eighty-three, the same age his father had been when he died. The last year or two had been difficult. He lost total sight in one eye after a fall. He joked that at least it was his bad eye, and when anything sad takes place he only sheds half as many tears. He also suffered a number of strokes. Near the end he was placed on dialysis but when it became clear it was not helping him, the family decided to stop the treatment. His son Pat and other members of the family were there with him to help him through his last months. At the time of his death, a newspaper article said, "Historians are likely to characterize Richard Hughes as a man of action who was instrumental in shaping modern New Jersey. But those who knew him said they saw much more—gentleness, compassion, and a good-natured sense of humor that guaranteed him a special place in the life of his state long after he had shed his last official title."[48]

New Jersey Network, which Hughes helped to create, covered his funeral live. Hundreds of people crowded the church for the funeral Mass. All of the governors who succeeded him were present for the ceremony. Hughes had specifically requested that the song "Sunrise Sunset" from *Fiddler on the Roof* be sung at his funeral. The song focuses on family and how quickly time goes by as children grow. When making the request he noted that it was one of Betty's favorites and had been sung at her funeral. Cissy Rebich, a personal friend of the family and a Broadway performer, was chosen to sing. Hughes and Betty had a daily Scrabble game for many years and Hughes requested that the Scrabble board and scores be buried with him. Judge John Hughes, his son, spoke at the funeral. He remembered his father's fondness for St. Thomas More and said: "Richard Hughes was more than a man for all seasons . . . he was a man, but for all people. It is no exaggeration to say that, with his passing, the people of New Jersey have lost a best friend."[49] After the final prayers at the grave, a bagpiper played the Irish song "Danny Boy."

Conclusion

In the courtyard in front of the New Jersey Bar Association Building in New Brunswick, as well as in the lobby of Seton Hall Law School in Newark, stand statues of Hughes. The artist, Brian Hanlon, studied Hughes's life before creating the identical sculptures. He interviewed a number of people as he attempted to discover the real Hughes. The most striking part of Hanlon's sculpture is the outstretched arm of Hughes waiting to shake the hand of the next person to come by. The statue caught the essence of the man. He was always happy to meet new people or people he had known for years. He made friends all over the state and throughout the nation. The statue depicts Hughes in a rather rumpled suit, reflecting the fact that clothes were not important to him. People were important to him. Ideas for improving his state were important to him, as was justice and family.

That statue is not the only monument to Hughes. The Justice Center in Trenton, which houses the Supreme Court and its administrative offices, as well as the offices of the attorney general and the public defender, is named for Hughes. Many other awards and recognitions, including the Hughes Chair at Seton Hall University, continue to be given today, reflecting the esteem in which this popular New Jerseyan was held.

Hughes's zest for life showed in all that he did. He was a strong advocate for the principles by which he lived, but at the same time he treated everyone with respect and consideration. This did not mean that he did not strongly assert his positions and often strongly criticize his opponents for their positions, but in his personal relationships with these people he treated them with deference and concern.

He, like most people, played numerous roles in his personal life—son, friend, husband, father, brother, uncle, godfather, and grandfather. He played them all well, especially considering his public and professional commitments, even though he, himself, felt that he could have done better in some situations.

Hughes lived a full life. He lived it with zest, enthusiasm and optimism. He loved his family, his church, his state, his country, and his party. His ability to remember those whom he met was legendary. Even years after his death many who were touched by Hughes remember him with great fondness. He worked hard to make things better for his state. He served as a judge, a governor, and a chief justice. He served his country as an Assistant United States Attorney. He served his profession as a practicing attorney. Even when he was not in office, he devoted himself to the public through his work with numerous commissions and boards.

He served his party by his work hosting the 1964 Democratic National Convention and by his yeoman service as chair of the Credentials Committee at the 1968 Democratic National Convention. He campaigned across the state and the country on behalf of those candidates whom he believed would make a difference. And he worked vigorously even in his later years for causes to which he was devoted.

He changed the political landscape of New Jersey considerably, expanding the role of government in the lives of New Jersey citizens. He also brought the state into the twentieth century in many ways. He increased the money available for public works by getting a sales tax enacted and later by helping in the creation of an income tax through his activities as chief justice. In conjunction with the state legislature, but leading the charge, he saw the creation of a county college system, a vastly expanded state college system, a revitalized Hackensack Meadowlands, an expanded transportation system, a public radio and television network, a public defender office, a community affairs department, a new corporation law, and an expanded commitment to civil rights for women and African Americans. Some might argue that some of the decisions he made as both governor and chief justice led to higher taxes, and there is no question that it is true. He made those decisions, however, because he thought that the state owed a greater commitment to education, to transportation, to the poor, and to the mentally ill. In his last speech to the legislature while he was governor, he said that he hoped history would record his administration as "devoted to hearing those who have no voice, who do not belong to a powerful organization with heavy treasure chests and long membership lists. The government should have a special care for those who have no power to speak for themselves."[50]

Hughes was an honest man who never profited from his political roles although occasionally he would seemingly look the other way when others in the state used their political influence to help themselves. This was partially the result of his extreme confidence in, and loyalty to, his friends and partially the result of growing up in a political system that he knew he had to live with if he was going to succeed in achieving his goals for the state. If politics is the art of the possible, he was a political artist. He used the bosses to help him achieve what he felt was best for the state. The fact that they were bosses and not just leaders was immaterial to him.

On the national stage Hughes also played a role. His work as chairman of the Credentials Committee at the 1968 Democratic Convention led to dramatic changes in the methods used to choose presidential candidates. His role in setting up the summit meeting between President Johnson and Premier Kosygin at Glassboro was another important contribution to the search for peace. He also served as an emissary for President Johnson when Johnson asked him to be part of a delegation to monitor the elections in Vietnam

This is the story of a man who, without wealth or an impressive educational background, was able by dint of his own efforts and a good bit of luck to achieve great things. Perhaps, his greatest, however, was his ability to depersonalize political disagreements and to demonstrate civility in his dealings with all.

Notes

Introduction

1. Joseph F. Sullivan, "Richard J. Hughes, Governor and Judge, Dies at 83," *New York Times*, December 8, 1992. On file with author.
2. Document prepared by Robert Hughes entitled "Two Buckets Hughes." On file with author.
3. Kevin R. Richardson, "Night for Richard Hughes," *Star-Ledger*, December 13, 1990.

Chapter 1: The Early Days

1. Dermot Quinn, *The Irish in New Jersey: Four Centuries of American Life* (Piscataway, NJ: Rutgers University Press, 2004), 203.
2. Virginia D. Sederis, "Mr. Hughes Remembers," *New Jersey Reporter*, April 1985, 13.
3. Interview with Thomas More Hughes, the youngest son of Hughes, June 26, 2006.
4. Alvin S. Felzenberg, "The Impact of Gubernatorial Style on Policy Outcomes: An In Depth Study of Three New Jersey Governors" (Diss., Princeton University, 1978), 159. (Hereafter cited as "Felzenberg").
5. "Fielder Names Florence Man Prison Keeper," newspaper article, n.d. On file with author.
6. In 1982, George Amick and John Kolesar interviewed Governor Hughes. The transcripts of the interviews were made available to the author by John Hughes, son and executor of Richard J. Hughes. (Hereafter cited as "Amick and Kolesar"), First Session, 4–5.
7. Letter to the Editor from a Convict of Trenton State Prison, *Newark Evening News*, n.d., Burlington County Regional Edition, 7. On file with author.
8. Ibid.
9. Felzenberg, 161.
10. Interview with Alice Hulse, sister of Richard Hughes, June 25, 2004.

11. Interview with James McLaughlin, former law partner of Governor Hughes, July 12, 2004.
12. Amick and Kolesar, First Session, 12.
13. Ibid.
14. Alvin S. Felzenberg, "The Making of a Governor: The Early Political Career of Richard J. Hughes," *New Jersey History* 101 (1983): 2.
15. Amick and Kolesar, First Session, 8.
16. Ibid.
17. Felzenberg, 161.
18. Amick and Kolesar, Third Session, 75.
19. *Courtier*, Yearbook of Georgian Court College (now Georgian Court University), 1933. Page from the yearbook on file with author.
20. Amick and Kolesar, First Session, 12.
21. Ibid.
22. Ibid., 13.
23. Felzenberg, 163.
24. Amick and Kolesar, First Session, 13.
25. Ibid., 12.
26. Lloyd Paul Stryker, *For the Defense, Thomas Erskine: The Most Enlightened Liberal of His Times, 1750–1823* (Garden City, NY: Doubleday, 1947), vii.
27. John D. Sheridan, introduction "Everyman" to *Handy Andy*, by Samuel Lover (New York: E.P. Dutton, 1954).
28. Amick and Kolesar, Third Session, 72.
29. Ibid., 73.
30. Ibid., First Session, 14.
31. Ibid. The dramatic change in grades is confirmed by the investigation carried out by the F.B.I. when Hughes was being considered for appointment as an Assistant United States Attorney. On file with author.
32. Fannie Steinberg, "Tribute to a Mother: Veronica Gallagher Hughes," 89th Cong., 1st sess., *Congressional Record* 111 (May 6, 1965): H 9382.
33. Amick and Kolesar, Third Session, 84.

Chapter 2: The Young Politician

1. Joseph Katz, "Dick Hughes: One of a Kind," *New Jersey Lawyer* 7, no. 40 (October 5, 1998): 6.
2. Ibid.
3. George Amick and John Kolesar interviewed Governor Hughes. The transcripts of the interviews were made available to the author. (Hereafter cited as "Amick and Kolesar.") Third Session, 74.
4. Ibid.
5. Interview with Alice Hulse, June 25, 2004.
6. Interview with Claire McQuade.
7. Interview with Robert Hughes.
8. Interview with Alice Hulse.
9. Amick and Kolesar, Third Session, 84.

10. Ibid., 85.

11. Ibid.

12. *Courier-Post*, "Hughes Announces for Congress from Fourth Jersey District," July 12, 1938, n.p.

13. Ibid.

14. Amick and Kolesar, Second Session, 49.

15. Richard J. Hughes, *Reflections: A Growing Court*, 11 Seton Hall L. Rev. 379, 381 (1981).

16. Amick and Kolesar, Second Session, 52.

17. Ibid., 51.

18. Letter from Hughes to Sis Rose Bernhardt, August 19, 1985. On file with author.

19. FBI file on Hughes in section dealing with investigation of Hughes for the position of Assistant U.S. Attorney at page 7. On file with author.

20. Amick and Kolesar, Second Session, 55.

21. *United States v. German-American Vocational League*, 153 F.2d 860 (3d Cir. 1946).

22. "Nazis' Nemesis in New Jersey Appears 'Nice and Innocent,'" n.d. Article on file with author.

23. Amick and Kolesar, Second Session, 62.

24. Joseph W. Katz, interview by G. Kurt Piehler and Darren Purtlebaugh, November 8, 1995, transcript, Oral History Archives of WW-II, Rutgers University History Department, New Brunswick, NJ, http://oralhistory.rutgers.edu/Interviews/katz_joseph_part_2.html.

25. Ronald Grele, "Structural Development of Urban Liberalism in the Democratic Party of the Fourth Congressional District of New Jersey, 1930–1960" (Diss., Rutgers University, 1971), 169.

26. Interview with Joel Sterns.

27. Alvin S. Felzenberg, "The Impact of Gubernatorial Style on Policy Outcomes: An In Depth Study of Three New Jersey Governors" (Diss., Princeton University, 1978), 168.

28. Grele, "Structural Development," 12–13.

29. Richard Carl Leone, "The Politics of Gubernatorial Leadership: Tax and Education Reform in New Jersey" (Diss., Princeton University, 1969), 44.

30. *Trenton Evening Times*, June 28, 1945. On file with author.

31. Ibid.

32. Ibid.

33. Amick and Kolesar, Third Session, 95.

34. Ibid., Second Session, 57.

35. Ibid., 57–58.

36. Ibid., 59.

37. Ibid., Fourth Session, 106.

38. Grele, "Structural Development," 168–69.

39. Ibid., 169.

40. Ibid.

41. Ibid., 170.

42. Ibid.

43. Amick and Kolesar, Second Session, 42.

44. *Newsday*, "Frank Thompson Jr., 70, Abscam Figure," July 24, 1989, City edition, 31.

45. Amick and Kolesar, Second Session, 43.

46. Ibid., 44.

47. Interview with W. Michael Murphy, July 9, 2006.

48. Leone, "Politics of Gubernatorial Leadership," 24–5.

49. Fleming, *Mysteries of My Father: An Irish-American Memoir* (Hoboken, NJ: Wiley, 2005), 181–182.

50. Ibid., 182.

51. Ibid.

52. Amick and Kolesar, Third Session, 86. See also Dayton David McKean, *The Boss: The Hague Machine in Action* (Boston: Houghton Mifflin/Riverside Press Cambridge, 1940), 97–98.

53. John T. Cunnigham, *New Jersey: America's Main Road* (Garden City, NY: Doubleday, 1966), 293.

54. Amick and Kolesar, Third Session, 86.

55. Ibid., Third Session, 86–87. See also Grele, "Structural Development," 214–217.

56. Amick and Kolesar, Second Session, 46–47. See generally McKean, *The Boss*, 166–167.

57. John McLaughlin, "The Arrangement: Hughes and the Party Bosses," *Sunday Times Advertiser*, January 18, 1970, 3.

58. Richard J. Hughes, editorial, "Skeleton in the Closet," *New Jersey L. J.*, August 5, 1948, 4.

Chapter 3: The Bench

1. Letter from Robert Hughes to the author. On file with author.

2. Barbara G. Salmore and Stephen A. Salmore, *New Jersey Politics and Government: Suburban Politics Comes of Age*, 2nd ed. (Lincoln: University of Nebraska Press, 1998), 128.

3. Ibid.

4. "The people of New Jersey will exchange America's worst court system for America's best." Arthur T. Vanderbilt II, *Changing Law: A Biography of Arthur T. Vanderbilt II* (New Brunswick, NJ: Rutgers University Press, 1976), 164.

5. G. Alan Tarr and Mary Cornelia Porter, *State Supreme Courts in State and Nation* (New Haven, CT: Yale University Press, 1988), 191.

6. Ibid., 188.

7. Ibid., 189. See also Dayton David McKean, *The Boss: The Hague Machine in Action* (Boston: Houghton Mifflin/Riverside Press Cambridge, 1940), 78–81

8. Arthur T. Vanderbilt II, *Changing Law*, 213.

9. George Amick and John Kolesar interviewed Governor Hughes. The transcripts of the interviews were made available to the author. (Hereafter cited as "Amick and Kolesar.") Fourth Session, 107.

10. Ibid., Third Session, 89–90.
11. Speech by Federal District Court Judge Katharine Sweeney Hayden at Seton Hall Law School on February 27, 2007. Copy of speech on file with author.
12. Ibid.
13. Interview with Robert Hughes.
14. Interview with Alice Hulse, June 25, 2004.
15. Amick and Kolesar, Fourth Session, 102–103.
16. Ibid., 98.
17. Pete Daly, "Chance Meeting with Sen. Biden Jars Memory," *Trentonian*, n.d. On file with author.
18. Robert Hughes to his siblings, memorandum, May 22, 1998, "In The Name of Our Father." Copy on file with author.
19. Prior to December 8, 1983, there was a distinction between judges sitting on the county court and judges sitting on Superior Court. In 1983, the New Jersey Constitution was amended, eliminating this distinction.
20. Amick and Kolesar, Fourth Session, 108–109.
21. Ibid., 109–110.
22. Letter from Hughes to Chief Justice Arthur T. Vanderbilt, June 4, 1952. On file with author.
23. Interview with The Honorable John Gibbons, April 11, 2006.
24. "Jersey Takes Over in Bergen Gambling," *New York Times*, December 2, 1950, 1.
25. Ibid.
26. "Takes Prosecutor's Job," *New York Times*, December 15, 1950, 44.
27. *State v. Winne*, 21 N.J. Super. 180, 186–187 (N.J. Super. Ct. Law Div. 1952).
28. Ibid.
29. Ibid., 192–193.
30. Ibid.
31. Ibid., 199–200.
32. Ibid., 210–211 (quoting *Curnow v. Kessler*, 67 N.W. 982, 984 (Mich. 1896)).
33. Ibid., 218.
34. Ibid., 222.
35. *State v. Winne*, 12 N.J. 152, 167 (1953).
36. Ibid., 169.
37. Ibid., 170.
38. Ibid., 181–182.
39. Robinson v. California, 370 U.S. 660 (1962).
40. "Winne is Cleared in Gambling Case," *New York Times*, May 15, 1954, 1.
41. Ibid.
42. Amick and Kolesar, Fourth Session, 111.
43. Interview with The Honorable Edward Beglin, June 16, 2006.
44. Interview with Governor Brendan Byrne, February 17, 2006.
45. Amick and Kolesar, Fourth Session, 98–99.
46. Interview with Joel Sterns.
47. Amick and Kolesar, Fourth Session, 99–100.
48. Ibid., 111–112.

49. Letter from Richard Paul Hughes to his son. On file with author.
50. Amick and Kolesar, Fourth Session, 112.

Chapter 4: Private Practitioner

1. Interview with James McLaughlin, July 12, 2004.
2. Ibid.
3. Joseph Katz, "Dick Hughes: One of a Kind," *New Jersey Lawyer* 7, no. 40 (October 5, 1998): 6.
4. Alvin S. Felzenberg, "The Impact of Gubernatorial Style on Policy Outcomes: An In Depth Study of Three New Jersey Governors" (Diss., Princeton University, 1978), 173 (hereafter cited as "Felzenberg").
5. George Amick and John Kolesar interviewed Governor Hughes. The transcripts of the interviews were made available to the author. (Hereafter cited as "Amick and Kolesar.") Fourth Session, 120.
6. John Seabrook, "Personal History: The Spinach King," *New Yorker*, February 20, 1995.
7. Interview with James McLaughlin.
8. Alan V. Lowenstein, *Alan V. Lowenstein, New Jersey Lawyer & Community Leader* (New Brunswick, NJ: Rutgers University Press, 2001), 241.
9. Amick and Kolesar, Fourth Session, 121–22.
10. Ibid., 121.
11. Interview with Agnes Reiss, daughter of William Reiss.
12. Amick and Kolesar, Fourth Session, 122.
13. Ibid., 127.
14. Ibid.
15. Ibid., 122.
16. Ibid., 123.
17. Ibid.
18. Ibid., 124.
19. Ibid., 119.
20. Interview with Joel Sterns.
21. Interview with Richard Coffee, February 22, 2005.
22. Interview with Joel Sterns.
23. Interview with The Honorable J. Wilson Noden.

Chapter 5: Governor Hughes: The Campaign

1. Lizabeth Cohen, *A Consumers' Republic: The Politics of Mass Consumption in Postwar America* (New York: Alfred A. Knopf, 2003), 195.
2. Ibid., 197.
3. Ibid., 229.
4. Ibid.
5. Richard Carl Leone, "The Politics of Gubernatorial Leadership: Tax and Education Reform in New Jersey" (Diss., Princeton University, 1969), 57.
6. Ibid., 60.

7. Paul A. Stellhorn and Michael J. Birkner, eds., *The Governors of New Jersey, 1664–1974* (Trenton, NJ: New Jersey Historical Commission, 1982), 221.

8. Alvin S. Felzenberg, "The Impact of Gubernatorial Style on Policy Outcomes: An In Depth Study of Three New Jersey Governors" (Diss., Princeton University, 1978), 175 (hereafter cited as "Felzenberg").

9. Theodore H. White, *The Making of the President, 1960* (Cutchogue, NY: Buccaneer Books, 1961), 159–160.

10. W. H. Lawrence, "Convention Opens," *New York Times*, July 12, 1960, 20.

11. Gary Shenfeld, "Meyner in Running for Vice President; Johnson Ties Cited," *Bulletin Staff*, December 28, 1963, 1.

12. Ibid.

13. Felzenberg, 175.

14. *Time*, "Battle for the Senate: Republicans Can Gain but Cannot Win Control," October 17, 1960, 25.

15. Ibid.

16. Interview with Joel Sterns.

17. John F. Kennedy, Presidential campaign speech, Bergen Mall, Paramus, NJ, September 15, 1960, http://www.jfklink.com/speeches/jfk/sept60/jfk150960_paramus02.html.

18. Robert Hughes, e-mail to author, 10/26/04. On file with author.

19. Interview with Joel Sterns.

20. Felzenberg, 176.

21. Ibid., 177.

22. Amick and Kolesar, Fourth Session, 113.

23. Ibid.

24. Interview with Joel Sterns, who indicated that he thought the meeting took place at Thorn Lord's house.

25. Amick and Kolesar, Fourth Session, 113.

26. Ibid., 113–114.

27. *Time*, "Battle for the Senate," 25.

28. Interview with Joel Sterns.

29. Grele tells a somewhat different version: "Meyner first proposed [Harrison] Williams as the party's candidate, with Lord and Wilentz favoring Thompson. Kennedy, however, convinced Thompson to remain in Congress, and on Kenny's suggestion, Hughes was chosen informally by party leaders. Meyner continued, however, to support Williams or William F. Hyland, then a New Jersey Public Utilities Commissioner. The impasse was resolved when the Democratic leaders of 20 of New Jersey's 21 counties in a meeting with Meyner chose Hughes—a decided 'rebuff' to Meyner." Ronald Grele, "Structural Development of Urban Liberalism in the Democratic Party of the Fourth Congressional District of New Jersey, 1930–1960" (Diss., Rutgers University, 1971), 493–494.

30. Interview with Adrian "Bud" Foley, April 11, 2006.

31. Amick and Kolesar, Fourth Session, 114.

32. Joseph W. Katz, "Dennis Carey Not THEIR Valentine," *Newark Evening News*, February 1961, page 6.

33. "Top Hughes Aide: Bontempo Set to Head Campaign," *Newark Evening News*, February 28, 1961.

34. "Giordano Heads Hughes Campaign," *Newark Evening News*, August 1, 1961.
35. Dawes Thompson, "Hughes Ratified," *Newark Evening News*, February 13, 1961.
36. Interview with Congressman Peter Rodino, November 4, 2004.
37. "Hughes Post for Rodino," *Newark Evening News*, September 11, 1961.
38. Joseph W. Katz, interview by G. Kurt Piehler and Darren Purtlebaugh, November 8, 1995, transcript, Oral History Archives of WW-II, Rutgers University History Department, New Brunswick, NJ, http://oralhistory.rutgers.edu/Interviews/katz_joseph_part_2.html (hereafter "Katz Oral History").
39. Grele, "Structural Development," 495.
40. Interview with James McLaughlin, July 12, 2004.
41. Interview with Senator Raymond Bateman, former Assembly and Senate leader, and later candidate for governor, September 27, 2004.
42. Joseph Katz, "Dick Hughes: One of a Kind," *New Jersey Lawyer* 7, no. 40 (October 5, 1998): 6.
43. Ibid.
44. John J. Farmer, "GOP Conservative Hughes Contributor," *Newark Evening News*, November 28, 1961.
45. *Time*, "Jersey Joust," October 6, 1961.
46. "Hughes Does the Impossible," *Newark Evening News*, July 8, 1961.
47. Ibid.
48. Ibid.
49. Open letter from Mercer County Lawyers for Hughes to James Mitchell, November 3, 1961. On file with author.
50. "Mitchell for Governor," *Asbury Park Evening Press*, October 25, 1961, 18.
51. "Hughes for Governor," *Trenton Evening Times*, October 12, 1961.
52. Katz Oral History.
53. Amick and Kolesar, Second Session, 37–38.
54. Interview with Angelo Baglivo, October 14, 2004.
55. Katz Oral History.
56. "Hughes Highlights: A Fortnightly Review of the Democratic Party Campaign Happenings," September 21, 1961, Richard J. Hughes Archives, Seton Hall University. Copy on file with author.
57. "Hughes Bars Broad-Base Tax Program," Associated Press, n.d. On file with author.
58. George Kentera, "Did Hughes Offer Seat on Court to Cahill?" *Newark Sunday News*, September 17, 1961, 1.
59. Ibid.
60. Ibid.
61. "Hughes Continues Silence on Cahill," *Newark Evening News*, September 21, 1961.
62. "Mitchell Has No Job 'Offer' Data," *Newark Evening News*, September 18, 1961.
63. "Hughes Continues Silence on Cahill," *Newark Evening News*, September 21, 1961.
64. Alvin S. Felzenberg, "The Making of a Governor: The Early Political Career

of Richard J. Hughes," *New Jersey History* 101 (1983), 20 (hereafter cited as "Felzenberg, 'Governor Hughes' ").

65. Interview with The Honorable Patrick King, December 6, 2006.

66. Felzenberg, "Governor Hughes," 20.

67. Ibid.

68. "Campaign Funds Erupt as Issue," *Newark Evening News*, October 11, 1961, 1.

69. Ibid.

70. Angelo Baglivo, "Says Legal Aides 'Hit' for Funds," *Newark Evening News*, October 23, 1961, 1.

71. Ibid.

72. *Star-Ledger*, "Hughes Asks Vote on Issues, Says Mitchell is 'No Liberal,' " September 27, 1961.

73. George Cable Wright, "Rights Enforcing Urged by Hughes," *New York Times*, June 4, 1961, 46.

74. White, *Making of the President*, 261–262.

75. "It's a Long Way to Nov. 7," United Press International, n.d. On file with author.

76. Interview with Senator Raymond Bateman. See also Leo Egan, " 'Visibility' and Parties," *New York Times*, April 20, 1961, 25.

77. *Time*, "Hughes Who in New Jersey," November 17, 1961, 29.

78. Dawes Thompson, " 'Know No Finer Man,' Ike says of Mitchell," *Newark Evening News*, October 12, 1961, 1.

79. "Pentagon Will Lease 460 Acres On Sandy Hook for Jersey Park," *New York Times*, October 26, 1961, 71.

80. The Hughes girls also functioned in the second campaign and this time Beusse convinced leading designers to donate their time and effort to designing new outfits for the "girls." Interview with Jacqueline Beusse, May 31, 2006. "The outfits were buff dresses, A-Line style, by Stacy Ames. The hats were by Mr. John of Paris and New York. The hats were a one-of-a-kind: They were royal blue and buff—with a high crown." The designers donated the outfits. Jacqueline Beusse, letter to author, August 30, 2006. On file with author.

81. Edward J. Mullin, "The Campaigners: Some Love It and Some Hate It. And It Doesn't Have Much to Do With Their Ability to Fill the Office," *Herald-News*, October 31, 1969, 2T.

82. *Time*, "Hughes Who in New Jersey," 29.

83. Interview with Robert Hughes.

84. Alan L. Otten, "Jersey Governor Race Gets National Interest But Stirs Little Heat," *Wall Street Journal*, October 17, 1961, 1.

85. Felzenberg, "Governor Hughes," 19.

86. Interview with John Miller, December 1, 2006. Miller served as an assemblyman during Hughes' first two years in office and later became the long-time clerk of the General Assembly of New Jersey.

87. George Cable Wright, "Hughes Backed by Jersey C.I.O.," *New York Times*, September 25, 1961, 37.

88. *Politifax: A Weekly Electronic Newsletter on Politics in New Jersey*, "Legends," III, no. 5 (June 30, 1999).

89. "Richard J. Hughes Dead at 83 New Jersey's Greatest Citizen, Ex-Governor," *Bergen Record*, December 8, 1992, 1.

90. *Trenton Evening Times*, November 3, 1961, 22.

91. Richard J. Hughes, *A Few Recollections of JFK*, n.d. On file with author.

92. Cabell Philips, "Hughes Seeking Kennedy's Help In Race for Jersey Governorship," *New York Times*, October 25, 1961, 24.

93. Joseph A. Loftus, "Kennedy Expresses Support of Hughes in Jersey Contest," *New York Times*, October 26, 1961, 28.

94. John F. Kennedy, Presidential campaign speech, Trenton, NJ, November 2, 1961, http://www.jfklink.com/speeches/jfk/publicpapers/1961/jfk448_61.html.

95. Ibid.

96. Interview with W. Michael Murphy, July 9, 2006.

97. *Fitzgerald's New Jersey Legislative Manual 1962*, 186th sess. (Trenton, NJ: J. Joseph Gibbons, 1962), 652–737.

98. Richard J. Hughes, *A Few Recollections of JFK*, on file with the author.

99. "Mr. Hughes Triumphs" *Trenton Evening Times*, November 8, 1961.

100. Frank Lordan, "Happy Day at the Capital," *Camden Courier-Post*, January 20, 1962, 10–11.

101. First Inaugural Address of Governor Richard J. Hughes, January 16, 1962, found in *Fitzgerald's New Jersey Legislative Manual 1962*, 762.

102. Ibid., 763.

103. *New York Times*, "Hughes Comes to Aid of a Constituent, 16," January 5, 1962, 34.

Chapter 6: The Early Days as Governor

1. Inaugural Address by President John F. Kennedy, January 20, 1961.

2. Richard Connors, *A Cycle of Power* (Metuchen, NJ: The Scarecrow Press, 1971), 203.

3. Ibid.

4. Letter from Hughes to Webster Todd, June 14, 1965. On file with author.

5. Letter from Hughes to Webster Todd, December 21, 1965. On file with the author.

6. Raymond Bateman, "Richard J. Hughes was My Kind of Politician," *Courier-News*, December 18, 1992.

7. Ibid.

8. Ibid. These sentiments were further confirmed in an interview on September 27, 2004.

9. *Baker v. Carr*, 369 U.S. 186 (1962); *Reynolds v. Sims*, 377 U.S. 533 (1964).

10. *Fitzgerald's New Jersey Legislative Manual 1968*, 192th sess. (Trenton, NJ: J. Joseph Gibbons, 1968), 183.

11. Joseph W. Katz, interview by G. Kurt Piehler and Darren Purtlebaugh, November 8, 1995, transcript, Oral History Archives of WW-II, Rutgers University History Department, New Brunswick, N.J., http://oralhistory.rutgers.edu/Interviews/katz_joseph_part_2.html.

12. Robert Leckie, "What The Governor Does All Day." On file with author.

13. Interview with Larry Bilder, former secretary and counsel to the governor, September 22, 2004.

14. Alvin S. Felzenberg, "The Impact of Gubernatorial Style on Policy Outcomes: An In Depth Study of Three New Jersey Governors" (Diss., Princeton University, 1978), 211 (hereafter cited as "Felzenberg").

15. Interview with Governor Byrne, February 17, 2006.

16. Christopher Minicler, "Governor Hughes is Bustling Executive, Surprisingly Accessible and Usually Late," Associated Press, n.d. On file with author.

17. Edward J. Sullivan, "How to be Governor by Really Trying!" *The Sign*, 28.

18. *Trenton Evening Times*, "Does NJ Need a Lieutenant Governor?" January 26, 1986.

19. Interview with Stephen Wiley, March 6, 2007.

20. "Situated directly outside the Governor's inner office, [Larry] Bilder enjoyed the greatest access to Hughes. Among the functions delegated to him were that of 'gatekeeper' and 'dispenser of patronage.'" Felzenberg, 216.

21. Bill Dwyer, "Governor Hughes Had His Buddies in the Media, Too," *Times* (Trenton, NJ), Sunday, January 19, 1992.

22. Interview with James McLaughlin, July 12, 2004.

23. George Amick, "Hughes Enjoys Matching Wits with the Press," *Trenton Evening Times*, March 31, 1963.

24. Roger Cohen, "Casting Giant Shadows: The Politics of Building the World Trade Center," *Portfolio: A Quarterly Review of Trade and Transportation*, Winter 1990/1991, http://www.greatbuildings.com/buildings/World_Trade_Center_History.html.

25. Ibid., quoting Austin Tobin.

26. Ibid.

27. Ibid.

28. *Courtesy Sandwich Shop v. Port of New York Auth.*, 17 A.D.2d 590 (N.Y. App. Div. 1963).

29. Brief and Appendix for the Intervenor, Attorney General of the State of New Jersey in *Courtesy Sandwich Shop v. Port of New York Auth*, 12 N.Y.2d 379 (1963). On file with author.

30. *Courtesy Sandwich Shop v. Port of New York Auth*, 12 N.Y.2d 379 (1963).

31. George Cable Wright, "Rockefeller Wins a Tax Agreement with New Jersey," *New York Times*, May 6, 1962, 1.

32. *Camden Courier-Post*, March 8, 1962.

33. George Cable Wright, "Hughes Approves Shore Storm Aid," *New York Times*, March 30, 1962, 34.

34. *Camden Courier-Post*, "Storm Aid Hailed by Governor," May 2, 1962.

35. Ibid.

36. Richard Carl Leone, "The Politics of Gubernatorial Leadership: Tax and Education Reform in New Jersey" (Diss., Princeton University, 1969), 14.

37. *Engel v. Vitale*, 370 U.S. 421 (1962).

38. Ibid., 422.

39. *Camden Courier-Post*, July 25, 1962.

40. "For most of its history, public education in America had been unabashedly patriotic and unmistakably Protestant. . . . Civic leaders assumed 'that Americanism

and Protestantism were synonyms and that education and Protestantism were allies.' Early common schools featured Bible reading, prayer, hymns, and holiday observances, all reinforced by the exhortations of the teacher and the pervasive Protestantism of the texts." John C. Jeffries and James E. Ryan, *A Political History of the Establishment Clause,* 100 *Mich. L. Rev.* 276, 297–298 (2001), citing David B. Tyack, *Onward Christian Soldiers: Religion in the American Common School,* in *History and Education: The Educational Uses of the Past* 212, 217 (Paul Nash ed. 1970) and Timothy L. Smith, "Protestant Schooling and American Nationality, 1800–1850," 53, *Journal of American History* 679, 689 (1967).

41. *Sch. Dist. of Abington Twp. v. Schempp,* 374 U.S. 203 (1963).

42. "Trenton Is Silent: Hughes, Officials Want Time to Study Edict," *Newark Evening News,* June 17, 1963, 1; "State to Delay Ban on Prayer: Sills' Opinion Is Awaited," *Newark Evening News,* June 18, 1963, 1.

43. Bruce Bahrenburg, "Must Live Under Law, Hughes Says," *Newark Evening News,* June 19, 1963, 10.

44. "Bible Ban Backed by Jersey Board," *New York Times,* September 12, 1963, 29.

45. Ibid.

46. *Sills v. Bd. of Ed.,* 84 N.J. Super. 63 (Super. Ct. Ch. Div. 1963).

47. George Cable Wright, "Hatch Act Charge Fought by Jersey," *New York Times,* April 20, 1962, 54.

48. George Amick and John Kolesar interviewed Governor Hughes. The transcripts of the interviews were made available to the author. (Hereafter cited as "Amick and Kolesar.") Sixth Session, 27.

49. Ibid., 28.

50. "Jersey Official Denies Violation of Hatch Act," *New York Times,* November 30, 1962, 18.

51. "Jersey Aide Wins In Hatch Act Case," *New York Times,* August 7, 1963, 30.

52. Ibid.

53. Amick and Kolesar, Sixth Session, 28.

54. Bolton Schwartz, "Hughes: Jersey's Happy Warrior," *Passaic Herald-News,* July 5, 1981, B2.

55. Ibid.

56. Interview with William Hyland, March 9, 2007, and excerpt from the Hughes's remarks at the Regional Conference of Attorneys General, September 25, 1975. On file with author.

57. George Cable Wright, "Kennedy Gives 'Major Boost' To Party in Short Jersey Visit," *New York Times,* October 13, 1962, 9.

58. Copy of press release of the telegram from Governor Hughes to President Kennedy. On file with author.

59. Copy of press release of the telegram from President Kennedy to Governor Hughes. On file with author.

60. Ronald Grele, "Structural Development of Urban Liberalism in the Democratic Party of the Fourth Congressional District of New Jersey, 1930–1960" (Diss., Rutgers University, 1971), 397.

61. Ibid., 398.

62. Interview with Larry Bilder.

63. Ibid.

64. Bolton Schwartz, postscript to *A House Called Morven: Its Role in American History*, by Alfred Hoyt Bill and Walter E. Edge (Princeton, NJ: Princeton University Press, 1978), 205.

65. Interview with Jacqueline Beusse.

66. Ibid.

67. Amick and Kolesar, Third Session, 75–76.

68. "Richard J. Hughes Dead at 83 New Jersey's Greatest Citizen, Ex-Governor," *Bergen Record*, December 8, 1992, 1.

Chapter 7: Dallas, 1963—Atlantic City, 1964

1. George Amick and John Kolesar interviewed Governor Hughes. The transcripts of the interviews were made available to the author. (Hereafter cited as "Amick and Kolesar.") Sixth Session, 25.

2. Ibid.

3. John Hughes, speech to Catholic Charities, September 21, 2001. On file with author.

4. Amick and Kolesar, Sixth Session, 29.

5. Ibid., 30.

6. Ibid.

7. Ibid., 33.

8. Ibid.

9. Ibid., 34.

10. Ibid.

11. Lyndon B. Johnson, Remarks on the transfer to New Jersey of lands for the Sandy Hook State Park, The American Presidency Project, June 23, 1963, http://www.presidency.ucsb.edu/ws/print.php?pid=26335.

12. "Gov. Hughes Urges Rights Units to Bar Convention Protest," *New York Times*, August 23, 1964, 81.

13. Warren Weaver, "Democrats Pick Atlantic City for 1964 National Convention," *New York Times*, Junes 26, 1963, 26.

14. Oral history of Governor Hughes and Betty Hughes for the Lyndon Baines Johnson Presidential Library, November 27, 1978, 9. (Hereafter cited as "LBJ Oral History, Hughes.")

15. "New Jersey is Happy," *New York Times*, Junes 26, 1963, 26.

16. Nelson Johnson, *Boardwalk Empire: The Birth, High Times, and Corruption of Atlantic City* (Medford, NJ: Plexus Publishing, 2002), photograph insert opposite page 155.

17. Ibid.

18. Oral history of Jane Engelhard for the Lyndon Baines Johnson Presidential Library, February 19, 20, 1977 and January 6, 1978, 35. (Hereafter cited as "LBJ Oral History, Engelhard.")

19. Ibid., 47.

20. Amick and Kolesar, Fifth Session, 9.

21. Ibid., 10.

22. Lyndon B. Johnson, remarks, Dinner of the New Jersey State Democratic

Committee, Atlantic City, May 10, 1964, http://www.presidency.ucsb.edu/ws/index.php?pid=26241.

23. LBJ Oral History, Engelhard, 47.

24. Ibid., 48–49.

25. Ibid., 50–51. The close relationship between the Engelhards and Johnson is clearly demonstrated in a quote from Jack Valenti. "The Engelhards were longtime chums of the president and he liked to be with them." Jack Valenti, *A Very Human President* (New York: W.W. Norton, 1975), 281.

26. Theodore H. White, *The Making of the President, 1964* (New York: Atheneum, 1965), 276.

27. Ibid.

28. LBJ Oral History, Hughes, 10.

29. Ibid., 12–14.

30. Ibid., 14.

31. Betty Hughes, "After the Ball was Over," *Sunday Star-Ledger*, August 30, 1964, 5.

32. Ibid.

33. *New York Times*, "Hughes Makes Room for Two," August 24, 1964, 17.

34. E. W. Kenworthy, "Texas-Size Boardwalk Fete Honors Johnson on 56th Birthday," *New York Times*, August 28, 1964, 12.

35. LBJ Oral History, Hughes, 63.

36. LBJ Oral History, Hughes, 63–64.

37. Lyndon Baines Johnson, *The Vantage Point: Perspectives of the Presidency, 1963–1969* (New York: Holt, Rinehart and Winston, 1971), 96–97.

38. C. David Heymann, *RFK: A Candid Biography of Robert F. Kennedy* (New York: Dutton Books, 1998), 363.

39. LBJ Oral History, Hughes, 8–9. For support from others concerning the deference that Johnson showed to Kennedy, see Heymann, *RFK*, 364.

40. Lyndon Johnson as quoted in Doris Kearns Goodwin, *Lyndon Johnson and the American Dream* (New York: Harper and Row, 1976), 199–200.

41. Jules Witcover, *85 Days: The Last Campaign of Robert Kennedy* (New York: Putnam Books, 1969), 20–21.

42. Heymann, *RFK*, 364.

43. Johnson, *Vantage Point*, 100.

44. Interview with Lester Shapiro, February 22, 2005.

45. Robert Mann, *The Walls of Jericho: Lyndon Johnson, Hubert Humphrey, Richard Russell, and the Struggle for Civil Rights* (New York: Harcourt Brace, 1996), 433.

46. "The capricious part of Johnson's nature made it impossible for Humphrey ever to relax about the relationship." Max Kampelman as quoted in Mann, *Walls of Jericho*, 435.

47. White, *Making of the President*, 273. See also, Mann, *Walls of Jericho*, 434.

48. LBJ Oral History, Hughes, 65.

49. Mann, *Walls of Jericho*, 438.

50. Ibid.

51. Michael R. Beschloss, *Taking Charge: The Johnson White House Tapes, 1963–1964* (New York: Simon and Schuster, 1997), 466.

52. Ibid., 467.

53. Mann, *Walls of Jericho*, 438.

54. Beschloss, *Taking Charge*, 535.

55. Interview with Governor James J. Florio, February 2, 2005.

56. Mann, *Walls of Jericho*, 439.

57. Johnson, *Vantage Point*, 101.

58. Betty Hughes, "After the Ball was Over," *Sunday Star-Ledger*, August 30, 1964, 1–5.

59. LBJ Oral History, Hughes, 64.

60. Richard O. Shafer, "Hughes Blasts GOP," *Star-Ledger*, August 25, 1964, 1.

61. Interview with Adrian "Bud" Foley, April 11, 2006.

62. Harold Faber, ed., *The Road to the White House* (New York: The New York Times, 1965), 107.

63. Ibid., 110.

64. Ibid.; William Shakespeare, *The Tragedy of Romeo and Juliet* (New Haven, CT: Yale University Press, 1954), III, ii, 21–25.

65. Hughes, "After the Ball was Over," 1.

66. Amick and Kolesar, Sixth Session, 31.

67. Interview with William Hyland, March 9, 2007.

68. LBJ Oral History, Hughes, 68.

69. LBJ Oral History, Hughes, 68–69.

Chapter 8: Civil Rights

1. Chris Baud, "1963: Trenton Shares in the Dream," *Trentonian*, www.capitalcentury.com/1963.html.

2. Priscilla Reed Chenoweth, "Black and White Together: A Time to Remember" in *Interracial Bonds*, ed. Rhoda Goldstein Blumberg and Wendell James Roye (Bayside, NY: General Hall Publishers, 1979), 62.

3. George Amick and John Kolesar interviewed Governor Hughes. The transcripts of the interviews were made available to the author. (Hereafter cited as "Amick and Kolesar.") Sixth Session, 3.

4. Ibid., 2.

5. Joseph A. Loftus, "Governors Shut Off Civil Rights Debate, Send Issue to Panel," *New York Times*, July 24, 1963, 1.

6. Amick and Kolesar, Sixth Session, 3.

7. "Catholics Obliged to OK Housing Bill." Newspaper article on file with author.

8. Ronald Sullivan, "Fair-Housing Bill Signed by Hughes," *New York Times*, April 8, 1966, 34.

9. L. 1945, c. 17.

10. Ibid., § 1.

11. Ibid., § 2.

12. Sullivan, "Fair-Housing Bill Signed by Hughes," 34.

13. Ibid.

14. *Fitzgerald's New Jersey Legislative Manual 1966*, 190th sess. (Trenton, NJ: J. Joseph Gibbons, 1966), 744.

15. "Hughes Prods Schools to Curtail Racial Bias." Newspaper article on file with author.

16. *New York Times*, "Hughes Won't Intervene," August 5, 1962, 55.

17. George Cable Wright, "Englewood Trial Postponed," *New York Times*, April 20, 1963, 12.

18. Ronald Grele, "Structural Development of Urban Liberalism in the Democratic Party of the Fourth Congressional District of New Jersey, 1930–1960" (Diss., Rutgers University, 1971), 349.

19. Ibid.

20. Interview with Raymond A. Brown, July 20, 2007.

21. "Hughes Vetoes Bill to Force Salute to Flag in School," *New York Times*, June 23, 1964, 18.

22. *Governor's Code of Fair Practices*, N.J. Exec. Order No. 21, 1965 N.J. Laws 1125, 1126.

23. Ibid., 1127.

24. Office of the Governor Release, Remarks of Governor Richard J. Hughes at the Negro History Week Program, Broadway Methodist Church, Camden, New Jersey, February 21, 1965. On file with author.

25. Office of the Governor Release, Remarks of Governor Richard J. Hughes at State-wide Conference for All Municipal Civil Rights Commission in New Jersey, Rutgers University, New Brunswick, New Jersey, May 22, 1965. On file with author.

26. Letter from Hughes to David Frost, August 22, 1967. On file with author.

27. Ronald Sullivan, "Marburger Wins Jersey Backing," *New York Times*, April 18, 1967, 34.

28. 347 U.S. 483 (1954).

29. *Swann v. Charlotte-Mecklenburg Bd. of Ed.* 402 U.S. 1 (1971).

30. *Milliken v. Bradley,* 418 U.S. 717 (1974).

31. Ronald Sullivan, "Busing of Pupils a Top Jersey Issue," *New York Times*, October 29, 1967, 72.

32. Letter from Hughes to Benjamin Palumbo, January 11, 1985. On file with author.

33. Interview with The Honorable June Strelecki.

34. Letter from Hughes to James Pitney, May 16, 1985. On file with author.

Chapter 9: Making a Difference: Hughes Confronts New Jersey's Challenges

1. *Furman v. Ga.*, 408 U.S. 238 (1972).

2. *Gregg v. Ga.*, 428 U.S. 153 (1976).

3. Article V, § 2, ¶ 1 of the New Jersey Constitution provides: "The Governor may grant pardons and reprieves in all cases other than impeachment and treason, and may suspend and remit fines and forfeitures."

4. "Governor Hughes Turns Down Death Appeal," *Trentonian*, June 28, 1962, 10.

5. *State v. Sturdivant*, 31 N.J. 165 (1959).

6. Ibid., 182 (Proctor, J., dissenting).

7. *State v. Hudson*, 38 N.J. 364 (1962).

8. Testimony of W. Michael Murphy to the New Jersey Department of Corrections. February 4, 2005. On file with author.

9. Ronald Sullivan, "Jersey Supreme Court Nullifies 2 Death Terms Over Judge's Advice to Jury," *New York Times*, September 26, 1967, 50.

10. *United States v. Jackson*, 390 U.S. 570 (1968); *State v. Funicello*, 60 N.J. 60 (N.J. 1972).

11. *Gregg, supra*, 428 U.S. at 153.

12. "Brooklyn Man Wins Hughes's Clemency in Prison Escape," *New York Times*, December 23 1969, 24.

13. "Hughes Won't Send A 1943 Escapee to Alabama Prison," *New York Times*, November 16, 1968, 27.

14. John Sibley, "Jersey and Connecticut Reject a 3-State Drinking Age of 19 1/2," *New York Times*, February 16, 1966, L1.

15. Ronald Sullivan, "Voting At 18 Gets Support In Jersey," October 5, 1967, 39.

16. U.S. Const. amend. XXVI.

17. "Drunk Driving Law Curbs Jersey Youth," *New York Times*, July 7, 1965, 22.

18. Ibid.

19. Ibid., 1.

20. *N.J. Stat. Ann.* § 39:4–50.2 (West 1966).

21. "Parked Drunk Driver Bills Disappointing to Hughes," n.d. On file with author.

22. George Amick and John Kolesar interviewed Governor Hughes. The transcripts of the interviews were made available to the author. (Hereafter cited as "Amick and Kolesar.") Sixth Session, 11. *N.J. Stat. Ann.* § 39:3–76.7 (West 2008).

23. "Jersey Requires Safety Belts," *New York Times*, June 16, 1965, 45.

24. "Jersey Tightens Narcotics Laws," *New York Times*, July 18, 1962, 31.

25. Bruce Baufman, "Hughes Sees Birth Control as Outside State Concern," *Newark Evening News*, May 17, 1963, 16.

26. Ibid.

27. Ibid.

28. N.J. Const. art. VIII, § 2, cl. 2; N.J. Const. art. 8, § 2, ¶ 3, providing for a balanced budget and a limitation on indebtedness.

29. *Fitzgerald's New Jersey Legislative Manual 1964*, 188th sess. (Trenton, NJ: J. Joseph Gibbons, 1964), 748.

30. Alvin S. Felzenberg, "The Impact of Gubernatorial Style on Policy Outcomes: An In Depth Study of Three New Jersey Governors" (Diss., Princeton University, 1978), 228 (hereafter cited as "Felzenberg").

31. *Fitzgerald's New Jersey Legislative Manual 1964*, 748.

32. Interview with Alice Hulse, June 25, 2004.

33. George Cable Wright, "750-Million Bond Issue Backed by Hughes Enliven Campaign in New Jersey," *New York Times*, October 8, 1963, 35.

34. George Cable Wright, "Broad-Based Tax Barred in Jersey," *New York Times*, March 31, 1964, 1.

35. "Hughes Signs Bills for 2 Referendums On Bond Flotations," *New York Times*, July 14, 1964, 35.

36. "Jersey Approves Railroad Subsidies," *New York Times,* September 16, 1962, 34.

37. Walter H. Waggoner, "Jersey Battling Its Traffic Jams," *New York Times,* July 6, 1965, 35; "Hughes Asks Study of Ways to Expand Turnpike in North," *New York Times,* April 2, 1965, 37.

38. "Jersey Central Line Threatens to Drop Commuter Services," *New York Times,* April 30, 1963, 36.

39. "Jersey Railroads Seek $405 Million," *New York Times,* February 28, 1964, 15.

40. "$7 Million Proposed To Aid 6 Railroads For Year in Jersey," *New York Times,* July 23, 1964, 29.

41. "Jersey Central to Lay Off 100 in Elizabethport Shop," *New York Times,* July 10, 1964, 27.

42. Walter H. Waggoner, "Accord Reached on Tristate Plan," *New York Times,* March 10, 1965, 43.

43. Walter H. Waggoner, "Hughes Proposes Jersey Rail Plan," *New York Times,* April 5, 1965, 1.

44. *New York Times,* "$8.7 Million Grant For Rail Services In Jersey Approved," July 2, 1965, 12.

45. Walter H. Waggoner, "State Rail Unit Urged In Jersey," *New York Times,* December 1, 1965, 49.

46. Ronald Sullivan, "Gov. Hughes Asks Commuter Agency," *New York Times,* May 17, 1966, 1.

47. Ibid.

48. "Jersey Road Plans Total $176-Million," *New York Times,* October 30, 1966, 85.

49. Ronald Sullivan, "$30-Million Program is Begun in Jersey to Improve Railroads," *New York Times,* October 18, 1966, 90.

50. *N.J. Stat. Ann.* § 27:1A-1 (West 1966).

51. Walter H. Waggoner, "Hughes Picks His Counsel to Be Transport Chief," *New York Times,* December 13, 1966, 34.

52. Peter Carver, "Transit Post to Goldberg," *Newark Evening News,* December 12, 1966, 1.

53. Ibid.

54. Walter H. Waggoner, "Jersey Central In Bankruptcy," *New York Times,* March 23, 1967, 37.

55. Joseph C. Ingraham, "Turnpike is Being Widened in New Jersey," *New York Times,* January 11, 1968, 39.

56. Joseph C. Ingraham, "A Delaware Span to Open Thursday," *New York Times,* September 7, 1968, 58.

57. "Thorn Lord Case Is Ruled Suicide," *New York Times,* June 18, 1965, 16.

58. "Thorn Lord a Suicide," *Newark Evening News,* June 17, 1965, 10.

59. Amick and Kolesar, First Session, 34.

60. Seton Hall agreed to pay $275,000 a year to rent the space at the Jersey City Medical Center. "School Lease Signed," *New York Times,* December 11, 1954, 9.

61. Robert A. Schwartz, "The New Jersey Medical School: A 50-year Retrospect," *Acta Dermatoven APA* 14, no. 2 (2005): 69.

62. Interview with Senator Raymond Bateman, September 27, 2004.

63. "Jersey to Study Aid for Medical School," *New York Times,* March 31, 1964, 21.

64. Interview with Senator Raymond Bateman.

65. Schwartz, "New Jersey Medical School," 70.

66. Ibid.

67. Ibid., 71.

68. Interview with Larry Bilder, September 22, 2004.

69. Lady Bird Johnson, *A White House Diary* (New York: Holt Rinehart and Winston, 1970), 309.

70. Ibid.

71. Ibid., 310.

72. Ibid.

73. Ibid.

74. Ibid., 311.

75. George Cable Wright, "Meyner Puts Aide in Prosecutor Job," *New York Times*, February 12, 1959.

76. Interview with Governor Brendan Byrne, February 17, 2006.

77. Interview with The Honorable John Gibbons, April 11, 2006.

78. Ronald Sullivan, "Democrats Say Hughes Was Warned on DeVita's Alleged Ties to Mafia in 1966," *New York Times*, December 18, 1969, 54.

79. Richard J. H. Johnston, "Ex-Judge DeVita Gets 1 to 2 Years," *New York Times*, May 28, 1970, 32.

80. *In re Imbriani*, 149 N.J. 521 (1997).

Chapter 10: The Second Campaign

1. George Amick and John Kolesar interviewed Governor Hughes. The transcripts of the interviews were made available to the author. (Hereafter cited as "Amick and Kolesar.") Seventh Session, 1.

2. Ibid., 2.

3. *New York Times*, "Hughes and Rival Hold Debate No. 5," October 12, 1965, 39.

4. Ronald Sullivan, "Jersey Economy Offers 2 Faces," *New York Times*, January 17, 1966, 144.

5. Interview with Hunt Dumont, son of Wayne Dumont, October 13, 2004.

6. Michael Birkner, *McCormick of Rutgers: Scholar, Teacher, Public Historian* (Westport, CT: Greenwood Press, 2001), 30.

7. Interview with The Honorable John McLaughlin, July 12, 2004.

8. Ronald Sullivan, "Kennedy Defends Academic Freedom," *New York Times*, October 15, 1965, 33.

9. Amick and Kolesar, Sixth Session, 31–32.

10. *New York Times*, "For Hughes in New Jersey," October 21, 1965, 46.

11. Ronald Sullivan, "Jones Criticizes Dumont Campaign," *New York Times*, August 26, 1965, 41.

12. Senator Bradley represented New Jersey in the United States Senate for eighteen years.

13. Letter from Hughes to Senator Bill Bradley, June 19, 1990. On file with author. Senator Richard Coffee, who held numerous positions in New Jersey, said that

the Genovese issue was just one of many issues and that Hughes would have won with or without that issue. Interview with Richard Coffee, February 22, 2005.

14. Letter from Hughes to Catherine Graham, May 18, 1967. On file with author.

15. Ibid.

16. Ibid.

17. Ibid.

18. *New York Times*, "Hughes Vetoes Bill Barring Distribution of Obscene Matter," January 12, 1966, 86.

19. Ibid.

20. "Hughes and Son, 19, Are Safe in Jersey As Copter Falters," *New York Times*, August 30, 1965, 15; "Hughes Hurts Hand As Car Door Shuts," *New York Times*, August 31, 1965, 35.

21. "Who Will Be New Jersey's Next First Lady?" *Sunday Times Advertiser*, June 20, 1965, 3.

22. "Mrs. Hughes Sets Aside Her Hope for Retirement," *Asbury Park Press*, October 12, 1965, 15.

23. "Richard J. Hughes Dead at 83 New Jersey's Greatest Citizen Ex-Governor," *Bergen Record*, December 8, 1992, A01. See also interview with Stanley C. Van Ness, September 16, 2004.

24. Ibid.

25. Ronald Sullivan, "Hughes Calls Victory a Mandate for Programs Equaling Johnson's," *New York Times*, November 4, 1965, 51.

26. Walter H. Waggoner, "Hughes to Press Big Jersey Issues," *New York Times*, November 7, 1965, 48.

Chapter 11: The Second Term

1. Ronald Sullivan, "Hughes, Starting 2nd Term, Asks Jersey to Find Identity," *New York Times*, January 19, 1966, 1.

2. *Fitzgerald's New Jersey Legislative Manual 1966*, 190th sess. (Trenton, NJ: J. Joseph Gibbons, 1966), 742.

3. Ibid.

4. Ibid.

5. Ibid., 743.

6. Ronald Sullivan, "Hughes Maps a 'Great Society' for Jersey," *New York Times*, December 5, 1965, E4.

7. "Hughes Calls County Senate Bid to Mrs. Kennedy 'Discourteous,'" *New York Times*, January 18, 1966, 32.

8. Richard Carl Leone, "The Politics of Gubernatorial Leadership: Tax and Education Reform in New Jersey" (Diss., Princeton University, 1969), 100.

9. Ibid., 102–103.

10. Ibid., 104.

11. Ibid., 105.

12. Ibid.

13. Ronald Sullivan, "Jersey Economy Offers 2 Faces," *New York Times*, January 17, 1966, 144.

14. Leone, "Politics of Gubernatorial Leadership," 111.

15. Lester V. Chandler, *"An Income Tax or a Sales Tax for New Jersey?" A report to Governor Richard J. Hughes,* Princeton University, January 1966, was a brief monograph prepared by Chandler, a former director of the Woodrow Wilson School and public director of the Federal Reserve Bank of Philadelphia. On file with author.

16. Leone, "Politics of Gubernatorial Leadership," 112–113.

17. Ibid., 71.

18. Wilentz had become famous for prosecuting Bruno Hauptmann, the alleged kidnapper of the son of Charles Lindbergh.

19. Leone, "Politics of Gubernatorial Leadership," 92.

20. Ibid., 98.

21. Ibid., 130.

22. Ibid., 121.

23. Ibid., 125.

24. Ibid., 137.

25. Interview with Lawrence Bilder, September 22, 2004.

26. Leone, "Politics of Gubernatorial Leadership," 138.

27. Ibid., 138–139.

28. Ibid., 139.

29. Ronald Sullivan, "Jersey Postpones Senate Tax Vote," *New York Times*, March 18, 1966, 22.

30. Interview with Larry Bilder.

31. Interview with Thomas Giblin.

32. Ronald Sullivan, "Hughes Gives Up Income-Tax Fight," *New York Times*, March 24, 1966, 1.

33. Leone, "Politics of Gubernatorial Leadership," 148.

34. Ronald Sullivan, "Hughes's Tax Bill Voted by Assembly," *New York Times*, March 17, 1966, 29.

35. Interview with Senator Raymond Bateman, September 27, 2004.

36. Leone, "Politics of Gubernatorial Leadership," 151.

37. Ibid., 155.

38. Ibid., 158, quoting the *Newark Sunday News*, April 17, 1966.

39. Ibid., 159.

40. Interview with Senator Raymond Bateman.

41. L. 1966, c. 30.

42. Jennifer Plotkin, "Social Science and Leadership: Reflections on the Significance of the Leadership of Richard Hughes," (Ph.D. diss., Rutgers University, New Brunswick, N.J, 1978), 29.

43. Ibid.

Chapter 12: A Flood of Legislation

1. Ronald Sullivan, "Hughes Extolled As He Signs Bills," *New York Times*, June 18, 1966, 24.

2. Ibid.

3. Ibid.

4. Ibid.

5. Letter from Hughes to Congressman Peter W. Rodino, Jr., July 16, 1985. On file with author.

6. Ibid.

7. Ronald Sullivan, "Jersey Gun Control Bill Passed over Opposition of Republicans," *New York Times*, June 1, 1966, 44; *N.J. Stat. Ann.* § 2A:151–1 (West 1966) is a lengthy, comprehensive bill.

8. Sullivan, "Jersey Gun Control Bill Passed," 44.

9. "Jersey Gun Law Signed," *New York Times*, June 4, 1966, 42.

10. *Burton v. Sills*, 53 N.J. 86, 103–106 (1968).

11. Ronald Sullivan, "Hughes Criticizes Congress on Guns," *New York Times*, June 12, 1968, 32.

12. *N.J. Stat. Ann.* § 18:13–112.70 provided: "When a member [teacher] retires reaches age 65 or upon retirement of a member after the attainment of age 65, the board of trustees shall reduce the retirement allowance by the amount of the old age insurance benefit under Title II of the Social Security Act paid or payable to him whether received or not."

13. Interview with Senator Stephen B. Wiley, who had been counsel to Governor Meyner, March 3, 2007.

14. *N.J. Stat. Ann.* § 18:13–112.70f. The current statute *N.J. Stat. Ann.* § 18A:66–68, "Effect of abolition of Social Security Offset," mentions that the 1966 version repealed the prior statute and its supplements.

15. Richard O. Shafer, "Crowd Hears LBJ Flay GOP," *Star-Ledger*, October 8, 1966.

16. Ibid.

17. Betty Hughes, "Memo from Morven," *Herald-News*, November 16, 1966, 1.

18. Ibid., 5.

19. The Alabama Department of Archives and History, "Governor George Wallace," http://www.archives.state.al.us/govs_list/g_walllu.html.

20. Alan V. Lowenstein, *Alan V. Lowenstein: New Jersey Lawyer & Community Leader* (Piscataway, NJ: Rutgers University Press, 2001), 318.

21. For an in-depth study of the history of corporate law in New Jersey see Lawrence E. Mitchell, *The Speculation Economy: How Finance Triumphed Over Industry* (San Francisco: Berrett-Koehler, 2007).

22. John T. Cunningham, *New Jersey: America's Main Road* (Garden City, NY: Doubleday, 1966), 264.

23. Ibid., 264–265.

24. It can be argued that the elimination of a separate Chancery Court in New Jersey, with its expertise in corporate matters, could have added to the decline in New Jersey's prominence in corporate law. Edward Hartnett, Richard J. Hughes Professor of Law at Seton Hall Law School, discussion with author.

25. Senator Edward J. O'Mara, Donald B. Kipp, Alan V. Lowenstein, and James A. Hession were commissioners, and John R. McKay II was secretary to the commission. Lowenstein, *New Jersey Lawyer*, 319–20.

26. Ibid., 320.

27. Interview with Senator McDermott, November 16, 2004.

28. Statement of Governor Hughes as quoted in Lowenstein, *New Jersey Lawyer*, 325–326.

29. See Symposium, *The New Jersey Business Corporation Act*, 23 Rutgers L. Rev. 613 (1969).

30. *Everson v. Bd. of Educ.of Twp*, 330 U.S. 1 (1947).

31. N.J. Const. art. VIII, sec. 4, ¶3.

32. "School Busing Bill Signed by Hughes," *Newark Evening News*, May 26, 1967, 30.

33. Susan Braybrooke, "Whatever Happened to the Meadowlands?" (May 1, 1982), 5. On file with author.

34. Paul N. Ylvisaker, *Conscience & Community: The Legacy of Paul Ylvisaker*, ed. Virginia M. Esposito, American University Studies, Series XIV, Education 43 (New York: Peter Lang, 1999), xxvii.

35. Clifford A. Goldman, "The Hackensack Meadowlands: The Politics of Regional Planning and Development in the Metropolis" (Ph.D. diss., Princeton University, Princeton, NJ, 1975).

36. Ibid., 93.

37. John W. Gleeson, "Dick Hughes and the Meadowlands," *Meadowlands/USA*, Meadowlands Chamber of Commerce, 1982, 5–7. Copy on file with author.

38. Goldman, "Hachensack Meadowlands," 130.

39. Ibid., 131.

40. Ibid., 139.

41. Ibid., 140.

42. Ibid., 143.

43. Ibid., 145.

44. Ibid., 159.

45. For the process of amending the New Jersey Constitution see N.J. Const. art. IX, § 1. Amendment did not pass until 1981.

46. Goldman, "Hackensack Meadowlands," 163.

47. Ibid., 163–164.

48. Interview with Alan Marcus, January 23, 2007.

49. Ibid.

50. Goldman, "Hackensack Meadowlands," 191.

51. Ibid., 192.

52. Ibid, 212.

53. Governor Hughes, *Special Memorandum to the Legislature* (Trenton, NJ, February 13, 1969). On file with author.

54. Ibid., 4.

55. Governor Hughes, interview, 1982, transcript. On file with author.

56. Gleeson, *Dick Hughes and Meadowlands*, 7.

57. 369 U.S. 186 (1962).

58. That system was first included in the Constitution of 1776 and retained in the two following constitutions.

59. 78 N.J. Super. 414 (N.J. Super. Ct. Ch. Div. 1964).

60. 377 U.S. 533 (1964).

61. *Jackman v. Bodine*, 43 N.J. 453 (1964).

62. Ernest C. Reock, *Unfinished Business* (New Brunswick, NJ: Center for Urban Policy Research, 2003), 18.

63. Prior to voting, the Republican Senators had met with their counsel, former Senator Walter Jones, who gave an opinion that the weighted voting formula was constitutional. "Vote Planned Monday," *New York Times*, November 6, 1964, 1.

64. George Cable Wright, "Hughes Challenges Weighted Voting in a Court Action," *New York Times*, November 18, 1964, 39.

65. George Cable Wright, "Hughes Snubbed by Legislature," *New York Times*, December 1, 1964, 1.

66. Ibid.

67. *Jackman v. Bodine*, 43 N.J. 491, 491 (1964).

68. Ibid., 493.

69. Reock, *Unfinished Business*, 19.

70. *N.J. Stat. Ann.* § 52:10B-4 (West 1965). Repealed by L. 1979, c. 431, §1.

71. Reock, *Unfinished Business*, 22.

72. Ibid.

73. Ibid., 25.

74. *Constitutional Convention to Amend State Constitution*, L. 1965, c. 43, § 1.

75. Reock, *Unfinished Business*, 47.

76. Ibid., 36

77. Ibid., 214.

78. Ronald Sullivan, "Jersey Districting Plan Is Deadlocked," *New York Times*, June 14, 1966, 94.

79. Ronald Sullivan, "Jersey Democrats Agree on Districts," *New York Times*, June 16, 1966, 1.

80. *New York Times*, "Districting Plan for House Upset by Jersey Court," July 24, 1966, 1.

81. See e.g. *Jones v. Falcey*, 48 N.J. 25 (1966); *Koziol v. Burkhardt*, 51 N.J. 412 (1968).

82. *Gideon v. Wainwright*, 372 U.S. 335 (1963).

83. For example, New Jersey assigned private attorneys to represent indigents in criminal cases, but those attorneys only received compensation in murder cases.

84. *State v. Rush*, 46 N.J. 399 (1966).

85. Ibid., 414.

86. *Rodriguez v. Rosenblatt*, 58 N.J. 281, 295 (1971).

87. Betty Hughes, "Memo from Morven," *Herald-News*, July 13, 1966, 1.

88. Letter from Hughes to Lynn Edwards, October 24, 1985. On file with author.

89. Ibid.

90. Betty Hughes, "Memo from Morven," *Herald-News*, August 3, 1966, 1.

91. Peter Kerr, "Ex-Rep. Charles Sandman, Nixon Supporter, Dies," *New York Times*, August 27, 1985, A20.

92. Letter from Hughes to Marian and Charles Sandman, June 17, 1985. On file with author.

93. Ronald Sullivan, "Hughes to Seek a Heavy Fine to Help Curb Pollution Sources," *New York Times*, January 6, 1967, 1.

94. *N.J. Stat. Ann.* § 26:2C-3.1 (West 1967).

95. *N.J. Stat. Ann.* § 26:2C-9(e) (West 1967).

96. *N.J. Stat. Ann.* § 26:2C-19 (West 1967).

97. *N.J. Stat. Ann.* § 26:2C-22 (West 1967).

98. *N.J. Stat. Ann.* § 26:2C-24 (West 1967).

99. *N.J. Stat. Ann.* § 32:29–1 (West 1967).

100. *N.J. Stat. Ann.* § 32:29–16 (West 1967).

101. *N.J. Stat. Ann.* § 26:2E-11 West 1967).

102. "A Cabinet-Level Agency to Give N.J. Cities a Hand," *Star-Ledger,* April 31, 1966, 1.

103. Alvin S. Felzenberg, *Governor Tom Kean: From the New Jersey Statehouse to the 9–11 Commission* (New Brunswick, NJ: Rivergate Books, 2006), 470, n.12.

104. "New Force Focuses on Urban Ills," *Business Week,* June 24, 1967, 75.

105. Anthony J. Yudis, "Governors Planning More Involvement," *Sunday Globe,* April 16, 1967.

106. Ibid.

107. "No Place for the Amateur," *Bergen Record,* January 9, 1970, A26.

108. *Roe v. Wade,* 410 U.S. 113 (1973).

109. *Gleitman v. Cosgrove,* 49 N.J. 22 (1967).

110. Ibid., 30.

111. Ibid., 32–49. The concurring opinion of Justice Francis goes into detail concerning the history of the abortion statute and the fact that it was rewritten in 1849 to make clear that it was intended to broaden the scope of the statute to apply to the embryo/fetus at the earliest stages.

112. Ibid., 49–55.

113. Ronald Sullivan, "Jersey Prosecutors Will Review Enforcement of Abortion Curb," *New York Times,* March 8, 1967, 37.

114. "Jersey Legislature Approves a Panel to Study Abortion," *New York Times,* April 2, 1968, 49.

115. Ronald Sullivan, "Jersey Prosecutors Will Review Enforcement of Abortion Curb," *New York Times,* March 8, 1967, 37.

116. Ronald Sullivan, "Jersey Refuses Abortion Study," *New York Times,* March 14, 1967, 49.

117. Ronald Sullivan, "Jersey to Study Its Abortion Law," *New York Times,* April 8, 1967, 29.

118. "Jersey Legislature Approves a Panel to Study Abortion," *New York Times,* April 2, 1968, 49.

Chapter 13: Working for Peace: At Home and Abroad

1. Rowan University was founded in 1923 as Glassboro Normal School, became Glassboro State Teachers College in the 1930s, Glassboro State College in 1958, renamed Rowan College of New Jersey in 1992, and finally Rowan University in 1997.

2. Robert D. Bole, *Summit at Holly Bush* (Glassboro NJ: Glassboro State College Endowment Fund, 1969), 10.

3. Ibid., 12.

4. Ibid., 21. It should be noted that Judge Larry Bilder, who was with Hughes during the summit, says that Hughes did not call Johnson but instead Johnson called Hughes. Stephen Farber, who was also on Hughes's staff, agrees with the view of Professor Bole that Hughes initiated the process. Interviews with Larry Bilder and Stephen Farber. In his book, Dallek merely says "With the help of Governor Richard Hughes, the two sides settled on Glassboro, New Jersey. . . ." Robert Dallek, *Flawed Giant: Lyndon Johnson and His Times, 1961–1973* (Oxford: Oxford University Press, 1998), 434.

5. George Amick and John Kolesar interviewed Governor Hughes. The transcripts of the interviews were made available to the author. (Hereafter cited as "Amick and Kolesar.") Fifth Session, 18.

6. Lyndon Baines Johnson, *The Vantage Point: Perspectives of the Presidency, 1963–1969* (New York: Holt, Rinehart and Winston, 1971), 482.

7. Amick and Kolesar, Fifth Session, 17.

8. Johnson, *Vantage Point*, 482.

9. Interview with Judge Larry Bilder, September 22, 2004.

10. Oral history of Governor Hughes and Betty Hughes for the Lyndon Baines Johnson Presidential Library, November 27, 1978, 75. (Hereafter cited as "LBJ Oral History, Hughes.")

11. Bole, *Summit at Holly Bush*, 43.

12. Ibid., 71.

13. Ibid., 81.

14. Interview with Stephen Farber, February 10, 2005.

15. "Under Lyndon B. Johnson [as opposed to President Kennedy], however, it became gradually apparent that the White House staff was a staff—not a community. More of the President's staff, probably, had more immediate access to their chief than had been true in Kennedy's day, but only as staff servants." Theodore H. White, *The Making of the President, 1964* (New York: Atheneum, 1965), 245.

16. Johnson, *Vantage Point*, 483.

17. Lady Bird Johnson, *A White House Diary* (New York: Holt, Rinehart and Winston, 1970), 535.

18. LBJ Oral History, Hughes, 21

19. Ibid., 21–23.

20. Bole, *Summit at Holly Bush*, 139.

21. LBJ Oral History, Hughes, 25.

22. Johnson, *A White House Diary*, 537.

23. Ibid., 538.

24. See Pat Mack, "Winners with Ties to Politics," North Jersey Dining Guide. On file with author.

25. LBJ Oral History, Hughes, 27.

26. Johnson, *A White House Diary*, 539.

27. LBJ Oral History, Hughes, 29.

28. Bole, *Summit at Holly Bush*, 145.

29. LBJ Oral History, Hughes, 40.

30. Bole, *Summit at Holly Bush*, 151.

31. Dallek, *Flawed Giant*, 436.

32. Johnson, *A White House Diary*, 542.

33. Theodore H. White, *The Making of the President, 1968* (New York: Atheneum, 1969), 277.

34. Bole, *Summit at Holly Bush*, 197.

35. Ron Parambo, *No Cause for Indictment: An Autopsy of Newark* (New York: Holt, Rinehart and Winston, 1971), 5.

36. Ibid.

37. Ibid., 7.

38. Ibid., 8.

39. See Ronald Grele, "Structural Development of Urban Liberalism in the Democratic Party of the Fourth Congressional District of New Jersey, 1930–1960" (Diss., Rutgers University, 1971), 502.

40. Ibid., 497.

41. LBJ Oral History, Hughes, 82.

42. Joseph A. Califano, Jr., *The Triumph and Tragedy of Lyndon Johnson: The White House Years* (New York: Simon and Schuster, 1991), 209.

43. Ibid.

44. Letter from Hughes to Professor Stanley B. Winters, July 1, 1985. On file with author.

45. Tom Hayden, *Rebellion in Newark* (New York: Random House, 1967).

46. Homer Bigart, "Newark Riot Panel Calls Police Action 'Excessive,'" *New York Times*, February 11, 1968, 1.

47. Hayden, *Rebellion in Newark*, 38.

48. Interview with Raymond Brown, July 20, 2007.

49. Amick and Kolesar, Sixth Session, 36.

50. State of New Jersey, Governor's Select Commission on Civil Disorder, *Report for Action: An Investigation into the Causes and Events of the 1967 Newark Race Riots* (New York: Lemma Publishing, 1972), 123. Hereafter referred to as *Lilley Commission Report*.

51. Paul N. Ylvisaker, *Conscience & Community: The Legacy of Paul Ylvisaker*, ed. Virginia M. Esposito, American University Studies, Series XIV, Education 43 (New York: Peter Lang, 1999), xxvi.

52. Interview with Larry Bilder.

53. *Lilley Commission Report*, 151.

54. "Ylvisaker Defends Riot Role," *Trenton Evening Times*, December 8, 1967, 2. See also report from Commissioner Ylvisaker to Senator John L. McClellan describing the chronology of actions by the Department of Community Affairs during the riots. On file with author.

55. Sidney E. Zion, "The Search in Plainfield," *New York Times*, July 22, 1967, 10.

56. Thomas A. Johnson, "Troopers Search Plainfield Homes for Stolen Guns," *New York Times*, July 20, 1967, 28.

57. *Lilley Commission Report*, v. The report became known as the Lilley Commission Report because the chairman of the Commission was Robert Lilley, president of New Jersey Bell. The prominent African American attorney Raymond Brown was named as vice chairman.

58. Interview with Sanford Jaffee, April 4, 2006.

59. Letter from Hughes to Professor Stanley B. Winters, July 1, 1985. On file with author.

60. Interview with Judge John Gibbons, April 11, 2006.

61. *Lilley Commission Report*, 199.

62. Ibid., 20.

63. Martin Gansberg, "Top Newark Aides Score Riot Report," *New York Times*, February 12, 1968, 1.

64. Ibid., 30.

65. Ronald Sullivan, "Addonizio Given a 10-Year Term," *New York Times*, September 23, 1970, 1.

66. Ibid.

67. Lilley Commission Report, 66.

68. Ibid., 85.

69. Ibid., 97.

70. Walter H. Waggoner, "Jersey to Expand Police Training," *New York Times*, July 29, 1967, 11.

71. Ronald Sullivan, "Hughes Seeks State Jobs for Unskilled Negroes," *New York Times*, August 3, 1967, 1.

72. Ronald Sullivan, "Jersey Will Add Negroes to Guard," *New York Times*, August 17, 1967, 1.

73. Special Message from Governor Hughes, "A Moral Recommitment for New Jersey," (speech, Trenton, NJ, April 25, 1968), 1–2.

74. Alvin S. Felzenberg, *Governor Tom Kean: From the New Jersey Statehouse to the 9–11 Commission* (Piscataway, NJ: Rutgers University Press, 2006), 92.

75. Ibid., 95.

76. Dr. Carol A. McMillan-Lonesome, "The Educational Opportunity Program: An Historical Overview," New Jersey Educational Opportunity Fund, http://academic.shu.edu/eop/about/overview.htm.

77. Felzenberg, *Governor Kean*, 91.

78. Amy Schapiro, *Millicent Fenwick, Her Way* (Piscataway, NJ: Rutgers University Press, 2003), 121.

79. Ibid., 123.

80. Ibid.

81. Felzenberg, *Governor Kean*, 92.

82. Letter from Hughes to Stanley B. Winters, July 1, 1985. On file with author.

83. Ibid.

84. LBJ Oral History, Hughes, 15.

85. David Broder, "Governors' Talk Is Picnic, Politics and Policy," *New York Times*, August 1, 1965, E6.

86. Gladwin Hill, "Abel Tells Governors Inadequacies of State Are Scandalous," *New York Times*, July 6, 1966, 13.

87. Warren Weaver Jr., "Governors Link Loss to Johnson," *New York Times*, December 16, 1966, 1.

88. Amick and Kolesar, Fifth Session, 1.

89. Ibid., 1–2.

90. Johnson, *Vantage Point*, 264.

91. Ibid., 265.
92. Letter from Robert Hughes to the author. On file with author.
93. Johnson, *Vantage Point*, 265.
94. Interview with Stephen Farber.
95. Ibid.
96. Johnson, *Vantage Point*, 265.
97. Max Frankel, "Observers Tell Johnson that South Vietnam's Election was Fair," *New York Times*, September 7, 1967, 1.
98. Ibid.
99. LBJ Oral History, Hughes, 91.
100. Howard R. Penniman, *Elections in South Vietnam* (Washington, D.C.: American Enterprise Institute for Public Policy Research, 1972), 75.
101. Ibid., 75–76.
102. Ibid., 76.
103. Ibid., 76–77, n. 44 that starts on pg. 76.
104. Ibid., 66, n. 30.
105. LBJ Oral History, Hughes, 91.

Chapter 14: 1967–1968

1. *State v. Hatch*, 64 N.J. 179, 186–87 (1973).
2. Alvin S. Felzenberg, *Governor Tom Kean: From the New Jersey Statehouse to the 9–11 Commission* (New Brunswick, NJ: Rutgers University Press, 2006), 77.
3. Ernest C. Reock, *Unfinished Business* (New Brunswick, NJ: Center for Urban Policy Research, 2003), 231.
4. Oral history of Governor Hughes and Betty Hughes for the Lyndon Baines Johnson Presidential Library, November 27, 1978, 99. (Hereafter cited as "LBJ Oral History, Hughes.")
5. Ibid.
6. Ibid.
7. Ronald Sullivan, "Hughes Threatens Court Action Against Migrant Labor Camps," *New York Times*, August 26, 1967, 14.
8. Ibid.
9. Ronald Sullivan, "5 Migrant Farms Warned by Jersey," *New York Times*, August 29, 1967, 25.
10. Ronald Sullivan, "Five Jersey Migrant Camps Pass Series of Inspections," *New York Times*, September 7, 1967, 47.
11. Ronald Sullivan, "Migrant Report Scored in Jersey," *New York Times*, September 8, 1967, 21.
12. Interview with Claire McQuade.
13. Betty Hughes, "Memo from Morven," *Herald-News*, December 27, 1967, 5.
14. Ibid.
15. Interview with W. Michael Murphy, July 9, 2006.
16. Janet Mezzack, "'Without Manners You are Nothing': Lady Bird Johnson, Eartha Kitt, and the Women Doers' Luncheon of January 18, 1968," *Presidential Studies Quarterly*, Vol. 20, Fall 1990, 746.

17. LBJ Oral History, Hughes, 47.
18. Margaret Moore, Chair of the Indianapolis Anti-Crime Crusade, Mrs. Charles Coe, a VISTA worker, and Katherine Peden, a member of the National Advisory Commission on Civil Disorders.
19. Mezzack, "Without Manners," 746.
20. Lady Bird Johnson, *A White House Diary* (New York: Holt Rinehart and Winston, 1970), 622.
21. Mezzack, "Without Manners," 749.
22. LBJ Oral History, Hughes, 49.
23. Johnson, *A White House Diary*, 623.
24. Mezzack, "Without Manners," 749–750.
25. LBJ Oral History, Hughes, 51.
26. Johnson, *A White House Diary*, 623.
27. LBJ Oral History, Hughes, 52.
28. George Amick and John Kolesar interviewed Governor Hughes. The transcripts of the interviews were made available to the author. (Hereafter cited as "Amick and Kolesar.") Fifth Session, 13.
29. Ibid.
30. LBJ Oral History, Hughes, 54.
31. Ibid., 55.
32. Lyndon Baines Johnson, *The Vantage Point, Perspectives of the Presidency, 1963–196* (New York: Holt, Rinehart and Winston, 1971), 532.
33. Ibid., 536–537.
34. For a detailed discussion of the Pueblo incident see Mitchell B. Lerner, *The Pueblo Incident: A Spy Ship and the Failure of American Foreign Policy* (University Press of Kansas, 2002).
35. LBJ Oral History, Hughes, 101.
36. Ibid.
37. Ibid.
38. Ibid.
39. Amick and Kolesar, Fifth Session, 1.
40. Interview with W. Michael Murphy.
41. Interview with Stephen Farber, February 10, 2005.
42. Ibid.
43. LBJ Oral History, Hughes, 97–98.
44. Ibid., 98.
45. "Hughes Strongly Opposed to Kennedy Candidacy," *New York Times*, March 15, 1968, 26.
46. Ibid.
47. Betty Hughes, "Memo from Morven," April 10, 1968.
48. Ernest Johnson Jr., "King Spends Day in Newark: Promotes D.C. March," *Newark Star-Ledger*, March 28, 1968.
49. Hughes, "Memo from Morven," April 10, 1968.
50. William Doolittle, "Youth Killed in Trenton," *Newark Evening News*, August 10, 1968.

51. Jack Mehl, "Leaders of Both Races Commended by Hughes," *Newark Sunday News*, August 11, 1968, 8.

52. Peter Carter, "Hughes Firm on Law and Order," *Newark Evening News*, April 11, 1968, 11.

53. "As Sole Riot Cure Hughes Raps Shooting," *Newark Evening News*, April 17, 1968, 24.

54. Peter Carter, "Hughes Ghetto Aid Plan Will Cost $126 Million" *Newark Evening News*, April 25, 1968, 1.

55. Ibid.

56. Peter Carter, "GOP Vows City Aid; Wants Public Views," *Newark Evening News*, April 26, 1968, 1.

57. Special Message from Governor Hughes, "A Moral Recommitment for New Jersey" (speech, Trenton, NJ, April 25, 1968), 2.

58. "$1.75 Billion Bond Issue Vote Sought by Hughes," *Asbury Park Press*, May 6, 1968, 1.

59. "Hughes Hoping for GOP Switch on Aid Program," *Asbury Park Press*, May 27, 1968, 2.

60. "GOP Hit by Split on Plans," *Asbury Park Press*, May 28, 1968, 1.

61. Interview with Raymond Bateman, September 27, 2004.

62. *Fitzgerald's New Jersey Legislative Manual 1969*, 193rd sess. (Trenton, NJ: J. Joseph Gibbons, 1969), 782–783.

63. "Governors Parley Divided over New Spending," *Newark Evening News*, July 23, 1968, 7.

64. Ibid.

65. Interview with Stephen Farber.

66. Betty Hughes, "Memo from Morven," *Herald-News*, July 24, 1968.

Chapter 15: The 1968 Democratic National Convention

1. Theodore H. White, *The Making of the President, 1968* (New York: Atheneum, 1969), 96.

2. Interview with Daniel M. Gaby, June 6, 2007.

3. Jules Witcover, *85 Days: The Last Campaign of Robert Kennedy* (New York: Putnam Books, 1969), 88.

4. Ibid., 128.

5. Sylvan Fox, "Political Chiefs Stunned; Kennedy Sets News Parley," *New York Times*, April 1, 1968, 27.

6. "Governor Hughes Resists Any Bandwagon Moves," *New York Times*, April 2, 1968, 30.

7. Ibid.

8. Oral history of Governor Hughes and Betty Hughes for the Lyndon Baines Johnson Presidential Library, November 27, 1978, 99.

9. Carl Solberg, *Hubert Humphrey: A Biography* (New York: W.W. Norton, 1984), 326.

10. White, *Making of the President, 1968*, 150.

11. Edward Kennedy, Eulogy for Robert F. Kennedy (St. Patrick's Cathedral, New York, NY, June 8, 1968).

12. "Dedication is Urged by Hughes," *Newark Evening News*, June 6, 1968, 16.

13. Robert Dallek, *Flawed Giant: Lyndon Johnson and His Times, 1961–1973* (Oxford: Oxford University Press, 1998), 572.

14. Warren Weaver Jr., "2 Governors Back Kennedy as No. 2," *New York Times*, July 22, 1968, 1; see also *Newark Evening News*, July 23, 1968, 7.

15. Weaver Jr., "2 Governors."

16. Ibid.

17. William May, "Wallace State Total Seen Topping Barry," *Newark Evening News*, July 22, 1968, 4.

18. Ronald Sullivan, "Hughes Says He Would Take 2d Spot if it is Offered Him," *New York Times*, August 11, 1968, 50.

19. Lewis L. Gould, *1968: The Election that Changed America* (Chicago: Ivan R. Dee, 1993), 121–122.

20. For an extended discussion of the problems in the selection of the delegates for the convention, see: Reid Peyton Chambers and Ronald Rotunda, *Reform of Presidential Nominating Conventions*, 56 Va. L. Rev. 179 (1970).

21. "Challenged Delegates Given Convention Okay by Hughes," *Atlantic City Press*, August 20, 1968.

22. "Hughes in Spotlight in Convention Post," *Asbury Park Evening Press*, August 20, 1968.

23. James Richardson, *Willie Brown: A Biography* (Berkeley: University of California Press, 1996), 158.

24. Interview with Angelo Baglivo, October 14, 2004.

25. It should be noted that some others were not satisfied. James Richardson's biography of Willie Brown, who also served on the credentials committee, indicated that many felt that Lyndon Johnson controlled the entire convention and that despite the questioning of the Texas delegation by Brown, it was preordained that the white delegation would be seated. Hughes had permitted Brown to do the questioning, but the committee voted to permit the Texas delegation to sit. Richardson, *Willie Brown*.

26. White, *Making of the President*, 273–274.

27. Governor Maddox owned a restaurant and, during the battles over desegregation, refused to allow African Americans into his restaurant. He was caught on camera with a number of supporters wielding ax handles to block the entry of African American activists. *New Georgia Encyclopedia*, s.v. "Governor Maddox."

28. Letter from Hughes to George Amick, July 23, 1990. On file with author.

29. White, *Making of the President*, 274.

30. Betty Hughes, "Memo from Morven," *Herald-News*, August 28, 1968. Interestingly, John Hughes believes that his mother did not want him to run for vice president, whereas, Tom Hughes believes that his mother was more anxious for him to become vice president than he was.

31. Gould, *1968: The Election*, 121.

32. Chambers and Rotunda, *Reform of Presidential Nominating*, 208.

33. Gould, *1968: The Election*, 121.

34. White, *Making of the President*, 277.

35. Ibid., 279.

36. Ibid., 281.

37. Ibid., 304.

38. *New Jersey Reporter*, "Dick Hughes and the 1968 Vice Presidency," New Jersey Oral History, September 2000, 35.

39. "Labor Chief Urges Hughes for VP," *Star-Ledger*, August 20, 1968.

40. "Hughes Seen As 'Liability' to Humphrey," *Philadelphia Bulletin*, August 16, 1968.

41. Bolton Schwartz, "Hughes Boom Worries Democrats; Nomination at Chicago Would Pose Problems," *Herald-News*, August 17, 1968.

42. Hubert H. Humphrey, *The Education of a Public Man: My Life and Politics* (London: Weidenfeld and Nicolson, 1976), 390.

43. Ibid., 390–91.

44. Ibid., 391.

45. White, *Making of the President*, 304.

46. Solberg, *Hubert Humphrey*, 367.

47. Ibid.

48. Betty Hughes, "Memo from Morven," *Herald-News*, August 27, 1968.

49. White, *Making of the President*, 358–359.

50. Ibid.

51. Ibid.

52. Betty Hughes, "Memo from Morven," *Herald-News*, July 13, 1966, 12.

53. Interview with W. Michael Murphy, July 9, 2006.

54. Ibid.

55. Betty Hughes, "Memo from Morven," *Herald-News*, n.d. On file with author.

56. George Amick and John Kolesar interviewed Governor Hughes. The transcripts of the interviews were made available to the author. (Hereafter cited as "Amick and Kolesar.") Sixth Session, 20.

57. Humphrey, *Education of a Public Man*, 11.

58. Amick and Kolesar, Sixth Session, 21.

59. Ibid., 22.

60. Ibid.

61. Ibid.

62. Interview with Stephen Farber, February 10, 2005.

63. Ibid.

64. Gould, *1968: The Election*, 164.

65. Ibid.

66. Interview with Daniel Gaby, 6/6/07.

67. Ibid.

68. Betty Hughes, "Memo from Morven," *Herald-News*, January 23, 1969.

69. Ibid.

70. Betty Hughes, "Memo from Morven,' *Herald-News*, June 9, 1969.

71. Betty Hughes, "Memo from Morven," *Herald-News*, May 19, 1969, 1.

72. Interview with Joel Sterns.

73. Betty Hughes, "Memo from Morven," *Herald-News*, January 16, 1969.

74. The Museum of Broadcast Communications, "Space Program and Television," http://www.museum.tv/archives/etv/S/space program/spaceprogram.htm.
75. Betty Hughes, "Memo from Morven," *Herald-News*, July 16, 1969, 1.
76. Betty Hughes, "Memo from Morven," *Herald-News*, August 14, 1969, 5.
77. Betty Hughes, "Memo from Morven," *Herald-News*, September 11, 1969, 5.
78. Colonel Edwin E. "Buzz" Aldrin, Jr. with Wayne Warga, *Return to Earth* (New York: Random House, 1973), 42.
79. Betty Hughes, "Memo from Morven," *Herald-News*, August 21, 1969, 6.
80. Betty Hughes, "Memo from Morven," *Herald-News*, September 19, 1969, 4.

Chapter 16: An Education Governor

1. Herman D. James, "Don't Let Brain-Drain Myth Guide Higher Ed. Plan," *Star-Ledger*, July 18, 2003, 21.
2. *N.J. Stat. Ann.* § 18:22–100 through 18:22–124 (West 1962).
3. Ibid., § 18:22–100.
4. Ibid., § 18:22–101.
5. Interview with Senator Richard Coffee, February 22, 2005.
6. Michael Birkner, *McCormick of Rutgers: Scholar, Teacher, Public Historian* (Westport, CT: Greenwood Press, 2001), 138.
7. McCormick used his access to Hughes to expand opportunities for historical research, especially with regard to the history of New Jersey. He said that Hughes "liked me. But he liked everybody . . . he was just a delightful, warm, wonderful person." Ibid., 139.
8. Richard C. Leone, "The Politics of Gubernatorial Leadership: Tax and Education Reform in New Jersey" (Diss., Princeton University, 1969), 173–340.
9. First Inaugural Address of Governor Richard J. Hughes, January 16, 1962, found in *Fitzgerald's New Jersey Legislative Manual 1962*, 186th sess. (Trenton, NJ: J. Joseph Gibbons, 1962), 764.
10. Leone, "Politics of Gubernatorial Leadership," 203.
11. Ibid., 211–212.
12. Ibid.
13. Richard C. Leone, "Back to Cuckooland," *New Jersey Reporter*, May/June, 1994, 21.
14. George D. Strayer and Charles R. Kelley, *The Needs of New Jersey in Higher Education, 1962–1970* (Trenton, NJ: New Jersey Dept. of Ed., 1962), 12. Copy on file with author.
15. Ibid., 60–61.
16. Governor Hughes, "Special Message to the Legislature," January 28, 1963. On file with author.
17. Dr. Carroll V. Newsom and others, "A Report Prepared by the Governor's Committee on New Jersey Higher Education," Englewood Cliffs, NJ, May 14, 1963, i. Copy on file with author.
18. Ibid., 1.
19. Ibid.
20. Leone, "Politics of Gubernatorial Leadership," 227.

21. Ibid., 235.

22. Ibid., 235–236.

23. Ibid., 217.

24. Ibid., 220.

25. Ibid., 218.

26. Ibid., 219.

27. Ibid., 242.

28. Ibid., 249.

29. Ibid., 251.

30. Interview with Judge Larry Bilder, September 22, 2004.

31. Leone, "Politics of Gubernatorial Leadership," 256–258.

32. Second Inaugural Address of Governor Richard J. Hughes, January 16, 1966, found in *Fitzgerald's New Jersey Legislative Manual 1966*, 190th sess. (Trenton, NJ: J. Joseph Gibbons, 1966), 744.

33. Ibid., 723.

34. Interview with Stephen Farber, February 10, 2005.

35. Leone, "Politics of Gubernatorial Leadership," 274.

36. Ibid. 274–275.

37. Robert F. Palmer, "Education Dispute Sure at Governor's Conference," *Newark Evening News*, April 1, 1966.

38. Leone, "Politics of Gubernatorial Leadership," 279.

39. Ibid., 271.

40. Ibid., 272.

41. Ibid., 285.

42. "Recommendations Adopted by the New Jersey Citizens Committee for Higher Education in New Jersey," Princeton, NJ, May 14, 1966, 1. Copy on file with author.

43. George F. Smith and others, "Position of the State Board of Education on the Report of the Governor's Committee on New Jersey Higher Education," Trenton, NJ, April 1965, 1. On file with author.

44. Ibid.

45. Ronald Sullivan, "Raubinger Resigning as Jersey's Education Chief," *New York Times*, May 20, 1966, 35.

46. Leone, "Politics of Gubernatorial Leadership," 289.

47. Governor Hughes, Special Message to Legislature, 1966, 1. Copy on file with author.

48. Francis T. Sidoti, "The History of State-Supported Higher Education in New Jersey," Seton Hall University School of Law, Fall 2006, 20–21. Unpublished seminar paper on file with author.

49. Leone, "Politics of Gubernatorial Leadership," 295.

50. Ibid.

51. Ibid., 296.

52. "Report on New Jersey Higher Education: Some Pertinent Facts Prepared by the New Jersey State Board of Education," Trenton, NJ, July 1966, 20.

53. Leone, "Politics of Gubernatorial Leadership," 307.

54. Ibid., 315.

55. Ibid., 319.
56. Interview with Joel Sterns.
57. Alvin S. Felzenberg, *Governor Tom Kean: From the New Jersey Statehouse to the 9–11 Commission* (New Brunswick, NJ: Rutgers University Press, 2006), 96.
58. Ibid.
59. For an extended discussion of the process and the results see Cynthia Hickman and Laurence R. Marcus, *The Outcomes of New Jersey's Higher Education Restructuring Act of 1994. ASHE Annual Meeting Paper* (ERIC Database, U.S. Dep. of Ed., 1998).
60. Matthew Reilly, "Dismantling Proposed for Higher Education," *Star-Ledger*, March 16, 1994.
61. Ibid.
62. Leone, "Back to Cuckooland," 20.
63. Robert J. Braun, "Whitman Must Rethink Killing off a Good Idea," *Star-Ledger*, March 20, 1994.
64. Editorial, "No Magic in a Merger," *Star-Ledger*, August 24, 2006, 18. "For more than a year, UMDNJ and the hospital it operates in Newark have been battered by evidence of Medicaid fraud, revelations about the awarding of millions of dollars in no-bid contracts to politically connected consultants, and allegations of patronage and abuse of expense accounts by senior administrators." Ted Sherman and Kelly Heyboer, "Merger Seen As Antidote for UMDNJ: Lawmakers Revive Idea of Unifying State Colleges," *Star-Ledger*, August 23, 2006, 1.
65. *Star-Ledger*, May 9, 2005, 13. See also Bob Braun, "'Synergy' Misses Mark as a Quick Fix for Higher Education," *Star-Ledger*, September, 23, 2002, 13.
66. New Jersey Policy Perspective, "Testimony of Jon Shure, President, NJPP Assembly Higher Education Committee," June 12, 2006, http://www.njpp.org/test_ahec_js.html.
67. Ibid.
68. *N.J. Stat. Ann.* § 48:23–7 (West 1967).
69. "Jersey Panel to Aid Radio-TV Education," *New York Times*, October 17, 1967, 95.

Chapter 17: The Hugheses Leaving Morven and Returning to Private Life

1. Betty Hughes, "Rose Kennedy: America's Lady," *Herald-News*, February 16, 1970.
2. Ibid.
3. Betty Hughes, "Memo from Morven," June 26, 1968. Copy on file with author.
4. Betty Hughes, "Memo from Morven," *Herald-News*, February 26, 1969, 42.
5. Betty Hughes, "Memo from Morven," *Herald-News*, September 11, 1969, 1.
6. Betty Hughes, "80 Pounds in 19 Weeks," August 1, 1968. Draft of article on file with author.
7. Ibid.
8. Betty Hughes, "Memo from Morven," *Herald-News*, March 13, 1968.
9. Betty Hughes, "Memo from Morven," *Herald-News*, March 20, 1968.
10. Betty Hughes, "Memo from Morven," *Herald-News*, April 4, 1968.
11. Betty Hughes, "Memo from Morven," *Herald-News*, August 10, 1968.

12. Betty Hughes, "Memo from Morven," *Herald-News*, January 8, 1969.

13. Ibid.

14. Interview with Kenneth Kunzman, a partner at Connell Foley who worked very closely with Hughes during his years at the firm, March 21, 2006.

15. Letter from Hughes to Bob Burkhardt, June 27, 1985. On file with author.

16. Those candidates were Charles W. Sandman, Harry L. Sears, Francis X. McDermott, and William E. Ozzard.

17. Ronald Sullivan, "Representative Cahill to Enter Jersey Gubernatorial Primary," *New York Times*, February 26, 1969, 40.

18. Interview with William T. Cahill, the son of Governor Cahill, July 6, 2005.

19. William F. Kelly, Henry Helstoski, Louis D. Tonti, Ned J. Parsekian, and John L. Hennessey.

20. Alvin S. Felzenberg, *Governor Tom Kean: From the New Jersey Statehouse to the 9–11 Commission* (Piscataway, NJ: Rutgers University Press, 2006), 109–110.

21. "Gov Hughes' Eighth Annual Message," *Fitzgerald's New Jersey Legislative Manual 1970*, 194th sess. (Trenton, NJ: J. Joseph Gibbons, 1970), 799.

22. Letter from Hughes to Governor Kean, September 12, 1985. On file with author.

23. Letter from Hughes to George Amick, October 18, 1985. On file with author.

24. Ibid.

25. Earl Josephson, "Label Him Unlabelable," *Evening Times*, January 22, 1970, 1.

26. Ibid.

27. Ronald Sullivan, "Jersey Legislators Block Closed Hearing on Mafia," *New York Times*, December 17, 1968, 1.

28. Interview with William F. Hyland, March 9, 2007.

29. Ibid.

30. John McLaughlin, "The Arrangement: Hughes and the Party Bosses," *Sunday Times Advertiser*, January 18, 1970, 3.

31. Roland Sullivan, "Sills Applauds Report in New Jersey," *New York Times*, January 16, 1969, 42.

32. Sidney E. Zion, "Brennan Recital is Called Flimsy," *New York Times*, December 31, 1968, 30.

33. Ibid.

34. Joel R. Jacobson, "The Tragedy of David Friedland," *New York Times*, February 7, 1988, A1.

35. Felzenberg, *Governor Kean*, 118.

36. Michael Marriott, "Flashy Life as Fugitive Led Agents to Ex-Senator," *New York Times*, December 28, 1987, B1.

37. Ronald Sullivan, "Hughes Condemns Release of Tapes," *New York Times*, January 9, 1970, 1.

38. Ibid.

39. Ibid.

40. John McLaughlin, "The Arrangement: Hughes and the Party Bosses," *Sunday Times Advertiser*, January 18, 1970, 3.

41. Ibid.

42. Editorial, *Bergen Record*, n.d. Copy on file with author.

43. Betty Hughes, "8 Years of Objectivity End; Betty Lauds Husband," *Herald-News*, January 22, 1970, 7.
44. Remarks by Richard J. Hughes at luncheon following the Red Mass, Newark, New Jersey, October 6, 1985. On file with author.
45. Interview with Kenneth Kunzman.
46. Interview with Edward Deutsch, June 10, 2008.
47. "Betty Hughes," *Asbury Park Press*, October 14, 1983.
48. Interview with Kenneth Kunzman, 3/21/2006.
49. Richard J. Hughes, "Open Letter from the Orient," Bulletin from Betty, *Trentonian*, September 5, 1970.
50. Daniel L. Skoler, "When Society Pronounces Judgment: The Work of the Commission on Correctional Facilities and Services: Five Year Report, 1970–1975" (Chicago: American Bar Association, 1975), iii. The preface was written by Robert McKay, the then dean of New York University Law School.
51. Ibid., 4.
52. Ibid., 7.
53. The author served on the New Jersey State Bar Association Correctional Reform Committee.
54. Hughes, "Open Letter from the Orient."
55. Interview with James Kellogg, July 11, 2006.
56. Robert Slater, "Ex-NJ governor's Life Now Happier, More Comfortable," *Houston Post*, November 5, 1970.
57. Interview with Governor Brendan Byrne, February 17, 2006.
58. William J. Menardi, "Politics in Essex," n.d. On file with author.
59. Dermot Quinn, *The Irish in New Jersey: Four Centuries of American Life* (Piscataway, NJ: Rutgers University Press, 2004), 204–205.
60. Paul Hoffman, *Tiger in the Court* (Chicago: Playboy Press, 1973), 278–279.
61. Ibid., 194.
62. Letter from Hughes to Governor Mario Cuomo, May 28, 1985. On file with author.

Chapter 18: Chief Justice

1. An article similar to this chapter was published in the Seton Hall University Law School Law Review. Reproduced with permission of the Seton Hall Law Review. John B. Wefing, *Chief Justice Richard J. Hughes and His Contributions to the Judiciary of New Jersey*, 36 Seton Hall L. Rev. 1287 (2006).
2. Richard J. Hughes, *Reflections: A Growing Court*, 11 Seton Hall L. Rev. 379, 383 (1981).
3. Cahill served as congressman from the First District in New Jersey from 1959 to 1967.
4. Alvin S. Felzenberg, *Governor Tom Kean: From the New Jersey Statehouse to the 9–11 Commission* (Piscataway, NJ: Rutgers University Press, 2006), 126.
5. Ibid., 126–127.
6. One story is that Hughes was having dinner with Colonel Kelly in Trenton and casually mentioned that he would love to be chief justice. Kelly then carried that story to Governor Cahill and he then made the decision. Another story is that

John McCarthy, a lawyer in Trenton who was good friends with both Hughes and Cahill, suggested it. A third story was that George Kugler, the attorney general under Cahill, came up with the idea at Morven one evening.

7. Richard Leone would later serve as the state treasurer in the Byrne administration and subsequently chairman of the Port Authority. Richard DeKorte was an assemblyman from Bergen County from 1968 to 1973 and also served as Republican majority leader.

8. Interview with Richard C. Leone, December 6, 2004.

9. Interview with Governor Brendan Byrne, February 17, 2006.

10. Ibid.

11. Morris Pashman, *A Tribute to Richard J. Hughes: Judge and Administrator,* 10 Seton Hall L. Rev. 86, 89 (1979).

12. Daniel J. O'Hern, *Brennan and Weintraub: Two Stars to Guide Us,* 46 Rutgers L. Rev. 1049, 1050 (1994).

13. Ibid., 1063.

14. Interview with Stanley C. Van Ness, September 16, 2004.

15. Morris Pashman, *Tribute to Richard J. Hughes,* 90.

16. The rule was adopted by the court in December 1971 to be effective January 31, 1972.

17. *Am. Trial Lawyers Ass'n., N.J. Branch v. N.J. Sup. Ct.,* 66 N.J. 258, 259 (1974).

18. N.J. Const. art. IV, § 2.

19. *Am. Trial Lawyers,* 66 N.J. at 267.

20. *Application of Ellen Gaulkin,* 61 N.J. 185, 193 (1976).

21. Ibid., 195–196.

22. Ibid., 199.

23. Interview with Rosemary Higgins Cass, June 14, 2007.

24. *Robinson v. Cahill,* 62 N.J. 473 (1973). "*Robinson I.*"

25. *NAACP v. Mount Laurel,* 67 N.J. 151 (1975). "*Mount Laurel I.*"

26. Barbara G. Salmore and Stephen A. Salmore, *New Jersey Politics and Government: Suburban Politics Comes of Age,* 2nd ed. (Lincoln: University of Nebraska Press, 1998), 259–265.

27. *San Antonio Indep. Sch. Dist. v. Rodriguez,* 411 U.S. 1 (1973).

28. In 1875 the New Jersey Constitution of 1844 was amended by adding, "The Legislature shall provide for the maintenance and support of a thorough and efficient system of free public schools for the instruction of all children in this State between the ages of five and eighteen years." N.J. Const. art. IV, § 6, 7.

29. *Robinson v. Cahill,* 63 N.J. 196 (1973). "*Robinson II.*"

30. *Robinson v. Cahill,* 67 N.J. 333 (1975). "*Robinson III.*"

31. *Robinson v. Cahill,* 69 N.J. 133 (1975). "*Robinson IV.*"

32. Ibid., 145.

33. N.J. Stat. Ann. § 18A:7A-1 (West 1975).

34. *Robinson v. Cahill,* 69 N.J. 449 (1976). "*Robinson V.*"

35. *Robinson V,* 69 N.J. at 475.

36. Salmore and Salmore, *New Jersey Politics and Government,* 196.

37. *Robinson v. Cahill,* 70 N.J. 175, 161–178 (1976). "*Robinson VI.*"

38. Salmore and Salmore, *New Jersey Politics and Government,* 197.

39. Robert J. Braun, "Judges Are In the Wrong Court When It Comes to Setting Education Policy," *Star-Ledger*, May 19, 1997.

40. Ibid.

41. Alexandra Greif, *Politics, Practicalities and Priorities: New Jersey's Experience Implementing the Abbott V Mandate*, 22 Yale L. & Pol. Rev. 615 (2004); Paul Tractenberg, *The Evolution and Implementation of Education Rights Under the New Jersey Constitution of 1947*, 29 Rutgers L. Rev. 827 (1998).

42. *Abbott v. Burke*, 119 N.J. 287 (1990). *Abbott v. Burke I* had been a procedural case to decide whether the case should be handled in the Superior Court or through the administrative process. *Abbott v. Burke*, 100 N.J. 269 (1985).

43. *Abbott II*, 119 N.J. at 384–85.

44. Ibid., 385.

45. New Jersey Department of Education—Comparative Funding Guide. For example in 2005, Newark, which is in Essex County, received 84 percent of its funding from the State of New Jersey, 9 percent from local property taxes, and 6 percent from the Federal Government. On the other hand, Glen Ridge, which is also in Essex County, received only 5 percent of its funding from New Jersey and 91 percent of its funding from local property taxes.

46. Abby Goodnough, "Rural Schools Feel Ignored by Trenton Aid To Poor," *New York Times*, June 23, 1997, A1.

47. "Some states have experienced protracted serial litigation that has extended for decades." John Dayton and Anne Dupre, *School Funding Litigation: Who's Winning the War?* 57 Vand. L. Rev. 2351, 2353–54 (2004); citing to the seven *Robinson v. Cahill* cases and the first two *Abbott v. Burke* cases.

48. *Twp. of Mt. Laurel v. S. Burlington County NAACP*, 67 N.J. 151(1975), *cert. denied*, 423 U.S. 808 (1975).

49. *S. Burlington County NAACP v. Twp. of Mt. Laurel*, 92 N.J. 158 (1983).

50. L. 1985, c. 222.

51. *Hills Dev. Co. v. Bernards Twp. in Somerset County*, 103 N.J. 1 (1986).

52. "On the night of April 15, 1975, [for reasons still unclear, Karen Quinlan] ceased breathing for at least two 15-minute periods." She received some ineffective mouth-to-mouth resuscitation from friends. ". . . [S]he was taken to Newton Memorial hospital." *In re Quinlan*, 137 N.J. Super. 227, 237 (N.J. Super. Ct. Ch. Div. 1975)

53. Peter G. Filene, *In the Arms of Others: A Cultural History of the Right-to-Die in America* (Chicago: Ivan R. Dee, 1998), 25. This book details some of the early history of Karen and her family.

54. Ibid., 76.

55. Ibid., xv.

56. Ibid., 10.

57. Paul Armstrong would later become a superior court judge in New Jersey.

58. Filene, *In the Arms of Others*, 44.

59. N.J. Ct. R. 2:12–1.

60. The chief justice of New Jersey has the power to assign the writing of opinions when s/he is in the majority.

61. Letter from Hughes to Neil E. McMillan, Esq., June 27 1985. On file with author.

62. Regina Waldron Murray, *Profiles in the Wind, A Potpourri of People* (Princeton, NJ: R. W. Murray, 1998), 62.
63. Interview with Patrick Murphy.
64. *In re Quinlan*, 70 N.J. 10, 24 (1976).
65. Ibid.
66. Ibid., 26.
67. Free Exercise of Religion and Cruel and Unusual Punishment.
68. *Griswold v. Connecticut*, 381 U.S. 479 (1965).
69. N.J. Const. art. I, § 1.
70. *In re Quinlan*, 70 N.J. at 41.
71. Ibid., 55.
72. Ibid., 33.
73. Filene, *In the Arms of Others*, 93.
74. Ibid., 125.
75. *Cruzan v. Dir., Mo. Dep. of Health*, 497 U.S. 261, 270 (1990). See John E. Nowak and Ronald D. Rotunda, *Constitutional Law*, 6th ed., Hornbook Series (St. Paul, MN: West, 2000), 922.
76. Interview with Julia Quinlan, April 27, 2005.
77. Interview with Julia Quinlan.
78. *In re Farber*, 78 N.J. 259 (1978).
79. N.J. Const. art. 1, § 10.
80. *In re Farber*, 78 N.J. at 282.
81. Ibid., 282–283.
82. Letter from Hughes to Edward Bloustein, August 25, 1982. On file with author.
83. Ibid.
84. *N.J. Stat. Ann.* § 2A:113–1 (1975), repealed by L.1978, c. 95, § 2C:98–2, eff. Sept. 1, 1979.
85. *State v. Canola*, 135 N.J. Super. 224, 235 (N.J. Super. Ct. App. Div. 1975).
86. *State v. Canola*, 73 N.J. 206, 227 (1977) (quoting *Canola* 135 N.J. Super. at 235).
87. *N.J. Stat. Ann.* § 2C:11–3(a)(3) (West 2008). Enacted by L.1978, c. 95.
88. N.J. Const. art. IV, § 5, cl. 1.
89. *N.J. Stat. Ann.* § 2A:1A-8. Repealed by L.1991, c. 119, § 4, effective April 25, 1991.
90. *Vreeland v. Byrne*, 72 N.J. 292, 835 (1977) (citing *U.S. v. Am. Trucking Ass'ns*, 310 U.S. 534, 543–44 (1940).
91. Ibid. (citing *Richman v. Ligham*, 22 N.J. 40, 44–52 (1956)).
92. Hughes, *Reflections: "A Growing Court,"* 11 Seton Hall L.R. 379 (1981).
93. Ibid., 382.
94. Ibid., 384.
95. Ibid., 386.
96. Letter from Gary A. Ehrlich, former clerk of Chief Justice Hughes, to the author, February 17, 2005. On file with author.
97. J. B. Wefing and J. G. Miles, *Consent Searches and the Fourth Amendment: Voluntariness and Third Party Problems*, 5 Seton Hall L. Rev. 211, 251–252 (1974).
98. *State v. Johnson*, 68 N.J. 349 (1975).

99. "Remarks of former Chief Justice Hughes at Memorial for Justice Nathan Jacobs" (Hughes Justice Complex, Trenton, NJ, May 8, 1989). On file with author.

100. Ibid.

101. Sidney M. Schreiber, *Statutory Interpretation: Some Comments on Two Judicial Viewpoints*, 10 Seton Hall L. Rev. 94, 101 (1979).

102. Ibid.

103. Letter from Gary A. Ehrlich to the author, February 17, 2005. On file with author.

104. Letter from John M. Donnelly, former clerk of Chief Justice Hughes, to the author, April 13, 2005. On file with author.

105. Letter on file with author.

106. Joseph F. Sullivan, "Hughes to Screen All State Prisoners in Battle Against Disparate Sentences," *New York Times*, April 5, 1974, 79.

107. Interview with Earl Josephson, December 8, 2006.

108. Arthur J. Simpson, Jr., Acting Administrative Director of the Courts, "Release from the Administrative Office of the Court," November 17, 1975, 2. On file with author.

109. Chief Justice Richard J. Hughes, "State of the Judiciary Address to the Legislature," Trenton, NJ, November 21, 1977, 1.

110. Ibid., 33–34.

111. Letter from Hughes to Brendan Byrne, May 4, 1978. On file with author.

112. Ibid.

113. *N.J. Stat. Ann.* § 17:34–3.13 (1953). Renumbered in 1971 as *N.J. Stat.* § 17B:18–19.

114. Ronald Sullivan, "Cahill Assailed on $20,000 Job," *New York Times*, March 23, 1975.

115. Bolton Schwartz, "If Age Bothers You, Think of the Alternative," August 5, 1979. On file with author.

Chapter 19: The Later Years

1. Richard J. Hughes, "Reflections: A Growing Court," 11 *Seton Hall L. Rev.* 379 (1981).

2. Interview with Jane Kelly, April 5, 2005.

3. Interview with Adrian "Bud" Foley, April 11, 2006.

4. Robert Schwaneberg, "Unlocking the Keys to Success at DEP," *Star-Ledger*, March 24, 1991.

5. Alvin S. Felzenberg, *Governor Tom Kean: From the New Jersey Statehouse to the 9–11 Commission* (New Brunswick, NJ: Rivergate Books, 2006), 205.

6. Ibid., 307.

7. Letter from Hughes to Governor Kean and others, February 20, 1985. On file with author. Pub. L. No. 98–399—§ 4(b), 98 Stat. 1473, 1474 (1984); N.J. Exec. Order No. 83, 1984 N.J. Laws 1334, 1335.

8. Interview with Robert O'Brien, Jr., April 18, 2006.

9. Letter from Hughes to C. Stewart Hausmann, April 26, 1985. On file with author.

10. Letter from Hughes to Paul N. Ylvisaker, April 22, 1963.
11. Letter from Hughes to Dr. and Mrs. Hyman Lewis, October 31, 1983. On file with author.
12. Numerous letters from Hughes to many different friends.
13. Letter from Lady Bird Johnson to Hughes, July 13, 1984. On file with author.
14. Interview with Thomas More Hughes, June 25, 2006.
15. Letter from Hughes to Mr. and Mrs. J. Duncan Pitney, November 2, 1983. On file with author.
16. Letter from Hughes to Betty, May 7, 1980. On file with author.
17. Interview with Mary "Devey" Abbott, July 6, 2005.
18. Letter from Hughes to Pauline and Albert Dunne. On file with author.
19. Letter from Hughes to Merv Griffin, January 13, 1985. On file with author.
20. Letter from Hughes to Reverend James J. Kortendick, S.S., April 18, 1985. On file with author.
21. Letter from Hughes to Mort Pye, August 22, 1985. On file with author.
22. Letter from Hughes to Tim Murphy, February 20, 1985. On file with author.
23. Ibid.
24. Robert Hughes to his siblings, memorandum, May 22, 1998, "In The Name of Our Father." Copy on file with author.
25. Letter from Hughes to his brother, Joe. April 1, 1985. On file with author.
26. Letter from Hughes to Reverend James J. Kortendick, S.S., April 18, 1985. On file with author.
27. For a detailed discussion see Felzenberg, *Governor Kean*, 347–358.
28. Ibid., 350.
29. 1991 N.J. Sess. Law Serv. 510 (West); see also *N.J. Stat. Ann.* § 19:46–7 (West 1991).
30. Interview with Michael Cole, December 20, 2005.
31. Ibid.
32. Joseph F. Sullivan, "Uncompromising Chief Justice: Robert Nathan Wilentz," *New York Times*, August 2, 1986, 26.
33. Joseph F. Sullivan, "Politics; Senate Is Forced to Modify its Blackball Privilege," *New York Times* New Jersey Section 1, column 2, July 27, 1986. For a thorough discussion of the issue of senatorial courtesy see *De Vesa v. Dorsey*, 134 N.J. 420 (1993).
34. John Cichowski, "Powerful GOP Senator Loses in Morris Democrat MacInnes Defeats Dorsey in Squeaker," *Bergen Record*, November 1993, a16.
35. Letter from Hughes to Senator Gerald Cardinale, July 6, 1984. On file with author.
36. Ibid.
37. Letter from Chief Justice Wilentz to Hughes, July 13, 1984. On file with author.
38. *Gen. Assembly of N.J. v. Byrne*, 90 N.J. 376 (1982).
39. Statement of Richard J. Hughes in Opposition to Question 7—"Legislative Oversight," October 21, 1970. Copy on file with author.
40. Ibid., 2.
41. Regina Murray, "Hughes Fought Lid on Budget," *Trentonian*, January 24, 1988.

42. Letter from Hughes to his son Brian Hughes, March 13, 1992. On file with author.
43. Interview with Michael Cole.
44. "Knights of St. Gregory: Guide to the Collection," McNeese State University, http://library.mcneese.edu/depts/archive/stgregory142.htm.
45. Jacqueline Beusse, a good friend of Hughes, organized the event.
46. Mailgram from Lady Bird Johnson to Hughes, September 6, 1989. On file with author.
47. Letter from Senator Edward Kennedy to Hughes, September 11, 1989. On file with author.
48. "Richard J. Hughes Dead at 83 New Jersey's Greatest Citizen Ex-Governor," *Bergen Record*, December 8, 1992, A01.
49. John Hughes's eulogy for his father. On file with author.
50. Regina Murray, "Hughes Made Few Political Foes," *Trentonian*, July 23, 1989.

Index

About the Author

IN HIS FORTY-YEAR CAREER as a professor of law at Seton Hall University, John B. Wefing has written many law review articles and taught numerous courses including those on the New Jersey Supreme Court and the New Jersey Court system. During his tenure at Seton Hall, he has served as associate dean and acting dean and held the Richard J. Hughes Chair for many years. He has received many awards including Young Lawyer of the Year from the New Jersey State Bar Association, the McQuade Medal, presented for outstanding contributions to Seton Hall University and the Thomas More Medal for his devotion to the law and the Catholic Church. He has received gubernatorial appointments to various state commissions and has been active in many community organizations. He was recently inducted into the Mount Saint Dominic Academy Hall of Fame for his work on its board. He is "of counsel" to the firm of Waters McPherson McNeill in Secaucus, New Jersey.